NEW DEAL JUSTICE

Studies in American Constitutionalism
General Editors: Gary J. Jacobsohn and Richard E. Morgan

NEW DEAL JUSTICE

The Constitutional Jurisprudence of Hugo L. Black, Felix Frankfurter, and Robert H. Jackson

Jeffrey D. Hockett

ROWMAN & LITTLEFIELD PUBLISHERS, INC.

ROWMAN & LITTLEFIELD PUBLISHERS, INC.

Published in the United States of America
by Rowman & Littlefield Publishers, Inc.
4720 Boston Way, Lanham, Maryland 20706

3 Henrietta Street
London WC2E 8LU, England

British Cataloging in Publication Information Available

Library of Congress Cataloging-in-Publication Data
Hockett, Jeffrey D.
New Deal justice : the constitutional jurisprudence of Hugo L.
Black, Felix Frankfurter, and Robert H. Jackson / Jeffrey D.
Hockett.
p.   cm. — (Studies in American constitutionalism)
Includes bibliographical references and index.
1. Black, Hugo LaFayette, 1886–1971.   2. Frankfurter, Felix,
1882–1965.   3. Jackson, Robert Houghwout, 1892–1954.   4. Judicial
review—United States—History.   5. Judicial process—United States-
-History.   6. New Deal, 1933–1939.   I. Title.   II. Series.
KF8744.H63   1996   347.73'2634—dc20   [347.3073534]   95-52944   CIP

ISBN 0–8476–8210-2 (cloth : alk. paper)
ISBN 0–8476–8211-0 (pbk : alk. paper)

Printed in the United States of America

⊗ ™ The paper used in this publication meets the minimum requirements of
American National Standard for Information Sciences—Permanence of
Paper for Printed Library Materials, ANSI Z39.48–1984.

For Laura and Evan

Contents

Preface

This book began as an analysis of the constitutional jurisprudence of Robert H. Jackson, a justice who, unfortunately, has not received his due in the literature of public law. I soon realized, however, that Jackson is best understood when compared with his more celebrated brethren, Hugo L. Black and Felix Frankfurter. Together, the justices revealed the remarkable jurisprudential diversity of Franklin Roosevelt's New Deal coalition. More generally, they illuminated jurisprudential implications of varying political and intellectual responses to one of the most significant events of the late nineteenth and early twentieth centuries: the urban-industrial transformation.

Although a sizable literature already exists on Justices Black and Frankfurter, I wrote this book believing that there is much more to be said about the underpinnings of each man's constitutional jurisprudence. My hope is that anyone who later examines one or more of these justices will find my study as helpful as I found the works of those scholars who preceded me.

For the reader's convenience, references—for both quotations and paraphrased material—are gathered in one endnote at the end of the paragraph. Within each paragraph, the sequence of referenced material corresponds to the sequence of sources in the endnote.

Portions of Chapters 4 through 7 appeared in volume 107 of *The Political Science Quarterly*. (Copyright © 1992 by the American Academy of Political Science. All rights reserved.) Portions of Chapters 8 and 9 appeared in *The Supreme Court Review* (1990), published by the University of Chicago Press. (Copyright © 1991 by the University of Chicago. All rights reserved.)

During the years spent writing this book, I received support from a number of sources. I am very pleased to express my gratitude to those who made this study possible. I benefited from the insights and encouragement of the following members of the faculty of the University of Virginia: Henry Abraham, Robert Morgan, George Klosko, James Ceaser, and Charles McCurdy. I am indebted, especially, to David O'Brien, who suggested Robert Jackson as a subject for study and who offered helpful comments on an early version of the manuscript. (I, of course, assume full responsibility for any remaining errors.)

I am also very grateful for the advice and support of a number of my colleagues at the University of Tulsa. I mention, in particular, Paul Rahe, Eldon Eisenach, Bill Caferro, Ed Dreyer, Tom Horne, and Michael Mosher. Maria Hahalis provided able bibliographic and editorial assistance, and Jeanne Ronda liberated me from the task of compiling an index. Donna Smith, Lara Lee Byerly, and, especially, Toy Kelley were very helpful with the production of the manuscript.

I thank Hugo Black Jr. and William Jackson for providing access to the collected papers of their respective fathers. The staff of the manuscript division of the Library of Congress was kind as well as helpful. A Fellowship for College Teachers from the National Endowment for the Humanities relieved me of teaching responsibilities for one year, while the University of Tulsa supported my research during the summer months over a period of years. I thank Gerald Rosenberg for his encouragement and Martha Babb for her research-related gifts. James Stoner and Gary Jacobsohn offered valuable comments and criticism, while the staff of Rowman & Littlefield Publishers (especially Julie Kuzneski) made the final stages of the project particularly enjoyable. My editor, Stephen Wrinn, was understanding as well as immensely helpful.

Finally, I thank my wife, Laura, and my son, Evan, who were partners in this enterprise. They were more supportive and patient than I ever could have hoped. It is with much love that I dedicate this book to them.

1

Introduction

The New Deal and the Supreme Court

Near the beginning of his second term as president of the United States, Franklin Roosevelt submitted to Congress a plan to reorganize the federal judiciary. The bill would have given him authority to appoint "additional judges in all Federal courts, without exception, where there are incumbent judges of retirement age who do not choose to retire or resign." Had the plan become law, Roosevelt would have been able to name six jurists to the Supreme Court alone. He desired this legislation because the Court had actively opposed his efforts to restore national economic health during the deepest depression in American history. As yet, he had had no opportunities to place his supporters on the nation's highest tribunal. Many important New Deal measures, including the Railroad Retirement Act, the Agricultural Adjustment Act, the Bituminous Coal Act, and the National Industrial Recovery Act, had become casualties of judicial review.[1]

Roosevelt denied that the justices spoke for the Constitution in these cases. In a national radio address touting the reorganization proposal, he said that the Court had "been acting not as a judicial body, but as a policy-making body." It had "improperly set itself up as a third House of the Congress—a super-legislature . . . —reading into the Constitution words and implications which are not there, and which were never intended to be there." Finding "no basis for the claim made by some members of the Court that something in the Constitution [had] compelled them regretfully to thwart the will of the people," he implored his listeners not to yield their "constitutional destiny to the personal judgment of a few men who, being fearful of the future, would deny us the necessary means of dealing with the present."[2]

1

In spite of Roosevelt's efforts, Congress declined to support his bill. Several factors contributed to the measure's demise. Initially, the president did not portray the proposal as a means to restore constitutional government. Rather than emphasize the point that the justices had infused their economic preferences into vague constitutional language, he offered the apology that the "need for legislative action [arose] because the personnel of the Federal judiciary [were] insufficient to meet the business before them." With the punitive nature of the proposal obvious to everyone, Roosevelt's rationale appeared guileful. The rhetoric of efficiency seemed even more disingenuous when Chief Justice Charles Evans Hughes (with the support of the Court's most liberal member, Louis Brandeis) denied the charge that the Court had lost control of its docket. Shortly after the president shifted strategies to stem growing opposition, the constitutional crisis of which he now spoke dissipated. In a series of cases, the Court revealed that it had submitted to public pressure. It upheld Washington state's minimum-wage law for women, the National Labor Relations Act of 1935, and portions of the Social Security Act of 1935. Understandably, Congress was loath to support the president's controversial measure when it no longer seemed necessary.[3]

Even if the Court had remained intransigent in the face of increasing pressure to support the New Deal, Roosevelt's extraordinary electoral achievements had given him numerous opportunities to affect the direction of constitutional law. Indeed, by the end of his second term, he had made five appointments to the Court. In 1937, he nominated Senator Hugo L. Black of Alabama to fill the seat that Willis Van Devanter vacated. The following year, when George Sutherland retired, the president appointed the solicitor general, Stanley F. Reed. In 1939, Roosevelt made two appointments: Felix Frankfurter of the Harvard Law School and William O. Douglas, chairman of the Securities and Exchange Commission. These men replaced the liberal justices, Benjamin Cardozo and Louis Brandeis. In the final year of his second term, Roosevelt achieved a judicial majority when he named his attorney general, Frank Murphy, to succeed Pierce Butler.

In the first year of his third term, the president made three changes on the Court. He first named Senator James F. Byrnes of South Carolina to replace James McReynolds. Then, with the retirement of Charles Evans Hughes, he elevated Justice Harlan F. Stone (a Republican) to the chief justiceship and nominated Attorney General Robert H. Jackson to fill the slot that Stone had occupied. Finally, in the third year of his third term, Roosevelt named the federal appeals court judge

Wiley B. Rutledge to replace James Byrnes, who had resigned to serve as the administration's director of economic stabilization.

Unquestionably, Hugo Black and Felix Frankfurter were Roosevelt's most conspicuous appointees. One commentator suggests that "[f]ew men not candidates for national office have been the object of either as much hatred or as much praise as [Hugo] Black."[4] As a description of most others, this statement would contain at least an element of hyperbole. However, many academics regard Black as one of the "greatest" justices ever to have served on the Court and as the "dean of American judicial liberalism," while other scholars see him as "absurd," "irresponsible," and "liberal without being intelligent."[5]

Black's extraordinary opinions in First and Fourteenth Amendment cases—areas of law that moved to the center of the Court's docket after the late 1930s—largely explain this marked divergence in valuation. He maintained that the only legitimate influences in constitutional adjudication are the document's language and, where the language is not explicit, the history of the adoption of the provision in question. Using this method of interpretation, he concluded that the First Amendment protects all forms of speech and press, including obscenity and libel. He also argued that, while the founders intended the provisions of the Bill of Rights to apply only against the national government, the framers and ratifiers of the Fourteenth Amendment meant to apply them against the states as well. Although this interpretation would have required that states bear the expense of such procedural niceties as trial by jury in civil cases involving as little as twenty dollars, Black did not doubt the accuracy of his historical argument or the wisdom of such a policy. It is not surprising, then, that he inspires fervent expressions of praise from individuals who regard themselves as friends of liberty, while he provokes equally passionate denunciations from those who emphasize the importance of effective, democratic governance.

Scholarly estimations of Felix Frankfurter's judicial performance also vary widely. Many individuals regard him as one of the "greatest" figures in the Court's history and as a "scholar on the bench."[6] Yet other academics describe him as "a textbook case of a neurotic personality" and as "the New Deal Court's most controversial and unhappy figure, its most tragically wasted brilliant mind."[7]

One can attribute Frankfurter's checkered reputation to a constitutional jurisprudence that was as extraordinary as Justice Black's. In sharp contrast to Black, however, Frankfurter was an "architect of a passive model of appellate judging. . . . [H]e was slow to find necessity for Court intervention even when the recourse of a minority to the political process seemed to be unavailable."[8] Besides rejecting Black's contention that the freedoms of speech and press are absolute and should suffer no compromise, he disparaged the notion that the First Amendment is composed of "preferred freedoms." This doctrine holds that the freedoms of speech and press, while not absolute, are so fundamental to a democratic form of government that the Court should presume legislation infringing upon them to be unconstitutional. Frankfurter maintained instead that the Court should only interpose its veto in those rare instances when no rational person could regard the legislation as constitutional. His Fourteenth Amendment decisions were equally deferential to lawmakers. In addition to rejecting Black's total-incorporation position, he forswore the view that at least the most important provisions in the Bill of Rights should apply against the states. He argued instead that the justices should exercise judicial review only when no reasonable person could regard the state action in question as fair. The extraordinary deference that resulted from Frankfurter's use of his First and Fourteenth Amendment standards prompts extravagant praise from those supportive of an active state and harsh criticism from civil libertarians.

If Black and Frankfurter were Roosevelt's best known justices, William O. Douglas, Robert H. Jackson, and Wiley B. Rutledge were only slightly less celebrated members of the Court. (Scholars typically regard Reed, Murphy, and Byrnes as less than eminent judicial figures.)[9] While students of the Court view Douglas and Rutledge as worthy associates of Black, they usually find the substance of Jackson's performance less impressive than his inimitable form. As one scholar observes, "Jackson entertained with his style," but "his solutions [to constitutional controversies] were idiosyncratic and not particularly influential."[10]

The quality that made Jackson's decisions "idiosyncratic" accounts for the lack of scholarly attention to the substance of his work. Numerous scholars suggest that a "pragmatic," or "middle-of-the-road," approach to constitutional decision making was the distinguishing feature of his jurisprudence.[11] Indeed, one scholar goes so far as to say that "[t]he unpredictability of Jackson's performance leads one to question whether he has developed any systematic theories about civil liberties or the judicial function." Like Frankfurter, Jackson avoided an absolutist interpretation of the freedoms of speech and press. But, like Black, he made no use of a rational-basis test in First Amendment contexts. With regard to the Fourteenth Amendment, Jackson rejected

Black's total-incorporation position, but he refused to join Frankfurter's critique of the doctrine of selective incorporation. As a consequence of these positions, Jackson reached results that placed him "sometimes in Frankfurter's and sometimes in Black's camp." Because "those who take extreme positions tend to get disproportionate attention," Black and Frankfurter became the objects of stronger praise (and blame) than their pragmatic colleague. In short, "the typical judgment on Jackson the Judge" is that he was "[b]rilliant, eloquent, but erratic" and thus "an enigma."[12]

The jurisprudential dissonance of the New Deal justices has inspired an extensive literature on this period of the Court's history. The spectacle of such disunity among individuals who had promoted Franklin Roosevelt's legislative agenda, and who had criticized the Court's hostility toward economic legislation, invited scholarly analysis and explanation. Not surprisingly, much scholarship has focused on the two justices who staked out the jurisprudential extremes on the New Deal Court: Black and Frankfurter.[13] Regrettably, comparatively few studies have examined Jackson, whose pragmatism presented a marked contrast to the constitutional views of his more celebrated brethren.[14] In neglecting Jackson, scholars have not only failed to appreciate fully the diversity of the New Deal justices; they have also overlooked the insights of an individual who saw both merit and flaws in the opinions of Black and Frankfurter.

Students of the Court should have anticipated a certain amount of disagreement among the three justices, given the diverse public and professional backgrounds of these men. Prior to his appointment, Black had served for ten years as a United States senator from Alabama. In this capacity, he had been a forceful advocate for, and avid participant in, the New Deal. Before becoming a national figure, he had been a part-time police court judge, a public prosecutor, and a personal injury and labor lawyer.

Frankfurter had been a professor of law at the Harvard Law School for twenty-five years before joining the Court. From his academic post, he had counseled Roosevelt on political matters and had recommended a number of Harvard graduates for positions in the administration. As an academician, he had also pursued several causes and projects. He had been involved in the Zionist movement, the founding of the *New Republic*, the scholarly indictment of the trial of Sacco and Vanzetti, the work of the National Association for the Advancement of Colored People, and the founding of the American Civil Liberties Union. He had been active in Progressive politics in the second decade of this century and had held numerous public posts before and during his years at Harvard. He had been assistant U.S. attorney for the Southern District of New York, legal officer in the War Department's Bureau of Insular Affairs, assistant to the secretary of War, assistant to the secretary of Labor, and chairman of the War Labor Policies Board.

Robert Jackson had served the Roosevelt administration in numerous capacities before joining the Court. He had been assistant general counsel for the Bureau of Internal Revenue; assistant attorney general for the tax, and then the antitrust, divisions in the Department of Justice; solicitor general; and, finally, attorney general. Before coming to Washington, he had established a lucrative legal practice in Jamestown, New York. His clients ranged from electric utility corporations and banks to labor organizations and small merchants and manufacturers.

While variation in public and professional experience undoubtedly explained some of the disharmony among the New Deal justices, this factor alone could not have accounted for the range of constitutional opinions displayed. Indeed, aspects of the backgrounds of Black and Frankfurter made the judicial performances of these men appear anomalous. Shortly after Black's appointment, the media discovered that the new justice had once been a member of the Ku Klux Klan. This finding caused civil libertarians considerable angst. They looked to Frankfurter, whose record on civil liberties was unimpeachable, to champion the cause of individual rights. "Ironically, the former member of the Ku Klux Klan . . . would become the libertarian hero and liberal leader of the Court—not Frankfurter." Many individuals wondered how Frankfurter—a Jew, a defender of Sacco and Vanzetti, and a founder of the American Civil Liberties Union—could display "so little sensitivity to the plight of left-wing dissenters" and other minorities.[15]

Recent studies that more thoroughly explore the backgrounds of Black, Frankfurter, and Jackson afford promising avenues for explaining the jurisprudential conflicts of the New Deal Court. Yet, despite an extensive literature on at least two of these men, scholars have not elucidated fully each justice's constitutional jurisprudence. Current explanations for the justices' disparate rulings are conflicting, problematic, and, in Jackson's case, dishearteningly incomplete.

The Scholarly Record

Several recent studies suggest that Hugo Black's efforts to tie judicial decision making under the Constitution to the document's language and history disclosed a belief that exercises of judicial discretion are inherently dangerous.[16] The more searching analyses of the underpinnings of his jurisprudence attribute this fear of discretion to the influence of the Populist movement that swept through the South and West at the end of the nineteenth century. Black, the argument runs, possessed a Populist's distrust of unchecked governmental power, and this distrust extended to judicial, as well as accountable, political institutions.[17]

Proponents of this argument strongly oppose an older, competing view: that Black was result oriented and sought to use judicial power for the liberal purpose of combating social and political hierarchy.[18] As proof that the justice's interpretations of the First and Fourteenth Amendments did not betray a desire to aid marginal social and political groups, these scholars point to the fact that his constitutional jurisprudence at times precluded liberal or antihierarchical results. Black's refusal to acknowledge a right of privacy in the Fourteenth Amendment, his reluctance to impede the imposition of capital punishment, and his marked deference to public authority in Fourth Amendment ("unreasonable" search and seizure) cases were the more notable examples of his judicial conservatism.

Yet several considerations militate against an argument that traces Black's jurisprudential uniqueness to a Populist-inspired belief that exercises of discretion are inherently dangerous. The most significant criticism of this view is that Populism cultivated within its adherents a desire to use power as a political and social corrective, rather than a fear of exercises of discretion. It is true that the Populists feared unchecked governmental authority, including judicial authority; however, this statement leaves much unsaid. Curiously, proponents of the view that Black was result oriented fail to provide a more elaborate treatment of this movement (or of aspects of Black's jurisprudence that reveal anything but a fear of discretion). Indeed, they make only fleeting reference to the possibility that Populism explained Black's judicial performance.[19] It would be appropriate for them to note that the Populists specifically feared the political and economic exploitation of the masses by the propertied few. The agrarian insurgents sought restraints on power, not because they feared discretion per se, but because they hoped to secure antihierarchical results. Those whom this movement influenced would thus welcome exercises of judicial discretion so long as these rulings supported marginal social and political groups.

Tellingly, Black at times disregarded the boundaries of his constitutional jurisprudence and used judicial discretion for antihierarchical purposes. Consider, for example, his acceptance of the argument that government violates due process when it secures convictions under vague statutes or through perjured testimony or suppressed evidence. He (wisely) made no effort to justify these rulings through recourse to history. Also, consider his support of decisions that engineered the reapportionment of electoral districts. The Court based some of these rulings upon the equal protection clause of the Fourteenth Amendment. Yet, neither the language of nor the intent behind that provision requires reapportionment.

Black's willingness to exercise discretion aside, the contention that he was, at base, a result-oriented jurist has some appeal simply because his constitutional jurisprudence, overall, was profoundly antihierarchical. His absolute protection for the freedoms of speech and press, and his support for an immensely increased federal judicial presence on the state level for antihierarchical purposes,[20] more than offset the conservative aspects of his judicial philosophy. Even some of those who maintain that Black feared judicial discretion acknowledge the antihierarchical thrust of his jurisprudence. In the words of one scholar, Black's judicial philosophy "produced the [supposed] anomaly of vastly increasing the impact of the Court in modern life."[21] Of course, those who would defend the view that Black was a result-oriented jurist need to explain why he did not pursue antihierarchical results in every case. In many instances, he accepted the conservative implications of his judicial philosophy.

Scholarship regarding Felix Frankfurter is as indeterminate as the literature on Black. Explanations for Frankfurter's extraordinary judicial reserve are several and usually complementary. Some studies suggest that he distrusted judicial power; specifically, he found fault with the process of judicial fact-finding, and he believed that frequent exercises of judicial review enervate the democratic process.[22] Unfortunately, proponents of this view present hypotheses rather than developed arguments.

One study adds that Frankfurter regarded the United States as an "open polity" (i.e., an order in which the availability of political and economic reform ensures social mobility) and thus saw no need for an active judiciary. The study identifies Frankfurter's association with Progressivism as the source of his democratic faith: like the Progressives, he had enormous confidence in the capacity of administrative expertise and political leadership to articulate a unifying national purpose.[23] Yet explanation is wanting for the fact that his faith in democracy persisted even after events appeared to disconfirm the openness of the American polity.

More recent and extensive studies suggest that Frankfurter's marked deference to other political bodies in no way indicated a distrust of judicial power. These works emphasize that the justice, although reserved, promoted discretionary over legalistic standards of decision making. In due process cases, for example, he invalidated governmental actions that "shocked the conscience" or violated "fundamental notions of fairness and justice"; in Fourth Amendment cases, he was not averse to finding federal searches and seizures "unreasonable." In allowing such discretion, the argument runs, he extended to the judiciary his Progressive confidence in trained governmental experts. Put another way, he embraced the statesmanlike task of balancing principles of individual liberty against considerations of effective, democratic governance.[24]

Proponents of this view identify the spread of totalitarianism in Europe during the 1930s as the impetus behind Frankfurter's extension to the judiciary of his faith in public power. Communism and fascism alerted him to the need for a branch of government that would ensure a consonance between social and economic change and enduring principles of liberty. Yet "so great was his faith in the harmonious operation of the democratic state under leadership such as [Franklin] Roosevelt's that rarely would the great power of judicial review be necessary to protect those immutable principles."[25] Once again, explanation is wanting for the fact that Frankfurter's faith did not wane even when the operation of the democratic state appeared anything but harmonious.

Several considerations detract from the argument that Frankfurter's Progressive confidence in power extended to the judiciary. First, Progressivism inspired within its adherents a profound distrust of judicial institutions rather than a faith therein. Ironically, defenders of the view that Frankfurter feared judicial power fail to examine the standing of courts in the ideology of the administrative state. (They also fail to illuminate those aspects of the justice's jurisprudence that coincide with this institutional critique). The Progressives viewed a strong executive and a developed administrative apparatus as a way to compensate for the deficiencies of a government theretofore dominated by parties and courts. They believed that patronage-obsessed politicians provided the nation with inadequate leadership, and that outmoded techniques for informing the judicial mind rendered the decisions of courts dangerously abstract in an interdependent age.

Frankfurter reiterated this critique of the judiciary throughout his tenure on the bench, and his constitutional jurisprudence reflected his assessment of judicial power. Most obviously, he rejected the notion of judicial supremacy, which had prevailed since the end of the nineteenth century. To his mind, exponents of this doctrine could offer no compelling historical or policy arguments to support the idea that courts should be the final arbiters of constitutional controversies. The executive and legislative branches, he thought, have as much responsibility as the judiciary to ensure the integrity of constitutional boundaries.[26]

Frankfurter's promotion of discretionary standards of decision making followed from his repudiation of judicial supremacy, for the discretion he allowed was very narrow in scope. In identifying governmental actions that "shock the conscience" as violations of due process, he merely rephrased the standard he used in other constitutional contexts: the Court should only interpose its veto when a rational person could not believe in the constitutionality of the challenged act. Needless to say, Frankfurter rarely concluded that the circumstances before the Court warranted an exercise of judicial review.

Still, proponents of the view that Frankfurter distrusted judicial power must account for limited areas of constitutional law (most notably, Fourth Amendment controversies at the federal level) in which he dispensed with his usual deference to the decisions of nonjudicial authorities. For that matter, supporters of this view need to explain why he trusted judges with any amount of discretion.

In contrast to the extensive literature on Black and Frankfurter, the relatively few studies that examine Robert Jackson reveal no consensus on the distinguishing features of his judicial performance, let alone on an explanation for his behavior. Some of the scholars who suggest that Jackson's rulings were pragmatic emphasize his scrupulous attention to the differences among circumstances prompting governmental action. As at least one scholar also notes, the justice did not believe his regard for factual distinctness rendered his decisions a collection of isolated instances; he thought "that judges could respond to the exigencies of practical problems while at the same time basing their resolutions on principles of law that transcended merely pragmatic judgments."[27] Unfortunately, this literature provides no explanation for Jackson's efforts to find a balance between continuity in the law and judicial responsiveness to a multiplicity of circumstances.

A competing interpretation of Jackson's judicial performance holds that he was pragmatic in appearance only; he actually experienced a violent shift from an early, marked concern with the protection of individual rights to a later, profound constitutional conservatism.[28] Proponents of this view identify his well-known and controversial involvement in the Nuremberg War Crimes Trial as the cause of this jurisprudential inversion, for the onetime United States chief of counsel for the prosecution of Axis war criminals came to believe that the German government's failure to crack down on radical dissenters and extremist groups explained the downfall of the Weimar Republic. His attentiveness to the circumstances of cases thus served merely to justify challenged governmental actions in his post-Nuremberg opinions. His early opinions, by contrast, contained some of the Court's most eloquent statements of the need to secure constitutional liberties.

Supporters of the view that Jackson was a pragmatic jurist must concede that Nuremberg inspired a change in the tone of his opinions and had some impact upon his jurisprudence. Yet they do not have to abandon their thesis and accept the war crimes trial as the prime determinant of his judicial performance. They could (but fail to) note that Jackson discriminated among cases (and, at times, reached conservative conclusions) well before Nuremberg. Moreover, he continued after the event to act upon a strong belief in the need for judicial protection of constitutional liberties.

To say that Nuremberg does not account for Jackson's pragmatism, however, is not to offer an explanation for his behavior. The virtue of the literature emphasizing Nuremberg's significance is that it at least seeks an account of the Justice's performance. Scholarly inattention to the source of Jackson's responsiveness to differences in factual settings (and to his competing concern for legal stability) leaves a regrettable lacuna in our understanding of this important judicial figure. In the same way that scholars have attempted to understand the aims of Black's and Frankfurter's conceptions of the judicial function, Jackson scholars must seek the purposes underpinning his judicial pragmatism.

Overview

The purpose of this book is to explain the judicial performances of Black, Frankfurter, and Jackson and, in so doing, to resolve the indeterminacy pervading the literature on these men. Following the lead of earlier works, the present study explores the justices' ideological backgrounds to explain their behavior on the Court.[29] It argues that the justices revealed jurisprudential implications of varying political and intellectual responses to the American industrial transformation: Black and Frankfurter illuminated differences in constitutional thinking between the most progressive political movements that industrialization inspired, namely, Populism and Progressivism. By contrast, Jackson was a transitional figure, caught between the jurisprudential changes of the modern age and the legal culture of pre-industrial America. The book contributes to the literature on the justices by affording a corrective to earlier studies that also link Black and Frankfurter to Populism and Progressivism, respectively. Specifically, it challenges the view that Black regarded judicial discretion as inherently dangerous, and it disputes the contention that Frankfurter possessed great faith in judicial power. Perhaps more important, the book provides an explanation for Jackson's constitutional pragmatism and thus helps to remedy the scholarly neglect of this significant member of the New Deal Court.

In view of the justices' jurisprudential differences, the book's title is not a reference to a shared ideal of constitutional justice toward which Roosevelt's appointees strove. Rather, each man was a "New Deal justice" who illustrated one of several distinct jurisprudential tendencies compatible with the reform politics of the 1930s. The coalitional character of the New Deal enabled the president to place on the Court individuals who together provided, not only an idea of the variance between jurisprudential responses to the massive social and economic transformation of the late nineteenth and early twentieth centuries, but also a sense of the distance between pre- and postindustrial constitutional thought. Put another way, the specific performances of the New Deal justices reflected regional, cultural, and ideological tensions that characterized the New Deal generally. The jurisprudential differences among these men were not apparent when issues of economic liberty dominated the Court's docket, because New Deal proponents united in opposition to the power of northern industrialists. As issues of nonproprietarian rights became prominent, however, conflict replaced consensus, and the Court's constitutional opinions became indices of the diversity of the New Deal coalition.

As suggested earlier, a failure among scholars to explore sufficiently the history of the era preceding the New Deal led to conflicting interpretations of the judicial behavior of Black, Frankfurter, and Jackson. In light of this consideration, Chapter 2 provides the groundwork for an analysis of the industrial age. It examines the system of parties and courts that performed the operational functions of governing in the nineteenth century. Political parties assumed responsibility for staffing public offices, while the judiciary engaged in economic surveillance. The chapter also discusses how federal courts gradually acquired hegemony over the resolution of constitutional questions. Jurists supported this notion of judicial supremacy with two claims: that permanent tenure insulates federal judges from the influence of oppressive majorities, and that analogical or common-law reasoning achieves a balance in the law between the competing principles of continuity and growth.

Chapter 3 examines regional variations in the social and political effects of industrialism. In the last third of the nineteenth century, an interregional division of labor developed between the economically advanced North and the underdeveloped South. This division of labor inspired intense sectional conflict. Southern farmers collectively opposed the commercial policies of northern industrialists because these policies established a colonial economic pattern within the nation and bled the South of scarce capital. The competition between the Republican party (the "party of the North") and the Southern Democracy reflected this sectional strife.

Within the Democratic party, an intrasectional rivalry between the South's wealthy Black Belt planters (known as "Bourbon Democrats") and the region's poor, upland yeomen fostered radical agrarianism and, ultimately, the insurgent politics of Populism. Yeomen or agrarians sought to escape a locally administered system of credit, which kept them in a virtual state of slavery. The dominant Bourbons resisted the reform of a financial scheme that benefited their associates in the financial and mercantile communities. When the agrarians scored modest legislative victories, judicial decisions frustrated these efforts to ameliorate the harsh existence of the region's rural poor. Convinced of the hierarchical nature of national and state politics, poor farmers formed the Populist party and adopted a platform that denounced the anti-agrarian rulings of the courts and called for clear demarcations on the use of public power. The Populists sought the discontinuation of political favors to northern industrialists and advocated the affirmative use of government to restore "equal rights to all."

Northeastern Progressives of the early twentieth century also called for a new public philosophy, but they sought certain institutional innovations rather than clear demarcations on power. This political movement addressed middle-class concerns over the inflationary effects of concentrated wealth and the instability of an increasingly discontented labor movement. Progressive social theory emphasized the concept of economic interdependence and the danger of abstraction, that is, the danger of isolating a problem or concept from the web of social factors with which it interacts. Progressives contended that the interdependent nature of industrial society rendered abstract the nineteenth-century notions of self-mastery and rights to property. They thus called for the replacement of the politics and jurisprudence of individualism with a new public philosophy: a welfare-oriented humanitarianism administered by a positive state. The Progressives viewed the establishment of a powerful executive and a developed administrative apparatus as the only sure way to prevent abstraction in governing. They hoped these institutional reforms would avoid the inaptitude and abstraction inhering in the old system of parties and courts that had theretofore performed the operational tasks of governing.

Administrative institutions did not address completely the problem of abstraction in governing; the Progressives also sought to deprive courts of the means to justify abstract rulings. More specifically, Progressive scholars criticized a theory of judicial decision making that denied the reality of judicial lawmaking. In the nineteenth century, the theory of analogical or common-law reasoning had allowed for a measure of judicial creativity or responsiveness to changed social circumstances. By the twentieth century, however, a rhetoric of abnegation masked judicial innovation. By depriving judges of the argument that their rulings were not exercises of will, the Progressives sought to compel judicial deference in the face of constitutional challenges to legislative and administrative efforts to meet the complex problems of an interdependent social order.

When the Great Depression prompted the next major reform effort (i.e., the New Deal), Franklin Roosevelt drew his primary support from the regional political cultures that industrialism had formed. However, the president did not merely resume the reform politics of the past, for northern labor and southern plantation elites represented the major branches of the fragile New Deal coalition. (Organized labor had benefited from Progressivism but was not of the movement, while wealthy southern planters had been the bitter enemies of Populism.) Yet former Progressives and southern yeomen also supported the New Deal because they shared with the dominant elements of Roosevelt's coalition an antipathy for northern, corporate power.

Chapter 4 locates Hugo Black within the history of the American industrial transformation. It reveals that, like the Populists, Black developed a hierarchical view of society and politics. As an Alabama youth, he witnessed Bourbon efforts to frustrate Populist reform measures. Later, he would champion the cause of the state's yeomen and laborers, first, as a lawyer and, then, as a member of Congress. In the Senate, he also devoted himself to fighting the systematic redistribution of national income that occurred at the turn of the century, when the South had to finance northern industrial development through tariffs and inflated prices for domestic goods. As a consequence of these events, he developed increasing regard for antihierarchical rights. Chapter four compares his use of the freedoms of speech and press in his political battles to the earlier efforts of agrarian editors to expose Bourbon corruption.

The next chapter relates Black's constitutional jurisprudence to his ideological background. In contrast to the view that he feared judicial discretion, chapter five suggests that he was profoundly result oriented: he believed that courts must assume an aggressive role in maintaining avenues, external to established national and state political institutions, for the expression of social discontent. He promoted a literal reading of the First Amendment and the application of the provisions of the Bill of Rights against the states, but not because he distrusted all exercises of judicial will. Rather, his jurisprudence exhibited strategic considerations. In the same way that the Populists sought clear demarcations on power to secure antihierarchical results, Black sought to curtail judicial discretion to prevent courts from impeding social reform and to ensure judicial involvement for important antihierarchical objectives. Furthermore, his efforts to tie judicial decision making under the Constitution to the language of the document and the intent behind its provisions enabled him to reconcile his belief that the Court should serve as a political and social corrective with a strong tradition of bounded judicial decision making. (While the Progressives deprived judges of the rationalization that decisions based upon precedent are purely deductive, the social expectation remained that judges would render decisions according to objective, legal criteria.) The fact that Black's jurisprudence led to results that were, on the whole, antihierarchical made the cost of respecting this tradition (i.e., periodic rulings in favor of the status quo) acceptable to him.[30] Still, he resorted occasionally to exercises of discretion because of a strong belief in the need for judicial promotion of social change.

Although Black conveyed the misleading impression that he distrusted all exercises of judicial discretion, he demonstrated convincingly through his absolutist interpretation of the First Amendment that he had little fear of judicial abstraction. This study suggests that he could not have believed that abstraction occurs only in cases involving proprietarian rights, for the move toward interdependence greatly complicated noneconomic, as well as economic, relationships. Nor could he have been entirely unfamiliar with the source of abstract thought; every part of the nation experienced the heightened interconnectedness that accompanied industrialism. Yet the hierarchical impact of interdependence within and among the nation's regions was the very reason he appreciated the antihierarchical value of abstract conceptions of rights. Moreover, the South was not nearly as economically developed or interdependent as the more industrialized North. One should not be surprised, then, that he was more alive to the injustices of the hierarchical politics he had witnessed than to the potential negative effects of abstract thinking in an interdependent society.

By contrast, Chapter 6 demonstrates that Felix Frankfurter rooted his thought in the interdependent conditions of the industrialized Northeast and in the views of intellectuals who emphasized the dangers of abstraction. Involvement in Progressive politics and membership in an academic community familiarized him with innovations in social and political thought that profoundly affected his assessment of the judicial process as a means for resolving controversies. He believed that, unlike legislative and administrative determinations, judicial decisions in an interdependent age are inherently abstract and, therefore, dangerous: limitations of human reason and inadequacies inhering in the process of judicial fact-finding make it impossible for judges to grasp the collective experience and knowledge of an interdependent culture.

In sharp contrast to the view that Frankfurter's constitutional jurisprudence manifested a faith in judicial power, this study suggests (in Chapter 7) that his rulings revealed a desire to reduce radically the Court's influence in American life. He employed discretionary standards in his decisions, but not because he had great faith in judicial power and expertise. Quite the contrary. As Justice Black demonstrated, adherence to rigid rules in constitutional contexts serves to force the exercise of judicial review in many instances and thus contravenes the principle that legislatures and administrative bodies represent superior forums for resolving social and political conflicts. By contrast, employment of a standard that specifically limits application of the judicial veto to situations in which no rational person could maintain the constitutionality of a challenged act is the only way to approximate legislative and administrative supremacy in a constitutional system that allows for judicial review. When Frankfurter aggressively used the power of review in certain areas of law, he simply held in abeyance his pronounced fear of judicial abstraction in order to secure values he regarded as especially important.

Frankfurter is, of course, remembered more for his refusal to use judicial review when effective means of inducing political change seemed unavailable to minorities than for his resort to that power. Unlike Black, he possessed no recognition that the political process might be unreceptive to minority demands to alter unjust policies. Frankfurter's faith in politics reflected further implications that Progressive social theorists drew from the fact of interdependence: the same phenomenon that led Progressives to fear judicial resolution of controversies inspired them to believe in a social predisposition toward integration or harmony. In the same way that the separate-but-interrelated components of biological organisms are naturally harmonious, they argued, the constituent elements of an interdependent society tend toward consensus and integration.

Chapter 8 reveals that Robert Jackson did not share Frankfurter's faith in the integrative nature of society and politics. Far from belonging to the Progressive intelligentsia, Jackson had no college training. Furthermore, he learned his law largely in the traditional manner, as an apprentice. (He attended law school for one year.) In his professional life prior to governmental service, he exemplified the mainstay of the nineteenth-century legal community: the generalist country lawyer. From his traditional legal background, he acquired a fear of majority oppression and a belief that constitutional adjudication provides an essential limit on politics, for he read and embraced the works of nineteenth-century jurists who presented this argument for judicial supremacy.

While Jackson shared with Black a belief in judicial hegemony over constitutional interpretation, he had in common with Frankfurter a fear of judicial abstraction. In spite of his unfamiliarity with Progressive social thought, Jackson perceived the interdependent nature of the society in which he lived. After defending New Deal policies against charges of unconstitutionality, he concluded that the process of judicial fact-finding is inadequate to collect and summarize the experience of an interdependent culture. Jackson had actually acquired a fear of abstraction (if not a belief that judicial decisions are inherently abstract) well before becoming a public servant. He had come from a practical people, had studied as an apprentice the empirical method of the common law, and had developed as a country lawyer an appreciation for the varying contexts surrounding cases.

If Jackson's traditional legal background contributed to his fear of judicial abstraction, Chapter 9 suggests that it also afforded the means by which he attempted to ease the tension in his thought between this fear and his belief in the importance of constitutional adjudication. In deciding constitutional controversies, he employed the method of the common law. If the Court could not avoid abstraction entirely because of the deficiencies inhering in its fact-finding process, he believed, it could at least avoid compounding the problem: adherence to the common-law method would ensure judicial attentiveness to the particular circumstances of cases. Judges could reduce further the possibility that enduring harm might result from their decision making if they de-emphasized in constitutional contexts the other component of the common law: the principle of *stare decisis*, or continuity in the law. Jackson's pragmatism, then, was a consequence not of the Nuremberg trial, as some scholars suggest, but of his efforts to minimize the peculiarly modern problem of abstraction through resort to a traditional method of decision making—one that demands of judges an appreciation of the novelty of the circumstances of cases.

The final chapter suggests that the significance of this study extends beyond its contributions to historical narrative and the support it lends the observation that a judge's values and attributes influence his or her rulings. Black, Frankfurter, and Jackson afforded insights into considerations that remain at the center of the debate over the Court's proper role in constitutional controversies. These considerations include both the warrant for a judicial corrective to democratic government and the competency of courts to address constitutional problems of the modern age. Moreover, the justices revealed the inadequacy of models of judicial behavior that neglect the cultural context in which American judges operate, for these men acknowledged the social demand that judges render decisions according to legal (as opposed to personal) criteria. Each man's performance on the Court reflected an interplay between personal values and external pressures to exclude such values from judicial rulings. One will find the origin of these pressures or expectations in the history of the early American republic. This history also provides the groundwork necessary for an analysis of the ideological backgrounds of the New Deal justices.

Notes

1. Robert H. Jackson, *The Struggle for Judicial Supremacy: A Study of a Crisis in American Power Politics* (New York: Knopf, 1941), 86–175, 333

(quoting Franklin Roosevelt); C. Herman Pritchett, *The Roosevelt Court* (New York: Macmillan, 1948), 1–7.

2. As quoted in Jackson, *Struggle for Judicial Supremacy*, 343–45, 349.

3. Ibid., 197–235, 329 (quoting Roosevelt); Henry J. Abraham, *Justices and Presidents: A Political History of Appointments to the Supreme Court*, 2d ed. (New York: Oxford University Press, 1985), 207–9; Robert G. McCloskey, *The American Supreme Court* (Chicago: University of Chicago Press, 1960), 174–79.

4. John P. Frank, *Mr. Justice Black: The Man and His Opinions* (New York: Knopf, 1949), xv.

5. Abraham, *Justices and Presidents*, 377 (survey quoted); James Magee, *Mr. Justice Black: Absolutist on the Court* (Charlottesville: University Press of Virginia, 1980), xii (unidentified academics quoted)

6. Abraham, *Justices and Presidents*, 377 (quoted); Helen Shirley Thomas, *Felix Frankfurter: Scholar on the Bench* (Baltimore: Johns Hopkins University Press, 1960), viii.

7. H. N. Hirsch, *The Enigma of Felix Frankfurter* (New York: Basic Books, 1981), 5; Fred Rodell, *Nine Men: A Political History of the Supreme Court from 1790—1955* (New York: Random House, 1955), 269.

8. G. Edward White, *The American Judicial Tradition: Profiles of Leading American Judges* (New York: Oxford University Press, 1976), 331.

9. In 1970, sixty-five scholars participated in a survey that asked them to evaluate the ninety-six justices who served on the Supreme Court between 1789 and 1969. They identified Hugo Black and Felix Frankfurter as "great," while they classified Robert Jackson, William Douglas, and Wiley Rutledge as "near great." Roosevelt's remaining appointees—Stanley Reed, Frank Murphy, and James F. Byrnes—earned the descriptive adjectives "average," "average," and "failure," respectively. Abraham, *Justices and Presidents*, 377–79.

10. White, *American Judicial Tradition*, 231–32. See also Abraham, *Justices and Presidents*, 233–34; Richard A. Posner, *Cardozo: A Study in Reputation* (Chicago: University of Chicago Press, 1990), 140–41; Felix Frankfurter, "Mr. Justice Jackson," *Harvard Law Review* 68 (1955): 938; Philip Halpern, "Robert H. Jackson, 1892–1954," *Stanford Law Review* 8 (1955): 4.

11. White, *American Judicial Tradition*, 231, 233, 243, 245–46; Paul A. Weidner, "Justice Jackson and the Judicial Function," *Michigan Law Review* 53 (1955): 590; Vincent M. Barnett Jr., "Mr. Justice Jackson and the Supreme Court," *Western Political Quarterly* 1 (1948): 240–41; Charles Fairman, "Associate Justice of the Supreme Court," *Columbia Law Review* 55 (1955): 487; James A. Nielson, "Robert H. Jackson: The Middle Ground," *Louisiana Law Review* 6 (1945): 395, 401; Glendon Schubert, "Jackson's Judicial Philosophy: An Exploration in Value Analysis," *American Political Science Review* 59 (1965): 957, 963; Robert J. Steamer, "Mr. Justice Jackson and the First Amendment," *University of Pittsburgh Law Review* 15 (1954): 194.

12. C. Herman Pritchett, *Civil Liberties and the Vinson Court* (Chicago: University of Chicago Press, 1954), 228–29; Wallace Mendelson, "Justices Black and Frankfurter: Supreme Court Majority and Minority Trends," *Journal of Politics* 12 (1950): 74 n. 28; Posner, *Cardozo*, 66; Walter F. Murphy, "Mr. Justice Jackson, Free Speech, and the Judicial Function," *Vanderbilt Law Review* 12 (1959): 1019.

13. For a listing of works on the New Deal Court, see Henry J. Abraham, *The Judicial Process: An Introductory Analysis of the Courts of the United States, England, and France*, 5th ed. (New York: Oxford University Press, 1986), 425–26. For a listing of works on Black and Frankfurter, see ibid., 471, 475–76.

14. See note 11 above.

15. James F. Simon, *The Antagonists: Hugo Black, Felix Frankfurter and Civil Liberties in Modern America* (New York: Simon & Schuster, 1989), 18; Michael E. Parrish, *Felix Frankfurter and His Times: The Reform Years* (New York: Free Press, 1982), 177.

16. Mark Silverstein, *Constitutional Faiths: Felix Frankfurter, Hugo Black, and the Process of Judicial Decision Making* (Ithaca: Cornell University Press, 1984); Tinsley E. Yarbrough, *Mr. Justice Black and His Critics* (Durham: Duke University Press, 1988); Howard Ball and Phillip J. Cooper, *Of Power and Right: Hugo Black, William O. Douglas, and America's Constitutional Revolution* (New York: Oxford University Press, 1992).

17. Silverstein, *Constitutional Faiths*; Ball and Cooper, *Of Power and Right*. Although Yarbrough does not examine Black's background, he apparently accepts the view that the justice's jurisprudence was the product of Alabama's Populist culture, because he refers approvingly to Silverstein's work. Yarbrough, *Black and His Critics*, 160–61.

18. For advocates of the older view, see Wallace Mendelson, "Hugo Black and Judicial Discretion," *Political Science Quarterly* 85 (1970): 17–39; Glendon Schubert, *The Constitutional Polity* (Boston: Boston University Press, 1970), 75–129.

19. See Mendelson, "Hugo Black and Judicial Discretion," 38.

20. He believed that, while history supports the application of the Bill of Rights against the states, it precludes judicial use of the Fourteenth Amendment's due process clause to protect property interests against state regulation.

21. Silverstein, *Constitutional Faiths*, 130.

22. White, *American Judicial Tradition*, 320, 327; Wallace Mendelson, "Mr. Justice Frankfurter: Law and Choice," *Vanderbilt Law Review* 10 (1957): 349–50; Alexander M. Bickel, "Justice Frankfurter at Seventy-Five," *New Republic* 137 (18 November 1957): 7–9; Sanford V. Levinson, "The Democratic Faith of Felix Frankfurter," *Stanford Law Review* 25 (1973): 439–40.

23. Levinson, "Democratic Faith of Felix Frankfurter," 430–48.

24. Silverstein, *Constitutional Faiths*; Gary J. Jacobsohn, *Pragmatism,*

Statesmanship and the Supreme Court (Ithaca: Cornell University Press, 1977); Melvin I. Urofsky, *Felix Frankfurter: Judicial Restraint and Individual Liberties* (Boston: Twayne Publishers, 1991), 148–49.

25. Silverstein, *Constitutional Faiths*, 89.

26. Silverstein attempts to reconcile Frankfurter's rejection of the doctrine of judicial supremacy with the argument that the justice had great faith in judicial power. See *Constitutional Faiths*, 145–46, where he says Frankfurter believed that entrusting the Court with the primary responsibility of protecting rights "would severely restrict [its] flexibility. . . . If the Court was to assume the primary responsibility for protecting civil liberties in the United States, the ability to weigh and balance, critical elements of judicial statesmanship would be lost." Jacobsohn makes a similar point in *Pragmatism, Statesmanship and the Supreme Court*, 125, 131. I criticize this argument in Chapter 7.

27. White, *American Judicial Tradition*, 247. See also ibid., 234, 238, 249–50.

28. Abraham, *Justices and Presidents*, 232–33; Paul A. Freund, "Individual and Commonwealth in the Thought of Mr. Justice Jackson," *Stanford Law Review* 8 (1955): 16–19; Louis L. Jaffe, "Mr. Justice Jackson," *Harvard Law Review* 68 (1955): 967–70.

29. Psychological analysis represents an alternative method of investigation. Harry Hirsch, for example, claims that "Frankfurter can only be understood politically if we understand him psychologically, and . . . we can understand him psychologically as representing a textbook case of a neurotic personality: someone whose self-image is overblown and yet, at the same time, essential to his sense of well-being." Hirsch continues, "The hypotheses offered here do not deny the importance of Frankfurter's political beliefs; they are not meant as a substitute for traditional ideological analysis, but rather as its complement." Yet Hirsch also maintains that "*the key* to Frankfurter's political behavior was his attitude toward opposition, and . . . the vehemence with which he reacted to opposition was a function of the psychological process involved in the formation of his self-image." *Enigma of Felix Frankfurter*, 5, 9–10, 201 (emphasis added). While I concede that psychological investigation complements ideological analysis, I believe that the latter affords a better understanding of Frankfurter's performance than Hirsch allows. I agree, however, that existing studies of the justice are inadequate.

30. Some scholars emphasize the communitarian aspects of late-nineteenth- and early-twentieth-century southern life to explain Black's conservative rulings. They view the justice's jurisprudence, not as antihierarchical, but as an effort to balance the competing concerns of individual liberty and community welfare. See Tony Freyer, ed., *Justice Hugo Black and Modern America* (Tuscaloosa: University of Alabama Press, 1990). I address this argument in Chapter 5.

2

Early American Society and Politics

Decentralized Politics in a Society of Island Communities

Robert Wiebe aptly characterized early-nineteenth-century America as "a society of island communities." "Weak communication," he noted, "severely restricted the interaction among these islands and dispersed the power to form opinion and enact public policy. . . . The heart of American democracy was local autonomy. A century after France had developed a reasonably efficient, centralized public administration, Americans could not even conceive of a managerial government."[1]

American rejection of the organizational qualities of the imperial powers of Europe in the preceding century accounted for the radical decentralization of nineteenth-century politics. The United States had its beginnings in a war fought to throw off such elements of European rule as standing armies, centralized and unaccountable taxing authorities, and growing numbers of imperial administrators. The political landscape of the post-Revolutionary era reflected the new nation's antipathy toward concentrated and centralized political forms: Americans located sovereignty in thirteen separate state legislatures and used frequent elections to ensure representation of majority sentiment. These arrangements avoided the dangers that centralized and unaccountable authority posed, but the resulting destabilization revealed the need to invest some degree of power in a national body. The Articles of Confederation represented an attempt to secure effective government without betraying revolutionary ideals. But the limitations of the confederation in providing adequate force, finance, and commercial regulation necessitated further institutional reorganization.[2]

The great achievement of the founders of the Constitution was to compensate for the deficiencies of the Articles without engendering the abuses of power that had prompted the break with imperial rule. Fearful of concentrated political authority, the founders separated power on the national level among a bicameral legislature, an executive, and a judiciary and made these branches accountable to public will, either directly or indirectly. They also provided the members of each branch with the necessary will and constitutional means to resist encroachments from the other branches, thus minimizing the danger that any single national institution would dominate.[3]

The framers further confined national power by dividing sovereignty between the central government and the old state governments. This system of federalism severely "inhibited the penetration of central power throughout the nation by ensuring the integrity of those states, each with its own institutional organization, legal code, and law enforcement apparatus."[4] Constitutional federalism thus preserved in the new American state the radical decentralization that had been present in revolutionary political forms.

Throughout the nineteenth century, the national government assumed a subordinate position in American political life. Central authorities fought the country's wars, engaged in international relations, acquired new territories, and aided economic development. But Americans experienced the national political presence primarily through such nonthreatening, service-oriented institutions as land offices, post offices, and customhouses. The states assumed the substantive tasks of domestic governance; their legal codes embodied the most important social choices, including the structure of the economy and the regulation of the family. Decentralization even characterized the nation's system of defense; the central government "relied upon a militia system of citizen-soldiers organized and controlled by the several states."[5]

The Importance of Parties and Courts

National penetration of the country in the nineteenth century may have been slight, but the central government still had to find a way to deliver its support services to the states. Moreover, both levels of government had to implement legislative directives. The American distaste for European political forms complicated these tasks because neither a developed administrative apparatus nor a trained civil service existed to perform the operational functions of governing.[6]

Political parties presented a partial solution to the nation's bureaucratic deficiencies. After an early flirtation with nonpartisanship, Americans came to see the value of permanent partisan competition. State and local party organizations formed first, perfecting techniques for gaining power. Parties gradually connected their machinery to national politics during the presidencies of Andrew Jackson and Martin Van Buren. Whig recognition of the need for solidarity in opposition to the Democrats ensured the continued existence and development of national two-party competition. Within different levels of government, parties promoted working relationships between the legislative and executive branches. And between governmental levels, parties delivered national support services to the states. Local party organizations staffed and oversaw the operation of the federal government's regional post offices, land offices, and customhouses. "[T]he federal patronage appointee became the embodiment of a series of concrete ties between President and Congress and between local and national governments."[7]

Indeed, the political patronage that was integral to partisan management of these operational tasks, and which came to be known as the "spoils system," became the connective tissue within each party. In order to appeal to a broad, heterogeneous electorate, parties could only promote the most general policy preferences in their platforms. Political coalitions thus formed around partisan promises of a broad distribution of federal offices, rather than substantive programs for governing the nation. The lack of comprehensive programs revealed the limitations of partisan politics. Yet parties demonstrated a capacity to promote moderate national majorities and to compensate somewhat for the bureaucratic deficiencies of the early American state.[8]

While partisanship solved certain of the new state's operational problems, it did not aid in the administration of law. In fact, it exacerbated this problem. One would expect vagueness to characterize statutes issuing from legislatures composed of numerous, diverse interests. The natural impulse of parties to maintain broad coalitions reinforced the tendency toward statutory imprecision and fostered a logrolling politics.[9]

Although government in the nineteenth century was passive relative to its twentieth-century counterpart, the national and state legislatures of the early 1800s managed to create a sizable administrative burden. The national government was less to blame for this situation, of course, since it was largely inactive, although not entirely passive. (Some states and interests pressed the federal government for large internal improvements.) The states were responsible for many more forms of intervention, including quality control over export commodities, regulation of weights and measures, preliminary efforts at conservation, and public health regulations.[10]

Much business of state legislatures was promotional rather than regulatory. Such work usually involved granting charters to corporations and amending these charters. At this time, "the business corporation [was] a unique, *ad hoc* creation, vesting exclusive control over a public asset or natural resource in one group of favorites or investors." The overwhelming majority of early corporations were banks, insurance companies, water companies, and bridges; legislatures granted charters to these interests by statute, one by one. As entrepreneurs increasingly made use of the corporation (over the less efficient partnership) to structure and finance their ventures, the nature of this legal institution began to change. Over the course of the first half of the nineteenth century, the corporation became "a general form for organizing a business, legally open to all, and with few real restrictions on entry, duration, and management." Whereas legislatures initially scrutinized each charter and tailored clauses to the particular case, this method proved impractical after requests for corporate charters grew. The method also inhibited the logrolling essential to partisan politics. Routinization and standardization of charters helped remedy this situation somewhat, but passage of general incorporation laws ultimately became necessary. Resort to these laws meant, however, that legislatures could no longer supervise or adequately control the corporations they created.[11]

The American judiciary assumed this administrative burden. As corporations multiplied, so did litigation involving them. Courts ruled on controversies regarding the internal life of corporations, that is, the relations among officers, directors, shareholders, and creditors. Moreover, legislatures virtually delegated to courts responsibility to oversee the relations of corporations to the rest of society. Many charters included reserve clauses for the protection of the public interest, which heavily involved courts in the exercise of the states' police powers. Indeed, "the judiciary became the chief source of economic surveillance in the nineteenth century." Along with parties, the "courts had become the American surrogate for a more fully developed administrative apparatus." The magnitude of the courts' administrative obligations can only be appreciated when one realizes that existing law on corporations was not relevant to the new situations judges faced. The courts essentially had to recreate corporate law in the nineteenth century.[12]

Judges were able to accomplish this task only because of an earlier change in their perception of the nature of the common law. In the *eighteenth* century, "the common law was conceived of as a body of essentially fixed doctrine to be applied in order to achieve a fair result between private litigants in individual cases." American judges "almost never self-consciously employed the common law as a creative instrument for directing men's energies toward social change"; they equated the common law with a static, customary standard and regarded their function as merely that of discovering and applying preexisting legal rules. Viewing judicial innovation as neither permissible nor necessary, judges sought to adhere strictly to precedent.[13]

As Americans sought after the Revolution to redefine the basis of legal obligation in terms of popular sovereignty, law that was not the product of popular will began to lose its legitimacy. The common law also drew criticism for being unpredictable; reality did not correspond with judicial rhetoric concerning the static nature of court decisions. Over time, judges had modified English law to fit American circumstances. Moreover, with no system for recording indigenous rulings, judges simply operated from memory. Many individuals, including judges and lawyers, thus came to view the common law as an exercise of judicial will. Although considerable sentiment developed in favor of codification, efforts in this regard failed to supplant the common law. Legal reformers themselves soon realized the impossibility of formulating a comprehensive code, and they accepted the inevitability of a degree of judicial innovation.[14]

The changed perception of the common law served the judiciary well when, during the first two decades of the nineteenth century, courts faced controversies involving new corporate structures. "Law was no longer conceived of as an eternal set of principles expressed in custom and derived from natural law. Nor was it regarded primarily as a body of rules designed to achieve justice only in the individual case. Instead, judges came to think of the common law as equally responsible with legislation for governing society and promoting socially desirable conduct. The emphasis on law as an instrument of policy encouraged innovation and allowed judges to formulate legal doctrine with the self-conscious goal of bringing about social change." Abandoning subservience to the doctrine of precedent, judges felt free to disregard the authority of prior cases for functional or policy reasons. When they adhered to precedent, they now did so to enable individuals to anticipate the consequences of particular forms of conduct, not to preclude judicial innovation.[15]

During the Jacksonian era of the 1820s and 1830s, judicial creativity once again became the object of sustained public criticism. Reappearance of the view that law must be a product of the people's will was one manifestation of the democratic ethos of this period. As in the past, this sentiment inspired efforts to codify the common law. Codifiers also sought to emulate, if not reproduce, French achievements in legal systematization and to follow the teachings of the English utilitarian—and enemy of indeterminate judicial decision making—Jeremy Bentham.[16]

The codification movement induced certain defensive responses within the elite legal community. Establishment of the treatise tradition was the most notable effort to defend the legal status quo. Such legal luminaries as James Kent, Joseph Story, and Joseph Angell attempted to demonstrate the "scientific" nature of judge-made law, and the legal treatise was their vehicle. "Through classification of subjects, [the treatise] sought to show that law [is 'scientific' because it] proceeds not from will but from reason. Through its 'black letter' presentation of supposed 'general principles' of law it sought to suppress all controversy over policy while promoting the comfortable ideal of a logical, symmetrical, and most important, inexorable system of law."[17]

Although treatise writers portrayed the common law as "scientific," they did not return to the eighteenth-century view of law as static and unchanging. Rather, by systematizing, or bringing conceptual order to, a multitude of rulings, these jurists sought to demonstrate that, when addressing the seemingly infinite variations in human conflicts that found their way into litigation, judges acted, not by fiat, but by common-law reasoning. "[T]he most typical nineteenth-century defense of the common law against the charge of the codifiers that 'judge-made law . . . [,] from its nature, must always be *ex post facto*' was the reply that there really was no common law 'case of first impression' because analogical reasoning from similar cases or principles provided a self-executing process of discovery, at least for those learned in the law." Lemuel Shaw, chief justice of the Supreme Judicial Court of Massachusetts from 1830 to 1860, commented on the "genius" of the common law, that is, the achievement of a balance between the competing poles of continuity and growth: "It is one of the great merits and advantages of the common law that instead of a series of detailed practical rules . . . [it] consists of a few broad and comprehensive principles founded on reason, natural justice, and enlightened public policy modified and adapted to the circumstances of all the particular cases which fall within it. . . . [When new cases arise, they are] governed by the general principle . . . , modified and adapted to new circumstances by considerations of fitness and propriety, of reason and justice."[18]

The importance of courts to American politics was not limited to the function of molding the common law to meet new economic circumstances. During the early nineteenth century, the federal judiciary also became involved, however haltingly, in disputes between branches and levels of government. The great chief justice John Marshall sought to use the United States Supreme Court to promote Federalist ideology, especially an expansive notion of national authority and the corollary view that exercises of state power must fall when in conflict with federal prerogatives. The latter doctrine was immediately relevant, while the former principle would become germane when the national government assumed greater responsibilities in the next century. Both doctrines were antithetical to the profound localism of early-nineteenth-century politics.[19]

With power over neither purse nor sword, Marshall could not hope that Americans would heed the Court's rulings unless they viewed the judiciary as the ultimate arbiter of constitutional questions. Although he secured for courts the power of judicial review,[20] he did not see the fulfillment of the doctrine of judicial supremacy during his tenure. The chief justice met strong opposition in Thomas Jefferson and Andrew Jackson. Both presidents subscribed to a departmental theory of constitutional interpretation. Each branch of the government, they argued, is obliged to determine for itself the constitutionality of matters before it; the Court has no claim to superiority over determinations of the other branches.[21]

Yet toward the end of the nineteenth century, the federal judiciary would achieve hegemony over resolution of constitutional questions. Marshall's statesmanlike alternation between boldness and prudence, which gradually accustomed the nation to the Court's rulings, was partly responsible for eventual widespread acceptance of judicial supremacy. Marshall also aided his cause by portraying judicial decision making as an application of reason rather than will. In the manner of the treatise writers, he insisted that "judicial power, as contradistinguished from the power of the law, has no existence. Courts are the mere instruments of the law, and can will nothing."[22]

In spite of Marshall's statesmanship, widespread acceptance of judicial supremacy occurred only after people came to believe that legislatures were undeserving of public trust. As far back as the late eighteenth century, Americans exhibited a "growing mistrust of legislative assemblies." "The legislatures seemed to many to be simply another kind of magistracy, promulgating decrees to which the collective people, standing outside the entire government, had never really given their full and unqualified assent. Thus all the acts of the legislature, it could now be argued, were still 'liable to examination and scrutiny by the people, that is, by the Supreme Judiciary, their servants for this purpose; and those that militate with the fundamental laws, or impugn the principles of the constitution, are to be judicially set aside as void, and of no effect.' "[23]

Marshall's Federalist associate, Alexander Hamilton, articulated a functional justification for judicial supremacy that aided the doctrine's eventual triumph. In the seventy-eighth number of the *Federalist*, he characterized courts as "faithful guardians of the Constitution, where legislative invasions of it had been instigated by the major voice of the community." Federal judges are uniquely qualified to serve as "bulwarks of a limited Constitution," he argued, because, among public officials, only they possess permanent tenure. Indeed, "[w]ithout [an independent judiciary], all the reservations of particular rights or privileges would amount to nothing." "Limitations of this kind can be preserved in practice no other way than through the medium of courts of justice, whose duty it must be to declare all acts contrary to the manifest tenor of the Constitution void."[24] By emphasizing the judiciary's political insularity, *Federalist* 78 added to prevailing concerns (over legislative inattention to majority sentiment) the observation that political majorities themselves are oppressive. Because the latter problem is not politically resolvable, the essay presented the most compelling argument in favor of judicial hegemony over constitutional questions.

Echoing Hamilton, the treatise writers worked to disseminate the concept of judicial supremacy. Story made the doctrine a prominent theme in his *Commentaries*. The theme of judicial supremacy also ran throughout part 2 of Kent's *Commentaries*. Kent "held fast to the conviction that majorities are fierce and pitiless, that they are prone to destroy, not only chartered rights, but the freedom of decision and the independence of the mind. Against these dangers of majority rule [he] interposed 'an independent judiciary, venerable by its gravity, its dignity, and its wisdom'; and for example of such a judiciary he pointed to the Supreme Court of the United States under Chief Justice Marshall." Like Marshall, Kent also envisioned an important role for the Court in resolving federalism questions. He could not "conceive of anything more grand and imposing in the whole administration of human justice than the spectacle of the Supreme Court sitting in solemn judgement upon the conflicting claims of the national and state sovereignties and tranquilizing all jealous and angry passions."[25]

Early American Lawyers

The judiciary's significance to American politics in the arbitration of jurisdictional disputes and in economic surveillance ensured an important place in governance for the prime constituents of courts— lawyers. Attorneys in the late eighteenth and early nineteenth centuries were an interesting mix. The country lawyer, the mainstay of the profession, was a colorful figure who, by virtue of the scarcity of legal source materials, had to rely heavily upon native wit in handling cases. "An independent generalist, he served all comers, with no large fees to turn his head toward a favored few. He moved easily between his casual, cluttered office, where informality (it was assumed) nurtured trust and loyalty, and the courtroom, where skill as an advocate earned him local renown. Self-reliant and persevering, he was the common man's lawyer in a pre-urban, pre-industrial society."[26]

Statesmen-lawyers represented a much different segment of the profession. These attorneys were the aristocracy of the bar that Toc-queville described and admired. Marshall, Story, Kent, and Daniel Webster personified this type of attorney. Usually of elite back-grounds, statesmen-lawyers advised mercantile houses on matters of insurance and international trade, and they formed a small but sophisticated bar of commerce. Like their rural counterparts, states-men-lawyers were usually solo practitioners who established their reputations through courtroom oratory. These attorneys also em-ployed their legal expertise on behalf of significant political causes; they felt an obligation to serve in public affairs and filled many posts in the early American state.[27]

At this time, lawyers acquired training almost exclusively through apprenticeship. An apprentice usually performed certain clerical duties in his master's office, read from the works of the oracles of the common law—Blackstone, Coke, and Kent—and learned from observ-ing his master at his work. The quality of instruction varied greatly. "At worst, an apprentice went through a haphazard course of drudgery and copywork, with a few glances, catch-as-catch-can, at the law

books." Some apprentices (most certainly a minority) had the good
fortune to be under the tutelage of masters who were committed
and competent instructors. Whatever the quality of teaching, by the
beginning of the nineteenth century, few individuals would have considered becoming lawyers without some period of apprenticeship.
Indeed, of the thirteen original states, twelve required some period of
training; in 1800, fourteen out of nineteen states or organized territories did so.[28]

In the first two decades of the nineteenth century, states began to
reduce or even abolish requirements for apprenticeship. The need for
a large, open-ended legal profession in a nation of widespread land,
and (to a lesser extent) capital, ownership explained this policy change.
Pressure to lower requirements for entrance to the trade intensified
with the spread of the egalitarian ideology of the Jacksonian era. By
1840, only eleven out of thirty jurisdictions required a period of
preparation. "Even at the low point of professional self-government,
[however,] no one practiced law without some pretense at qualification," that is, without some time spent in a lawyer's office.[29]

Jacksonianism may have had a rather limited impact upon legal
training, but it inspired further division within the legal community.
With the rise of partisan politics, the statesman-lawyer was no longer
dominant in government; he became a casualty of the spoils system
and its underlying philosophy that any person of intelligence and
probity could hold office. Attorneys still entered politics, but they now
considered themselves professional politicians first and lawyers
second.[30]

Despite the value to American politics of permanent party competition, partisan electioneering for the sake of patronage convinced
many Americans that parties were composed of vulgar, self-interested
individuals. Those attorneys not involved in partisan politics thus
regarded professional politicians as damaging to the prestige of the
legal trade. To avoid the taint of partisanship, the former declared
themselves apolitical, the possessors of a technical mastery of the law
and the suppliers of specialized litigation skills.[31]

Also, because of the pervasiveness of Jacksonian sentiment, nonpa-
trician lawyers attempted to dissociate themselves from the elitist
image that attached to the aristocracy of the bar. They emphasized
that they did not acquire expertise through privilege or an undue
reliance upon book learning. In sharp contrast to the anti-Jacksonian
treatise writers, who stressed the esoteric, scientific nature of law,
journeymen of the bar maintained that legal expertise, while not

achievable through mere dilettantism, is largely a product of common sense or a firsthand acquaintance with everyday life. They also portrayed themselves as paragons of industry and fortitude, as examples of self-made men.[32] By midcentury, then, the American legal community displayed a widening gulf between statesmen-lawyers and general practitioners, as well as a fresh split between professional politicians and the remainder of the bar.

The bar's composition, as well as its method of instruction, would undergo further changes during the urban-industrial transformation of the late nineteenth and early twentieth centuries. This massive social shift, "undoubtedly the most profound and rapid alteration in the material conditions of life that human society has ever experienced,"[33] would also have a tremendous impact on the system of parties and courts that, to this point, had assumed the operational tasks of governing.

Notes

1. Robert H. Wiebe, *The Search for Order, 1877–1920,* (New York: Hill & Wang, 1967), xiii.

2. Stephen Skowronek, *Building a New American State: The Expansion of Administrative Capacities, 1877–1920* (New York: Cambridge University Press, 1982), 20–21; Gordon S. Wood, *The Creation of the American Republic, 1776–1787* (Chapel Hill: University of North Carolina Press, 1969), 1–429.

3. Skowronek, *Building a New American State,* 21; Wood, *Creation of the American Republic,* 430–564.

4. Skowronek, *Building a New American State,* 21–22.

5. Ibid., 22–23 (quoted); Lawrence Friedman, *A History of American Law,* 2d ed. (New York: Simon & Schuster, 1985), 177–85.

6. Friedman, *History of American Law,* 185–87; James Willard Hurst, *The Legitimacy of the Business Corporation in the Law of the United States, 1780–1970* (Charlottesville: University Press of Virginia, 1970), 40.

7. James W. Ceaser, *Presidential Selection: Theory and Development* (Princeton: Princeton University Press, 1979), 77, 90–92; Richard Hofstadter, *The Idea of a Party System* (Berkeley: University of California Press, 1969), 2; Skowronek, *Building a New American State,* 24–25 (quoted).

8. Skowronek, *Building a New American State,* 25–26; Ceaser, *Presidential Selection,* 123–69.

9. Skowronek, *Building a New American State,* 29.

10. Friedman, *History of American Law,* 182–85.

11. Ibid., 177–95, 511–31 (p. 191 quoted); Skowronek, *Building a New*

American State, 27; Kermit L. Hall, *The Magic Mirror: Law in American History* (New York: Oxford University Press, 1989), 109–11.

12. Skowronek, *Building a New American State*, 27–28 (quoted); Friedman, *History of American Law*, 187, 198–99.

13. Morton J. Horwitz, *The Transformation of American Law, 1780–1860* (Cambridge: Harvard University Press, 1977), 1, 8–9.

14. Ibid., 9–30; Wood, *Creation of the American Republic*, 291–305; Hall, *Magic Mirror*, 79–80; Richard E. Ellis, *The Jeffersonian Crisis: Courts and Politics in the Young Republic* (New York: W. W. Norton, 1971).

15. Horwitz, *Transformation of American Law, 1780–1860*, 25–27, 30 (quoted).

16. Charles M. Cook, *The American Codification Movement: A Study of Antebellum Legal Reform* (Westport, Conn.: Greenwood Press, 1981), 46–95.

17. Horwitz, *Transformation of American Law, 1780–1860*, 257–58 (quoted); Friedman, *History of American Law*, 329–33; David Sugarman, "Legal Theory, the Common Law Mind and the Making of the Textbook Tradition," in *Legal Theory and Common Law*, ed. William Twining (London: Basil Blackwell, 1986), 33–44.

18. Morton J. Horwitz, *The Transformation of American Law, 1870–1960* (New York: Oxford University Press, 1992), 202–3 (quoted); Robert W. Gordon, "Legal Thought and Legal Practice in the Age of American Enterprise, 1870–1920," in *Professions and Professional Ideologies in America*, ed. Gerald L. Geison (Chapel Hill: University of North Carolina Press, 1983), 83–84; Robert W. Gordon, "Historicism in Legal Scholarship," *Yale Law Journal* 90 (1981): 1039; Sugarman, "Making of the Textbook Tradition," 40–41; Alexis de Tocqueville, *Democracy in America*, ed. J. P. Mayer, trans. George Lawrence (Garden City, N.Y.: Anchor Books, 1969), 268; G. Edward White, *The American Judicial Tradition: Profiles of Leading American Judges* (New York: Oxford University Press, 1976), 60 (quoting Lemuel Shaw).

19. See, e.g., *Marbury v. Madison*, 5 U.S. (1 Cranch) 137 (1803); *Fletcher v. Peck*, 10 U.S. (6 Cranch) 87 (1810); *McCulloch v. Maryland*, 17 U.S. (4 Wheaton) 316 (1819); *Gibbons v. Ogden*, 22 U.S. (9 Wheaton) 1 (1824). See also Robert G. McCloskey, *The American Supreme Court* (Chicago: University of Chicago Press, 1960), 26–80.

20. *Marbury v. Madison*, (see note 19 above).

21. Hall, *Magic Mirror*, 91; Ellis, *Jeffersonian Crisis*, 66; McCloskey, *American Supreme Court*, 30, 78–79; Adrienne Koch, *Jefferson and Madison: The Great Collaboration* (New York: Oxford University Press, 1977), 224–32; Robert H. Jackson, *The Struggle for Judicial Supremacy: A Study of a Crisis in American Power Politics* (New York: Knopf, 1941), 28–33. At midcentury, Abraham Lincoln echoed Jefferson's and Jackson's departmental theory of constitutional interpretation. Roy P. Basler, ed., *The Collected Works of Abraham Lincoln* (New Brunswick, N.J.: Rutgers University Press, 1953), 4: 268.

22. Friedman, *History of American Law*, 378; Jackson, *Struggle for Judicial Supremacy*, 37–38; McCloskey, *American Supreme Court*, 54, 56, 64–65, 78; White, *American Judicial Tradition*, 21–22, 33, 148; Arnold M. Paul, *Conservative Crisis and the Rule of Law: Attitudes of Bar and Bench, 1887–1895* (Gloucester, Mass.: Peter Smith, 1976), 230–31; Hall, *Magic Mirror*, 82–84; Robert Kenneth Faulkner, *The Jurisprudence of John Marshall* (Princeton: Princeton University Press, 1968); Shannon C. Stimson, *The American Revolution in the Law: Anglo-American Jurisprudence before John Marshall* (Princeton: Princeton University Press, 1990), 141; *Osborn v. United States Bank*, 865 22 U.S. (9 Wheaton) 738, 866 (1824) (quoted). The contemporaneous observations of Alexis de Tocqueville suggested that Marshall at least witnessed indications of increasing public acceptance of judicial supremacy. *Democracy in America*, 102, 150.

23. Wood, *Creation of the American Republic*, 304–05, 453–63 (p. 456 quoted).

24. Alexander Hamilton, John Jay, and James Madison, *The Federalist*, Modern Library (New York: Random House, n.d.), 509, 508, 505.

25. Joseph Story, *Commentaries on the Constitution of the United States* (1833; reprint, Durham: Carolina Academic Press, 1987), 122–33; John Theodore Horton, *James Kent: A Study in Conservatism, 1763–1847* (New York: Da Capo Press, 1969), (286–87 quoted; 289, quoting James Kent).

26. Jerold S. Auerbach, *Unequal Justice: Lawyers and Social Change in Modern America* (New York: Oxford University Press, 1976), 15 (quoted); Friedman, *History of American Law*, 157–76, 306–10.

27. Friedman, *History of American Law*, 310–14; Skowronek, *Building a New American State*, 31–32; Tocqueville, *Democracy in America*, 263–70.

28. Friedman, *History of American Law*, 98 (quoted), 316–19; Gordon, "Legal Thought and Legal Practice," 85; Auerbach, *Unequal Justice*, 15; Horton, *James Kent*, 304; Robert Stevens, "Two Cheers for 1870: The American Law School," *Perspectives in American History* 5 (1971): 412–13.

29. Friedman, *History of American Law*, 316–18 (p. 318 quoted); Stevens, "Two Cheers for 1870," 416–17.

30. Maxwell Bloomfield, *American Lawyers in a Changing Society, 1776–1876* (Cambridge: Harvard University Press, 1976), 148–49; Maxwell Bloomfield, "Law vs. Politics: The Self-Image of the American Bar (1830–1860)," *American Journal of Legal History* 12 (1968): 314–15; Skowronek, *Building a New American State*, 32–33; Friedman, *History of American Law*, 186–87; Ceaser, *Presidential Selection*, 156–57.

31. Bloomfield, *American Lawyers in a Changing Society*, 148–50; Skowronek, *Building a New American State*, 33; Bloomfield, "Law vs. Politics," 314–17.

32. Bloomfield, *American Lawyers in a Changing Society*, 145–46, 151; Bloomfield, "Law vs. Politics," 311–13, 316; Gordon, "Legal Thought and Legal Practice," 85–87.

33. Thomas L. Haskell, *The Emergence of Professional Social Science: The American Social Science Association and the Nineteenth-Century Crisis of Authority* (Urbana: University of Illinois Press, 1977), 1. Many scholars share this assessment of the significance of the urban-industrial transformation. Ibid., 3–4.

3

The American Industrial Transformation

Industrialism, Interdependence, and Sectionalism

The mid-nineteenth century witnessed the most cataclysmic event in the nation's short history. The Civil War and its antecedents had significant, albeit short-term, implications for the structure of the American state. The Supreme Court's notorious *Dred Scott* ruling temporarily compromised judicial prestige and helped precipitate the disintegration of the two-party system. Furthermore, the localism of the early nineteenth century gave way to "national military conscription, a military occupation of the South, a national welfare agency for former slaves, a national income tax, national monetary controls, and national citizenship."[1]

These structural changes vanished soon after the war concluded. Although the national government had demonstrated power sufficient to mobilize an enormous quantity of resources, maintenance of this authority depended entirely upon the new Republican Party and its ability and willingness to organize men and means. When the South returned to national politics in the 1870s, the federal government rapidly disassembled the war's institutional achievements. Americans demanded an expeditious return to localism and laissez-faire, and politics once again involved a minimal federal presence and the delegation of significant operational tasks to parties and courts.[2]

The return to the politics of the early part of the century coincided with a massive social and economic transformation. The rise of industrialism in the last third of the nineteenth century brought urbanization, increased economic productivity, and a corresponding rise in the standard of living of many Americans. Less obviously, although more significantly, it marked the point at which America moved from a

37

society of island communities to a complex and interdependent social order. Now, "action in one part of society [was] transmitted in the form of direct or indirect consequences to other parts of society with accelerating rapidity, widening scope, and increasing intensity."[3]

Increased interdependence had three sources: a developed commercial market, a revolution in transportation and communications, and increased economic specialization. From early on, the United States possessed the requisite elements for a commercial market. The land afforded abundant resources that individuals could exploit with relatively little effort and capital. Immigrants seeking economic opportunity in America provided entrepreneurs with a ready and cheap supply of labor. Adequate capital, domestic and European, afforded funds for internal development. And finally, economic activity encountered few political barriers. Commercial exchange involved market participants in a network of mutually dependent relationships. But in the early nineteenth century, Americans entered the market only occasionally; most people lived on scattered farms and were virtually self-sufficient.[4]

Technological advances in transportation and communication greatly extended the discipline and interdependence of the market. An explosion of canal building in the second decade of the nineteenth century initiated economic expansion. But the introduction of steamboats and, especially, railroads dramatically increased the reach of market forces. First constructed in the 1830s, railroad lines grew rapidly between 1868 and the depression of 1893; merchants came to see the potential for creating a mass clientele with a form of transportation that was fast and relatively invulnerable to weather. Mid- to late-nineteenth-century communications innovations also promoted economic activity. The telegraph, the telephone, and the modern press each helped coordinate the activities of distant sellers and buyers.[5]

A heightened division of labor attended market expansion. Specialization enabled individuals to escape the competition of outsiders who invaded local economies. At the same time, it gave people the opportunity to move beyond their customary market and exploit a competitive advantage. Although specialization of function afforded tactical advantages, it could not restore the autonomy that preceded market growth. "Far from being an escape from interdependence, it furthered the process, for the specialist became dependent on others to supply his needs. The process was circular: interdependence encouraged specialization, which in turn reinforced and crystallized interdependent relationships."[6]

An interregional division of labor developed within this general pattern of social and economic change. For several reasons, industry concentrated in the Northeast. This region possessed plentiful resources, including coal, lumber, and waterpower. It also had the nation's major transportation arteries, most notably, the Erie Canal. When the locomotive appeared, new rail lines followed these established patterns of transport. The region thus became the hub of a growing rail-transportation system. Finally, entrepreneurs found capital and labor more readily available in Boston, New York, Philadelphia, and Baltimore than in other parts of the country, since these seaport cities had a preexisting concentration of commercial activity.[7]

Lacking these advantages, the South and the West to Middle West remained economically underdeveloped. Manufacturing appeared in a few isolated places, but agriculture and mining dominated the economies of these regions. The South produced tobacco, rice, and, of course, cotton, while the West supplied iron, copper, lead, zinc, lumber, beef, and wheat. These peripheral economies functioned essentially as colonies; they served as sources of food and raw materials for the industrialized Northeast and as markets for northeastern manufactured goods. The new rail network bound this regional division of labor into a national economy.[8]

Inherent regional advantages and disadvantages did not entirely explain sectional differences in levels of economic development. Northeastern economic policies also retarded growth in the South and West to Middle West. Large northern corporations, for example, commanded prices that reinforced a colonial economic pattern within the nation. These business entities emerged in the late nineteenth century, in part, because the mass production techniques and standardization of parts and processes needed to produce goods on a national scale demanded a huge amount of capital. Once established, corporations grew as they sought in numerous ways to protect and control their markets. Vertical integration, or the purchasing of, say, relevant extractive industries and transport facilities, reduced corporate dependence upon others for essential materials and services. Other techniques, such as pools, trusts, and holding companies, represented attempts to control or reduce competition. Once these combinations became monopolistic, they were able to inflate prices artificially and thus bleed scarce funds from the nation's periphery.[9]

Railroads were the corporations most responsible for stunting development in peripheral economies and cementing a colonial relationship among regions. (Indeed, until the turn of the century, most large corporations were railroads.) Cooperating with northeastern industrialists, the railroads established rate differentials to restrict peripheral industrial competition and to reserve peripheral markets for core industries. Shipments of raw materials from the periphery to the northeastern core enjoyed lower rail rates than those sent in the opposite direction. And transfers of manufactured products from the Northeast to the South and West received lower rates than those shipped from the periphery to the core.[10]

To some degree, northerners invested in southern industry. The Civil War had devastated the South, leaving it starved for capital. Southern promoters attracted northern investors with such devices as low taxes and tax exemptions, municipal subsidies, and cheap labor. The manufacturing that developed, however, involved merely the initial processing of crops and resources. Southern industrialists shipped most of these products to the Northeast or abroad. "Value added to them by manufacture, usually the largest proportion of the total value of the finished product, went not to the South or West but to the industrial East or Europe."[11]

Governmental policies reinforced private economic behavior that disadvantaged the nation's periphery. Indeed, sectional economic competition became the dominant influence in American politics. "Emerging from the Civil War and Reconstruction as both agent and product of northern economic development, the American state's close identification with the interests of northern industry and finance created a political economy in which the South was systematically impoverished." Tariffs on manufactured imports caused the most bitter sectional animosity. Northeastern industrialists proposed the protective tariff as a means by which American industry could develop and ultimately compete with the advanced nations of Europe. But these interests alone were not strong enough to secure passage of the tariff. Industrial labor and Civil War veterans afforded additional support for the measure. Labor hoped to secure higher wages through import duties; veterans favored the tariff because it created a budgetary surplus that funded military pensions. Since all of the pro-tariff interests were from the North, "this section retrieved the 'taxes' it paid through imposition of the tariff. The tax imposed by the higher costs of manufactured goods was recaptured by regionally repatriated profits and customs duties were recaptured by the payment of military pensions. The developmental engine left the southern periphery to shoulder almost the entire cost of industrialization; Confederate veterans were not eligible for federal pensions and no indigenous product (save sugar) was protected by the tariff. The periphery was drained while the core prospered."[12]

Federal banking policy also diminished the periphery's position in the national economy. War had destroyed southern banking, and charter restrictions on entry into the national banking system hindered the formation of new banks in peripheral regions. Furthermore, reserve requirements promoted the concentration of capital in northeastern financial centers. Together with governmental subsidies to railroads and waterways, the national banking system promoted the formation of national markets. But the "concentration of capital in the Northeast meant that only the North would be able to exploit the opportunities thus created; national market formation meant northeastern penetration of southern and western periphery economies."[13]

The Populist Revolt: Hierarchy in Society and Politics

Sectional or interregional economic competition was not the only form of social conflict that occurred in the late nineteenth century. Intraregional economic strife was also a significant social fact. Although industry had come to the South to some degree, conflict in this region did not assume the form one would expect in an industrializing economy, namely, the struggle between capital and labor. Rather, southern economic strife involved antagonistic segments of an agricultural population. More specifically, plantation elites from the region's fertile Black Belts clashed with independent yeomen from the upland portions of the southern states. Plantation elites were large agricultural operators who supervised the work of numerous (mostly black) tenants, sharecroppers, and laborers. These wealthy planters were very concerned with maintaining a supply of subordinate black labor. By contrast, upland yeomen were generally poor and less concerned with the maintenance of white supremacy because upcountry soil could not support a plantation economy.[14]

This intrasectional economic rivalry dated from antebellum times, when it had been manifested in a lively two-party competition. The plantation elites had been members of the Whig party, while the small, upcountry farmers had been Democrats in the Jeffersonian and Jacksonian tradition. When the war approached, splits within the southern states over secession paralleled these party divisions. "In every state, the people of the hills, those who had few slaves, and those who had been little blessed in the distribution of this world's

goods, manifested restrained enthusiasm for secession." The "independent yeomanry had no overwhelming desire to take up arms to
defend the slave property of the lowland planters."[15]

Certain factors contributed to the failed reemergence in the postwar
South of partisan competition mirroring the plantation elite—yeoman
division. One-party southern politics was a product, first, of Radical
Republicanism and Reconstruction. These factors bound most of the
region's whites together. Southerners, like the "people of an[y] occupied land[,] bur[ied] their differences and join[ed] forces to repel the
alien." They "retain[ed] an antipathy toward the occupying power"
well after the withdrawal of northern forces in 1877. This enmity
cultivated a strong social taboo against disloyalty to the Democratic
party.[16]

One-party politics also represented the South's only hope of over-
coming sectional government. Southerners united to oppose the self-
serving economic policies of the Northeast. Monopolistic pricing,
discriminatory railroad rates, protective tariffs, and insufficient capital
affected plantation elites and yeomen alike. And "political conflict
over interregional wealth redistribution tended to efface [intraregional]
class divisions."[17]

Moreover, "[u]nity on the national scene was essential in order that
the largest possible bloc could be mobilized to resist any national move
toward interference with southern authority to deal with the race
question as was desired locally." Just as yeomen eventually agreed to
fight to protect slave property, they also joined the plantation elites
after the war in the effort to maintain white supremacy. Such behavior
on the part of upland farmers might seem peculiar, given that only
lowland planters benefited economically from slavery and the institution's postwar incarnation, the notorious Black Codes. But yeomen
were hardly immune to racial prejudice. Indeed, the Negrophobia of
lower-class whites contrasted with the paternalism of wealthy plantation owners. "The conservatives [i.e., the plantation elites] acknowledged that the Negroes belonged in a subordinate role, but [in contrast
to the upland farmers] denied that subordinates had to be ostracized;
they believed that the Negro was inferior, but denied that it followed
that inferiors must be segregated or publicly humiliated. Negro degra-
dation was not a necessary corollary of white supremacy in the
conservative philosophy." The plantation elites even went so far as to
defend Negro suffrage.[18]

The slightly less offensive views of the lowland planters were not a
product of enlightenment so much as enlightened self-interest. For

these individuals sought to enlist black voters in their continued struggle with independent yeomen. Beneath the veneer of regional unity, the "chaotic factional politics" of the antebellum period continued to rage. "The one-party system [of the South was] purely an arrangement for national affairs."[19]

The latent divisions in the southern economy became overt when the elite-dominated Democratic Party proved unreceptive to the demands and concerns of upland farmers. Although sectional politics harmed the entire region, the lack of available capital hit independent yeomen especially hard. They became ensnared in a system of credit that operated as little more than a modified form of slavery. This system involved furnishing merchants who, after providing cash-short yeomen with supplies, took liens on the farmers' crops as security against their investments. Farmers faced a dual-pricing scheme under which cash customers (of which there were few) paid one amount, while credit customers paid a higher price. Merchants then charged interest, often at rates of 100 percent per annum and sometimes twice that figure, on the inflated base price. (The furnishing merchants themselves paid 18 percent or more for credit, usually extended through northeastern banks.) Farmers found repayment well-nigh impossible after the deflationary fiscal policy of the federal government led to a sustained postwar fall in the price of cotton. They would mortgage the following year's crop in a futile attempt to stave off foreclosure and landless tenantry. Not surprisingly, "the central reality in the lives of most [upland] Southern farmers in the late nineteenth century was the desire to escape the crop lien."[20]

The Farmers' Alliance of the 1880s attempted to liberate yeomen from usury with the "sub-treasury" plan. Under this scheme, the federal government would erect warehouses in rural counties, and yeomen would store their crops in these "sub-treasuries" to await higher prices before selling. Alliancemen also expected the federal government to extend them credit in the form of sub-treasury "certificates" or greenbacks. Farmers would receive 80 percent of the local market price for stored produce and pay interest at the rate of 2 percent per annum, plus incidental charges for storage and insurance. In short, the alliance sought to replace "the high-interest crop-mortgage of the furnishing merchant [and eastern banker] with a plan that mortgaged the crop to the federal government at low interest."[21]

At first, the Farmers' Alliance sought to attack the crop-lien system through existing political arrangements. Strong social pressures demanding loyalty to the Southern Democracy led most poor farmers to

look for "Alliance candidates" within the party. Yeomen soon realized, however, that they could not achieve their policy goals in this
manner. The Democrats repeatedly postponed decision on the sub-
treasury until they finally rejected the plan as a party goal. Resistance
to Alliance proposals came from merchants, southern bankers, and the
old antagonists of upland farmers: the plantation elites, or Bourbon
Democrats. Although this coalition represented a minority of party
members, it possessed overwhelming political power. These supporters of the status quo controlled the mechanisms of the parliamentary
process, most notably, the chairmanships of important legislative
committees.[22]

Yeomen were not entirely unsuccessful in their quest for ameliora-
tive legislation. In certain areas, the state Granges, which preceded
the Farmers' Alliance movement, obtained legislation controlling discriminatory rail rates. The Granges also secured laws establishing
maximum rates that operators of warehouse and grain-elevator monopolies could charge farmers who wanted to ship their produce by
rail. In *Munn v. Illinois*, grain-elevator legislation even received the
temporary imprimatur of the United States Supreme Court. There, the
Court held that state regulation of businesses "affected with a public
interest" was a valid exercise of the police power.[23]

These modest victories were short lived. Business interests that
were objects of governmental regulation sought legal representation,
and the bar responded accordingly. A new breed of attorney—the
corporation lawyer—appeared at this time. Unlike the independent,
general practitioner of the past, the corporate attorney practiced in a
large firm (albeit small by contemporary standards) and functioned
solely as "a servant and advisor to big business, an architect of
financial structures." Corporation attorneys fought state regulations,
urging the judiciary to declare these laws unconstitutional.[24]

The Supreme Court struck one blow to reform in 1886, when it held
that states have no power to regulate the rates of railways that are part
of an interstate system.[25] Four years later, in *Chicago, Milwaukee and
St. Paul Railway Co. v. Minnesota*, the Court once again disappointed
farmers when it held that the requirement of due process in the
Fourteenth Amendment precludes states from prohibiting judicial examination of the substance or reasonableness of state rail rates. Theretofore, the Court had said due process required of states only fair legal
procedure. Judicial resort to a substantive notion of due process
had profound implications because the *Munn* decision, although not
overruled, "was now in danger of being outflanked, and the way was

being opened for judicial supervision of [all] state regulation on the grounds of reasonableness.''[26]

These and other decisions made the Democratic Party's failure to pursue the Alliance's major goals seem all the more catastrophic to farmers. The situation was thus ripe for a third-party movement. The People's, or Populist, Party of the early 1890s materialized in large measure because yeomen viewed existing political arrangements as a mere reflection of a hierarchical social order. A Populist manifesto commented on the hierarchical nature of society and politics: ''There are but two sides in the conflict that is being waged in this country today. On the one side are the allied hosts of monopolies, the money power, great trusts and railroad corporations, who seek the enactment of laws to benefit them and impoverish the people. On the other are the farmers, laborers, . . . and all other people who produce wealth and bear the burdens of taxation. . . . Between these two there is no middle ground.'' The Republican Party and, now apparently, the party of the South were beholden to great industrial and financial interests, thus pointing up the critical need for a new party responsive to the humiliating conditions pervading American agriculture.[27]

Profound disillusionment with established political arrangements was a necessary, rather than a sufficient, condition for the formation of a new party. The emotional attachment of whites to the Southern Democracy was so powerful that many impoverished yeomen remained within the party. Democratic loyalties faded only in those areas that came under the influence of the Alliance lecturing system and the agrarian reform press. These institutions served the antihierarchical function of educating poor farmers about Alliance proposals for ending their misery. Itinerant lecturers and reform-press editors impugned the crop-lien system and explained the intricacies of the sub-treasury plan. ''Only through this process was it possible to develop sufficient political self-consciousness among farmers to overcome sectional loyalties and transfer large portions of the Alliance constituencies to the new third party.''[28]

The Populists rallied yeomen behind the effort to combat social and political hierarchy—''to restore the government of the Republic to the hands of 'the plain people' ''—with the Jacksonian motto: ''Equal rights to all, special privileges for none.'' The People's Party invoked as its symbol the paragon of agrarian virtue and philosopher of American democracy, Thomas Jefferson.[29] Populism thus embraced the language of rights, of equality and liberty. Such rhetoric suggested a strong trust in legalism, a reliance on law as a barrier to the oppressive use of political power.

The insurgents, however, did not merely restate an older, classical notion of liberalism. In the Omaha Platform of 1892, they did call for certain strict prohibitions on public power; they opposed "any subsidy or national aid to any private corporation for any purpose." Yet it was clear to them that equal economic opportunity also required the affirmative use of government. One plank of the platform, of course, demanded federal adoption of the sub-treasury plan. Another called for public ownership and operation of railroads and telephone and telegraph services. So, while the Populists drew emotional sustenance from the public icons of earlier eras, this third-party movement marked a significant departure from traditional political thought. "Rather than Jefferson's limited government, they proposed an expanded government, believing that only a new civic polity—augmented by a clear sense of its own mission to secure equity for the many—could cope with the demonstrated financial power of the few."[30]

The late-nineteenth-century division in the Southern Democracy opened the way for Republican gains in the region and thus threatened to end white supremacy. Predictably, plantation elites regarded Populism as a threat to their existence, and they responded accordingly. "The story is not well documented, yet it is apparent from scattered evidence that the Bourbon Democrats, to liquidate the opposition, must have applied with savagery all the social and economic sanctions available." They threatened and sometimes shot at insurgents, turned them out of church, drove them from their homes, and refused them credit. The plantation elites also engaged in electoral corruption, using such tactics as "wholesale ballot-box stuffing, open bribery, various forms of intimidation, and massive voting by dead or fictitious Negroes."[31]

Continued Populist strength convinced many Democrats that assimilation represented the only alternative to Republican ascendance. The Democratic platform of 1896 contained elements that the Bourbons hoped would secure fusion with the Populists. The free-silver plank was the most significant provision having this purpose. The Populists had included a similar inflationary proposal in the Omaha Platform. Democrats also inserted certain anticourt provisions in their formal political program. These planks addressed recent Supreme Court rulings that were contrary to the interests of the Populists, including the invalidation of the income tax (the Omaha Platform had demanded this tax), the evisceration of the Sherman Antitrust Law (also passed in response to agrarian pressure), and the use of this same antitrust legislation to combat labor unions (the Omaha Platform had declared unity with American labor). Like the Populist platform of that same year, the Democratic platform denounced the income-tax and labor-union rulings.[32]

The anticourt and, especially, the free-silver planks prompted the fusion of the two parties. The more radical members of the People's Party dismissed the Democratic platform as an empty gesture. They believed free silver to be a poor substitute for the sub-treasury plan because the former merely "tied the nation's monetary system to the fluctuating output of Western silver mines." To many farmers under the crush of debt, however, attainment of bimetallism through fusion with the Democrats seemed a more likely possibility than attainment of the sub-treasury through insurgent politics. The relief that inflation would bring, however mild, proved too alluring for most to resist.[33]

Following the collapse of the People's Party in 1896, the South returned to one-party politics. "The Populists . . . dispiritedly returned to the Democratic party which offered them more than the party of McKinley and Hanna." The demise of insurgent politics, however, did not mark the end of intraregional conflict. The third-party movement left "a residue of a belligerent attitude that for decades found expression in support for leaders who at least talked, if they did not always act, against the 'interests.' "[34]

The Populist revolt may have left a tradition of radicalism in upland areas, but the movement's decline coincided with Bourbon efforts to consolidate their position. The plantation elites now sought disfranchisement of blacks through such devices as poll taxes and literacy tests. During the period of insurgency, the Populists had managed to suppress temporarily their Negrophobic impulses and borrow from the plantation elites the technique of appealing to black voters for support. Fearing that the former insurgents would continue to attract black voters, the Bourbons used disfranchisement to remove the threat. Although yeomen pursued this same strategy in those states where they had achieved ascendancy, those states were few in number.[35]

Some yeomen in Bourbon-dominated states embraced the rhetoric of white supremacy that accompanied disfranchisement proposals; their numbers helped secure passage of the measures. But most poor farmers realized that white supremacy secured through black disfranchisement had indirect consequences for their own political standing. More significantly, they understood that disfranchisement by way of poll taxes and literacy tests had a direct effect upon their influence. Upcountrymen "suspected, at times rightly, that the black belt was trying to disfranchise [them] as well as the black man."[36]

The Progressive Movement: Interdependence and the Danger of Abstraction

Intraregional economic competition in the developed North exhibited characteristics more typical of those seen in industrialized societies: conflicts between capital and labor were much more evident here than in the underdeveloped South. But labor did not inspire the early twentieth century reform movement that had its center in this part of the country. In fact, the leaders of Progressivism were suspicious of, and kept their distance from, American workingmen. The explanation for this distrust lies in the fact that the Progressive movement responded primarily to the needs and concerns of a different economic group, namely, the middle class.[37]

The middle class grew within the urban-industrial areas of the Northeast in the latter part of the nineteenth century. This social stratum "included those with strong professional aspirations in such fields as medicine, administration, social work, and architecture," as well as "specialists in business, in labor, and in agriculture." "[C]onsciousness of unique skills and functions, an awareness that came to mold much of their lives, characterized all members of the class." The specialization that attended market expansion explained the possession and awareness of special skills and functions among these individuals. Northeastern markets were the most developed in the nation and were thus most conducive to the growth of a diverse and self-conscious middle class.[38]

The self-awareness of specialists stimulated efforts within different occupations to improve the quality of services to the community. Those individuals working toward this goal usually sought and obtained legally imposed standards on entry and proficiency. Not so incidentally, such efforts also restricted the numbers of those practicing the new professions.[39]

The professionalization of law illustrated middle-class efforts to improve services. The preceding section noted the appearance of corporation lawyers in the latter part of the nineteenth century. The contemporaneous appearance of house counsel (i.e., lawyers on the payroll of a company) indicated further specialization within the legal community. In the 1870s, these and other successful business attorneys began to work for higher standards of entry to the trade. They sought to overcome the laxness that had characterized admission to the bar since the Jacksonian era. The gradual formation of city and state bar associations and, most important, the American Bar Association represented the initial stage of their plan. Bar associations then pressed government to reverse the trend toward laxity in admission. Such pressure proved effective, for, by 1890, twenty-three jurisdictions required some period of preparation before practice, compared with only nine jurisdictions three decades earlier. Increasingly, states also made a written bar examination a requirement for entry into the legal trade.[40]

In the latter part of the nineteenth century, academic legal education began to expand. Equally significant, instruction through apprenticeship declined. The number of law schools increased gradually, from 15 in 1850, to 21 in 1860, and to 31 in 1870. Then, in the final decades of the century, the number jumped significantly to 51 in 1880, and to 102 by 1900. Early in the twentieth century, law school would become the dominant mode of preparation for practice. For law, as for many other occupations, the development of specific academic training represented the final stage in the process of professionalization, following specialization and the formation of professional associations. But, in contrast to earlier restrictions on entry to the trade, the increase in the number of law schools and the eclipse of apprenticeship were not the result of bar association pressure and legal compulsion. Prior to 1923, no state required entrants to attend law school. Perhaps the main reason for this shift in the method of legal instruction was the fact that "law school gave the student a prestige that law-office training could not match." As was the case with other professions (most notably, medicine), the claimed necessity of specific academic training for an occupation that served an indispensable social function marked the members of that profession as experts, or possessors of essential, esoteric knowledge.[41]

The waning of Jacksonian anti-elitism made professional expertise socially acceptable. And the innovations of Christopher Columbus Langdell at Harvard in the 1870s lent credence to the claims of law schools that only they provided students with such specialized knowledge. Echoing the treatise writers of the early part of the century, Langdell asserted that law is a "science." Judicial decision making, he believed, proceeds from reason rather than will. In the same way that scientists observe reality to discover natural laws, judges survey relevant empirical data—precedents—from which they induce principles to guide present decisions. Making legal instruction "scientific" in this sense was Langdell's great contribution to law schools. Early schools employed the lecture method of teaching, which presented law as a series of rules for students to transcribe and memorize. Langdell thought students should experience for themselves the inductive process of legal reasoning; they should learn the law, not by rote, but by analyzing a limited number of appellate court decisions collected in specially prepared casebooks. He believed that the function of law professors should change as well. Rather than state rules ex cathedra, legal instructors would now serve as Socratic guides whose questions facilitate the process of scientific discovery. Langdell noted the implications of his educational theory for distinctly unscientific apprenticeships: "[I]f printed books are the ultimate sources of all legal knowledge, . . . then a university, and a university alone, can afford every possible facility for teaching and learning law." As Langdell's students populated the faculties of other institutions and law schools came to appreciate the prestige attaching to "scientific" legal instruction, the case method began to spread. "By the early 20th century, the success of the method seemed assured. . . . Every major and most minor law schools ultimately swung over."[42]

Langdell argued that the success of academic legal education depended upon a particular type of instructor, the full-time professor: "What qualifies a person . . . to teach law . . . is not experience in the work of a lawyer's office, not experience in dealing with men, not experience in the trial or argument of causes, not experience, in short, in using law, but experience in learning law." As another of Langdell's legacies, full-time legal academics appeared very slowly. They were rare before the 1880s. Even by 1897, only 75 of the nation's 349 instructors taught full time. As this number expanded in the next century, however, the law professor would become another specialist within the legal profession and within the growing middle class.[43]

Middle-class concerns extended beyond a desire to enhance the income and prestige of various occupations. The appearance of large corporations greatly troubled professionals and small businessmen (save corporation attorneys). The steady, upward trend in the price cycle that occurred after 1897 and continued over the next two decades was largely responsible for this concern. Even though a combination of factors (including the discovery of new gold supplies and new refining processes) explained the increase in the cost of living, most members of the middle class connected the phenomenon with the trustification of American industry. They viewed as more than mere coincidence the simultaneous appearance of inflation and such frighteningly large organizations as United States Steel, Standard Oil, and Amalgamated Copper.[44]

Middle-class anxiousness over the organization of labor matched the concern over trust growth. Between 1897 and 1911, union membership increased from 447,000 to 2,382,000. Many people came to view the wage demands of organized labor as a contributing factor to higher prices. More significantly, they feared that union growth would cause social disruption and, ultimately, disintegration. An increase in the number of strikes punctuated the rise of unions, and this occurrence made many worry "about the lengths to which union power might go if labor-unionism became the sole counterpoise to the power of business."[45]

While members of the middle class feared the restlessness of American labor, they acknowledged the legitimate grievances of workers. Urban slums, the exploitation of women and children, and appalling working conditions—all exposed in the muckraking press of the period—filled people "with concern both because they felt a sincere interest in the welfare of the victims of industrialism and because they feared that to neglect them would invite social disintegration and ultimate catastrophe."[46]

Middle-class restiveness over the conditions of labor and capital did not translate immediately into public action. The notion that governmental power should be used to alter significantly the economic conditions of life was foreign to most minds in the nineteenth century; the ethic of self-mastery or self-reliance was the dominant theme in social thought. With regard to the issue of poverty, for example, government held indigent individuals responsible for their situation in life. Paupers had to endure degrading, stigmatic forms of public assistance designed to compel them to become more responsible. Only the "worthy poor"—the blind, children, disabled veterans, the deaf and dumb, and the epileptic—received public compassion. If people viewed poverty as an indication of indolence and lack of thrift, they regarded wealth as a sign of assiduousness and frugality. "Since each man was ordinarily master of his own fate, he himself—his will, character, and inner merit—was seen as the primary cause of his place in society. If a man was of high position, that in itself was evidence of merit; if he was lowly, that showed a lack of merit."[47]

The controversial writings of the English philosopher Herbert Spencer contributed to a social disinclination to use governmental power in the economic realm. Drawing upon Charles Darwin's evolutionary hypotheses, Spencer denied the worth for social progress of the conscious decisions of individual agents. He maintained that development of the human race proceeds instead through the unconscious, undirected process of natural selection, the struggle for existence in which the less fit perish and the more capable survive. Efforts to ameliorate poverty, he argued, interfere with nature's laws and thus impede the progress of society. The public should thus view slums, poor working conditions, and low living standards as sacrifices for a larger, long-term good.[48]

Self-mastery and social Darwinism did not go unchallenged as social philosophies, for a changing of the guard began in American higher education in the final decades of the nineteenth century. As in other middle-class occupations, specialization occurred within academia. The appearance of the American Historical Association, the American Economics Association, the American Statistics Association, the American Political Science Association, and the American Sociological Society revealed significant differentiation among scholars. The emergence of professional social sciences indicated deep dissatisfaction in academia with existing social thought and represented a concerted effort to offer alternative, more credible explanations of social reality.[49]

Spencer's secular determinism fascinated the new generation of professional academics, but its bleak toleration of the status quo as the necessary price for a better, but very remote, future impelled them to search for a more voluntaristic explanation of social progress. Scholars ultimately rejected this rigid theory of social evolution because they became convinced that mankind develops as much through rational planning as through evolution. "[I]f evolution were really the result of an adaptation of organism to environment, ran the implicit argument, then the process could be made more efficient and humane if the adaptation were conscious and if each stage of environmental development were organized consistently."[50]

Although scholars rejected social Darwinism, they did not dismiss Spencer's work. The philosopher's insight concerning the organic nature of society was separable from his discussion of the process of natural selection. While society is composed of discrete individuals, he maintained, social differentiation has become so pervasive that, like the constituent parts of an organism, the members of society are now mutually dependent. An individual depends upon others for survival while contributing to the welfare of all by fulfilling a specialized function. Social scientists embraced Spencer's organicist metaphor because it illuminated the significance of certain prominent social facts: the transportation-communication revolution, the attendant expansion of the impersonal capitalist marketplace, and the process of the division of labor. Exposure to and involvement in these occurrences made social thinkers very receptive to the claim that society was becoming increasingly organic or interdependent. In the words of the sociologist Charles Horton Cooley, "If we are to take society to include the whole of human life, this may be said to be organic, in the sense that influences may be and are transmitted from one part to any other part, so that all parts are bound together into an interdependent whole."[51]

The organicist metaphor had significant implications for political thought, since it destroyed the dominant rationalization for laissez-faire politics. To insist on the interconnectedness of social phenomena was to insist that such individualistic concepts as self-mastery and self-reliance were anachronistic. As a consequence of replacing the assumption of individual potency with the notion of social interdependence, "merit was partially divorced from status: the powerful were seen as the beneficiaries of external circumstance, and the weak were seen as its victims. Neither were fully responsible for their places in life." Social scientists were quick to point out the ultimate implications of interdependence; they linked this social fact to a humanitarian public philosophy whose "emphasis fell on redistribution of wealth or the design of institutional shelters where the poor might be shielded from life's worst hazards."[52]

The belief that the major source of error and misunderstanding in an interdependent society is the tendency to think abstractly—to isolate a phenomenon or idea from its social context—informed the call for a new public philosophy. Because human affairs form a seamless web, virtually uninterrupted by distinct boundaries, to remove one thing from the network of factors with which it interacts is to neglect the multiplicity and mutuality of causal influences at work in society. In other words, abstraction disregards the difficulty involved in determining causation in an interdependent culture; it overlooks the primary cause of an event or occurrence and neglects the secondary effects of any action. In the past, abstract thinking was responsible for the erroneous belief that the distribution of wealth in society is entirely a measure of individual effort or merit. Abstract thought also disregarded the fact that concentrations of economic power perpetrate certain social harms.[53]

The middle-class Progressive movement that emerged around 1900 gave life to the heretical ideas of the new generation of intellectuals. Drawing upon insights concerning the organic or interdependent nature of society, Progressives insisted upon the need for governmental intervention into the economy. "Representing as they did the spirit and the desires of the middle class, the Progressives stood for a dual program of economic remedies designed to minimize the dangers from the extreme left and right." With respect to the former threat, they sought to ameliorate the harsh conditions under which American workers toiled. They proposed legislation dealing with workers' compensation, the labor of women and children, maximum hours, minimum wages for women, and old-age pensions. With regard to the danger from the right (the trustification of industry), they worked to prevent corporate dominance over competitors and prices.[54]

Progressives were of two minds concerning the means appropriate to secure these shared political goals. One group, which Herbert Croly and Theodore Roosevelt best represented, held that the pervasiveness of economic interdependence made the national government the appropriate political forum. They also regarded business consolidation as an inevitable aspect of modern life and the most efficient form of economic organization. They thus argued that the national government should regulate concentrations of economic power in the interest of workers and consumers. A second group of Progressives, which Louis Brandeis and Woodrow Wilson typified, regarded state governments as the primary agents of reform. They maintained that states were best able to address the unique problems of the specialized economies of the nation's regions. The principal role of the national government was to restore and maintain competition—to approximate the old, competitive order among small entrepreneurs that had preceded business consolidation. This group denied the inevitability and efficiency of concentrated economic power.[55]

While Progressives exhibited differences on certain aspects of their political program, they shared the same views concerning the obstacles to effective reform. These reformers believed that political parties, as then organized, were inimical to progressive measures. Constructed in a pre-industrial age, parties failed to offer the strong leadership required in an interdependent society. Their primary purpose—winning power in order to distribute patronage among a broad, heterogeneous electorate—prevented the delineation and pursuit of a substantive political program. Issueless platforms were testimony to the impotence of parties. Furthermore, the spoils system did nothing to ensure competence in government; loyalty to the party (rather than personal qualification) had become the primary requisite for appointment.[56]

The Progressives also viewed the judiciary as an impediment to social and economic reform. As in the late nineteenth century, courts in the early twentieth century ruled on controversies that the increased activities of legislatures had inspired. In addressing cases involving governmental attempts to regulate property interests, judges became increasingly formal in their reasoning. Continued efforts among judges to demonstrate the autonomy, or "scientific" nature, of judge-made law explained their indifference to context. Whereas the treatise writers of the early nineteenth century had sought a balance between the value of continuity and that of growth through the adaptation of legal principles to changed circumstances, jurists of the early twentieth century merely continued the process of legal generalization and abstraction. In the course of making their decisions appear less partisan, courts freed "legal rules from the reality testing that regular encounters with the concrete particularities of social life might entail." For example, judges would "apply the same set of rules that were applicable between sophisticated businessmen of relatively equal information and bargaining power to labor and consumer contracts between vastly unequal parties."[57] And when courts, under the due process clause of the Fourteenth Amendment, examined the substance or reasonableness of regulations of contracts between unequal partners, they often declared such reform legislation unconstitutional.

The most notorious instance of this form of judicial abstraction occurred in *Lochner v. New York*, where the United States Supreme Court invalidated a law limiting bakers to a sixty-hour workweek. It was unreasonable for the state to assume, the Court held, that bakers "are not able to assert their rights and care for themselves [in disputes with their employers] without the protecting arm of the state." In conformity with the prevailing theory of judicial decision making, the Court justified its ruling with the apology, "This is not a question of substituting the judgment of the court for that of the legislature." While neither the Supreme Court nor the state courts were dogmatic proponents of laissez-faire, judges at both levels of government became increasingly hostile toward legislative efforts to cope with social and economic change.[58]

Like the Populists before them, the Progressives objected strongly to such judicial behavior. In contrast to the reaction of the Populists, however, the Progressive response went well beyond protests against particular rulings. A critique (if not a disavowal) of the view that judicial decisions proceed from reason rather than will was a major component of sociological jurisprudence, the jurisprudential analogue to Progressivism. (Ironically, those who benefited from Langdell's claim that law is an esoteric "science"—law professors and jurists— eventually attacked the notion.) Sociological jurisprudents emphasized the significant role that discretion plays in judicial decision making. They also reproved judges for engaging in abstraction, for rendering decisions on the basis of legal principles or notions of rights divorced from the interdependent environment in which legal conflicts originate. Roscoe Pound pointed up the need for "a scientific apprehension of the relations of law to society and of the needs and interests and opinions of society of today." "More than anything else," he maintained, "ignorance of the actual situations of fact for which legislation was provided and supposed lack of legal warrant for knowing them, have been responsible for the overthrowing of so much social legislation."[59]

The Progressives were skeptical that judges could ever entirely avoid abstraction, given the inadequacies that inhered in the judicial process. They argued that a lack of familiarity among judges with the specialized technologies and complex matters of an urban-industrial age partly explained the incapacity of courts to render rulings grounded in reality. Instead of receiving a sizable number of cases on a particular matter, judges typically confronted insufficient quantities of cases in numerous policy areas. The Progressives also noted that courts could not seek out cases; instead, judges had to wait for litigants to sue. As a result, the judiciary could not provide continual oversight or management of changing social problems. The process of judicial fact-finding also contributed to abstraction. This method for informing the judicial mind had its origin in a pre-industrial age, when people did not expect the context of litigation or the effects of judicial actions to extend beyond the immediate parties to a suit. The sluggish pace of litigation represented a final source of abstract rulings, according to the Progressives. The intricate rules of court procedure created the possibility that decisions, when finally rendered, would meet with changed circumstances.[60]

The Progressives viewed a powerful executive and a developed administrative apparatus as the institutional remedy for a government of political parties and courts. They thought that a dynamic executive would provide the nation with the vitality and direction needed to meet the conflicts and challenges of an urban-industrial age. Whereas parties bought unity through issueless politics and patronage, leaving serious social and economic conflicts unresolved, statesmanlike leadership would transcend divisions within the national community. The statesman would possess the capacity or charisma to convince the populace (and thus the legislature) that the true interest of particular groups is to put aside narrow, selfish goals so as to accomplish a larger, national purpose. In order to allow the statesman-president to emerge, the Progressives sought to break the discipline of parties, to take from them the power to nominate candidates. Specifically, direct democracy through primaries would enable a national constituency to form around the substantive program of a statesman. This nomination method contrasted with the old caucus system, which forced candidates to accept the parties' issueless platforms.[61]

The Progressives also sought an expansive administrative arm for the government. The statesman-president would depend upon expert administrators to provide him with policies that in fact transcended social and economic divisions. Moreover, Progressives looked to bureaucratic institutions to implement these policies, to compensate for the inaptitude and abstraction inherent in the system of political parties and courts that had theretofore staffed federal offices and performed the task of economic surveillance. In lieu of the patronage system, a civil service commission would use competitive examinations to select qualified individuals for administrative positions. Once appointed, administrators would concentrate on particular areas of policy and thus enhance their expertise. To ensure continual oversight with an adequate factual basis, administrators would have the power of investigation; they would be able to require reports, call in witnesses or documents, and conduct searches. Finally, bureaucratic institutions would dispense with the Byzantine internal procedures of courts, thus ensuring prompt resolution of controversies arising under new legislation.[62]

The mere creation of bureaucratic institutions, the Progressives realized, would not entirely remove judicial impediments to social and economic reform. As noted earlier, the Court had held in the late nineteenth century that judges have the power, under the due process clauses of the Fifth and Fourteenth Amendments, to assess the reasonableness of administrative rulings. The courts, of course, also had the power to declare unconstitutional the very legislation creating administrative bodies. Some Progressives sought to minimize the judicial threat through popular recall of judicial decisions. Theodore Roosevelt took up this proposal in the presidential campaign of 1912. The call for self-restraint in the exercise of judicial power was a more moderate, more widely accepted response. This plea for deference toward the decisions of legislatures and administrative agencies followed from the critique of the notion that judicial decision making is a purely deductive process. Progressive jurists maintained that, because the imprecision inherent in legal language allows for the infusion of personal predilections, judges should hesitate before invalidating laws that the representatives of a majority of citizens thought necessary. If the demystification of the interpretive process would not convince judges to embrace deference, at the very least it would deprive them of the rationalization that their rulings proceeded from reason, rather than will.[63]

James Bradley Thayer's essay, "The Origin and Scope of the American Doctrine of Constitutional Law," was the most influential statement of the Progressive period on the importance of judicial deference. Thayer derided the notion that the judicial duty is "merely and nakedly to ascertain the meaning of the text of the constitution and of the impeached Act of the legislature, and to determine, as an academic question, whether in the court's judgment the two were in conflict." "[T]he constitution," he argued, "often admits of different interpretations; . . . there is often a range of choice and judgment." In view of this fact, and to help secure to legislatures their proper power under the Constitution, he contended that courts "can only disregard the Act when those who have the right to make laws have not merely made a mistake, but have made a very clear one,—so clear that it is not open to rational question." Put another way, judges should recognize that "whatever choice is rational is constitutional"; they should interpose their veto only when a person could not rationally believe in the constitutionality of the challenged act.[64]

Thayer defended his call for judicial deference with a critique of judicial supremacy. Hamilton, Marshall, Story, and Kent had believed that judges possess the responsibility of constitutional guardianship because elected officials tend to heed the desires of majorities to the detriment of constitutional limitations. By contrast, Thayer denied categorically that the founding generation gave courts this duty: "The judiciary may well reflect that if they had been regarded by the people as the chief protection against legislative violation of the constitution, they would not have been allowed merely incidental and postponed control. They would have been let in, as it was sometimes endeavored in the conventions to let them in, to a revision of the laws before they began to operate."[65]

Thayer argued that, in fact, legislators—state as well as national—

have primary responsibility to defend the Constitution. The oath provision in Article 6 of the Constitution obligates officials at both levels of government to support that document; legislators "cannot act without making [a determination of constitutionality]." Placing considerably more faith in the efficacy of oaths than did Hamilton, Thayer argued that "virtue, sense, and competent knowledge are always to be attributed to [the legislature]." Judges must assume that the lawmaker is "a competent and duly instructed person who has carefully applied his faculties to the [constitutional] question." Thayer concluded "that where a power so momentous as this primary authority to interpret is given, the actual determinations of the body to whom it is intrusted are entitled to a corresponding respect; and this not on mere grounds of conventional respect, but on very solid and significant grounds of policy and law."[66]

The New Deal Coalition

American participation in the First World War put an end to the Progressive movement. "Not long after they began to pay the price of war, the people began to feel that they had been gulled by its promoters both among the allies and in the United States." Progressive domestic politics was a casualty of the isolationism that developed at the war's end. After the Senate rejected the Treaty of Versailles (and, therefore, the League of Nations), the public repudiated President Wilson in 1920.[67] The election of Harding did not signal the passing of middle-class concerns, but the new president's conservatism did represent the end of this group's hold on national politics.

The Great Depression, of course, prompted the next major reform effort. Franklin Roosevelt's New Deal did not suggest a mere resumption of the reform politics of the past. The president sought neither to destroy the old party structure nor (initially) to make the subject of monopoly the focus of his administration. Moreover, northern labor and southern conservative elites formed the nucleus of the New Deal coalition. Organized labor had benefited from Progressivism but was not of the movement, while the Bourbons were the mortal enemies of those upland whites who had been the wellspring of Populist sentiment.[68]

Nevertheless, those individuals having Progressive credentials joined poor southern whites, and together they further diversified the coalition supporting Roosevelt. Given the one-party politics of the South, indigent yeomen had no viable choice but to join the coalition.

The president, however, did not take them for granted; he displayed great concern for the plight of the rural poor. Understandably, former Progressives found the New Deal attractive, what with its attack upon "economic royalists" and its recognition of the continued need for governmental regulation and income redistribution in an interdependent society. Indeed, at one time or another, Roosevelt appealed to Progressives of all stripes. The New Deal initially took its bearings from Theodore Roosevelt's policy of regulating concentrations of economic power. But the corporatism of the National Recovery Administration later gave way to a Wilsonian antitrust strategy. The disparate elements of the New Deal coalition shared an antipathy for the privileges of northern capital.[69]

President Roosevelt selected his Supreme Court nominees from this diverse aggregation of people. All of his appointees had witnessed the Court's renewed use of the power of judicial review, directed this time against the New Deal. Some of these men objected to the president's disingenuous characterization of his ill-fated attempt to pack the Supreme Court as a move to improve judicial efficiency. Yet these same individuals offered varying degrees of support for the measure.[70] All of the New Deal justices shared the conviction that judicial formalism is hazardous, especially when courts examine the constitutionality of governmental efforts to address the economic crises of an industrial society.

Ironically, the Roosevelt Court would demonstrate little jurisprudential harmony. Instead of facing challenges to the constitutionality of economic legislation, they confronted novel civil liberties issues. Unanimity vanished as the justices struggled with such matters as political dissent, criminal justice, and racial equality. The fact that judges could no longer claim that their interpretations of legal language and precedent proceeded entirely from reason rather than will made the task of these men even more formidable. This traditional view of judicial decision making did not survive the assaults that the Progressive jurists initiated and the legal realists of the 1930s expanded. Yet the social expectation remained that judges would render decisions according to legal, as opposed to personal, criteria.[71]

Thayer's counsel of deference and his repudiation of judicial supremacy represented one method of contending with this widespread expectation. Other interpretive models would compete with Thayer's influential proposal. The controversial constitutional absolutism of Hugo Black, Roosevelt's first Supreme Court appointee, represented an alternative means for preserving judicial power and prestige in an age of jurisprudential realism. Black grounded his approach to constitutional interpretation in a perception of reality acquired through exposure to and involvement in the agrarian and industrial conflicts of his native Alabama.

Notes

1. *Dred Scott v. Sandford*, 60 U.S. (19 Howard) 393 (1857); Robert G. McCloskey, *The American Supreme Court* (Chicago: University of Chicago Press, 1960), 93–96; Lawrence Friedman, *A History of American Law*, 2d ed. (New York: Simon & Schuster, 1985), 378; Stephen Skowronek, *Building a New American State: The Expansion of Administrative Capacities, 1877–1920* (New York: Cambridge University Press, 1982), 29–30 (quoted). In *Dred Scott*, the Court held that individuals of African descent could not bring suit in federal courts, because they could never become citizens in the meaning of the federal Constitution. Chief Justice Roger B. Taney suggested in dictum that Congress had no right to exclude slavery from any territory. The decision struck at the roots of the Republican Party, which opposed the extension of slavery into the territories.

2. Skowronek, *Building a New American State*, 30; Morton Keller, *Affairs of State: Public Life in Late Nineteenth Century America* (Cambridge: Harvard University Press, Belknap Press, 1977), 37–285; Richard Franklin Bensel, *Yankee Leviathan: The Origins of Central State Authority in America, 1859–1877* (New York: Cambridge University Press, 1990).

3. Thomas L. Haskell, *The Emergence of Professional Social Science: The American Social Science Association and the Nineteenth-Century Crisis of Authority* (Urbana: University of Illinois Press, 1977), 28–29 (quoted); Samuel P. Hays, *The Response to Industrialism, 1885–1914* (Chicago: University of Chicago Press, 1957), 4; Keller, *Affairs of State*, 289, 371.

4. Hays, *Response to Industrialism*, 4–5; Haskell, *Emergence of Professional Social Science*, 30–33.

5. Haskell, *Emergence of Professional Social Science*, 33; Hays, *Response to Industrialism*, 5–8.

6. Haskell, *Emergence of Professional Social Science*, 36 (quoted); Hays, *Response to Industrialism*, 11.

7. Hays, *Response to Industrialism*, 15–16.

8. Ibid.

9. Hays, *Response to Industrialism*, 10, 48–52; Robert H. Wiebe, *The Search for Order, 1877–1787* (Chapel Hill: University of North Carolina Press, 1969), 23–24; Richard Hofstadter, *The Age of Reform: From Bryan to F.D.R.* (New York: Vintage Books, 1955), 169.

10. Hays, *Response to Industrialism*, 128; R. Jeffrey Lustig, *Corporate*

Liberalism: The Origins of Modern American Political Theory, 1890–1920 (Berkeley: University of California Press, 1982), 43.

11. Bensel, *Yankee Leviathan*, 416; Hays, *Response to Industrialism*, 121–26 (p. 126 quoted).

12. Bensel, *Yankee Leviathan*, 416; Richard Franklin Bensel, *Sectionalism and American Political Development, 1880–1980* (Madison: University of Wisconsin Press, 1984), 62–63. See also Hays, *Response to Industrialism*, 132.

13. Bensel, *Yankee Leviathan*, 416–18 (p. 418 quoted); Lawrence Goodwyn, *Democratic Promise: The Populist Moment in America* (New York: Oxford University Press, 1976), 27.

14. V. O. Key Jr., *Southern Politics in State and Nation*, new ed. (Knoxville: University of Tennessee Press, 1977), 5–6; Bensel, *Sectionalism*, 12–13.

15. Key, *Southern Politics*, 551, 6.

16. Ibid., 552, 7 (quoted); Goodwyn, *Democratic Promise*, 179.

17. Bensel, *Yankee Leviathan*, 428–29 (quoted); Bensel, *Sectionalism*.

18. Key, *Southern Politics*, 9 (quoted); C. Vann Woodward, *The Strange Career of Jim Crow*, 3d ed. (New York: Oxford University Press, 1974), 23, 31–65 (p. 48 quoted); Goodwyn, *Democratic Promise*, 83, 212.

19. Woodward, *Strange Career of Jim Crow*, 56–57; Key, *Southern Politics*, 11–12, 16 (quoted).

20. Bensel, *Yankee Leviathan*, 417; Goodwyn, *Democratic Promise*, 25–31, 117–19, 131 (quoted).

21. Goodwyn, *Democratic Promise*, 135–36, 152–53, 167–68 (quoted).

22. Ibid., 8, 110–12, 168, 178, 216–17, 222–23, 225–29, 234, 241–43, 248, 651; Key, *Southern Politics*, 8, 553.

23. *Munn v. Illinois*, 94 U.S. 113, 134 (1877) (quoted); McCloskey, *American Supreme Court*, 128.

24. Friedman, *History of American Law*, 635–40 (p. 637 quoted); Richard L. Abel, *American Lawyers* (New York: Oxford University Press, 1989), 182–84; Arnold M. Paul, *Conservative Crisis and the Rule of Law: Attitudes of Bar and Bench, 1887–1895* (Gloucester, Mass.: Peter Smith, 1976), 5–7; Benjamin R. Twiss, *Lawyers and the Constitution: How Laissez Faire Came to the Supreme Court* (Westport, Conn.: Greenwood Press, 1973), 63–92.

25. *Wabash, St. L. & Pac. Ry. v. Illinois*, 118 U.S. 557 (1886).

26. *Chicago, M. & St. P. Ry. v. Minnesota*, 134 U.S. 418 (1890); Paul, *Conservative Crisis*, 39–42 (pp. 41–42 quoted); Alan Furman Westin, "The Supreme Court, the Populist Movement and the Campaign of 1896," *Journal of Politics* 15 (1953): 14–15; Kermit L. Hall, *The Magic Mirror: Law in American History* (New York: Oxford University Press, 1989), 235–36; Lustig, *Corporate Liberalism*, 92, 95.

27. Westin, "Supreme Court, Populist Movement and Campaign of 1896," 3–19, 39–41; Hofstadter, *Age of Reform*, 64 (quoted); Goodwyn, *Democratic Promise*, 173, 244–72, 651–52; Norman Pollack, ed., *The Populist Mind* (New York: Bobbs-Merrill, 1967), 61.

28. Goodwyn, *Democratic Promise*, 242, 351–86, 652 (quoted).

29. Pollack, ed., *Populist Mind*, 61 (quoted), 63; Hofstadter, *Age of Reform*, 62–63; Goodwyn, *Democratic Promise*, 374–77.

30. Pollack, ed., *Populist Mind*, 63–65 (p. 65 quoted); Goodwyn, *Democratic Promise*, 386 (quoted), 593–96; Lustig, *Corporate Liberalism*, 69–74.

31. Key, *Southern Politics*, 553 (quoted); Goodwyn, *Democratic Promise*, 299, 332–36, 342, 422, 478, 480 (p. 332 quoted).

32. Paul, *Conservative Crisis*, 225; Pollack, ed., *Populist Mind*, 63, 65; Bensel, *Yankee Leviathan*, 16; Westin, "Supreme Court, Populist Movement, Campaign of 1896," 22–41. The relevant Supreme Court rulings are: *Pollack v. Farmer's Loan Co.*, 157 U.S. 429 (1895); *United States v. E.C. Knight Co.*, 156 U.S. 1 (1895); and *In re Debs*, 158 U.S. 564 (1895).

33. Goodwyn, *Democratic Promise*, 433–34 (quoted), 426–514.

34. Key, *Southern Politics*, 554, 8 (quoted); Keller, *Affairs of State*, 579–80.

35. Woodward, *Strange Career of Jim Crow*, 60–64, 79, 86–90; Key, *Southern Politics*, 8, 541, 548–550. Yeomen prevailed only in South Carolina and Georgia.

36. Key, *Southern Politics*, 8 (quoted), 531–643; Woodward, *Strange Career of Jim Crow*, 82–85.

37. Progressivism was national in scope but emanated from the Northeast. Moreover, its southern manifestation was narrow, given the lack of a developed middle class. Wiebe, *Search for Order*, 111–32, 164–95, 206; Hofstadter, *Age of Reform*, 131, 217–18.

38. Wiebe, *Search for Order*, 112 (quoted); Hofstadter, *Age of Reform*, 217–18.

39. Wiebe, *Search for Order*, 111–32; Abel, *American Lawyers*, 14–39; Haskell, *Emergence of Professional Social Science*, 26; Burton J. Bledstein, *The Culture of Professionalism: The Middle Class and the Development of Higher Education in America* (New York: W. W. Norton, 1978); Magali Sarfatti Larson, *The Rise of Professionalism: A Sociological Analysis* (Berkeley: University of California Press, 1977).

40. Friedman, *History of American Law*, 633–54; Wiebe, *Search for Order*, 116–17.

41. Friedman, *History of American Law*, 607 (quoted); Abel, *American Lawyers*, 41–43, 277; Wiebe, *Search for Order*, 113–16.

42. Christopher Columbus Langdell, "Harvard Celebration Speeches," *Law Quarterly Review* 9 (1887): 124 (quoted); Friedman, *History of American Law*, 606–20 (pp. 616–17 quoted); Robert Stevens, *Law School: Legal Education in America from the 1850s to the 1890s* (Chapel Hill: University of North Carolina Press, 1983), 35–72; Calvin Woodard, "The Limits of Legal Realism: An Historical Perspective," *Virginia Law Review* 54 (1968): 709–18; Hofstadter, *Age of Reform*, 157–58; Robert W. Gordon, review of *Tort Law in America: An Intellectual History*, by G. Edward White, *Harvard Law Review* 94 (1981): 909 n. 21.

43. Langdell, "Harvard Celebration Speeches," 124 (quoted); Abel, *American Lawyers*, 172–73; Friedman, *History of American Law*, 609.

44. Hofstadter, *Age of Reform*, 168–71, 217, 219–22; Hays, *Response to Industrialism*, 84–85.

45. Hofstadter, *Age of Reform*, 168–70, 241 (quoted).

46. Ibid., 186–98, 238 (quoted), 241–42; Hays, *Response to Industrialism*, 85–86.

47. Friedman, *History of American Law*, 488–95; Haskell, *Emergence of Professional Social Science*, 254–55 (quoted); John G. Cawelti, *Apostles of the Self-Made Man* (Chicago: University of Chicago Press, 1965).

48. Hays, *Response to Industrialism*, 39; Haskell, *Emergence of Professional Social Science*, 243–44; Wiebe, *Search for Order*, 134–36.

49. Wiebe, *Search for Order*, 121; Hofstadter, *Age of Reform*, 152–55; Haskell, *Emergence of Professional Social Science*, vii, 27.

50. Haskell, *Emergence of Professional Social Science*, 2, 244–45; Lustig, *Corporate Liberalism*, 158 (quoted); Richard Hofstadter, *Social Darwinism in American Thought* (Philadelphia: University of Pennsylvania Press, 1945), 52–67.

51. Alvin Boskoff, "From Social Thought to Sociological Theory," in *Modern Sociological Theory: In Continuity and Change*, ed. Howard Becker and Alvin Boskoff (New York: Holt, Rinehart & Winston, 1957), 11; Jean B. Quandt, *From the Small Town to the Great Community: The Social Thought of Progressive Intellectuals* (New Brunswick, N.J.: Rutgers University Press, 1970), 27–28; Albion W. Small, *General Sociology: An Exposition of the Main Developments in Sociological Theory From Spencer to Ratzenhofer* (Chicago: University of Chicago Press, 1905), 109–53; Haskell, *Emergence of Professional Social Science*, 24–47; Wiebe, *Search for Order*, 140–44; Charles Horton Cooley, *Social Process* (New York: Charles Scribner's Sons, 1926), 26 (quoted); Albion W. Small and George E. Vincent, *An Introduction to the Study of Society* (New York: American Book Company, 1894), 87–96; John Dewey, *The Public and Its Problems* (1927; reprint, Chicago: Athens Press, 1954), 141.

52. Haskell, *Emergence of Professional Social Science*, 13–14, 17, 23, 241–42, 254–55 (quoted); Hofstadter, *Age of Reform*, 238, 242; Hays, *Response to Industrialism*, 76–83.

53. Haskell, *Emergence of Professional Social Science*, 10–13, 253–54.

54. Hofstadter, *Age of Reform*, 217, 238 (quoted), 242.

55. Ibid., 134, 224–56.

56. James W. Ceaser, *Presidential Selection: Theory and Development* (Princeton: Princeton University Press, 1979), 197–201; Skowronek, *Building a New American State*, 43; Hofstadter, *Age of Reform*, 257.

57. Morton J. Horwitz, *The Transformation of American Law, 1870–1960* (New York: Oxford University Press, 1992), 15.

58. *Lochner v. New York*, 198 U.S. 45, 47, 46 (1905) (quoted); McCloskey,

American Supreme Court, 136–57; Robert W. Gordon, "Legal Thought and Legal Practice in the Age of American Enterprise, 1870–1920," in *Professions and Professional Ideologies in America*, ed. Gerald L. Geison (Chapel Hill: University of North Carolina Press, 1983), 88–90; Gordon, review of *Tort Law*, by White, 916; Morton J. Horwitz, *The Transformation of American Law, 1780–1860* (Cambridge: Harvard University Press, 1977), 253–66; Hall, *Magic Mirror*, 226–46; Paul, *Conservative Crisis*.

59. Oliver Wendell Holmes, "The Path of the Law," *Harvard Law Review* 10 (1897): 465–68; Roscoe Pound, "Mechanical Jurisprudence," *Columbia Law Review* 8 (1908): 605–23; Roscoe Pound, "The Need of a Sociological Jurisprudence," *The Green Bag* 19 (1907): 611 (quoted); Roscoe Pound, "Liberty of Contract," *Yale Law Journal* 18 (1909): 470 (quoted); Roscoe Pound, *An Introduction to the Philosophy of Law* (1922; reprint, New Haven: Yale University Press, 1954), 1–47; Dewey, *Public and Its Problems*, 86–87, 102, 145; G. Edward White, *Patterns of American Legal Thought* (Charlottesville, Virginia: Michie, 1978), 99–115; Wilfrid E. Rumble Jr., *American Legal Realism: Skepticism, Reform, and the Judicial Process* (Ithaca: Cornell University Press, 1968), 9–13, 52; Horwitz, *Transformation of American Law, 1870–1960*, 33–63.

60. Horwitz, *Transformation of American Law, 1870–1960*, 213–46; William C. Chase, *The American Law School and the Rise of Administrative Government* (Madison: University of Wisconsin Press, 1982), 5–6; Skowronek, *Building a New American State*, 42, 152.

61. Herbert Croly, *The Promise of American Life* (1909; reprint, Indianapolis: Bobbs-Merrill, 1975); Charles Forcey, *The Crossroads of Liberalism: Croly, Weyl, Lippmann, and the Progressive Era, 1900–1925* (New York: Oxford University Press, 1961), 3–51; Ceaser, *Presidential Selection*, 170–212; Wiebe, *Search for Order*, 159–63.

62. Wiebe, *Search for Order*, 145, 160, 169–70, 174; Chase, *Law School and the Rise of Administrative Government*, 7–10, 130–32; Lustig, *Corporate Liberalism*, 150–51; Horwitz, *Transformation of American Law, 1870–1960*, 213–46; James T. Kloppenberg, *Uncertain Victory: Social Democracy and Progressivism in European and American Thought, 1870–1920* (New York: Oxford University Press, 1986), 361; Skowronek, *Building a New American State*.

63. Hays, *Response to Industrialism*, 160–61; Hofstadter, *Age of Reform*, 311; Skowronek, *Building a New American State*, 254–55; G. Edward White, *The American Judicial Tradition: Profiles of Leading American Judges* (New York: Oxford University Press, 1976), 154–55.

64. James Bradley Thayer, "The Origin and Scope of the American Doctrine of Constitutional Law," *Harvard Law Review* 7 (1893): 143–44. Ironically, Thayer did not argue that the rational-basis test precludes substantive due process. Ibid., 148. It is certainly rational to believe that due process requires only what the phrase implies: fair legal procedure. Although Thayer

misapplied the rational-basis standard in this instance, he maintained that judges should employ the test when examining the reasonableness of governmental action. Ibid.

65. Ibid., 136.

66. Ibid., 135, 149, 136. Thayer acknowledged only one exception to the principle of judicial deference: he believed that the supremacy clause of Article 6 requires federal judges to apply independent judgment in cases involving state action allegedly in conflict with the constitutional exercise of national power. Ibid., 154–55; Sanford Byron Gabin, *Judicial Review and the Reasonable Doubt Test* (London: Kennikat Press, 1980), 40–42.

67. Hofstadter, *Age of Reform*, 272–82.

68. Ibid., 302–28; Bensel, *Sectionalism*, 26, 30, 105, 148–52, 369–72.

69. Basil Rauch, *The History of the New Deal* (New York: Creative Age Press, 1944); Alan Brinkley, "The New Deal and the Idea of the State," in *The Rise of the New Deal Order, 1930–1980*, ed. Steve Fraser and Gary Gerstle (Princeton: Princeton University Press, 1989): 85–121; Bensel, *Yankee Leviathan*, 433.

70. McCloskey, *American Supreme Court*, 161–69, 174–79; Henry J. Abraham, *Justices and Presidents: A Political History of Appointments to the Supreme Court*, 2d ed. (New York: Oxford University Press, 1985), 208; Robert H. Jackson, *The Struggle for Judicial Supremacy: A Study of a Crisis in American Power Politics* (New York: Knopf, 1941), 328–37; Peter H. Irons, *The New Deal Lawyers* (Princeton: Princeton University Press, 1982), 272–80.

71. Horwitz, *Transformation of American Law, 1870–1960*, 169–212; Rumble, *American Legal Realism*; William Twining, *Karl Llewellyn and the Realist Movement* (South Hackensack, N.J.: Rothman, 1973).

4

Hugo L. Black and Hierarchy in Society and Politics

Hugo Black prefaced his memoirs with an observation that, had he left it unsaid, still would have been apparent to his readers: "I am what might be called an unadulterated product of the South, a fact that I recall with pride."[1] Although he made this observation in reference to the purity of his southern pedigree, the relevance of his statement went beyond mere matters of lineage. An examination of the contours of his life reveals that he was very much a part of the inter- and intraregional conflicts that plagued southern society at the turn of the century and for some time thereafter. Indeed, he came to possess a hierarchical view of society and politics, and thus developed a strong appreciation for antihierarchical rights, as a consequence of his exposure to the enduring sectionalism of the national political process and to the abuses of power that Alabama plantation and industrial elites committed.

Political Insurgency in Alabama

Black's education in southern politics began early in his life. He was born in 1886; his boyhood thus coincided with the decade of Populist turmoil. The Alabama of his youth, especially his native Clay County, was a hotbed of insurgency. He recalled that the "Populist Party at that time had a thriving active membership in the County and State." Because his father was a successful furnishing merchant, he discovered firsthand the significance (if not the intricacies) of the crop-lien system that was at the center of this political maelstrom. His father, a passionate opponent of the Populists, "became the most prosperous merchant" and "owned more property than any other person in the county."[2]

Not surprisingly, young Hugo shared his father's antipathy for the Populists: "Before I could articulate my syllables distinctly, I recall how angry people could make me by saying: 'You are a Populist, a third party-ite.' My reply in those early days . . . was 'I am *not* a tird [*sic*] party—I a democrat.' " His "father was so much against the Populists that he would not support the Bryan ticket in 1896 because he felt that Bryan was too near being a Populist." Following his father's lead, ten-year-old Hugo supported the independent ticket of Palmer and Buckner.[3]

Yet a marked political curiosity accompanied Hugo's professed distaste for Populism. While his father scrupulously avoided insurgent gatherings, the boy found his entertainment primarily in Populist rallies, torchlight parades, and stump speeches. He later recalled going "to most political meetings" held and attending "practically all the speeches that were ever made in Ashland [i.e., Black's hometown] during [his] boyhood."[4] It is not surprising that a precocious boy would find these events fascinating, since in few states was the conflict between the forces of reform and reaction fought more intensely or bitterly. While young Hugo could not have understood all that was at issue in the gatherings he attended, one must still examine the social and political conflicts that were the focus of the charged rhetoric to which he was exposed. The events of the late nineteenth century carved out a political landscape in Alabama that would persist for decades and in which Black would be forced to take sides. Informed insights would replace his childhood impressions after he learned the history of the struggle he had joined.

In the latter part of the nineteenth century, between 80 and 90 percent of Alabama cotton growers were dependent upon the crop-lien system. The first attack on this usurious credit scheme came, ironically, from the plantation elites of the state's Black Belt region, rather than from the yeomen who suffered under the system. A desire to aid those less fortunate did not inspire this attack. Rather, the Black Belt planters were incensed that Alabama law made the liens of merchants superior to the liens of landowners, because this provision lessened the control of the plantation elites over their black tenants. The landowners thus worked to secure a prior lien on tenants' crops. Although the potential for further conflict between merchants and large landowners existed, "[n]o serious difficulty developed." "[G]radually landowners opened stores on their land and became merchants, while merchants acquired land and became planters. The two groups soon developed mutual interests. Although the landholder was willing to make an arrangement with the merchant, all he offered to the tenant was the advice to 'let retrenchment in expenses be his watchword.' "[5]

The unresponsiveness of those benefiting from the crop lien to the complaints of those ensnared in the system ensured that the state would present fertile ground for Farmers' Alliance teachings. An overwhelming response greeted this Texas-based movement when it dispatched six lecturers to Alabama in 1887. The demand for assistance in forming county organizations and suballiances became so great that not enough lecturers could be supplied. The appearance in the state of a group of newspapers dedicated to the agrarian cause also demonstrated receptiveness to alliance principles. The *Alliance News* (later renamed the *Alliance Advocate*) became the Alabama Alliancemen's first and most important newspaper.[6]

With yeomen across the South, Alabama Alliancemen sought at first to secure reforms through the Democratic Party. The farmers understood the need for sectional unity on the national level and were thus averse to insurgent politics. They promoted Democratic candidates for state office who would amend usury laws to ameliorate the harsher aspects of the crop lien; and they sought candidates for national office who would replace the crop lien with the sub-treasury plan. In 1890, efforts to secure reform through existing political arrangements held some promise because the Farmers' Alliance gained a majority of seats in the Alabama House of Representatives and was strong in the Alabama Senate.[7]

Tangible reform through the Democratic Party proved illusory, however, because the Bourbons exercised a disproportionate and controlling influence in state politics. These defenders of the political status quo consistently and strongly resisted efforts to reapportion the Alabama legislature. As a result, the underrepresentation of nine upland counties and the overrepresentation of eleven Black Belt counties occurred by 1890. More important, "[p]arty positions and places were dictated by the bourbons." Alabama Democrats nominated their candidates for major offices at a biennial state convention, and the plantation elites made the event "an instrument for machine government." The county vote for the last governor determined representation at the convention. This procedure ensured large Black Belt delegations because the state's lowland counties always gave the Democratic candidate a lop-sided margin. The state's upland counties were more likely to vote Republican, since yeomen were less concerned with maintaining white supremacy than were the plantation elites. Moreover, the Bourbons controlled black votes in the Black Belt region.[8]

As a consequence of Bourbon influence, poor Alabama farmers could secure neither the nominations of Farmers' Alliance candidates for important offices nor significant legislation addressing their concerns. In 1890, Bourbon political maneuvering denied the Democratic nomination to Reuben F. Kolb, the Farmers' Alliance candidate for governor. And the sub-treasury plan never became a part of the state party platform. Except for the theme of white supremacy, party platforms were virtually contentless; they were "phrased in the most general terms possible and seldom mentioned any controversial issues." Legislation favoring plantation elites exacerbated the yeomen's sense of injustice. Once, after a proposal to exempt small farms from taxation for five years failed, the Alabama legislature revised the tax laws to benefit large planters: the new legislation allowed Black Belt planters to exempt property worth five thousand dollars or more, while small farmers could not exempt even five hundred dollars' worth of property.[9]

Not surprisingly, the poor farmers of Alabama, like yeomen all across the South, eventually became convinced "that a new party, divorced from the corruptive influence of the old would be more responsive to the needs of the people and would deliver them from their oppressors." Failing to seize control of the machinery of the Democratic Party and enact their program from within, some farmers declared themselves the true party, adopted the name Jeffersonian Democrats, and, led by Kolb, entered the gubernatorial campaign of 1892. Other Alliancemen, refusing even a token attachment to the Southern Democracy, joined the Populist movement that was sweeping through the South and West. Although the two reform parties remained formally separate until 1894, opposition to the elite-dominated Democratic Party united them. The Populists supported Kolb for the governorship, and the Jeffersonians supported James B. Weaver, the Populist candidate for president.[10]

Seeking strength in numbers, insurgent agrarians attempted to enlist the support of the state's fledgling labor movement. Before 1900, only the largest cities, most notably, Birmingham, were sites of significant labor activity. Northerners had invested capital in Birmingham to exploit the state's mineral deposits, and the city experienced a rapid growth in population as the steel industry burgeoned. The prosperity that attended industrialization, however, was limited geographically within the state. Furthermore, relatively few persons enjoyed its blessings. Those who did not share in the new wealth included those who were largely responsible for its creation: Alabama miners. Government and industry dealt harshly with the efforts of workers to improve their situation through combination. The state convict-lease system also presented an impediment to the goals of organized labor. While Alabama officials justified the leasing of convicts to private industries as a method of making the state penal system self-sustaining and as a means of obtaining public revenue, the system, not so incidentally, provided industrialists with a hedge against labor unrest.[11]

In order to harness labor discontent, the agrarians emphasized the similarities between the plight of the farmer and that of the worker. Joseph C. Manning, a native of Clay County and the founder of the People's, or Populist, Party in Alabama, divided society into "the 'better classes' and the 'ordinary folk.' " The latter class included "the great mass of the people among the farmers, the laboring men, miners and mechanics of the state." Agrarian rhetoric declared that the common people were a victimized majority who needed to gain control of the state to protect the weaker portions of society from the stronger elements. Yet it was the willingness of the Jeffersonian Democrats and the Populists to incorporate into their respective platforms statements condemning competition between convict and free labor (among other pro-labor planks) that transformed a shared sentiment (i.e., a common belief in the value of labor and a common sense of exploitation) into a working relationship aimed at achieving substantial reform.[12]

The union of reformist groups prompted a counteralliance of forces supporting the status quo; the resources of the state's new industrialists supplemented those of the merchants and plantation elites. The Black Belt Bourbons initially regarded the "Big Mules" (i.e., the leaders in steel, coal, iron, insurance, and utilities) as antagonists. Intermittent conflict over industry demands for internal improvements and other forms of governmental assistance had characterized the relationship between the two groups. There were instances of agreement when policies were mutually beneficial, such as the fashioning of the convict-lease system. But the industrial and plantation elites sought a closing of ranks and close cooperation only after the onslaught of insurgent politics.[13]

The supervision and management of elections was the most important form of partnership between the two groups of elites. In the same way that the Bourbons took advantage of laws organizing the nominating conventions, the Big Mule–Black Belt coalition exploited electoral laws which assured that "only Democrats would appoint the registrars and other officials, conduct the elections, and count the votes": through the manipulation of elections, the Bourbons and their allies frustrated agrarian efforts to win political office. Electoral corruption, evident in most of the South, could not have been more flagrant or egregious than it was in Alabama. In legislative and gubernatorial contests in the 1890s, the forces defending the status quo stole ballot boxes containing agrarian majorities, registered false ballots for Bourbon candidates, and influenced votes through the use of money, whiskey, intimidation, and threats. On the basis of available evidence concerning the gubernatorial contest of 1892, it appears that Reuben Kolb received the most votes, but Bourbon machinations denied him his office. The 1894 gubernatorial election was so tainted that even several Democratic newspapers protested, fearing that Alabamians would refuse to accept the results. The absence of an election-contest law further limited the agrarians' options to achieve reform.[14]

The reform press, which had grown to some one hundred papers in Alabama, represented one recourse left open to the agrarians. The papers had served initially to disseminate Farmers' Alliance principles, which made the creation of new parties possible. The press now served the critical antihierarchical functions of criticizing incumbents, promoting agrarian candidates, and exposing Bourbon corruption. Through the efforts of reformers generally and agrarian editors specifically, "the state was made aware of long-standing corrupt election practices, and the evils of machine politics were brought home as never before." Statewide newspapers and smaller, but equally important, county journals were so censorious of the Bourbons that some editors faced libel charges while others saw their offices ransacked. Although the reform newspapers did not succeed in wresting political control from the Bourbons, they had a significant impact upon Alabama politics. "That the papers added color is undeniable; that they angered the Democrats is certain; that they influenced voters is probable." Most important, the papers helped to create pressure for the passage of an election-contest law and certain modest legislation addressing the concerns of yeomen and laborers.[15]

After the nationwide decline of the Populist movement in 1896, the Alabama Bourbons moved to consolidate their position. Ostensibly seeking Negro disfranchisement, they managed to pare the ranks of poor white voters through the use of a literacy test and the harshest cumulative poll tax in the South (i.e., a tax an individual must pay for each in a series of years in order to qualify to vote). The poll tax alone disfranchised around 24 percent of the total white male voting-age population in the state.[16]

Workingman's Lawyer and Opponent of Convict Leasing

The waning of Populism and the political enfeeblement of Alabama's yeomen did not mark an end to intrastate conflict. Quite the contrary. As V. O. Key noted in his classic study of southern politics, "[t]he north Alabama region . . . retains to this day [1949] a strident radical agrarian tone in its politics and tends to be the source of movements disturbing to the [state's plantation and industrial elites]." "There[,] a wholesome contempt for authority and a spirit of rebellion akin to that of the Populist days resist the efforts of the big farmers and 'big mules' . . . to control the state."[17]

As an adult, Black demonstrated a keen awareness of this conflict, a grasp of its history, and, in sharp contrast to his father, an allegiance to Alabama's yeomen and laborers:

In the days before the war between the states, the "Black Belt" of Alabama was a Whig stronghold. This was on account of the fact that the land was divided up among a few large plantation holders, who constituted what was then called "Alabama Aristocracy." Our section of the State and that further North, was the home of Jacksonian Democracy. Our people owned few slaves. They owned small tracts of ground and cultivated it themselves. . . . The political philosophy of these two sections, has not changed with the arrival of new generations. While there is at present an artificial coalition, called the Democratic Party, the Black Belt is not at heart sympathetic with the rights and privileges of the average citizen, nor have they ever joined with Governor Comer or any other man who sought to stem the rising tide of Plutocracy.[18]

Black provided this analysis in 1929 when he was serving in the United States Senate and was in the thick of the conflict he described. But his abandonment of his father's politics and his involvement in this intrasectional rivalry occurred well before he moved to the nation's capital. To understand his metamorphosis, one must examine the initial stages of his career, starting with the fulfillment of his childhood ambition to become a trial lawyer.

"It is hard for me to remember when I did not want to be a lawyer," Black recalled. "This desire increased year by year as I attended the regular sessions of Court in Ashland. Few sessions occurred at which a small boy, meaning me, was not present, looking and listening eagerly to find out what the lawyers said and did." He had considered following in the footsteps of his older brother, Orlando, who was a doctor. But, after a year of medical school, he decided, on Orlando's advice, that he would be happiest pursuing his heartfelt interest in the law.[19]

In 1904, Black entered the University of Alabama Law School, whose faculty then consisted of two instructors. He spent two years under the tutelage of these men, who helped him "to learn the basic principles of the law as it then existed." He recalled that they stressed the traditional view "that legislators not judges should make the laws." He performed so well as a law student that his instructors recommended him for membership in Phi Beta Kappa when he graduated in 1906.[20]

Black returned to his hometown of Ashland to offer his services. He found that a disheartening shortage of clients was the price to be paid for familiar surroundings. The town "already [had] five lawyers, not one of whom . . . was earning more than enough to afford him a skimpy living." Moreover, "the people of Clay County saw [him] not as a lawyer but as the same marble-shooting boy whom they had watched grow up in their midst. . . . It was therefore no surprise to [him] that litigants did not crowd into [his] law office." Adding injury to insult, he also had the misfortune of losing his law library in a fire. He had purchased the books with money inherited after the death of his father in 1899, but he had not had the foresight to use some of his inheritance to insure the investment.[21]

Black managed to find some work collecting old debts. After a year and three months in Ashland, however, he decided to leave for Birmingham. Debt collection "was not the type of law practice for which [he] yearned," and he welcomed the increased opportunities that an industrial economy would afford.[22]

Although Black looked forward to the move, he cherished the bond he had established with the people of Ashland. Many of the individuals he saw in his practice had been customers of his father. Indeed, his first debt collections were against farmers who owed money to his father's estate. These yeomen paid the debts even though they knew that the statute of limitations already barred collection. Black explained: "Many of those debtors told me that my father had dealt too fairly or leniently with them for them to be willing to plead a technicality of any kind to escape paying what they owed his estate." This made him "very proud" of his father; it also caused him to admire greatly the yeomen of Clay County. "It now seems to me," Black reflected, "that I had planned far wiser than I knew when, in mapping out my program, I somehow stumbled upon the idea of spending my first few years [*sic*] as a lawyer in Clay County. They were a people of rugged, sturdy, honest, and patriotic character, and I hope that by virtue of living among them in my early formative years, and also as a part of my heritage, I was able to absorb some of these fine qualities."[23]

If the time spent in Ashland disposed Black toward Alabama's yeomen, his years in Birmingham would sensitize him to the plight of the other wellspring of Populist sentiment, namely, urban laborers. "He saw in Birmingham the industrial system at its rawest and most brutal"; he witnessed "the drama of helpless people confronting the power of big absentee corporations that dominated their lives." The effects of urban poverty—prostitution, gambling, intemperance, and murder—were all too common in the lives of the city's slum dwelling laborers. Birmingham had developed "the reputation of the nation's most crime-filled city"; some individuals even referred to it as "the murder capital of the world."[24]

The city's dispossessed may have taken heart at the turn of the century with the ascendance of Progressivism in the state. The Progressives, like the agrarian insurgents, opposed the Big Mule–Black Belt coalition. This movement also prompted certain legislative initiatives favorable to labor, such as regulation of child labor and abolition of the convict-lease system. "In contrast to Populism," however, "Progressivism's narrow commitment excluded any but the most traditional humanitarian concern for the working classes." "[T]he cutting edge of the Progressive movement in Alabama [as in the Northeast] was primarily concerned with material progress and with changing the distribution of wealth to favor the middle range of the economic hierarchy." If virtual neglect of workers' concerns was not enough to convince laborers that they would have to await new champions, involvement of Progressive administrations in strikebreaking and antilabor legislation (such as an antiboycott act) dashed any hopes workingmen may have had for significant reform.[25]

Black witnessed a deplorable instance of Progressive hostility toward labor soon after he arrived in Birmingham. In the summer of 1908, Progressive Governor B. B. Comer "performed just as his Big Mule enemies would have performed" when he helped crush a United Mine Workers strike against the Tennessee Coal, Iron, and Railroad

Company. The company recently had become a subsidiary of United States Steel, which was an aggressive opponent of organized labor. At contract time, Tennessee Coal announced a wage cut from fifty-seven to forty-seven cents per ton mined. This wage reduction followed a cutback in operations and a reduction in the workforce. Moved to militancy, union miners sought to convince or coerce nonunion miners to join them in striking. Escalating violence between miners and their opponents (scabs and company guards) eventually prompted the governor to take action. Although Comer refused company requests for guns, he employed state troopers to escort trainloads of strike-breakers to the mines and to raze union tent-villages (ostensibly for health reasons). The collapse of this strike and the memory of a failed strike in 1904 left labor in Birmingham demoralized.[26]

Although of the same social stratum as the Progressives, Black became an advocate almost exclusively for workingmen. As a young stranger in Birmingham with "[no] entree into any law firm," he developed a symbiotic relationship with the city's less fortunate individuals and groups. "They could not afford better; he could not afford to turn them away." He played a role in the effort of the United Mine Workers to reorganize their dispirited Birmingham district. Later, he "represented [the unionists] as a special attorney in quite a number of cases, [although he] was never their regularly retained lawyer." He "*was* the regularly retained lawyer of the Local Carpenters' Union, for many years, and also represented the Brotherhood of Railroad Trainmen in all of their business for several years."[27]

Black had some relations with the business community, but this contact was nominal. Recognizing that "[w]hat [he] needed more than anything else [early in his legal career] were clients," he had sought to build his practice by joining such business conduits as the Masons, the Knights of Pythias, and the Odd Fellows. He became "the attorney for the Zurich Insurance Co. of Switzerland, which did a large amount of business in the Birmingham vicinity." Yet, in 1914, he declined an opportunity to become a corporate lawyer. By this time, he "had acquired a reputation for winning lawsuits," and the senior member of one of the city's top corporate firms thought it wise to tender him a partnership. The offer flattered Black, and he was well aware that partnership in that firm would place him in an elite social group. But serious misgivings occupied his thinking: "I reminded [the attorney] . . . that I had watched him argue cases for the street car company and other companies defending serious personal injury and death cases, and that I had always wondered if he could be wholly happy with that kind of practice. I expressed some doubt as to whether I could enjoy a practice limited to that kind of trial work.'' Black had come to identify with those interests that, at the outset of his career, he had merely represented. In refusing the partnership offer, he chose to concentrate on the business of organized labor and the claims of individuals harmed in industrial accidents. At a time when workers' compensation programs did not exist, he accepted personal injury suits on a contingent fee basis to ensure that workers alone did not bear the costs of industrial development.[28]

Black also demonstrated his commitment to labor through his perpetual hostility toward convict leasing. His first exposure to this system came soon after he began his law practice in Birmingham. On a referral, he took up a lawsuit involving Willie Morton, a black convict whom the state had leased to the Sloss Sheffield Steel and Iron Company. As a result of poor record keeping, the steel company had held Morton twenty-two days beyond his sentence. Black tried the case before Judge A. O. Lane. William I. Grubb, a leading attorney in Birmingham's largest corporate law firm, defended the steel company. Grubb sought to overwhelm the tenderfoot Black with a series of complex common-law pleadings, thus preventing the issue from ever reaching the jury. Black, however, proved equal to the challenge and, in addition to impressing Judge Lane, managed to obtain a jury verdict of one hundred fifty dollars in Morton's favor.[29]

As a consequence of this initial contact with convict leasing and Judge Lane, Black managed, in 1911, to secure an appointment to a police court judgeship. This position enabled him to combat indirectly the leasing system. Judge Lane eventually became one of four Birmingham city commissioners; to save the city money, he consolidated five police court judgeships into one. Seeking an appointee with the capacity to make this administrative change a success, he called upon the "quick, enterprising, and smart" attorney who had earlier argued the Morton case before him. Black accepted the position only after Lane assured him that he could continue his law practice. The twenty-five-year-old judge then began to preside over cases involving the city's nocturnal miscreants. While the dispatch with which Black handled cases did not disappoint Commissioner Lane, the new judge's methods appeared to other individuals as a recipe for arbitrary justice. (Black disposed of 118 cases in 150 minutes on one day.) It is likely, however, that much of this censure was motivated less by compassion for the accused than by concern over the effect that Black's methods had upon both the convict-lease system and the fees that the state paid to court clerks and sheriffs for housing prisoners. Since the state required defendants to work off the costs of their pretrial incarceration, private enterprises benefited from inefficient judges who maintained the supply of convict-labor. Incarceration costs took the form of fees paid to law officers responsible for prisoner care. (Sheriffs and court clerks profited through not spending the entire amount that the state allocated.) By disposing of most cases within twenty-four hours, Black ensured that defendants had no costs charged against them and, therefore, that there would be less competition between convict and free labor and no fees paid to sheriffs.[30]

When he became solicitor (prosecutor) for Jefferson County, Black continued to alienate companies using convict labor and individuals dependent upon the fee system. He assumed this post in 1914, about two years after resigning as police court judge. Trumpeting his allegiance to Alabama's working classes, he campaigned for the position as the candidate of the plain folk, rather than of a "few capitalists or a ring of politicians." In his first significant action as prosecutor, he sought and received the dismissal of approximately five hundred cases involving industrial workers whom the state had charged with illegal gaming. He viewed the defendants as hapless victims of a corrupt system because police informants had instigated the crapshooting so that the sheriff could arrest the workers and draw state fees. Subsequent threats to impeach the prosecutor for this incident came to nothing. But Black's continued hostility toward powerful interests would make his political situation precarious.[31]

Some law officers had reason to resent Black for more than his attack on the fee system. When he noticed that police in the town of Bessemer had obtained an unusually large number of confessions, he called for a grand jury investigation of the matter. This inquest resulted in a finding that officers had secured confessions from suspects through third-degree methods "so cruel that . . . [they] would bring discredit and shame upon the most uncivilized and barbarous community."[32]

Black also challenged coal and insurance companies. He prosecuted a coal company for short-weighting its miners. (The United Mine Workers had long protested this practice.) And when insurance companies pressed him to halt ambulance chasing, he responded that he would do so as soon as the companies supported a law permitting courts to set aside settlements that insurers obtained before workers realized the full extent of their injuries.[33]

Black made some of his most bitter political enemies through aggressive enforcement of Alabama's prohibition laws. He pursued prohibition violators for personal as well as professional reasons. Liquor offended his deep religious convictions and was the source of some sorrowful childhood memories. These incidents included his father's drinking (and subsequent expulsion from the Baptist church) and the alcohol-related death of his brother, Pelham. At times, the solicitor's aversion to alcohol inspired him to take controversial actions. Once, when the leaders of a whiskey ring failed to appear at their trial, he immediately ordered the destruction of six hundred thousand dollars' worth of confiscated alcohol. He also strictly enforced a law that banned the publication of advertisements about intoxicating liquors. Newspaper owners had requested that he delay prosecutions until they could challenge the constitutionality of the law. He did much more than refuse such requests; he went so far as to defend (successfully) the constitutionality of the law in the state supreme court.[34]

Predictably, Black's numerous enemies sought his ouster. They secured his removal through a legal battle, which ultimately gave the circuit solicitor (who, at the time, was an adversary of Black) the authority to name the county solicitor's deputies. Realizing the futility of his situation, Black resigned his post in 1917. He decided instead to join the effort to make the world safe for democracy. After successfully completing an officers' training course, he became a captain in the field artillery. As an assistant to a colonel in charge of training regiments for battle, he never saw the front. But he served his country until the Armistice.[35]

At the end of the First World War, Black returned to his legal practice in Birmingham. A bad investment he had made prior to the war had left him "practically dead broke," but he did not remain in this condition for long. "Clients began to hire me immediately," he recalled. In a short time, he had a lucrative practice. He also improved his situation by marrying Josephine Foster, the daughter of a prominent Birmingham couple. He greeted his new bride with a home in a fashionable section of Birmingham, a new car, and a country club membership.[36]

Although Black refined his lifestyle, he did not change his philosophy. He still served as an advocate for workingmen. Personal injury lawsuits and union business remained the focus of his practice. The Fosters, especially, were aware of his convictions; they referred to their new relation as the "young Bolshevik." Black enhanced his reputation as a friend of labor when he served as president of the Anti-Convict-Lease Association. Reformers established this organization in 1885 to publicize the evils of the leasing system, especially the impact of leasing upon the wages of miners. Black's contributions as association president were instrumental in persuading the Alabama legislature to abolish the system, although this reform occurred after his tenure.[37]

Senator Black, Candidate of the "Unorganized Mass"

An Allegiance to Yeomen and Laborers

Black made his most visible and significant efforts to aid Alabama's working classes as a United States senator. After deciding to run for office in 1925, he said to a relative: "I am personally of the opinion that there have been so many millionaires and corporation lawyers in the United States Senate that the people rarely ever have a representative. It is my ambition to give them one."[38]

Black's decision to seek office may have seemed quixotic, in view of the fact that his connections to labor and his involvement in many personal injury suits against large corporations distanced him from the Democratic leadership. Certain considerations, however, favored his candidacy. In 1902, the Democratic state executive committee had abandoned the traditional convention method of nominating candidates and had instituted a statewide primary. The agrarian insurgents had long pressed this reform in response to Bourbon overrepresentation and political maneuvering at state conventions. The executive committee's eventual acceptance of the primary did not denote a greater sensitivity to the concerns of small farmers and laborers. Rather, the Democratic leadership hoped to prevent defections from the party. Republican growth seemed likely at the turn of the century, given the enmity that Alabama's yeomen and laborers still felt for the state's plantation and industrial elites. The Big Mule–Black Belt coalition was confident that reform of the nominating system would quell restiveness within the party without threatening Bourbon dominance, because disfranchisement and post–Populist-era apathy worked against those desiring further reform. By the time Black decided to run, however, poor whites in Alabama had mobilized behind a resurgent Ku Klux Klan. This "mass protest movement of poorer and more marginalized whites, whether urban, small town, or rural," was intent on flexing its political muscle.[39]

An electoral reform the state adopted in 1915 to prevent costly runoff primaries also aided Black. This law provided that, when there were more than two candidates for an office, voters should indicate both their first and their second choices. In the event that no candidate received a majority of first-choice votes, election officials would add the first- and second-choice votes together and declare as the winner the candidate with the largest total. This reform favored minority candidates and those with fewer resources because it permitted an individual to win the nomination on one ballot, despite polling less than a majority of the total votes cast.[40]

Hoping to take advantage of these changed circumstances, Black plunged into his campaign. He joined a field of four other candidates in which he was the youngest, had the least money, was the least experienced in the larger affairs of government, and was the least known outside of his own county. Lacking the resources of his opponents, he depended upon circulars, posters, and face-to-face contact to familiarize voters with his name and message. Like the Populists, he fought the status quo with the spoken and written word. In order to distinguish himself from the field, he emphasized his unique commitment to the concerns of Alabama's working classes and indirectly referred to the backgrounds of two of his opponents, Thomas E. Kilby and John Bankhead: "I am not now, and have never been a railroad, power company, or corporation lawyer. They have never shaped my ideals, fashioned my political creed, nor helped in my aspirations for public office. They have not been a part of my environment. I am not a millionaire [like Kilby]. I am not a Coal Operator. My father was not a United States Senator [as was Bankhead's father] and I am not running on his record." Black stressed his Clay County origins and emphasized his solicitude toward the problems of Alabama's farmers and laborers: "I have served the needs of the poor and unfortunate. In my practice I have represented the injured and broken, the widows and orphans of men killed beneath the wheels of trains or buried in the falls of rock down in the mines of coal and iron. . . . My law practice is in line with my natural sympathies and my conception of a lawyer . . . is one to whom the plain people can take their troubles in trust and confidence . . . and whose intellect is devoted to the task of giving the humble and poor their chance before the bar of justice."[41]

In a series of concrete proposals, Black made explicit his allegiance to yeomen and laborers and his willingness to confront the Big Mule–Black Belt alliance. To attract the labor vote, he expressed support for immigration restrictions. He maintained that "[s]elfish interests have imported [immigrant workers] here to obtain the temporary benefits of cheap labor in mines and other industries and have placed them in competition with American citizens." Addressing farmers, he proposed using the federally financed Wilson Dam on the Tennessee River near Muscle Shoals to manufacture fertilizer: "Everybody knows that cheap fertilizer means profit and prosperity to the farmer and that high-priced fertilizer means debt at the end of the harvest." By contrast, John Bankhead advocated that the government make Muscle Shoals available to the Alabama Power Company so that the company could provide citizens with cheap electricity. Black found this policy doubly disturbing: it failed to address the farmer's priority (fertilizer) and subsidized those who least needed governmental assistance (powerful utilities). Bankhead, he argued, was advocating "socialism or communism turned upside down. The Socialist or Communist would take from the few rich to give to the many poor. Mr. Bankhead's plan would take from the many poor toilers to give to the few and mighty rich." While the other three candidates had not expressed their opinion of the Bankhead plan, Black wanted voters to know that he at least was "forever opposed to any such dangerous device" as subsidizing powerful corporations. Adopting the motto of the Populists, he championed instead "justice to all and special favor to none."[42]

Black's efforts to portray himself as the candidate of the "unorganized mass" proved a successful strategy. Although he received only 32 percent of first-choice votes, he won the Democratic nomination under the primary rules of 1915. (He had been the first or second choice of more voters than any other candidate.) His organized support included the Women's Christian Temperance Union (he backed national prohibition), many labor unions, and a portion of the Ku Klux Klan (Klansmen also supported L. Breckenridge Musgrove).[43]

Since marginalized whites (small farmers and urban laborers) were the rank and file of the Klan, it is not surprising that this organization would find Black an attractive candidate. Klan members, however, had a special reason to vote for him: he had been a Klansman himself! He had joined the organization in 1923 because, as he explained it, his livelihood depended upon his doing so. He tried many cases before juries made up largely of Klan members, and many defendants, as well as most of the lawyers who opposed him, were also Klansmen. It is also worth noting that "the Alabama Klan was about the only organization that could provide help for an aspiring politician cut off from the campaign treasure chests of the 'Big Mules' [and Bourbons]. . . . The industrial unions, though active, were not powerful enough. Besides, their strength did not reach into the countryside." Although Black made "no *definite* decision to run for the Senate until 1925," he had long hoped to go to Congress. Most likely, his efforts to win office began with his decision to join the Klan. He resigned from the organization before beginning his campaign. But this move conformed with the sentiment of most Klansmen that members should not be candidates for office. Since his was a friendly resignation, he had the advantages of Klan support without the liabilities that came with membership in such a controversial organization. In a primary victory speech before a large group of Klansmen, he acknowledged his indebtedness to his audience: "I know that without the support of the members of this organization, I would not have been called, even by my enemies, the 'Junior Senator from Alabama.' "[44]

Political Tightrope Walk

After arriving in the nation's capital, Black sought to fulfill his campaign promises. He directed his energy toward suspending immigration and using Muscle Shoals to produce fertilizer instead of electricity. With respect to the latter issue, he told the Senate:

> I am talking in the interest of the people, not the big farmer who owns 18 cows and has his cows milked by electricity. I am talking in the interest of the great unorganized mass of farmers, many of them rental farmers. I want to state to the Senate that in my own experience I have known farmers in the county in which I was reared who came to town in the fall of the year and sold their cotton, and when they paid off the mortgage that was already on the crop and paid for the fertilizer they did not have a dime left to buy food and clothes for the children in the next year. . . . What we want is not power. We want fertilizer.[45]

While Black promoted the interests of his constituents, events conspired to make more difficult any future actions on behalf of Alabama's workingmen. Soon after his arrival in Washington, Klan membership dropped precipitously, from 94,301 in 1926 to 10,431 by the end of 1927. This exodus, most likely a reaction against the increasingly brutal tactics that certain elements in the Klan used, left him politically vulnerable. Such a drop in his organized support meant that he would have to be more solicitous of the concerns of his enemies if he hoped to remain in the Senate.[46]

Black's political tightrope walk began when the Democrats nominated Al Smith for president in 1928. Smith's urban-Catholic background and antiprohibition stance offended many southerners, especially Black's principal constituents. Fearing desertions to the Republicans, the chairman of the Bourbon-dominated Democratic executive committee in Alabama warned that the party would institute a loyalty oath and not allow Democrats who voted against Smith to participate in upcoming primaries. Black took the warning seriously and supported Smith, although he campaigned very quietly. His only statement in favor of the nominee was that Smith's views, except on the issues of immigration and prohibition, were "a clarion call to progressive democracy." Black regretted that prohibition had become the dominant issue because this concern created "a noisy division of wets and drys, submerging party issues of Jeffersonian progress and equal opportunity as opposed to Hamiltonian reaction and special privilege."[47]

Soon after Smith's defeat, Black's allegiance would be tested once again. Alabama's senior senator, Thomas Heflin, shared the anti-Catholic sentiments of the Klan and had voted against Smith's presidential bid. As a consequence, the executive committee excluded the senator from the 1930 primary. Black thought Heflin should have anticipated this result. Nevertheless, Black spoke out against the "political skulduggery" of the Democratic Party. The committee's action, he maintained, "boldly attempts to limit *all voters*, to a choice of candidates from a specially privileged class named by the Committee." He denied "that an effort thus to restrict and hamper the exercise of the right of suffrage is either morally or legally sound. Viewed from the voter's standpoint it is bureacratic [*sic*] robbery." In order to prevent this "small clique" from assuming "control of Alabama for and by the clique, and in the interest of special privilege and plunder," he called upon his constituents to vote the committee members out of office. He also urged Heflin to challenge the loyalty oath in the courts.[48]

Neither Black's constituents nor Heflin followed this advice. Instead, Heflin launched a third-party candidacy. Black now had to decide whether to support Heflin's insurgent campaign or remain within the party and back the Bourbon candidate, John Bankhead. Once again, Black thought better of defying the party. "I would . . . regret to jeopardize my own political future," he explained, "at a time when I believe I am just becoming of some real service to the people of the State."[49]

Another reason for Black's reluctance to support an insurgent candidate was the same reason that explained the nineteenth-century agrarians' hesitancy to pursue reform outside of the Democratic Party: a profound distrust of the party of the North matched Black's marked suspicion of the Bourbons. As his brief statement supporting Smith's presidential bid had suggested, he regarded the Republican party as the "party of sectionalism and plutocracy." He contended that it "is now and has always been sectional in its rewards and in its punishments." Because of Republican conduct toward the South, "[i]ndustrial progress was stopped" and "agricultural development was stayed" after the Civil War. He maintained that the southern economy still suffered greatly in the twentieth century from continued use of the favorite economic weapon of Republicanism, the protective tariff: "Four Eastern Republican states, thanks largely to a Republican Sectional tariff, obtain 43% of our National income for only 23% of the total population." The Hoover-Grundy Tariff Bill served "to hold up the price of every industrial commodity the farmer must buy if that commodity happen[ed] to be produced in a strong Republican state." (When he later spoke on the Hawley-Smoot Tariff Act of 1930, he would argue that its sponsors "had never stood for a fair and equitable spread of tariffs to both raw products and manufactured products." He would express pride in having "voted against that iniquitous, sectional, robbing, extortionate measure.") The sectionalism of the national political process thus led him to oppose any measure aimed at combating the power of the Alabama plantation elites that would redound to the benefit of the Republican Party. Reform of the Democratic Party ("the traditional friend of the South"), he believed, must come from within.[50]

Black's sense of political insecurity, the other reason for his abandonment of Heflin, increased in the early 1930s. His organized support deteriorated further when prohibition forces weakened and sentiment grew for revoking the Eighteenth Amendment. Also, Alabama did away with the primary reforms of 1915, returning to a run-off primary in the event that no candidate received a majority.[51]

These happenings prompted further complicity on Black's part in matters essential to the Bourbons. When Heflin obtained a congressional investigation of Bankhead's election to the Senate, for example, Black vigorously defended his state against charges of massive voting fraud. Indeed, his support of Bankhead served "in large measure as his campaign for renomination. . . . [I]t was a world turned upside down as the attacker of the Bankhead ascendancy in 1926 won reelection in 1932 in the role of its ardent defender." In that same year, Senators Robert M. LaFollette Jr. and Edward P. Costigan offered a bipartisan bill authorizing a Federal Emergency Relief Board to allocate $375 million to Depression-weary Americans. Presumably, many of Black's constituents would have qualified for relief. Black, however, led the floor fight against the proposal. He identified as the bill's deficiencies the likelihood that it would create an immortal bureau and the fact that federal officials, who had little knowledge of Alabama's special needs and concerns, would administer the program. His call for state distribution of relief money, however, was most likely a bow to the Bourbons, who were instinctively wary of any federal program that might upset race relations. He evidenced a similar solicitousness of Bourbon racial concerns when he participated in a 1935 filibuster against an antilynching bill.[52]

New Deal Champion

Although Black cooperated with his political enemies, he more than offset his concessions to the Bourbons by using federal power to promote working-class interests. After securing a second term in the Senate, he became absorbed with the problems of laborers. Ironically, his efforts on behalf of workers at first brought him into conflict with another champion of labor, Franklin Roosevelt. Soon after Roosevelt became president, Black sought his support for a bill that would prohibit interstate commerce in the goods of firms whose employees worked more than thirty hours per week. Black hoped that a limitation of hours would distribute income more widely, producing an economic stimulus through a consequent increase in consumer demand. Although labor strongly supported the bill, Roosevelt thought the proposal was extreme. As a countermeasure, he put forth his National Industrial Recovery Act (NIRA) in 1933. Black, in turn, opposed this legislation, objecting strongly to its antitrust exemption. After the Supreme Court declared the NIRA unconstitutional in 1935, Black reintroduced his thirty-hour bill. Again, he lacked sufficient congressional support. At this point, he saw fit to compromise with the president, and the Fair Labor Standards Act (FLSA) of 1938 was the fruit of their rapprochement.[53]

The Black-Connery Bill, as the FLSA was otherwise known, brought its Senate sponsor into open conflict with Alabama's propertied classes. Black's opponents charged him with complicity in northern efforts to sabotage southern industry. Requirements of minimum wages, maximum hours, and the abolition of child labor, the bill's detractors argued, would deprive the South's manufacturers of advantages that would enable them to compete with northern industry. When one critic sarcastically noted that the bill had "a lot of lovely poetry in it," Black retorted: "Thank God it has! All through the ages, poets have raised their voices in behalf of the weak."[54]

The FLSA was not an isolated instance of agreement between Black and the president on appropriate means for achieving economic reform. Among southern senators who were part of a fragile New Deal coalition with northern labor, none ranked higher than Black (near 80 percent) in terms of voting with nonsouthern Democrats in support of New Deal agricultural and labor policies. Senator Bankhead, by contrast, joined nonsouthern Democrats only 23 percent of the time.[55] Much to the dismay of Alabama's Bourbons and Big Mules, Black's voting record revealed that political expedience accounted for his earlier concessions to conservatism.

Black demonstrated opposition to corporate power in other ways as well. Over a period of years, he conducted a series of investigations that earned him the enmity of big business. These formal inquiries also enhanced his appreciation for antihierarchical rights. In 1933, he looked into the performance of the marine-shipping industry in executing federal mail contracts. His highly publicized hearings uncovered rampant mismanagement, contracts obtained without competitive bidding, and questionable perquisites that industry leaders offered to legislators and executive officials. He followed this effort with an investigation of federal-airmail-contract recipients. In hearings receiving even more media attention than the shipping industry investigation, he discovered that the noncompetitive bidding practices of Hoover's postmaster general had supported the development of airline industry giants at the expense of smaller, more efficient air carriers. He "reported to a nationwide radio audience that a web of collusion existed in which twenty-four of twenty-seven airmail contracts were divided among three giant holding companies."[56]

Black's most spectacular investigation occurred in 1935, when he inquired into the lobbying activities of the opponents of the Public Utility Holding Company Act. Through this bill, the Roosevelt administration sought to destroy public utility holding companies, some of which controlled utilities in dozens of states. When a supposedly grassroots protest greeted the bill, the president requested congressional investigations into the lobbying efforts of utility companies. Heading up the Senate inquiry, Black made aggressive use of subpoenas to acquire relevant testimony and documents. Although his methods were controversial, he revealed that one holding company orchestrated a seven-hundred-thousand-dollar bogus telegram- and letter-writing campaign against the legislation. He also disclosed that the president of the Associated Gas and Electric Company bullied newspaper editors with threats of decreased advertising and, on several occasions, provided papers with editorials he wanted printed. In a radio address, Black defended the aggressive investigative tactics used against the "high-powered, deceptive, telegram-fixing, letter-framing, Washington-visiting five million dollar [utilities] lobby." "[C]ontrary to tradition, against the public morals, and hostile to good Government," he asserted, "the lobby has reached such a position of power that it threatens Government itself." His vindication, the dismantling of the holding companies, followed soon after passage of the Public Utility Holding Company Act.[57]

Black provided a final measure of his opposition to corporate wealth with his defense of the president's controversial Court-packing plan. When Roosevelt attempted to enlarge the Supreme Court in response to the judicial invalidation of much of his legislative program, Black supported him in an impassioned radio address. The Court had "changed the basic theory of our Constitution" when "it protected wealth at the expense of poverty," the Senator declared. Fortunately, Congress had the means to remedy this "clear usurpation of legislative power": "With wise forethought, the framers of the Constitution carefully provided checks for use by Congress to prevent the courts from becoming too powerful, and to give assurance that the Congress could prevent judicial usurpation. The Constitution, therefore, left to Congress, among other powers, the right to increase or decrease the number of Supreme and inferior court judges and complete power to fix the appellate jurisdiction of the Supreme Court."[58]

Unlike his investigations of industry, Black's attack on the Court did not lead to remedial legislative action. The retirement of one conservative justice (Willis Van Devanter) only months after the defeat of the Court-packing bill, however, gave some consolation to the president and his champion in the Senate. Roosevelt made good use of the opportunity and selected Black as his first Supreme Court nominee. Black was, no doubt, grateful for the nomination, since he had said he was anticipating "the toughest primary fight of [his] life." In response to his strong support of workingmen during his second term, "[l]eaders of Alabama's business, industrial, and timber interests . . . had been gearing up to oppose [his] reelection."[59] Roosevelt made certain that Black would never again have to worry about his precarious political situation.

Soon after Roosevelt announced his choice for the vacant Court seat, rumors about Black's Klan membership began to circulate.

Black, who had earlier insisted on full disclosure from witnesses during Senate investigations, was not entirely forthcoming with the truth. He told the Senate Judiciary Committee that he was not at present a member of the Klan but suggested that anyone concerned about his former membership should vote against him. Senator Borah of Idaho took this statement as a denial of any association with the Klan. When Borah said as much in defense of the nomination, Black did not correct him. After Senate confirmation, Black expedited the administration of the judicial oath. His second wife provided his explanation for this move; she recalled that he had said: "I wasn't taking any chances. I knew that my enemies in big business and the press would influence the public against me so much that they might get a judge to enjoin me from taking the oath."[60]

Black's fears of press revelations materialized with an article in the Pittsburgh *Post-Gazette*. Reporter Ray Springle charged that the new justice was a member of the Ku Klux Klan. Black recognized that his credibility as a justice hinged upon his response to the charge, and he confronted the issue in a dramatic eleven-minute radio address. He admitted having joined the Klan but insisted that he was no longer a member of the organization and had never been a proponent of its racial or religious doctrines. He said that his "record as a Senator refute[d] every implication of racial or religious intolerance" and revealed that he "was of that group of liberal Senators who have consistently fought for the civil, economic and religious rights of all Americans, without regard to race or creed."[61] (Black, of course, failed to take into account his concessions to Bourbon racial concerns.)

Black's assurance that his erstwhile Klan membership would not affect his performance as a justice was borne out in a judicial tenure lasting thirty-four years. In addition to defending vigilantly the rights of black criminal defendants, he participated in the historic school desegregation ruling, *Brown v. Board of Education*.[62] His willingness to sacrifice his reputation with many southerners removed any suspicions that his jurisprudence reflected anything but a belief in human equality.[63] Yet to say that southern racial mores did not figure in his judicial performance is not to say that he escaped his past entirely.

Notes

1. Hugo L. Black and Elizabeth Black, *Mr. Justice and Mrs. Black: The Memoirs of Hugo L. Black and Elizabeth Black* (New York: Random House, 1986), 4.

2. Ibid., 7; Hugo L. Black to Irving Dilliard, 25 July 1962, Papers of Hugo L. Black, Library of Congress, Manuscript Division (hereafter cited as HLBP), Box 25. See also William Warren Rogers, *The One-Gallused Rebellion: Agrarianism in Alabama, 1865–1896* (Baton Rouge: Louisiana State University Press, 1970), 205, 316; James F. Simon, *The Antagonists: Hugo Black, Felix Frankfurter and Civil Liberties in Modern America* (New York: Simon & Schuster, 1989), 69; Gerald T. Dunne, *Hugo Black and the Judicial Revolution* (New York: Simon & Schuster, 1977), 88.

3. Black and Black, *Mr. Justice and Mrs. Black*, 7–8; Hugo L. Black to Irving Dilliard, 13 July 1962, HLBP, Box 25.

4. Hugo L. Black to Irving Dilliard, 13 July 1962, HLBP, Box 25; Hugo L. Black to John Frank, 20 January 1948, HLBP, Box 460. See also Virginia Van der Veer Hamilton, *Hugo Black: The Alabama Years* (Baton Rouge: Louisiana State University Press, 1972), 15.

5. Allen Johnston Going, *Bourbon Democracy in Alabama: 1874–1890* (Tuscaloosa: University of Alabama Press, 1951), 93–95; Rogers, *One-Gallused Rebellion*, 3–30 (pp. 17–18 quoted).

6. Lawrence Goodwyn, *Democratic Promise: The Populist Moment in America* (New York: Oxford University Press, 1976), 87–94, 102, 253–54; Rogers, *One-Gallused Rebellion*, 249–52; Going, *Bourbon Democracy in Alabama*, 107.

7. Rogers, *One-Gallused Rebellion*, 176, 185–86.

8. Ibid., 55, 178 (quoted); Going, *Bourbon Democracy in Alabama*, 28–30, 44, 211.

9. Rogers, *One-Gallused Rebellion*, 19–20, 164, 178–87; Going, *Bourbon Democracy in Alabama*, 31 (quoted), 60, 95, 99, 108, 209.

10. Theodore Saloutos, "The Professors and the Populists," *Agricultural History* 40 (1966): 235 (quoted); Rogers, *One-Gallused Rebellion*, 189, 193–94, 205, 217, 220, 229, 231–32, 271–72, 290; Goodwyn, *Democratic Promise*, 323–24.

11. Rogers, *One-Gallused Rebellion*, 93–97, 139, 274; Goodwyn, *Democratic Promise*, 382–83; Sheldon Hackney, *Populism to Progressivism in Alabama* (Princeton: Princeton University Press, 1969), 59–60; Going, *Bourbon Democracy in Alabama*, 170–90.

12. Hackney, *Populism to Progressivism in Alabama*, 23–24, 30 (quoted), 58–59, 61, 78, 81, 83–84, 282; Rogers, *One-Gallused Rebellion*, 213, 215, 271–73, 275, 293, 331.

13. Rogers, *One-Gallused Rebellion*, 92–93; Hackney, *Populism to Progressivism in Alabama*, 10 n. 12, 118, 133, 210, 226; Going, *Bourbon Democracy in Alabama*, 109, 117, 125; V. O. Key Jr., *Southern Politics in State and Nation*, new ed. (Knoxville: University of Tennessee Press, 1977), 42–44, 56.

14. Rogers, *One-Gallused Rebellion*, 45 (quoted), 217–35, 271–92; Goodwyn, *Democratic Promise*, 244–45, 323–25, 382; Hackney, *Populism to Progressivism in Alabama*, 18, 48, 63, 67.

15. Goodwyn, *Democratic Promise*, 355–56; Rogers, *One-Gallused Rebellion*, 249–70, 294, 331, 334 (pp. 331, 270 quoted).

16. Hackney, *Populism to Progressivism in Alabama*, 147–79, 180–208; Key, *Southern Politics*, 542–44, 578–98, 599–618; Rogers, *One-Gallused Rebellion*, 236–48, 333.

17. Key, *Southern Politics*, 42, 36 (quoted); Rogers, *One-Gallused Rebellion*, 335; Hackney, *Populism to Progressivism in Alabama*, 332.

18. Hugo L. Black to John R. McCain, 30 December 1929, HLBP, Box 104.

19. Black and Black, *Mr. Justice and Mrs. Black*, 15–16 (quoted); Hugo L. Black, "Reminiscences," *Alabama Law Review* 18 (1965): 4–5, 15–16.

20. Black, "Reminiscences," 8–11 (p. 10 quoted); Black and Black, *Mr. Justice and Mrs. Black*, 17–19.

21. Black and Black, *Mr. Justice and Mrs. Black*, 20, 22.

22. Ibid., 22, 25.

23. Ibid., 22–23.

24. Clifford J. Durr, "Hugo Black, Southerner: The Southern Background," *American University Law Review* 10 (1961): 30 (quoted); Hamilton, *Hugo Black*, 30 (quoted); Dunne, *Black and the Judicial Revolution*, 92–94.

25. Hackney, *Populism to Progressivism in Alabama*, 122–46, 230–54, 264, 278, 310, 316–23, 327–28 (pp. 327–28, 264 quoted).

26. Ibid., 316–23 (p. 316 quoted); Hamilton, *Hugo Black*, 33–35.

27. Black and Black, *Mr. Justice and Mrs. Black*, 31 (quoted); Bertram Wyatt-Brown, "Ethical Background of Hugo Black's Career: Thoughts Prompted by the Articles of Sheldon Hackney and Paul L. Murphy," *Alabama Law Review* 36 (1985): 919 (quoted); Hamilton, *Hugo Black*, 33; Hugo L. Black to Irving Dilliard, 13 July 1962, HLBP, Box 25 (quoted third and fourth, emphasis added).

28. Black and Black, *Mr. Justice and Mrs. Black*, 27 (quoted), 31–32, 39 (quoted third and fourth); Hugo L. Black to Irving Dilliard, 13 July 1962, HLBP, Box 25 (quoted); Hugo Black Jr., *My Father: A Remembrance* (New York: Random House, 1975), 23, 44–45.

29. Black and Black, *Mr. Justice and Mrs. Black*, 35; Hamilton, *Hugo Black*, 32–33; John P. Frank, *Mr. Justice Black: The Man and His Opinions* (New York: Knopf, 1949), 16.

30. Hamilton, *Hugo Black*, 37–45 (quoting Judge Lane, p. 37); Frank, *Justice Black: Man and Opinions*, 16–21; Black and Black, *Mr. Justice and Mrs. Black*, 36–37.

31. Hamilton, *Hugo Black*, 46–59 (quoting Black, p. 52); Simon, *The Antagonists*, 73–74; Frank, *Justice Black: Man and Opinions*, 22–23; Black and Black, *Mr. Justice and Mrs. Black*, 38–48.

32. Hamilton, *Hugo Black*, 62 (quoting Black); Frank, *Justice Black: Man and Opinions*, 27–30; Daniel M. Berman, "Hugo L. Black: The Early Years," *Catholic University Law Review* 8 (1959): 110.

33. Hamilton, *Hugo Black*, 61; Frank, *Justice Black: Man and Opinions*, 23–24.

34. Hamilton, *Hugo Black*, 61–62, 66–67; Frank, *Justice Black: Man and

Opinions, 26; Simon, *Antagonists*, 74–75; Black and Black, *Mr. Justice and Mrs. Black*, 8, 12, 48–49; Paul L. Murphy, "The Early Social and Political Philosophy of Hugo Black: Liquor as a Test Case," *Alabama Law Review* 36 (1985): 874–75.

35. Black and Black, *Mr. Justice and Mrs. Black*, 48–56; Frank, *Justice Black: Man and Opinions*, 30–31; Hamilton, *Hugo Black*, 67–69.

36. Black and Black, *Mr. Justice and Mrs. Black*, 57–59 (quoted), 62–63; Simon, *Antagonists*, 80–81; Sheldon Hackney, "The Clay County Origins of Mr. Justice Black: The Populist as Insider," *Alabama Law Review* 36 (1985): 840.

37. Frank, *Justice Black: Man and Opinions*, 34–35; Hamilton, *Hugo Black*, 70–71, 110–11; Black and Black, *Mr. Justice and Mrs. Black*, 35, 51–61; Dunne, *Black and the Judicial Revolution*, 100–101 (quoting the Fosters); Going, *Bourbon Democracy in Alabama*, 187–88; Hackney, *Populism to Progressivism in Alabama*, 314.

38. As quoted in Simon, *Antagonists*, 84.

39. Rogers, *One-Gallused Rebellion*, 178, 331; Hackney, *Populism to Progressivism in Alabama*, 232–34; Hamilton, *Hugo Black*, 95–104; Berman, "Black: The Early Years," 111–12; J. Mills Thornton III, "Hugo Black and the Golden Age," *Alabama Law Review* 36 (1985): 904 (quoted).

40. Hamilton, *Hugo Black*, 64–65, 76, 134.

41. Frank, *Justice Black: Man and Opinions*, 38–43; Hamilton, *Hugo Black*, 116–33; Hugo L. Black, "Opening Speech of the Hon. Hugo L. Black in His Campaign for United States Senator from Alabama," 20 March 1926, HLBP, Box 476 (quoted); Hugo L. Black, "Principles Advocated by Hugo Black, Candidate for United States Senate," undated, HLBP, Box 476 (quoted).

42. Black, "Opening Speech," HLBP, Box 476; Black, "Principles Advocated by Hugo Black," HLBP, Box 476. See also Richard Franklin Bensel, *Sectionalism and American Political Development, 1880–1980* (Madison: University of Wisconsin Press, 1984), 128, 130–31, 137.

43. Black, "Opening Speech," HLBP, Box 476 (quoted); Hamilton, *Hugo Black*, 134; Virginia Van der Veer Hamilton, "Lester Hill, Hugo Black, and the Albatross of Race," *Alabama Law Review* 36 (1985): 844–48; Frank, *Justice Black: Man and Opinions*, 39, 42.

44. Black and Black, *Mr. Justice and Mrs. Black*, 20, 70; Wyatt-Brown, "Ethical Background of Black's Career," 922–23 (quoted); Dunne, *Black and the Judicial Revolution*, 111–14, 117; Hugo L. Black to John Frank, 20 January 1948, HLBP, Box 460 (quoted, emphasis added); Frank, *Justice Black: Man and Opinions*, 38, 43–44; Hamilton, *Hugo Black*, 98–100, 119–20, 136–39 (quoting Black, pp. 136–37).

45. Hugo L. Black, "Muscle Shoals Should Be Used in the Interest of the Farmers of this Nation through the Manufacture of Cheap Fertilizer," 5 and 6 March 1928, 22–23, HLBP, Box 476 (quoted); Frank, *Justice Black: Man and Opinions*, 51–55; Dunne, *Black and the Judicial Revolution*, 127–32.

46. Hamilton, *Hugo Black*, 143–49.

47. Frank, *Justice Black: Man and Opinions*, 48–49; Hamilton, *Hugo Black*, 149–53, 155–56 (quoting Black).

48. Hugo L. Black, untitled, undated, handwritten essay, HLBP, Box 102 (emphasis in original); Hugo L. Black to John R. McCain, 30 December 1929, HLBP, Box 104; Hugo L. Black to J. Johnston Moore, 28 June 1930, HLBP, Box 104; Hugo L. Black to Hugh H. Ellis, 28 August 1930, HLBP, Box 195.

49. Hugo L. Black to John R. McCain, 30 December 1929, HLBP, Box 104.

50. Hugo L. Black, untitled speech given in Montgomery, Alabama, 1930, HLBP, Box 476; Hugo L. Black, "Senator Black's Record on the Tariff," 13 May 1930, HLBP, Box 476; Hugo L. Black to J. Johnston Moore, 28 June 1930, HLBP, Box 104; Hugo L. Black to Theo. F. May, 17 June 1930, HLBP, Box 104; Hugo L. Black to Hugh H. Ellis, 28 August 1930, HLBP, Box 195.

51. Hamilton, *Hugo Black*, 157, 206.

52. Hugo L. Black, "In Defense of the State of Alabama in the Bankhead-Heflin Senatorial Contest," 23 April 1932, HLBP, Box 477; Hamilton, *Hugo Black*, 189–91, 198–204; Dunne, *Black and the Judicial Revolution*, 140–41 (quoted), 167; Hugo L. Black, "Emergency Relief—It Should Be Administered by the People, Not by Bureaus," 16 February 1932, HLBP, Box 477; Frank, *Justice Black: Man and Opinions*, 50, 57; Howard Ball and Phillip J. Cooper, *Of Power and Right: Hugo Black, William O. Douglas, and America's Constitutional Revolution* (New York: Oxford University Press, 1992), 66. The fragile New Deal coalition between northern labor and southern plantation elites was held together in large measure through decentralized policy implementation, which ensured that southern racial mores would not be threatened. Bensel, *Sectionalism*, 26, 30, 53, 105, 139, 149–50. While opposing the LaFollette-Costigan Relief Bill, Black did not oppose the creation of the Reconstruction Finance Corporation, which allocated billions to revive distressed corporations. Hamilton, *Hugo Black*, 199, 237–38.

53. Ball and Cooper, *Of Power and Right*, 64–66; Dunne, *Black and the Judicial Revolution*, 148–51, 169–72; David A. Shannon, "Hugo LaFayette Black as United States Senator," in *Justice Hugo Black and Modern America*, ed. Tony Freyer (Tuscaloosa: University of Alabama Press, 1990), 128–29. The Court declared the NIRA unconstitutional in *Schechter Poultry Corp. v. United States*, 295 U.S. 495 (1935).

54. Hamilton, *Hugo Black*, 264–72 (p. 267 quoted); Frank, *Justice Black: Man and Opinions*, 88–94.

55. Key, *Southern Politics*, 365–67.

56. Dunne, *Black and the Judicial Revolution*, 151–54; Ball and Cooper, *Of Power and Right*, 58–61; Simon, *Antagonists*, 90–93 (p. 91 quoted).

57. Dunne, *Black and the Judicial Revolution*, 154–57 (quoting Black, p. 157); Simon, *Antagonists*, 93–95; Ball and Cooper, *Of Power and Right*, 61–64 (quoting Black, p. 63); Frank, *Justice Black: Man and Opinions*, 63–88; Hamilton, *Hugo Black*, 222–34, 243–59.

58. Hugo L. Black, "Reorganization of the Federal Judiciary," 23 February 1937, 4, 2, HLBP, Box 478.

59. Dunne, *Black and the Judicial Revolution*, 43–51, 166 (quoting Black); Frank, *Justice Black: Man and Opinions*, 95–108; Hamilton, *Hugo Black*, 261–64, 273–82, 306–07; Hamilton, "Lester Hill, Hugo Black," 90–91 (quoted).

60. Black and Black, *Mr. Justice and Mrs. Black*, 69 (quoted); Dunne, *Black and the Judicial Revolution*, 51–59; Ball and Cooper, *Of Power and Right*, 26–28.

61. Hamilton, *Hugo Black*, 283–300; Hugo L. Black, "Text of Justice Black's Speech on October 1, 1937," HLBP, Box 478 (quoted); William E. Leuchtenberg, "A Klansman Joins the Court: The Appointment of Hugo L. Black," *University of Chicago Law Review* 41 (1973): 1–31.

62. *Brown v. Board of Educ.*, 347 U.S. 483 (1954).

63. Hugo Black Jr., *My Father*, 206–17.

5

The Antihierarchical Jurisprudence of Justice Black

"Havens of Refuge"

In his third year on the United States Supreme Court, Justice Black made clear that he repudiated the racist doctrine of the Klan. But if his beautiful opinion in *Chambers v. Florida*[1] demonstrated that this ignoble element of southern culture had no place in his jurisprudence, the same opinion suggested that the South's perennial inter- and intraregional conflicts continued to influence his thought. *Chambers* indicated that his constitutional jurisprudence flowed from a hierarchical vision of society and politics—that he viewed judicial authority in the same way he had viewed legislative authority: the function of both forms of power, he thought, is to protect society's weakest members from political and economic exploitation.

In *Chambers*, the Court reviewed a claim that Florida policemen had violated the due process requirement of the Fourteenth Amendment when they secured confessions to the brutal murder of an elderly white man. The officers had arrested the suspects (four young black males) without warrant and had subjected them to five days of questioning. The accused had confessed after the police deprived them of sleep on the fifth night. Speaking for the Court, Black held that the police had compelled the confessions and had thus violated due process. In voiding the men's death sentences, he emphasized that "[t]he very circumstances surrounding [the suspects'] confinement and their questioning without any formal charges having been brought, were such as to fill [them] with terror and frightful misgivings." The young men "never knew just when any one would be called back to the

95

fourth floor room, and there, surrounded by his accusers and others, interrogated by men who held their very lives—so far as these ignorant petitioners could know—in the balance."[2]

Black displayed his sympathies toward the accused and, more generally, toward society's less fortunate groups. He maintained that "they who have suffered most from secret and dictatorial proceedings have almost always been the poor, the ignorant, the numerically weak, the friendless, and the powerless." "Tyrannical governments," he continued, "had immemorially utilized dictatorial criminal procedure and punishment to make scapegoats of the weak, or of helpless political, religious, or racial minorities and those who differed, who would not conform and who resisted tyranny." His view of the Court's role followed from these observations: "Under our constitutional system, courts stand against any winds that blow as havens of refuge for those who might otherwise suffer because they are helpless, weak, outnumbered, or because they are nonconforming victims of prejudice and public excitement." He believed so deeply in the argument of *Chambers* that, according to his second wife, "he could never read aloud from his opinion without tears streaming down his face."[3]

Black located his view of the Court's role in something more substantial than personal preference. His 1960 James Madison lecture, "The Bill of Rights," provided a historical foundation for the notion that the Court serves as a political and social corrective: "The provisions of the Bill of Rights that safeguard fair legal procedure came about largely to protect the weak and the oppressed from punishment by the strong and powerful who wanted to stifle the voices of discontent raised in protest against oppression and injustice in public affairs." He then implicitly sided with Joseph Story and James Kent (over James Bradley Thayer) on the question of which branch the framers entrusted with the responsibility of maintaining these provisions. "In this country the judiciary was made independent," he argued, "because it has . . . the primary responsibility and duty of giving force and effect to constitutional liberties and limitations upon the executive and legislative branches."[4]

In defending judicial supremacy with respect to constitutional interpretation and enforcement, Black necessarily rejected the blanket application of Thayer's standard for constitutional adjudication. According to Thayer, the threshold requirement for an exercise of judicial review is an irrational belief on the part of legislators in the constitutionality of their policies. He based this standard upon the assumption that legislators are no less concerned than judges with ensuring the integrity of constitutional boundaries. By contrast, Black believed that the framers, in guaranteeing the political insularity of the judiciary, were skeptical of the capacity of elected officials to consider the nature and extent of constitutional limitations. The soundness of this distrust, he thought, makes very troubling the view "that all constitutional problems are questions of reasonableness, proximity, and degree." Judicial reference to the rational-basis test "comes close to the English doctrine of legislative omnipotence," since lawmakers almost always have *reason* to believe that their policies respect constitutional boundaries. In his view, constitutionalism often requires exercises of judicial review in spite of the rational basis of the governmental practice at issue.[5]

Black did not go so far as to say that judges should be unrestrained in the pursuit of justice. He was very much aware of the traditional social expectation (which persisted after the Progressives dispelled the myth that judicial decision making is a purely deductive process) that judges should not incorporate their values into law. In his 1968 James S. Carpentier lectures, he said that he much "fear[ed] the rewriting of the Constitution by judges under the guise of interpretation." Avoidance of this form of constitutional adjudication, he maintained, requires an understanding on the part of judges that the only legitimate determinants in constitutional adjudication are the document's language and, where the language is unedifying, the history informing the adoption of the provision in question. Put another way, the Court should exercise judicial review only when those responsible for enacting a provision intended for the Court to use that power. For Black, then, historical analysis served to limit judicial power as much as it served to justify the doctrine of judicial supremacy. Indeed, this interpretive method would lead him to afford individuals slight protection under certain constitutional provisions.[6]

In spite of (and in some instances because of)[7] the slight constitutional protection that Black afforded at times, the strategy of tying judicial decision making to constitutional language and history proved a very effective means of combating hierarchy in society and politics. Black's decisions regarding the First Amendment freedoms of speech and press reveal the result-oriented nature of his jurisprudence.

"All Speech May Be Dangerous to the Status Quo"

An Unrestricted Freedom

Like the Farmers' Alliance lecturers and the editors of the agrarian reform press, Black possessed a marked appreciation of the antihierarchical qualities of the spoken and printed word. Recall that he had made use of the rights to free speech and press in his successful anti-Big Mule–Black Belt Senate campaign, his efforts to fight sectional tariffs, and his aggressive investigations into the activities of big business. He had observed in reference to the Senate investigations that "special privilege thrives in secrecy and darkness and is destroyed by the rays of pitiless publicity."[8]

The senator had provided more elaborate statements on the importance of open public discourse. Interestingly, he made these remarks while fighting to prevent public utilities from obtaining radio broadcast permits. In pursuing this effort, he did not hope to avoid the anticipated partisan use of the nation's airwaves; instead, he feared that the nature of broadcast technology made it "possible for a few great corporations to control the situation." Public or private control of the supply of public information, he believed, is "the most dangerous [form of monopoly] that can be imagined." It is imperative that the airwaves remain "equally open, to all sides"—"that the springs and channels of useful public opinion be unpoisoned and unpolluted by mercenary partisanship"—since "freedom and uncensored discussion of public men and events, are inseparably united." "Arbitrary and unjust power cannot thrive and prosper, in the face of hostile public opinion," he said. And in an observation that calls to mind Bourbon efforts to silence reform press editors, he noted that "[d]espots, modern and ancient, have endeavored to fix their arbitrary powers, by striking first at the right of their subjects to free assemblies and free speech."[9]

As a justice, Black was even more forthcoming with statements praising the anti-hierarchical properties of First Amendment freedoms. For example: "[A]ll speech criticizing government rulers and challenging current beliefs may be dangerous to the status quo." "Tyrannical totalitarian governments cannot safely allow their people to speak with complete freedom." Free speech "is always the deadliest enemy of tyranny" and represents "the best hope for the aspirations of freedom which men share everywhere." And again: "The right to think, speak, and write freely without governmental censorship or interference is the most precious privilege of citizens vested with power to select public policies and public officials." Black "strongly believe[d] that the First Amendment freedoms are indispensable safeguards to our country's safety and prosperity" and that censorship is the "deadly enemy of freedom."[10]

By using an interpretive strategy that ties judges to the language and history of the Constitution, Black promoted his policy preferences. He

stated in his Carpentier lectures that the authors of the First Amendment intended to accord absolute protection, "without deviation,
without exception, without any ifs, buts, or whereases," to the freedoms of speech and press. This interpretation, he said, follows from
"the clear wording of the First Amendment that 'Congress shall make
no law . . . abridging the freedom of speech or of the press.' . . . As I
have said innumerable times before[,] I simply believe that 'Congress
shall make no law' means Congress shall make no law." He also
emphasized the views of James Madison, who had "told Congress that
under [the First Amendment, the] 'right of freedom of speech is
secured; the liberty of the press is expressly *declared to be beyond the
reach of this Government.* . . .' Some years later Madison [had written]
that 'it would seem scarcely possible to doubt that *no power whatever*
over the press was supposed to be delegated by the Constitution, as it
originally stood, and that the amendment was intended as a *positive
and absolute reservation of it.*' " Madison and his compatriots "were
familiar with the sad and useless tragedies of countless people who
had had their tongues plucked out, their ears cut off or their hands
chopped off, or even worse things done to them, because they dared
to speak or write their opinions." As if echoing the voice of a crusading
editor of the agrarian reform press, Black declared that the First
Amendment's framers sought to secure for every American "an un-
restricted freedom to express his views, however odious they might be
to vested interests whose power they might challenge."[11]

Although Black emphasized the framers' understanding of the political significance of speech and press, he did not believe that the
protection of the First Amendment extends only to communications
involving matters of governing. "[T]o provide such protection was no
doubt a strong reason for the Amendment's passage," but the language
relating to the freedoms of speech and press "contains no exceptions."
Thus, the First Amendment compels the judicial invalidation even of
all laws relating to libel and to "so-called obscene materials." Black
supplemented his textual case for extending constitutional protection
to "non-political" speech and press with an argument drawn from
politics: "It is not difficult for ingenious minds to think up and continue
ways to escape even the plain prohibitions of the First Amendment.
This same kind of ingenuity existed in the days of Rome. For example,
it is said that Augustus punished people for criticizing the Emperor by
the simple device of calling such criticism obscene. So far as I am
concerned, I do not believe there is any halfway ground for protecting

freedom of speech and press. If you say it is half free, you can rest assured that it will not remain as much as half free.''[12]

In addition to eschewing efforts to deny constitutional protection to certain classes or forms of speech and press, Black criticized the judiciary for employing discretionary tests in First Amendment contexts. As with the identification of unprotected forms of expression, he thought that judicial use of such standards flies in the face of the categorical language of the First Amendment and ultimately eviscerates the amendment's protections. Among discretionary standards, Black believed, ''the most dangerous . . . is the so-called balancing test.'' Individuals who advocate balancing argue, in Thomas Emerson's words, ''that the court must, in each case, balance the individual and social interest in freedom of expression against the social interest sought by the regulation which restricts expression.'' In Black's view, ''[t]he great danger of the judiciary balancing process is that in times of emergency and stress it gives Government the power to do what it thinks necessary to protect itself, regardless of the rights of individuals. If the need is great, the right of Government can always be said to outweigh the rights of the individual. If 'balancing' is accepted as the test, it would be hard for any conscientious judge to hold otherwise in times of dire need. And laws in times of dire need are often very hasty and oppressive laws, especially when, as often happens, they are carried over and accepted as normal.''[13]

Black also disparaged the Court's other major First Amendment standard: Oliver Wendell Holmes's contention that the state can suppress speech or press when either poses a ''clear and present danger'' to society. ''The problem with this test,'' Black said, ''is that it can be used to justify the punishment of advocacy.'' The same concerns that led Black to reject balancing informed this criticism of ''clear and present danger'': he believed that the test violates the clear command of the First Amendment, and he feared that judicial use of the standard leads to the destruction of the freedoms of speech and press.[14]

Black's indictment of the Court's use of discretionary standards was anything but an academic exercise. He had not always been an absolutist with respect to First Amendment freedoms. He moved toward a method of interpretation that ties judges to constitutional text and history only after the Court used discretionary standards to shift from an expansive to a severely limited view of the freedoms of speech and press.[15]

The Making of an Absolutist

During the 1940s, Black saw fit to allow a measure of flexibility in his interpretation of the language of the First Amendment; he joined, and even wrote, opinions using the "clear and present danger" test. He employed this standard because a majority of the Court then accepted the "preferred freedoms" doctrine: the view that First Amendment (as opposed to economic) rights are fundamental to a democratic form of government and that the Court should presume legislation infringing upon these liberties to be unconstitutional. With the ascendance of the "preferred freedoms" doctrine, the Court used the "clear and present danger" test to reach libertarian conclusions. Only "imminent" dangers, Black and certain of his colleagues maintained, satisfy the "clear and present" requirement. This interpretation contrasted sharply with the Court's initial use of the standard in the early 1900s, when the words "clear and present danger" had served to justify convictions of individuals whose speech had had a mere "tendency" to cause harm to society.[16]

In the 1940s, Black also accepted the view that certain forms of speech and press do not receive constitutional protection. In *Chaplinsky v. New Hampshire*, he joined Justice Murphy's unanimous opinion, which held that laws prohibiting "fighting words" do not violate the First Amendment. In dictum, Murphy said that "the lewd and obscene, the profane, [and] the libelous" are unprotected as well.[17] In allowing for the discretion involved in determining which categories of expression remain outside the purview of the First Amendment, Black necessarily permitted the discretion involved in determining whether a particular use of speech belongs in these unprotected categories.

In accepting the constitutionality of obscenity laws, Black did not depart from his earlier professions on the importance of free speech and press. Indeed, while in Congress, he had sought to reconcile demands for limitations on expression with the principle of open public discourse. On one occasion, he had vehemently opposed a bill that would have allowed the federal government to ban the importation of obscene materials into the country. In denying that government officials should be entrusted with the responsibility of determining whether a publication is obscene, he had pointed out that "[t]here are some fundamentals which must not be overlooked or overstepped" and "which grow necessarily in a democracy if human liberty is to be preserved. . . . One of them is the freedom of speech." He had conceded that "[n]o good American is in favor of the indiscriminate distribution of obscene literature," but added that "[s]uch literature get[s] not very far in this country anyway. . . . Who is afraid of the distribution of literature injuring and breaking down the morals of the good, solid, substantial citizenship of America? That will never be so long as the churches are open; not so long as the schools continue to educate the young minds and teach these minds the way of truth and of light. Who fears that, with education spreading all over this land[,] we shall by admitting a few small books at the port of entry so corrupt those minds that we shall destroy American civilization?" At this time, however, he was willing to supplement his liberal faith in the power of reason with the arm of the law. "I have no hesitancy in saying that the jury should convict [an individual] when literature is so obscene as to be contrary to good morals and decent society," he asserted. "I do say, however, that until he stands and faces a jury of his peers no individual servant of this country ought to be given sufficient power to take away a single leaf or page from his book nor to put him to one penny's expense."[18]

The first signs of Black's discomfort with the use of discretionary standards in First Amendment cases appeared, ironically, shortly before he joined the *Chaplinsky* "fighting words" decision. In *Cox v. New Hampshire*, the Court upheld a license requirement for persons seeking to stage a parade or procession. In a draft of what would be a unanimous opinion, Chief Justice Hughes emphasized the reasonableness of the state's permit system. Black sent a letter to the chief justice suggesting that the "several references to reasonableness . . . are unnecessary and also inapplicable to the points raised here." He indicated that failure to "eliminate discussion as to reasonableness" would force him to write separately. In a draft concurrence (which Black did not publish because Hughes agreed to remove the challenged language), Black elaborated upon his concerns:

> Fully realizing the difficulties involved in enforcing observance of [the freedoms of speech, press, assembly, or religion] in instances where they apparently clash with exertions of an admitted state power, I am still not persuaded that invocation of the word "reasonable" offers a solution to the problem these difficulties present. Standards of reasonableness vary according to individual views. The broad, and might I say, limitless, range within the area of the differing concepts of the word "reasonable" cause me to fear its use in relation to the cherished privileges intended to be guaranteed by the First Amendment.[19]

He maintained that the Court did not have to consider the appropriateness of a deferential reasonableness standard, since the "petitioners [had] suffered no denial or abridgment of these constitutional guarantees." A law that regulates the conduct of individuals, as opposed to the content of their message, does not violate "the literal language of the First Amendment to our Constitution."[20]

Black first entertained an absolutist interpretation of the freedoms of speech and press in a case the Court decided before the "preferred freedoms" doctrine had become an explicit constitutional philosophy. *Bridges v. California* involved a contempt citation against a local labor leader for publishing a telegram that supposedly interfered with the administration of justice. The published telegram, which Bridges had sent to the United States secretary of labor, warned that a strike would result from enforcement of an "outrageous" state court ruling in a recent labor case. Initially, the Court narrowly voted to uphold the contempt citation and reject Bridges's First Amendment challenge. Black drafted a forceful dissent in which he implored his brethren to realize that

> the First Amendment was written in the form of a command so clear, so unequivocal, and so persuasive in its expressions and implications that it is impossible to deny that those who drafted it intended to mark off an inviolable area and dedicate it to the liberties there enumerated. It may be true that there are no such things as absolute liberties. It may be true that newspapers and others take undue and mischievous advantage of the privileges granted them by the Constitution. But even if the newspapers were guilty of all the offenses to which they have sometimes been accused, it was the theory of those responsible for our Bill of Rights that in the last analysis the solution would lie in censorship by public opinion rather than in censorship by a court of law.[21]

As Tinsley Yarbrough notes, "The fundamentally absolutist thrust of this passage is unmistakable: any limitation on the freedoms granted by the First Amendment could constitutionally be imposed only by 'public opinion,' not by government."[22]

Black acknowledged, however, that the Court had never viewed the First Amendment in absolute terms. Earlier cases had "held [not only] that the states do have the power to abridge freedom of expression in matters which relate to cases pending in courts," but that courts may hold authors in contempt for publications that have a mere "tendency" to interfere with the administration of justice. Believing that this standard affords insufficient protection to important constitutional liberties, Black argued "that state courts should never punish for contempt in such cases unless there [is] found to be a clear and present danger of an immediate interference which [cannot] be averted without the imposition of punishment."[23] He did not believe that Bridges had presented such a danger.

With the switch of Justice Murphy's vote, the retirement of Justice McReynolds, and the addition of the vote of McReynolds's replacement (Robert Jackson), the Court now sustained Bridges's First Amendment challenge. Writing for the majority, Black abandoned any reference to absolutism and, instead, illuminated the nature of the "clear and present danger" test. This standard, he opined, "is a working principle that the substantive evil must be extremely serious and the degree of imminence extremely high before utterances can be punished." Earlier judicial interpretations of the standard "do not purport to mark the furthermost constitutional boundaries of protected expression, nor do we here. They do no more than recognize a minimum compulsion of the Bill of Rights." Since "the First Amendment does not speak equivocally . . . [, i]t must be taken as a command of the broadest scope that explicit language, read in the context of a liberty-loving society, will allow."[24]

Black continued to employ the "clear and present danger" test, but only as long as a majority of the Court adhered to the notion of "preferred freedoms." This doctrine, implicit in *Bridges*, became explicit in the Court's rulings during the 1940s.[25] As the decade closed, however, Black's demonstrated suspicion of discretionary standards proved well founded. He moved toward, and finally embraced, an absolutist interpretation of the First Amendment when the Court, in response to public apprehensiveness over the Soviet threat, returned the "clear and present danger" test to its original function: justifying the punishment of those whose controversial ideas presented no immediate threat to society.

In *American Communications Ass'n v. Douds*, the Court approved federal regulations that required "non-Communist" affidavits of labor union officials. In his majority opinion, Chief Justice Vinson (citing *Bridges v. California*) conceded that the Court had interpreted the "clear and present danger" test to afford significant protection to the freedoms of speech and press. He maintained, however, that "it was never the intention of this Court to lay down an absolutist test measured in terms of danger to the Nation. When the effect of a statute or ordinance upon the exercise of First Amendment freedoms is relatively small and the public interest to be protected is substantial, it is obvious that a rigid test requiring a showing of imminent danger to the security of the Nation is an absurdity.''[26]

In contrast to Vinson's assertion that ''[w]e have never held that [First Amendment] freedoms are absolute,'' Black came close to making such a declaration in his dissent: ''Whether religious, political, or both, test oaths are implacable foes of free thought.'' ''By approving their imposition, this Court has injected compromise into a field where the First Amendment forbids compromise.''[27]

In the year following *Douds*, Black's disappointment with the ''clear and present danger'' test intensified. *Dennis v. United States* involved an appeal from a conviction of eleven Communist Party leaders for violating the Smith Act. The government had charged the Communists with conspiring to form a political party to teach violent overthrow of the government. In a plurality opinion, Chief Justice Vinson accepted Judge Learned Hand's revision of the ''clear and present danger'' test (the federal appeals court judge had subordinated the requirement of a ''present'' danger to a ''probable'' one) and upheld the convictions. In separate concurring opinions, Justices Frankfurter and Jackson accepted the convictions, but declined to apply the ''clear and present danger'' test.[28]

In a bitter dissent, Black noted that the ''opinions in this case show that the only way to affirm these convictions [was] to repudiate directly or indirectly the established 'clear and present danger' rule,'' for the petitioners had presented no imminent threat to society. Indeed, the Communists ''were not charged with overt acts of any kind designed to overthrow the Government. They were not even charged with saying anything or writing anything designed to overthrow the Government. The charge was that they [had] agreed to assemble and to talk and publish certain ideas at a later date.'' Black hoped ''that in calmer times, when present pressures, passions and fears subside, this or some later Court will restore the First Amendment liberties to the high preferred place where they belong in a free society.'' Drawing upon his *Bridges* opinion, he reminded his brethren ''that the 'clear and present danger' test does not 'mark the furthermost constitutional boundaries of protected expression' but does 'no more than recognize a minimum compulsion of the Bill of Rights.' ''[29]

In view of the limitless flexibility of the ''clear and present danger'' test, Black soon came to believe that the only way to secure the First Amendment's preferred position is to embrace an absolutist interpretation of the freedoms of speech and press. He first used absolutist language in his dissent in *Carlson v. Landon*, where the

Court permitted the attorney general, under the Internal Security Act, to hold in custody without bail aliens who were members of the Communist Party. Specifically, the Court concluded that the attorney general could hold such aliens, pending determination as to their deportability, if he had reasonable cause to believe that their release would endanger the safety and welfare of the United States.[30]

In dissent, Black argued that "the basis of holding these people in jail is a fear that they may indoctrinate people with Communist beliefs." He conceded that the government's policy was "a logical application of recent cases watering down constitutional speech." But he believed that putting "people in jail for fear of their talk seems . . . to be an abridgment of speech in flat violation of the First Amendment." The categorical language of that amendment "grants an absolute right to believe in any governmental system, discuss all governmental affairs, and argue for desired changes in the existing order."[31]

Black provided a more forceful statement supporting absolutism in a case decided one month after *Carlson*. In *Beauharnais v. Illinois*, the Court sustained the punishment of a man who had violated a group libel law. The accused had distributed racist leaflets that implored Chicago officials "to halt the further encroachment, harassment and invasion of white people, their property, neighborhoods and persons, by the Negro." The leaflets added: "If persuasion and the need to prevent the white race from becoming mongrelized by the negro will not unite us, then the aggressions[,] . . . rapes, robberies, knives, guns, and marijuana of the negro, surely will." Speaking for the majority, Justice Frankfurter invoked the *Chaplinsky* dictum excluding libel from the protections of the First Amendment: "[I]f an utterance directed at an individual may be the object of criminal sanctions, we cannot deny to a State power to punish the same utterance directed at a defined group, unless we can say that this is a wilful and purposeless restriction unrelated to the peace and well-being of the State."[32]

Black dissented and attempted to distinguish the present case from *Chaplinsky*. In contrast to Frankfurter, he thought that *Chaplinsky* permitted states to protect only identifiable individuals, as opposed to large groups of people, from harmful forms of speech. More important, he believed that the expression at issue in *Beauharnais* did not fall outside the purview of the First Amendment. "[T]he leaflet used here [as opposed to the "fighting" words spoken in *Chaplinsky*] was . . . the means adopted by an assembled group to enlist interest in their efforts to have legislation enacted." "To say that a legislative body can, with this Court's approval, make it a crime to petition for and publicly discuss proposed legislation seems as farfetched to me as it could be to say that a valid law could be enacted to punish a candidate for President for telling the people his views." In Black's view, the First Amendment " 'absolutely' forbids such laws without any 'ifs' or 'buts' or 'whereases.' Whatever the danger, if any, in such public discussions, it is a danger the Founders deemed outweighed by the danger incident to the stifling of thought and speech."[33]

In addition to calling for absolute protection of political communications, Black expressed concern over judicial efforts to determine whether particular uses of speech fall into unprotected categories: "Freedom of petition, assembly, speech and press could be greatly abridged by a practice of meticulously scrutinizing every editorial, speech, sermon, or other printed matter to extract two or three naughty words on which to hang charges of 'group libel.' "[34]

Black sparked considerable controversy when, in subsequent opinions and in his extrajudicial writings and speeches, he claimed that the text and history of the First Amendment preclude judicial efforts to distinguish between protected and unprotected categories of speech and press, as well as between threatening and nonthreatening forms of political expression. Because the words "freedom of speech or of the press" might suggest a category that is less inclusive than one containing any form of speech or press, some scholars maintained that the amendment's language is less edifying than Black believed. They also challenged Black's reading of the history surrounding the adoption of the First Amendment. Leonard Levy, for example, argued that there is no evidence to suggest "an understanding that a constitutional guarantee of free speech or press meant the impossibility of future prosecutions of seditious utterances," let alone prosecutions for the publishing of obscene or libelous materials.[35]

Undeterred by such criticism, Black insisted, "[A] careful review of all the evidence convinces me that my interpretation is accurate."[36] It is beyond the scope of this book to determine whether his arguments or those of his critics are more compelling. For purposes of this study, it is sufficient to note that he desired the results of his historical investigations. He believed deeply in the wisdom of an absolutist reading of the First Amendment.

"Essential Supplements to the First Amendment"

The "Original Purpose" of the Fourteenth Amendment

A further way in which Black attempted to aid marginal social groups was by limiting judicial discretion in incorporation controversies. This area of constitutional law addresses the extent to which the first section of the Fourteenth Amendment incorporates within its meaning the provisions of the first eight amendments, making those restrictions (which originally applied only against the national government) binding on the states. Black maintained that the provisions of the Bill of Rights "were designed to meet ancient evils . . . that have emerged from century to century wherever excessive power is sought by the few at the expense of the many."[37] As seen in the preceding chapter, the conflict between Alabama's economic elites and its working classes provided the context in which he usually spoke of the struggle between the few and the many. Undoubtedly, he regarded the procedural injustices that marked this intrasectional rivalry as contemporary illustrations of the "ancient evils" that inspired the protections of the Bill of Rights. The forcible termination of labor strikes, the unjustified arrests and detentions that accompanied the convict-lease and fee systems, and the use of the third degree against criminal suspects alerted him to the value of the Bill of Rights and the need to extend its protections to the state level.

Black thought that the role played by the procedural guarantees of the Bill of Rights as "essential supplements to the First Amendment" was the primary reason to incorporate these rights. He, of course, had looked favorably upon the incorporation in the early twentieth century of the freedoms of speech and press, what with his reliance on the spoken and written word in his battles with the Big Mule–Black Belt alliance. But the Court's application of these provisions against the states was, to him, a necessary, rather than a sufficient, step: "[H]istory teaches that attempted exercises of the freedoms of speech, press, and assembly have been the commonest occasions for oppression and persecution. Inevitably such persecutions have involved secret arrests, unlawful detentions, forced confessions, secret trials, and arbitrary punishments under oppressive laws." In view of this sorry record, he thought it "not surprising that the men behind the First Amendment also insisted upon the Fifth, Sixth, and Eighth Amendments, designed to protect all individuals against arbitrary punishment by definite procedural provisions guaranteeing fair public trials by juries." Although the threat of oppression always exists, "the people of no nation can lose their liberty so long as a Bill of Rights like ours survives and its basic purposes are conscientiously interpreted, enforced and respected."[38]

Once again, Black promoted his policy preferences with an interpretive strategy that permitted an analysis only of constitutional language and history: he took the position that the framers of the Fourteenth Amendment had intended total incorporation, or the application of all of the first eight Amendments against the states. In defending total incorporation, he emphasized the statements of the Fourteenth Amendment's principal spokesmen: Representative John A. Bingham ("the Madison of the first section of the Fourteenth Amendment") and Senator Jacob M. Howard. Black summarized his historical and textual arguments thus:

> My study of the events that culminated in the Fourteenth Amendment, and the expressions of those who sponsored and favored, as well as those who opposed[,] its submission and passage, persuades me that one of the chief objects [that] the Amendment's first section, separately, and as a whole, [was] intended to accomplish was to make the Bill of Rights . . . applicable to the states. With full knowledge of the import of the *Barron [v. Baltimore]* decision [where the Court had held in 1833 that the Bill of Rights applies only against the national government], the framers and backers of the Fourteenth Amendment proclaimed its purpose to be to overturn the constitutional rule that case had announced.[39]

Since Black favored application of the first eight Amendments against the states, he was understandably disappointed with the Court's past performance in incorporation controversies. He directed his harshest criticism at the approach taken in 1908 in *Twining v. New Jersey*. There, Justice Moody, who spoke for the Court, had gone "all the way to say that the 'privileges [or] immunities' clause of the Fourteenth Amendment 'did not forbid the States to abridge the personal rights enunciated in the first eight Amendments. . . .' " According to Black, *Twining* had "held that that question [of the meaning of the privileges-or-immunities clause] was 'no longer open' because of previous decisions." (Before *Twining*, the Court had restricted the meaning of this clause to a narrow list of privileges unconnected to the provisions of the Bill of Rights. Black noted, however, that these decisions "had not appraised the historical evidence on that subject.") The *Twining* majority had also "specifically rejected any connection between the Bill of Rights and the Due Process Clause [of the Fourteenth Amendment]." It had conceded that "some of the personal rights safeguarded by the first eight Amendments against National action may also be safeguarded against state action, because a denial of them would be a denial of due process of law," but had maintained that "[i]f this is so, it is not because those rights are enumerated in the first eight Amendments, but because they are of such a nature that they are included in the conception of due process of law.''[40]

Rather than tie the concept of due process to the specific provisions of the Bill of Rights, the *Twining* majority had asserted that the clause merely guards individuals "against the arbitrary action of government." Put another way, due process embodies only "immutable principle[s] of justice which [are] the inalienable possession of every citizen of a free government" and are "to be ascertained from time to time by judicial action." The problem with this interpretation, Black argued, is that it had "marked the beginning of the era when due process of law meant whatever a majority of the Supreme Court said it meant, and unfortunately . . . this meant too often that judges struck down everything they thought undesirable on economic or social grounds." (As noted above in Chapter 3, however, the pre-*Twining* Court had, in fact, already put due process to such use in, among other decisions, the anti-agrarian *Chicago, Milwaukee and St. Paul* rail rate case and *Lochner*.)[41] *Twining*, then, not only frustrated the incorporation of the antihierarchical provisions of the Bill of Rights but also provided judges with a weapon to defend the social and economic status quo.

Black also criticized, although less strenuously, the process of selective incorporation articulated in *Palko v. Connecticut*. Addressing the contention that the first eight amendments apply against the states, Justice Cardozo had concluded for the *Palko* majority that "[t]here is no such general rule." To account for a number of post-*Twining* decisions incorporating certain provisions of the Bill of Rights, Cardozo had explained: "[I]mmunities that are valid as against the federal government by force of the specific pledges of particular amendments have been found to be implicit in the concept of ordered liberty, and thus, through the Fourteenth Amendment, become valid as against the states." This "process of absorption has had its source in the belief that neither liberty nor justice would exist if [these rights] were sacrificed."[42]

Black said he "would choose the *Palko* selective process" over "the *Twining* rule of applying none of [the provisions of the Bill of Rights against the states]," since "the selective incorporation process . . . does limit the Supreme Court in the Fourteenth Amendment to specific Bill of Rights' protections only and keeps judges from roaming at will in their own notions of what policies outside the Bill of Rights are desirable and what are not." But he was "not completely happy with the selective incorporation theory since it still leaves to the determination of judges the decision as to which Bill of Rights' provisions are 'fundamental' and thus applicable to the states." He preferred to "follow what [he] believe[d] was the original purpose of the Fourteenth Amendment—to extend to all the people of the nation the complete protection of the Bill of Rights."[43]

As with his disparagement of the use of judicial discretion in First Amendment contexts, Black's criticism of the Court's standards in incorporation controversies was not an academic exercise. He had not always advocated total incorporation.[44] In Fourteenth Amendment cases, only after the Court failed to make substantial progress on the piecemeal application of the provisions of the Bill of Rights against the states did he embrace an interpretive strategy that limits judges to an analysis of constitutional language and history.

The Move toward Total Incorporation

Initially, Black allowed for a degree of flexibility in incorporation controversies. Indeed, he joined the *Palko* majority. His vote in this case was ironic for two reasons. First, the Court held that the Fifth Amendment's prohibition of double jeopardy did not apply against the states by force of the Fourteenth Amendment. Second, Black's statement to the contrary notwithstanding, *Palko* did not limit judges in Fourteenth Amendment cases to the specific provisions of the Bill of Rights. In *Palko*, Cardozo suggested that under the concept of due process, judges are to invalidate practices that violate " 'principle[s] of justice so rooted in the traditions and conscience of our people as to be ranked as fundamental.' " Put another way, courts should void "hardship[s] so acute and shocking that our polity will not endure [them]." In certain instances, this interpretation of due process involves the incorporation of specific provisions of the Bill of Rights. Yet, according to Cardozo, state actions that would not violate any of the provisions of the Bill of Rights might still be violations of due process. In short, the *Palko* standard gave judges the flexibility to go beyond the provisions of the Bill of Rights as well as to avoid applying all of these guarantees against the states.[45]

In spite of these considerations, Black's decision to join the *Palko* majority was not anomalous. One should not be surprised that a new member of the Court would demonstrate respect for a justice of Cardozo's stature. More important, *Palko* marked a significant departure from *Twining*. The *Palko* majority approved of the incorporation of certain provisions of the Bill of Rights, most notably, the crucial freedom of speech. Black agreed strongly with Cardozo's statement that the freedom of speech should be incorporated, since it "is the matrix, the indispensable condition of nearly every other form of freedom." Furthermore, *Palko* left open the possibility that the Court would find other portions of the Bill of Rights "of the very essence of a scheme of ordered liberty" and thus applicable against the states.[46]

Black had occasion, soon after *Palko*, to appreciate the antihierarchical potential of a concept of due process not confined to the provisions of the Bill of Rights. In *Chambers v. Florida* (a discussion of which began this chapter), he employed the *Palko* standard to overturn the murder convictions and death sentences of four young blacks whose confessions the police had coerced. The incorporation of the provisions of the Bill of Rights would not have helped the defendants, since, at that time, the rule concerning the inadmissibility of coerced confessions was independent of the privilege against self-incrimination. (The former proscription had developed as a rule of evidence having no connection to the Fifth Amendment.) Using the *Palko* standard, however, Black held, as the Court's spokesman, that the state had violated the due process clause of the Fourteenth Amendment by failing to conform to "fundamental standards of procedure in criminal trials."[47]

Although Black availed himself of a flexible concept of due process in this instance (among others), he evidenced a desire to move beyond *Palko*. In a footnote to *Chambers*, he noted "a current of opinion . . . that the Fourteenth Amendment [had been] intended to make secure against state invasion all the rights, privileges and immunities protected from federal violation by the Bill of Rights." He acknowledged that the Court had "declined to adopt [this view] in many previous cases. . . ." But in another part of his opinion, he stated "that the forfeiture of the lives, liberties or property of people accused of crime can only follow if procedural safeguards of due process have been obeyed," and in a footnote listing those safeguards, he cited, among other provisions, the "Bill of Rights (Amend. I to VIII)."[48]

Even before *Chambers*, Black may have voiced the view that the Fourteenth Amendment incorporates the Bill of Rights. In a memo to Black shortly after the Court voted to hear that case, Justice Frankfurter wrote:

Dear Hugo: Perhaps you will let me say quite simply and without any ulterior thought what I mean to say, and all I mean to say, regarding your position on the "Fourteenth Amendment" as an entirety.

(1) I *can* understand that the Bill of Rights—to wit Amendments 1–9 inclusive—applies to state action and not merely U.S. action, and that *Barron v. Baltimore* was wrong. I think [*Barron*] was rightly decided.

(2) What I am unable to appreciate is what are the criteria of selection as to the Amendments—which applies and which does not apply.[49]

Frankfurter's note reveals some confusion as to whether Black was contemplating complete or partial application of the Bill of Rights against the states. The first numbered point suggests the former possibility; the second point indicates the latter. In view of *Chambers*, however, it seems likely that, by 1939, Black indeed entertained the possibility of total incorporation.[50]

Black moved further toward total incorporation after judicial use of the flexible *Palko* standard served to frustrate the incorporation of the "essential supplements to the First Amendment," namely, the Fifth and Sixth Amendments. He might have been less quick to embrace total incorporation had the Court, in requiring states to respect "fundamental principles of justice," at least afforded protection to defendants in the cases before the Court. An affirmance of conviction, however, often followed the Court's refusal to force state compliance with the full scope of the provisions of the Bill of Rights.

Black first explicitly endorsed total incorporation in *Betts v. Brady*. The case involved a Fourteenth Amendment challenge to a conviction obtained after a Maryland court refused an indigent defendant's request for counsel. Speaking for the majority, Justice Roberts stated that "[t]he due process clause of the Fourteenth Amendment does not incorporate, as such, the specific guarantees found in the Sixth Amendment." Due process, he continued, "formulates a concept less rigid and more fluid than those envisaged in other specific and particular provisions of the Bill of Rights. Its application is less a matter of rule. Asserted denial is to be tested by an appraisal of the totality of the facts in a given case. That which may, in one setting, constitute a denial of fundamental fairness, shocking to the universal sense of justice may, in other circumstances, and in the light of other considerations, fall short of such denial." Applying this fluid concept of due process to the present case, the Court held that no constitutional violations had occurred. The Court conceded that "want of counsel in a particular case may result in a conviction lacking in . . . fundamental fairness," but denied that "the [Fourteenth] Amendment embodies an inexorable command that no trial for any offense, or in any court, can be fairly conducted and justice accorded a defendant who is not

represented by counsel." Here, "the accused was not helpless, but
was a man forty-three years old, of ordinary intelligence. . . ."
Moreover, he "had once before been in a criminal court, pleaded
guilty to larceny and served a sentence and was [thus] not wholly
unfamiliar with criminal procedure."[51]

Black penned a vigorous dissent in which he challenged the Court's
due process standard, as well as its application in this case. In contrast
to Roberts, Black "believe[d] that the Fourteenth Amendment made
the Sixth applicable to the states." Indeed, he went so far as to say
that "[d]iscussion of the Fourteenth Amendment by its sponsors in the
Senate and House shows their purpose to make secure against invasion
by the states the fundamental liberties and safeguards set out in the
Bill of Rights." Since Black's view had "never been accepted by a
majority of [the] Court," he decided that a "statement of the grounds
supporting it [was] . . . unnecessary at [the] time." Even "under the
prevailing view of due process," however, Black believed that "the
judgment below should be reversed," for a "practice cannot be recon-
ciled with 'common and fundamental ideas of fairness and right,'
which subjects innocent men to increased dangers of conviction merely
because of their poverty."[52]

Black did more than criticize his brethren for failing to protect the
petitioner and for refusing to incorporate the Sixth Amendment. With
the antihierarchical potential of *Palko* apparently waning, he fretted
over the demonstrated utility of the flexible concept of due process as
a tool to maintain the social and economic status quo: "[T]he prevailing view of due process . . . gives this Court such vast supervisory
powers that I am not prepared to accept it without grave doubts."[53]

The repudiation of a flexible concept of due process, of course, had
mixed results for one pursuing an antihierarchical agenda. In tying due
process to the provisions of the Bill of Rights, Black lost the ability to
afford protection against violations that those provisions do not cover.
Thus, it is not surprising that he sought to reconcile the result obtained
in *Chambers* with his new understanding of the Fourteenth Amendment. In *Lyons v. Oklahoma*, the Court upheld a murder conviction
against a claim that police had coerced the defendant's confession.
Black joined Justice Murphy's dissenting opinion, which, in contrast
to *Chambers*, located the right against coerced confessions in the
Fifth Amendment privilege against self-incrimination and deemed this
provision applicable against the states. Murphy, however, did not
claim originality when grounding his opinion in the language of the

Fifth Amendment; curiously, he invoked *Chambers* as support for his argument.[54]

In spite of his endorsement of total incorporation in *Betts*, Black remained willing to join, and even write, opinions that relied on a flexible concept of due process to invalidate convictions obtained with coerced confessions. Still, as he revealed in *Malinski v. New York*, he was very much dissatisfied with this approach. In that case, the Court voided a murder conviction tainted by a coerced confession. Black joined Justice Douglas's plurality opinion, which carefully avoided an excursus on the nature of due process. Unhappy with such a cursory treatment of the constitutional issue, Justice Frankfurter wrote a concurring opinion. Frankfurter praised "the wisdom of [his] predecessors in refusing to give a rigid scope" to due process, a concept that "expresses a demand for civilized standards of law" and is not "a compendious expression of the original federal Bill of Rights." When Frankfurter circulated his opinion, Black responded sharply:

> Mr. Justice Frankfurter has filed a concurring opinion which construes the Due Process Clause as authorizing this Court to invalidate state action on the ground of a belief that the state action fails to set "civilized standards." This seems to me to be a restoration of the natural law concept whereby the supreme constitutional law becomes this Court's views of "civilization" at a given moment. Five members of the Court, including Mr. Justice Frankfurter, have expressed their assent to this interpretation of the Due Process Clause.
>
> I disagree with that interpretation. Due Process, thus construed, seems to me to make the remainder of the Constitution mere surplusage. This Due Process interpretation permits the Court to reject all of those provisions of the Bill of Rights, and to substitute its own ideas of what legislatures can and cannot do. *In the past, this broad judicial power has been used, as I see it, to preserve the economic status quo and to block legislative efforts to cure its existing evils. At the same time, the Court has only grudgingly read into "civilized standards" the safeguards to individual liberty set out in the Bill of Rights.*[55]

Black could not have made a more revealing critique of the flexible concept of due process. But he decided not to make public his concerns over the hierarchical nature of this standard or to provide a justification for total incorporation. He thought *Malinski* "an improper case to debate this question," since the issue before the Court "could be decided without it." He promised a full treatment of the meaning of the Fourteenth Amendment "[w]hen the matter . . . [arose] in a proper case."[56]

Adamson v. California provided the appropriate context for this
discussion. This time, Black had no choice but to engage the proponents of a flexible concept of due process: besides explicitly refusing
to incorporate the Fifth Amendment privilege against self-incrimination, the Court failed to hold as a violation of due process the state
practice of permitting judges and prosecutors to comment adversely
on a defendant's refusal to testify on his own behalf.[57]

In an impassioned dissent, Black voiced the policy concerns he
had suppressed in *Malinski*: "[T]he natural-law—due-process formula,
which the Court today reaffirms, has been interpreted [in *Betts*, for
example,] to limit substantially this Court's power to prevent state
violations of the individual civil liberties guaranteed by the Bill of
Rights. But this formula also has been used in the past, and can be
used in the future, to license this Court, in considering regulatory
legislation, to roam at large in the broad expanses of policy and morals
and to trespass, all too freely, on the legislative domain of the States
as well as the Federal Government." He termed "an incongruous
excrescence on the Constitution" the notion that due process empowers judges to determine constitutionality independent of the provisions
of the Bill of Rights. This concept of due process contradicts "the
views expressed by [the] Court, at least for the first two decades
after the Fourteenth Amendment was adopted." In defense of his
alternative interpretation of the Fourteenth Amendment, Black
attached a thirty-four-page appendix detailing his historical argument
for total incorporation. To those concerned that the application of the
first eight amendments against the states "would unwisely increase the
sum total of the powers of [the] Court to invalidate state legislation,"
he answered: "The Federal Government has not been harmfully bur-
dened by the requirement that enforcement of federal laws affecting
civil liberty conform literally to the Bill of Rights. Who would advocate
its repeal?"[58]

Black's arguments supporting total incorporation drew sharp criticism. Indeed, at least one student of the Court accused him of
deliberately distorting the history of the Fourteenth Amendment.
Some scholars, critical of Black's reliance on the comments of Representative Bingham and Senator Howard, echoed Justice Frankfurter's
assessment that the "[r]emarks of a particular proponent of the
Amendment, no matter how influential, are not to be deemed part of
the Amendment." The intent that gives meaning to the language of a
constitutional amendment, Black's critics argued, is the intent of the
legislature that proposed it and of the legislatures that ratified it. And,

after investigating the matter, the critics found little evidence to suggest that the members of the Thirty-ninth Congress or of the relevant state legislatures sought to alter radically their systems of justice.[59]

Pointing to his legislative experience, Black defended his reading of the intentions behind the Fourteenth Amendment: "I served in the United States Senate for ten years and believe I have some knowledge of the legislative process. . . . [T]he attacks made upon my historical beliefs . . . simply have not convinced me that I am wrong." More than a few scholars have come to Black's defense on this matter.[60] It is unnecessary, however, to undertake the formidable task of evaluating the competing explanations of the purpose of the Fourteenth Amendment. As with the controversy over the meaning of the First Amendment, it is sufficient for this study to recall that Black much desired the results of his historical investigations.

A Fear of Judicial Discretion?

Conservative Implications

Although Black based his constitutional jurisprudence upon his policy preferences, he did not invariably pursue and render antihierarchical rulings. Indeed, in several areas of constitutional law, his jurisprudence prescribed rulings supporting the social status quo. While he believed that the categorical commands of the First Amendment suffer no compromise, he argued that the Constitution contains more imprecise or flexible clauses that authorize only a guarded use of judicial power.

With regard to the Eighth Amendment's ban on cruel and unusual punishments, Black demonstrated a certain deference to political authority. One should note that he did not limit the reach of the clause to forms of punishment its framers would have found cruel and unusual. In *Robinson v. California*, for example, he agreed that criminal punishment for the mere status of narcotics addiction is cruel and unusual. In subsequent cases, however, he hesitated to use the Eighth Amendment to invalidate less than extreme forms of punishment. In *Powell v. Texas*, he was part of a five-man majority that declined to declare unconstitutional the criminal conviction of a chronic alcoholic for public drunkenness. In a draft opinion for that case, he concluded that criminal punishment of a status is "particularly obnoxious" and could "reasonably be called cruel and unusual, because it involves punishment for a mere propensity, a desire to commit an offense." But he maintained that "legislatures have always been allowed wide freedom to determine the extent to which moral culpability should be a prerequisite to conviction of a crime." He thus refused to challenge the state's decision that Powell was responsible for being intoxicated in public.[61]

Judges who advocate fidelity to the text of the Constitution and its history would, of course, accept capital punishment: the founders accepted the death penalty, and the Fifth and Fourteenth Amendments explicitly permit the taking of life, so long as government accords defendants due process. Black revealed no jurisprudential inconsistency here.

> The Eighth Amendment forbids "cruel and unusual punishments." In my view, these words cannot be read to outlaw capital punishment because that penalty was in common use and authorized by law here and in the countries from which our ancestors came at the time the Amendment was adopted. It is inconceivable to me that the framers intended to end capital punishment by the Amendment. Although some people have urged that this Court should amend the Constitution by interpretation to keep it abreast of modern ideas, I have never believed that lifetime judges in our system have any such legislative power.[62]

Nor did he attempt to frustrate the use of capital punishment: he once recommended that the Court regard as "frivolous" an Eighth Amendment challenge to state imposition of the death penalty for common-law robbery; he concurred in a decision that upheld provisions leaving imposition of capital punishment to the discretion of juries; he dissented when the Court invalidated the practice of excluding from death penalty cases jurors who had scruples against capital punishment; and he agreed that a second attempt at an execution (after "an unforeseeable accident" foiled the state's initial effort to impose a death sentence) did not constitute "cruel and unusual punishment."[63]

The conservative implications of Black's jurisprudence were even more evident in his opinions on the Fourth Amendment's prohibition of unreasonable searches and seizures and its requirement of probable cause for the issuance of warrants. Interestingly, he accepted the exclusionary rule (i.e., the rule excluding from criminal proceedings evidence states obtain in unreasonable searches and seizures) despite conceding that it is "perhaps not required by the express language of the Constitution strictly construed.'' (He was unclear as to the constitutional basis of the rule. At times, he located it in the Fourth and Fifth Amendments; on other occasions, he grounded it in the Fifth Amendment protection against self-incrimination alone.) He pointed out, however, that the use of the word "unreasonable" in the Fourth Amendment means, of course, that ''not *all* searches and seizures are prohibited. Only those which are *unreasonable* are unlawful.'' And he proved very unreceptive to challenges to the reasonableness of warrantless police searches and seizures.[64]

When Black determined that circumstances required a warrant, he was very deferential to the decisions of lower courts as to the existence of "probable cause." In *Spinelli v. United States*, the Court invalidated a search warrant that a magistrate had issued on what the majority believed was an inadequate statement of the circumstances supporting an informant's tip. Black dissented:

> The existence of probable cause is a factual matter that calls for the determination of a factual question. While no statistics are immediately available, questions of probable cause to issue search warrants and to make arrests are doubtless involved in many thousands of cases in state courts. All of those probable-cause state cases are now potentially reviewable by this Court. It is, of course, physically impossible for this Court to review the evidence in all or even a substantial percentage of those cases. Consequently, whether desirable or not, we must inevitably accept most of the fact findings of the state courts, particularly when, as here in a federal case, both the trial and appellate courts have decided the facts the same way. It cannot be said that the trial judge and six members of the Court of Appeals committed flagrant error in finding from evidence that the magistrate had probable cause to issue the search warrant here. It seems to me that this Court would best serve itself and the administration of justice by accepting the judgment of the two courts below. After all, they too are lawyers and judges, and much closer to the practical, everyday affairs of life than we are.[65]

Besides believing that the vague phrases of the Fourth Amendment authorize only a guarded use of judicial power, Black argued that the amendment's explicit reference to "persons, houses, papers, and effects" precludes judges from extending the protection against unreasonable searches and seizures to evidence obtained through electronic surveillance. When, in *Katz v. United States*, the Court ruled that the protection of the Fourth Amendment extends beyond physical invasions and physical seizures, Black dissented forcefully:

Since I see no way in which the words of the Fourth Amendment can be construed to apply to eavesdropping, that closes the matter for me. In interpreting the Bill of Rights, I willingly go as far as a liberal construction of the language takes me, but I simply cannot in good conscience give a meaning to words which they have never before been thought to have and which they certainly do not have in common ordinary usage. I will not distort the words of the Amendment in order to "keep the Constitution up to date" or "to bring it into harmony with the times." It was never meant that this Court have such power, which in effect would make us a continuously functioning constitutional convention.[66]

Black's dissent in *Griswold v. Connecticut* is perhaps the most recognized instance of his jurisprudential conservatism. In that case, the Court held that a Connecticut statute prohibiting the use of birth control devices interfered excessively with the "right of privacy." Justice Douglas did not (because he could not) ground his majority opinion in specific constitutional language; instead, he found a right to privacy within "penumbras" emanating from the protections of the First, Third, Fourth, Fifth, and Ninth Amendments.[67]

The Court's reference to a general right of privacy prompted Black's vigorous dissent. "In order that there may be no room at all to doubt why I vote as I do," he declared at the outset of his opinion, "I feel constrained to add that the law is every bit as offensive to me as it is to my Brethren of the majority." But he found the ill-conceived statute less objectionable than the Court's "talk about a constitutional 'right of privacy' as an emanation from one or more constitutional provisions. I like my privacy as well as the next, but I am nevertheless compelled to admit that government has a right to invade it unless prohibited by some specific constitutional provision." Once again, he repudiated the notion that "the duty of this Court [is] to keep the Constitution in tune with the times."[68]

Black also directed his ire at Justices Harlan and White, who concurred in the Court's judgment. In contrast to Douglas, these men located the right to privacy in the concept of liberty that the due process clause of the Fourteenth Amendment protects. They regarded the Connecticut statute as a violation of due process because the law represented an "arbitrary or capricious" denial of privacy. Black responded caustically: "The Due Process Clause with an 'arbitrary and capricious' or 'shocking to the conscience' formula was liberally used by the Court to strike down economic legislation in the early decades of this century, threatening, many people thought, the tranquility and stability of the Nation. . . . That formula, based on subjective considerations of 'natural justice,' is no less dangerous when used to enforce this Court's views about personal rights than those about economic rights."[69]

Although these rulings appear to detract from the thesis that Black sought to use judicial power for antihierarchical purposes, one might reconcile them with this account of his jurisprudence. Black drew a distinction between the "ordinary criminal" and the dissenter who is caught in the criminal justice system because of his or her heretical views. Furthermore, he more than occasionally mentioned in his Fourth Amendment opinions the overwhelming evidence of a defendant's guilt.[70] In short, his belief in the culpability of criminal defendants may have been the operative principle in those cases in which he declined to use judicial power to secure antihierarchical provisions.

This explanation is problematic, however. It ignores the fact that the issue of culpability had "absolutely no impact on the justice's reaction to self-incrimination, counsel, and other procedural claims raised by petitioners whose guilt often seemed equally obvious." Black worked continually to secure these constitutional protections.[71] Furthermore, this explanation does not account for his dissent in *Griswold*. That case did not involve "ordinary criminals," as the phrase is commonly understood. It appears, then, that Black simply followed the logic of his constitutional jurisprudence, which permitted judicial intervention only where constitutional language or history gave clear support. His belief in the guilt of petitioners in Fourth Amendment cases was incidental to his rulings; in his view, the amendment's requirement of reasonableness does not warrant exercises of judicial review in cases involving less than extreme forms of police behavior.

Black's apparent willingness to decide cases in a manner inconsistent with his personal preferences raises the possibility that his jurisprudence reflected something more fundamental than ideological considerations: *Black may have feared and thus sought to curtail judicial discretion.* The justice's pronouncements concerning the wisdom of an absolutist interpretation of the freedoms of speech and press and of the incorporation of the Bill of Rights into the Fourteenth Amendment may have been incidental to his opinions. Similarly, his assertion that the Court functions to protect the weak and oppressed of society may have been a mere observation concerning the overall effect of his efforts to restrict judicial decision making to the language and history of the Constitution. In short, and in contrast to the argument of this chapter, Black's statement that the Court serves an antihierarchical role may not have served as the motivating principle behind his jurisprudence.

Scholars have offered various explanations for Black's supposed fear of judicial discretion. One student of the Court suggests that the justice followed the teachings of Jeremy Bentham. In an interview, Black professed to be a "great admirer" of the English philosopher. Moreover, "the elements of Black's judicial and constitutional philosophy bear a close resemblance to positivist [jurisprudential] theory. In fact, the Justice would appear to have been the preeminent positivist jurist." His fear of judicial revision of law under the guise of interpretation, his belief that the interpretation of law requires fidelity to the intent of the framers, and his consequent use of clear, consistent legal standards all accorded with the tenets of positivist jurisprudence, as contained in the writings of Bentham and John Austin.[72]

The problem with this interpretation is that virtually nothing suggests that Black was a proponent of the utilitarianism embedded in Bentham's legal positivism. Benthamites believe that the function of law is to reflect the will of the majority and to manipulate human behavior so as to maximize social utility, that is, to actualize the greatest happiness of the greatest number. They regard judicial discretion as inherently dangerous because unfettered, unaccountable judicial decision making would contravene the will of the majority. Benthamites thus seek clear, known, and consistent rules that instruct persons how to maximize social utility and preclude judges from pursuing a different goal when resolving social conflicts. Although Black may have expressed admiration for Bentham, one searches in vain for references to the concept of utility in the justice's writings and opinions. Moreover, his admiration for (or knowledge of) Bentham could not have been very great, since Bentham rejected devices for legal limitations on sovereignty, including bills of rights, the separation of governmental powers, and systems of checks and balances for restraining power. These devices present obstacles to the fulfillment of the needs and desires of a social majority. Black was thus hardly paying homage to Bentham when he said: "[The] Constitution is my legal Bible; its plan of our government is my plan and its destiny my destiny. I cherish every word of it, from the first to the last, and I personally deplore even the slightest deviation from its least important commands."[73]

In what would seem to be a more compelling explanation, some scholars argue that Black's Populist heritage and his hierarchical perception of society accounted for his apparent belief that judicial discretion is inherently dangerous. Those who point to Black's immersion in Populist culture to explain his conservative rulings emphasize the insurgents' mistrust of unchecked governmental power, including judicial power. In the words of one scholar, Black's "political education was shaped by a Populist understanding of the continuing conflict between the few and the many, the rich and the poor. . . . History, he believed, proved that men could not be trusted with power, and to assume that power could be employed in a disinterested fashion for the benefit of the many was naive." Black thus "sought continually to decrease the sphere of judicial judgment," to "check the discretion and will of the judiciary." Concurring in this explanation, the authors of a more recent study argue that Black "was a populist in the Senate who never forgot that he was from Clay County and represented the needs and aspirations of the citizens of Alabama. He was a populist on the Court in the sense that he kept in mind the importance of the little man [and] was fearful of centralized power (particularly in the hands of unelected judges)." He thus "vowed . . . to be religiously consistent in his decisions and to fight vigorously against a judiciary that used its discretion freely." This "commitment to avoid judicial discretion," the authors note, "disappointed many because it led to 'conservative' judgments."[74]

The proposition that Populism would explain a belief that judicial discretion is inherently dangerous is singularly unconvincing. Although those individuals having a Populist-inspired conception of reality would not favor constitutional protection for every antihierarchical social act or occurrence[75] (the Populists, after all, sought social reform through extant political institutions), they would not possess a fear of judicial discretion used for antihierarchical purposes. As demonstrated in the two preceding chapters, the Populists fundamentally feared the political and economic exploitation of the masses by the propertied few, and they resorted to legalism or clear demarcations upon public power because they wished *to secure antihierarchical results*, not because they feared discretion per se. The Populists, in short, were profoundly result oriented. Any concern over the excessive use of discretion for antihierarchical purposes figured much less prominently in Populist thought than did a desire to combat social and political hierarchy. Those whom the movement influenced would thus in most instances welcome exercises of judicial discretion that supported marginal social groups.

One should not be surprised, then, that Black at times ignored the confines of his jurisprudence and used discretion to further antihierarchical aims. His belief in the unconstitutionality of malapportionment would be anomalous if he had possessed a fear of judicial discretion per se, since neither the language nor the history of the Constitution requires the reapportionment of electoral districts. Speaking for the Court in *Wesberry v. Sanders*, Black attempted to locate the right to equipopulous congressional districts in the command of Article 1, section 2 (specifically, that representatives be chosen "by the people of the several States") and the historical background of that provision.[76] In an elaborate dissent, which Black made no effort to rebut, Justice Harlan argued that "the language of Art. I, . . . the surrounding text, and the relevant history are all in strong and consistent direct contradiction of the Court's holding." Sounding like the Justice Black of earlier decisions, Harlan stated that the "constitutional right which the Court creates is manufactured out of whole cloth."[77]

In *Hadley v. Junior College District*, Black did not even attempt a historical justification of the holding that the equal protection clause of the Fourteenth Amendment requires public college trustees to be elected from districts substantially equal in population.[78] Arguably, he should have provided such a discussion because the equal protection clause defies a literal interpretation. Moreover, in an earlier case, Harlan had penned a detailed historical critique of the holding that equal protection requires the seats in both houses of a bicameral state legislature to be apportioned on an equal population basis.[79] (Black had joined Chief Justice Warren's opinion for the Court, which was devoid of historical analysis.)

Far from suggesting a fear of judicial discretion, Black's position in these cases corroborates the view that he sought to use judicial power to aid marginal social groups. The reapportionment decisions weakened the hegemony of the plantation elites across the South by shifting the distribution of political power away from the rural Bourbons and toward the increasingly urbanized lower classes.[80]

Also, in numerous instances, Black disregarded his contention that the concept of due process does not extend beyond the provisions of the Bill of Rights and the procedural protections contained within the original Constitution. He took the position, for example, that government violates due process when it secures convictions through the use of vague statutes, perjured testimony, suppressed evidence, no evidence, or false evidence.[81] One might enlist historical arguments to justify looking beyond the text of the Constitution to ensure a defendant an opportunity to answer a charge through the service of process in proper form, that is, in due course. (Indeed, one scholar argues that the common-law definition of due process warrants *only* this protection.)[82] But history does not appear to support, nor did Black use historical arguments to defend, his positions in these cases. Black, of course, did not go so far as to suggest that the Court has a broad power under due process to judge the reasonableness of legislation. To do so would have been to approve the weapon the Court had used to defend the social and economic status quo. But he was more than willing to take advantage of the antihierarchical results that attend judicial application of the flexible *Palko* standard to criminal proceedings.

A Conflict More Apparent Than Real

Yet, if Black was a result-oriented jurist, one must ask why he did not use discretion more frequently to reach antihierarchical conclusions. His conservative rulings in *Griswold* and many other cases appear to speak against the view that he designed his jurisprudence to aid marginal social groups.[83]

The tension between his decisions supporting the social status quo and his efforts to use the Court as a social corrective is more apparent than real. These decisions do not seem anomalous if one recalls his experiences with judicial discretion and his acknowledgment of the social expectation that judges not engage in lawmaking. Discretionary standards would have enabled Black to reach antihierarchical conclusions he could not have derived from the explicit language of the Constitution or the history informing its provisions. But such standards open courts to the charge of judicial lawmaking. Moreover, as the two preceding sections demonstrate, he learned quickly that judicial discretion is a double-edged sword: it has the potential to support the social and economic status quo as much as to promote reform. James Bradley Thayer's deferential rational-basis test represents a form of judicial discretion that would meet the social expectation that judges should not infuse their values into law. Furthermore, Thayer's standard hinders judicial use of a substantive conception of due process to invalidate social and economic legislation. Yet Black would not accept a blanket application of this Progressive response to the problem of judicial legislation, because the rational-basis test also impedes judicial protection of antihierarchical rights.

Black embraced a legalistic jurisprudence, partly for the same reason the political program of the Populists featured rigid restraints upon the state: to secure the affirmative use of power for crucial antihierarchical purposes and to prevent government from supporting the social and economic status quo. As a senator, he had favored positive programs to aid the dispossessed and had said he was "forever opposed" to corporate subsidies. He was similarly result oriented in restraining judicial discretion: he hoped, first, by rejecting substantive due process, to prevent the judiciary from supporting extant power relations and, second, by advocating total incorporation, to secure a strong federal judicial presence on the state level for important antihierarchical purposes, namely, the protection of the crucial freedoms of speech and press. Specifically, he hoped to protect those freedoms through an absolutist interpretation of the First Amendment and an aggressive enforcement of the supporting procedural protections of the Fifth and Sixth Amendments. It is more than mere coincidence that he moved toward total incorporation and an absolutist interpretation of the freedoms of speech and press only after the Court's use of discretionary standards had conservative consequences. Because he thought that arbitrary and tyrannical rule cannot survive in the face of open discussion and a free press,[84] he was willing virtually to sacrifice the use of judicial discretion for other antihierarchical purposes. In the same way he had engaged in reciprocity with the Big Mule–Black Belt alliance to prolong his reformist political career, he sacrificed some goals as a justice for the ultimate accomplishment of larger, more lasting constitutional objectives.

The recollections of Black's son corroborate the view that Black's decisions supporting the status quo were part of a result-oriented approach to constitutional interpretation. Hugo Black Jr. remembered his father saying: " 'I believe we've got to tie the judges of this Court and the subordinate federal courts to something lasting, even if we've got to sacrifice doing some good through the federal courts.' " When his father

arrived . . . [in Washington,] he determined to do all he could to make the Supreme Court and the court system which it bestrides a haven for the helpless, weak, outnumbered and non-conforming victims of prejudice that he believed the founders of our government intended courts to be. And he intended to bring this about through a living law based on the Constitution, a law that would possess elements of permanency to withstand the shifting political winds which blow one day for the superprivileged and the next for the underprivileged, even though this frequently meant passing up opportunities based on the raw power of the Court to do right as its members saw it. If the liberals passed up the opportunity to use the raw power of the Court without regard to a philosophy of permanency ensured by the Constitution, Hugo believed that it would make it more difficult "for the reactionaries to do the right as they see it—the wrong as I see it—when they recapture the raw power of the Court, which they inevitably will."[85]

Black's conservative rulings were more than necessary sacrifices for securing important antihierarchical results: they were important elements in his effort to pay homage to the ideal of a non-policy-making judiciary. Time and again, he availed himself of the public relations advantage that his constitutional jurisprudence afforded; he pointed to the intent of the framers as support for his decisions and chastised his brethren for engaging in constitutional revision. But his decisions supporting the social status quo made most believable his claim that he was "not in that group" of people who think a judge "should interpret the Constitution and statutes according to his own belief of what they ought to prescribe." (He went so far as to refuse to support the Court's invalidation of a favorite political weapon of the Bourbons: the poll tax.) His usual faithfulness to the conservative implications of his jurisprudence led numerous scholars to agree with Justice Douglas's statement that one "find[s] plenty [in Black's opinions] to disprove the charge that he is an 'activist' and a devotee of judicial power." Black's demonstrated willingness to use judicial discretion for certain antihierarchical purposes, however, belied his profession that he was "attempting in all cases to resist reaching a result simply because [he thought] it . . . desirable."[86] More significantly, this tendency revealed that there was nothing paradoxical about the fact that, even when one accounts for the conservative implications of his jurisprudence, his unique attempt to meet the social expectation of a non-policy-making Court dramatically broadened the scope of judicial power in American political life.[87]

While Black's efforts to secure crucial antihierarchical results and to meet social expectations for the judiciary required him at times to suppress his reformist impulse, not all of his decisions supporting the social status quo contradicted his personal values. His ideology was not so uncomplicated. Recall that he sometimes expressed agreement with the criminal convictions at issue in Fourth Amendment cases.[88]

Black made the complexity of his ideology most apparent in his consistent refusal during the 1960s to extend constitutional protection to forms of demonstrative conduct. One can assume that these cases disclosed his values because his opinions stemmed from a willingness to exercise discretion, rather than from efforts to limit judges to an analysis of constitutional language and intent. True, he believed that the language of the Constitution distinguishes between speech and conduct: because only speech is mentioned explicitly, he did "not believe that the First Amendment grants a constitutional right to engage in the conduct of picketing or demonstrating, whether on publicly owned streets or on privately owned property. . . . Marching back and forth, though utilized to communicate ideas, is not speech and therefore is not protected by the First Amendment." (He essentially ignored the clause guaranteeing "the right of the people peaceably to assemble," given the untenability of an absolutist interpretation of this provision in a system of ordered liberty.) Yet, in spite of this reading of the First Amendment, he maintained that the Court must protect demonstrative conduct if (1) the regulation in question has an indirect effect on speech and the speech interest involved is more important than the interest that the state advances, or (2) the state can accomplish its goal through means that do not burden speech. For most of his tenure, he used these discretionary standards to protect conduct that conveys ideas. But he was unreceptive to demands for constitutional protection against governmental efforts to quell the social and political protests of the 1960s.[89]

At least one scholar suggests that these First Amendment opinions during the 1960s indicated a profound shift toward jurisprudential conservatism in Black's later years.[90] This interpretation is not compelling, however. Black continued to advocate an absolutist reading of the freedoms of speech and press and the protection of clearly delineated procedural safeguards, most notably, the protection against self-incrimination. He refused to protect demonstrative conduct in the 1960s because he discerned a difference in the forms of conduct at issue in these later cases. He thought that the "isolated incidents of labor picketing the Court confronted during [his] early years . . . were hardly comparable in frequency, general size, and burdens on government resources to the protest movements of the sixties."[91]

Alternatively, some scholars argue that Black's later opinions on demonstrative conduct (among other opinions supporting the social status quo) disclosed a belief in "the interdependency of [majoritarian democracy and broad guarantees of individual liberty]." In other words, "Black believed that personal freedom was not an end in itself. Instead, individual liberty was essential because it facilitated democratic self-government upon which community welfare depended."[92] This argument stresses the fact that Black's southern background involved issues of community and order, as well as claims of right against power. Recall that, although well aware of the poverty of Alabama's yeomen, he spent his youth (and continued to live) in fairly privileged circumstances. Also, recall that he was profoundly religious and took seriously the biblical injunction that communal concerns should take precedence over individual interests and gains. His support for prohibition and his attendant willingness to subordinate claims of right made against governmental efforts to regulate liquor were the most obvious manifestations of his religious upbringing.

That Black acknowledged limits to claims of right, even when those claims were antihierarchical, is incontestable. However, the contention that his judicial behavior represented an attempt to expound the organic relations between the principles of order and liberty cannot be maintained. Anyone engaged in such an enterprise would regard the cornerstone of Black's constitutional jurisprudence—an absolutist interpretation of the freedoms of speech and press—as anathema. By contrast, anyone whose primary (as opposed to sole) concern is to prevent government from stifling efforts to alter the status quo would regard the classifications of obscenity and libel as problematic. Although Black, at times, yielded to governmental efforts to defend the status quo, his jurisprudence, overall, was profoundly antihierarchical. This should not be surprising, since, in all fairness, one must conclude that he devoted his pre-Court years to promoting social and economic change. His personal wealth, his belief in the universal applicability of a Christian sense of duty, and even his periodic concessions to the Bourbons diminished neither the strength of his commitment to the laboring classes nor his reputation as a champion of the common man.

Little Fear of Judicial Abstraction

Black's aversion to the doctrine of judicial deference, at least in those instances where he believed the Constitution compels exercises of judicial review, suggested that the danger of judicial abstraction was not the focus of his jurisprudence. Recall that the Progressives viewed judicial deference as a way to reduce the threat posed to legislative and administrative determinations by an institution whose decisions are comparatively separated from a complex social reality.[93]

In view of the change in the composition of the Court's docket in the middle of this century, one is tempted to conclude that concerns over judicial abstraction became largely irrelevant. Interdependence, the principal source of abstract thinking, was primarily an economic phenomenon. The shift toward constitutional controversies involving nonproprietarian rights meant that the Court no longer had to worry that the intricacies of interdependent, economic relationships hid the exigencies prompting governmental action. Likewise, the justices did not have to concern themselves with tracing the effects of governmental policies or the reverberations of their own decisions through the same network of economic dependencies.

Those who viewed abstraction as a significant danger during the era of economic due process, however, would have remained concerned with the issue when constitutional controversies became largely nonproprietarian, for the move toward interdependence greatly complicated noneconomic, as well as economic, relationships. Urbanization followed heightened interdependence, and the increased physical proximity of individuals meant that one person's noneconomic behavior could now affect the lives of many others. Advances in communication technology, which also attended the move toward interdependence, enormously expanded the reach of ideas and images. Specialization, another element of interdependence, further complicated nonproprietarian relationships: In a heterogeneous society, noneconomic conflicts or problems (e.g., types of crime or the impact of certain forms of speech or press) vary with regions or localities. And, in those instances when similar problems affect different areas, nonuniform responses may be necessary. Finally, the development of expertise in human behavior and governance accompanied specialization. Such specialized knowledge contrasted with the generalized nature of the judicial mind. In short, those persons concerned with abstract judicial thinking in the early twentieth century would still fear at midcentury that judges might neglect the scale or severity of exigencies prompting governmental action and thus overlook the secondary effects of exercises of judicial review.

At times, Black fretted over the possibility of judicial abstraction in nonproprietarian contexts. Recall that his Fourth Amendment opinions revealed some concern over the inadequacies of appellate court fact-finding.[94] But his absolutist interpretation of the freedoms of speech and press proves conclusively that a fear of abstraction was not central to his jurisprudence. Indeed, a literal reading of the language of the First Amendment represents the worst form of abstraction because absolute rights cannot be qualified, regardless of the merit of any competing social claim.

Black also revealed his near indifference to the problem of abstraction in his approach to the concept of justiciability. This concept, which is composed of several doctrines rooted in the case-or-controversy requirement found in Article 3 of the Constitution, serves in part to ensure that the Court will not address abstract legal questions. The norm prohibiting the Court from rendering "advisory opinions" on questions not raised in an actual lawsuit and the doctrines of adverseness (that litigants to a controversy must have adverse interests in the outcome of the case), standing (that a petitioner must show injury to a legally protected interest or right), ripeness (that the injury claimed must have already occurred), and nonmootness (that pertinent facts or law must not have changed such that there is no longer real adverseness) all help to ensure that litigants will present judges with information adequate to weigh the contending interests in a case. Black, however, did not acknowledge this purpose behind the concept of justiciability. Indeed, he was apprehensive about judicial attentiveness to justiciability because such behavior restrains judicial power in constitutional controversies. He acknowledged that many people view this consequence as salutary, since it makes judicial revision of the Constitution under the guise of interpretation less likely. But he "believe[d] strongly that judges are restrained by the [language and history of the] Constitution." He thus worried that justiciability would interfere with the Court's responsibility to give force and effect to clear constitutional limitations: "[T]he Framers were right in believing that such judicial power is an essential feature of our type of free government and I believe it ill behooves the courts to restrict their usefulness in protecting constitutional rights by creating artificial judicial obstacles to the full performance of their duty. . . . [The essential protection of liberty] should not be hobbled by general and abstract judicial maxims created to deny litigants their just deserts in a court of law, perhaps when they need the court's help most desperately."[95]

Black's decision not to temper his concern for the protection of individual liberties with a fear of judicial abstraction could not have been the result of a lack of familiarity with social interdependence. Every part of the nation experienced the heightened interconnectedness that accompanied industrialism. And Black was fully aware that the economic problems of the South generally and the region's upland farmers and laborers specifically stemmed in considerable measure from northeastern economic policies. But he was alive to the antihierarchical value of abstract conceptions of rights precisely because of the hierarchical impact of social interdependence.

One must also remember that the southern economy remained

underdeveloped when the nation became interdependent. Although Black practiced law for many years in the most industrialized city in Alabama, a few major industries (primarily steel production and cotton textile manufacturing) dominated Birmingham's economy. Unlike northeastern cities, southern urban centers could not attract a large middle class composed of individuals representing a multitude of professions and possessing a quantity of specialized knowledge well beyond the reach of any one individual.[96] In view of the fact that southern society was not as dynamic or diverse as the mature, industrialized areas of the North, and given that Black saw much evidence of the conflict between those who possess economic and political power and the less fortunate who would use government to improve their lives, it is not surprising that he did not view abstract thinking as the greatest danger to the nation in the twentieth century. This belief, by contrast, served as the cardinal tenet of the judicial philosophy of his colleague and jurisprudential nemesis, Felix Frankfurter.

Notes

1. *Chambers v. Florida*, 309 U.S. 227 (1940).

2. Ibid., 239–40.

3. Ibid., 238, 236, 241; Hugo L. Black and Elizabeth Black, *Mr. Justice and Mrs. Black: The Memoirs of Hugo L. Black and Elizabeth Black* (New York: Random House, 1986), 73.

4. Hugo L. Black, "The Bill of Rights," *New York University Law Review* 35 (1960): 880, 870.

5. Ibid., 866, 878–79. Black employed the rational-basis standard in limited areas of constitutional law. See note 64 below and accompanying text.

6. Hugo LaFayette Black, *A Constitutional Faith* (New York: Knopf, 1968), 8, 14 (quoted). Black did not deny that judgment would be required under his approach; he suggested only that his interpretive strategy would minimize judicial discretion. See ibid., 35–36; *Adamson v. California*, 332 U.S. 46, 90–92 (1947) (Black, J., dissenting). For instances in which Black's interpretive method led him to advocate the exercise of judicial deference, see notes 61–69 below and accompanying text.

7. See notes 41–43 below and accompanying text.

8. As quoted in James F. Simon, *The Antagonists: Hugo Black, Felix Frankfurter and Civil Liberties in Modern America* (New York: Simon & Schuster, 1989),95.

9. Hugo L. Black, "No Broadcasting by Utilities," 1929, 688, 689, 691, 687, Papers of Hugo L. Black, Library of Congress, Manuscript Division (hereafter cited as HLBP), Box 476.

10. *Wieman v. Updegraf*, 344 U.S. 183, 194 (1952) (Black, J., concurring); Black, "The Bill of Rights," 881, 879; Black, *A Constitutional Faith*, 43, 48. See also ibid., 44.

11. Black, *A Constitutional Faith*, 45–46 (quoted first, second, and fourth); Black, "The Bill of Rights," 874 (quoted; footnotes omitted; Black's emphasis); *Feldman v. United States*, 332 U.S. 487, 501 (1944) (Black, J., dissenting); (quoted).

12. Black, *A Constitutional Faith*, 46–48 (quoted); Hugo L. Black, "Justice Black and First Amendment 'Absolutes': A Public Interview," interview by Edmond Cahn, *New York University Law Review* 37 (1962): 557–59.

13. Black, *A Constitutional Faith*, 50; Thomas I. Emerson, *Toward a General Theory of the First Amendment* (New York: Random House, 1966), 53–54; Black, "The Bill of Rights," 878. Interestingly, Black employed a discretionary standard in cases involving demonstrative conduct. See notes 89–93 below and accompanying text.

14. C. Herman Pritchett, *Constitutional Civil Liberties* (Englewood Cliffs, N.J.: Prentice-Hall, 1984), 20–23; Black, *A Constitutional Faith*, 52 (quoted).

15. Cf. Black, *A Constitutional Faith*, xv.

16. David M. O'Brien, *The Public's Right to Know: The Supreme Court and the First Amendment* (New York: Praeger, 1981), 76–79; Pritchett, *Constitutional Civil Liberties*, 25–28; Henry J. Abraham, *Freedom and the Court: Civil Rights and Liberties in the United States*, 5th ed. (New York: Oxford University Press, 1988), 21–28. For cases in which Black employed the "clear and present danger" test, see *Thornhill v. Alabama*, 310 U.S. 88 (1940); *Milk Wagon Drivers Union v. Meadowmoor Co.*, 312 U.S. 287, 299 (1941) (Black, J., dissenting); *Bridges v. California*, 314 U.S. 252 (1941); *Pennekamp v. Florida*, 328 U.S. 331 (1946); *Craig v. Harney*, 331 U.S. 367 (1947). The initial formulation of the "clear and present danger" test is found in *Schenck v. United States*, 249 U.S. 47 (1919), and *Abrams v. United States*, 250 U.S. 616 (1919).

17. *Chaplinsky v. New Hampshire*, 315 U.S. 568, 572 (1942).

18. Hugo L. Black, Senate speech, dated Oct. 11, HLBP, Box 476.

19. *Cox v. New Hampshire*, 312 U.S. 569 (1941); Hugo L. Black to Mr. Chief Justice Hughes, 27 March 1941, HLBP, Box 262; Hugo L. Black, undated memorandum, headed #2, HLBP, Box 262.

20. Hugo L. Black, undated memorandum, headed #2, HLBP, Box 262. For a discussion of the distinction Black made between speech and conduct in First Amendment cases, see notes 89—93 below and accompanying text.

21. *Bridges v. California*, (see note 16 above); Hugo L. Black, undated memorandum on *Bridges v. California*, HLBP, Box 256.

22. Tinsley E. Yarbrough, *Mr. Justice Black and His Critics* (Durham: Duke University Press, 1988), 161. See also Mark Silverstein, *Constitutional Faiths: Felix Frankfurter, Hugo Black, and the Process of Judicial Decision Making* (Ithaca: Cornell University Press, 1984), 183–84.

23. Hugo L. Black, undated memorandum on *Bridges v. California*, HLBP, Box 256.

24. Yarbrough, *Black and His Critics*, 161–62; Silverstein, *Constitutional Faiths*, 185; *Bridges v. California*, 263 (quoted).

25. See note 16 above.

26. *American Communications Ass'n v. Douds*, 339 U.S. 382, 397 (1950).

27. Ibid., 399; ibid., 448 (Black, J., dissenting).

28. *Dennis v. United States*, 341 U.S. 494, 510 (1951); ibid., 517 (Frankfurter, J., concurring); ibid., 561 (Jackson, J., concurring).

29. Ibid., 579–81 (Black, J., dissenting).

30. *Carlson v. Landon*, 342 U.S. 524 (1952).

31. Ibid., 555 (Black, J., dissenting).

32. *Beauharnais v. Illinois*, 343 U.S. 250, 252, 256–58 (1952).

33. Ibid., 272–73, 275 (Black, J., dissenting).

34. Ibid., 273 (Black, J., dissenting).

35. Leonard W. Levy, *Emergence of a Free Press* (first published as *Legacy of Suppression: Freedom of Speech and Press in Early American History*, 1960; rev. and enl. ed., New York: Oxford University Press, 1985), 268–69 (quoted), 271–73. See also ibid., 274, where Levy suggests that even James Madison did not hold forth an absolutist understanding of the freedom of speech. For interpretations of the intent behind the First Amendment that preceded, and are inconsistent with, Black's understanding, see Edward S. Corwin, "Freedom of Speech and Press under the First Amendment: A Resume," *Yale Law Journal* 30 (1920): 48–55; Zechariah Chafee Jr., *Free Speech in the United States* (Cambridge: Harvard University Press, 1941); and Alexander Meiklejohn, *Free Speech and Its Relation to Self-Government* (New York: Harper & Bros., 1948).

36. Black, *A Constitutional Faith*, 49.

37. Abraham, *Freedom and the Court*, 38–117; *Adamson v. California*, 89 (Black, J., dissenting); (quoted); Black, "The Bill of Rights," 880. Section 1 of the Fourteenth Amendment provides: "All persons born or naturalized in the United States, and subject to the jurisdiction thereof, are citizens of the United States and of the State wherein they reside. No State shall make or enforce any law which shall abridge the privileges or immunities of citizens of the United States; nor shall any State deprive any person of life, liberty, or property, without due process of law; nor deny to any person within its jurisdiction the equal protection of the laws."

38. *Adamson v. California*, 71, 89 (Black, J., dissenting) (quoted first and fourth); *Feldman v. United States*, 501 (Black, J., dissenting). By 1937, the Court had incorporated, among other provisions, the First Amendment rights to speech, press, free exercise of religion, peaceable assembly, and petition. Abraham, *Freedom and the Court*, 77.

39. *Adamson v. California*, 74, 71–72 (Black, J., dissenting).

40. *Adamson v. California*, 82, 74 (Black, J., dissenting) (quoted first, second, and third); *Twining v. New Jersey*, 211 U.S. 78, 99 (1908) (quoted fifth and sixth); Black, *A Constitutional Faith*, 38–39 (quoted fourth). The Court

had restricted the meaning of the privileges-or-immunities clause in *Butchers' Benevolent Ass'n v. Crescent City Livestock Landing & Slaughterhouse Co.*, 83 U.S. 36 (1873).

41. *Twining v. New Jersey*, 111, 113; Black, *A Constitutional Faith*, 39.

42. *Palko v. Connecticut*, 302 U.S. 319, 323–26 (1937).

43. *Adamson v. California*, 89 (Black, J., dissenting) (quoted first and fourth); Black, *A Constitutional Faith*, 39.

44. Cf. Black, *A Constitutional Faith*, xv.

45. *Palko v. Connecticut*, 325, quoting *Snyder v. Massachusetts*, 291 U.S. 97, 105 (1934), 328. See also Abraham, *Freedom and the Court*, 76.

46. Yarbrough, *Black and His Critics*, 82; Richard A. Posner, *Cardozo: A Study in Reputation* (Chicago: University of Chicago Press, 1990); *Palko v. Connecticut*, 327, 325 (quoted); Abraham, *Freedom and the Court*, 50.

47. Silverstein, *Constitutional Faiths*, 137; *Chambers v. Florida*, 238 (quoted). See also *Lisenba v. California*, 314 U.S. 219, 241 (1941) (Black, J., dissenting); *Hysler v. Florida*, 315 U.S. 411, 423 (1942) (Black, J., dissenting).

48. *Chambers v. Florida*, 235–36 n. 8, 237, 237 n. 10.

49. Felix Frankfurter to Hugo Black, 31 December 1939 (emphasis in original), Papers of Felix Frankfurter, Library of Congress, Manuscript Division (hereafter cited as FFP), Box 25.

50. Yarbrough, *Black and His Critics*, 83–84.

51. *Betts v. Brady*, 316 U.S. 455, 461–62, 473, 472 (1942).

52. Ibid., 474–76 (Black, J., dissenting).

53. Ibid., 475 (Black, J., dissenting).

54. *Lyons v. Oklahoma*, 322 U.S. 596, 605 (1944) (Murphy, J., dissenting). The Court formally incorporated the Fifth Amendment privilege against self-incrimination in *Malloy v. Hogan*, 378 U.S. 1 (1964), and *Murphy v. Waterfront Comm'n*, 378 U.S. 52 (1964).

55. *Malinski v. New York*, 324 U.S. 401, 414 (1945) (Frankfurter, J., concurring); Hugo L. Black, memorandum headed "Re: No. 367, Malinski and Rudish vs. People of State of New York," 23 March 1945, FFP, Box 218 (emphasis added). For an opinion in which Black used the flexible concept of due process, see *Ashcraft v. Tennessee*, 322 U.S. 143 (1944).

56. Hugo L. Black, memorandum headed "Re: No. 367, Malinski and Rudish vs. People of State of New York," 23 March 1945, FFP, Box 218.

57. *Adamson v. California*, (see note 6 above).

58. Ibid., 75, 81–83, 90, 92–123 (Black, J., dissenting) (pp. 75, 90 quoted).

59. Ibid., 64 (Frankfurter, J., concurring) (quoted); Charles Fairman, "Does the Fourteenth Amendment Incorporate the Bill of Rights? The Original Understanding," *Stanford Law Review* 2 (1949): 5–139; Stanley Morrison, "Does the Fourteenth Amendment Incorporate the Bill of Rights? The Judicial Interpretation," *Stanford Law Review* 2 (1949): 140–73. (On p. 162, Morrison accuses Black of distorting history.)

60. Black, *A Constitutional Faith*, 34. For an overview of the controversy

concerning the history of the adoption of the Fourteenth Amendment, see Abraham, *Freedom and the Court*, 49–54.

61. *Robinson v. California*, 370 U.S. 660 (1962); *Powell v. Texas*, 389 U.S. 810 (1968); Yarbrough, *Black and His Critics*, 208–9, quoting draft opinion of Hugo L. Black.

62. *McGautha v. California*, 402 U.S. 183, 225 (1971) (Black, J., separate opinion).

63. Yarbrough, *Black and His Critics*, 209 (common-law robbery); *McGautha v. California*, 225 (Black, J., separate opinion) (jury discretion); *Witherspoon v. Illinois*, 391 U.S. 510, 532 (1968) (Black, J., dissenting) (juror exclusion); *Francis v. Resweber*, 329 U.S. 459 (1947) (second attempt at execution).

64. *Mapp v. Ohio*, 367 U.S. 643, 662 (1961) (Black, J., concurring) (quoted); Yarbrough, *Black and His Critics*, 215–17; Black, "The Bill of Rights," 873 (quoted; emphasis in original). For cases in which Black approved of warrantless searches and seizures, see *Harris v. United States*, 331 U.S. 145 (1947); *Ker v. California*, 374 U.S. 23 (1963); *Terry v. Ohio*, 392 U.S. 1 (1968); *Sibron v. New York*, 392 U.S. 40, 79 (1968) (Black, J., concurring and dissenting); *Chimel v. California*, 395 U.S. 752, 770 (1969); *Vale v. Louisiana*, 399 U.S. 30, 36 (1970) (Black, J., dissenting).

65. *Spinelli v. United States*, 393 U.S. 410, 433–34 (1969) (Black, J., dissenting). See also *Aguilar v. Texas*, 378 U.S. 108, 116 (1964).

66. *Katz v. United States*, 389 U.S. 347, 373 (1967) (Black, J., dissenting).

67. *Griswold v. Connecticut*, 381 U.S. 479, 484–86 (1965).

68. Ibid., 507, 509–10, 522 (Black, J., dissenting).

69. Ibid., 499 (Harlan, J., concurring); ibid., 502 (White, J., concurring); ibid., 509–10, 522 (Black, J., dissenting).

70. See, e.g., *Feldman v. United States*, 502 (Black, J., dissenting); *Bumper v. North Carolina*, 391 U.S. 543, 558–59 (1968) (Black, J., dissenting). Sylvia Snowiss discusses the distinction Black made between dissenters and "ordinary criminals." "The Legacy of Justice Black," in *The Supreme Court Review*, ed. Philip B. Kurland (Chicago: University of Chicago Press, 1990), 220. Jacob Landynski notes Black's tendency to emphasize the evidence of a defendant's guilt. "In Search of Justice Black's Fourth Amendment," *Fordham Law Review* 45 (1976): 472.

71. Yarbrough, *Black and His Critics*, 222. See note 91 below.

72. Yarbrough, *Black and His Critics*, 21–33 (p. 25 quoted).

73. George H. Sabine, *A History of Political Theory*, 4th ed. (Hinsdale, Ill.: Dreyden Press, 1973), 612–22, 629; Black, *A Constitutional Faith*, 66 (quoted).

74. Silverstein, *Constitutional Faiths*, 16, 15; Howard Ball and Phillip J. Cooper, *Of Power and Right: Hugo Black, William O. Douglas, and America's Constitutional Revolution* (New York: Oxford University Press, 1992), 14, 319. See also Howard Ball, *The Vision and the Dream of Justice Hugo L. Black: An Examination of a Judicial Philosophy* (Tuscaloosa: University of Alabama Press, 1975); Howard Ball, "Hugo L. Black: A Twentieth Century Jefferson-

ian," *Southwestern University Law Review* 9 (1977): 1049–68; Howard Ball, "Justice Hugo L. Black: A Magnificent Product of the South," in *Justice Hugo Black and Modern America*, ed. Freyer, 31–74. Yarbrough does not examine Black's background. Yet he apparently accepts the view that the justice's jurisprudence was the product of Alabama Populism, since he refers approvingly to Silverstein's work. See *Black and His Critics*, 160–61.

75. See notes 88—93 below and accompanying text.

76. *Wesberry v. Sanders*, 376 U.S. 1, 7–8 (1964). See also *Colegrove v. Green*, 328 U.S. 549, 566 (1946) (Black, J., dissenting); *Baker v. Carr*, 369 U.S. 186 (1962); *Gray v. Sanders*, 372 U.S. 368 (1963); *Reynolds v. Sims*, 377 U.S. 533 (1964); *Hadley v. Junior College Dist.*, 397 U.S. 50 (1970). For an argument that the history of the adoption of the Fourteenth Amendment does not support reapportionment, see Raoul Berger, *Government by Judiciary: The Transformation of the Fourteenth Amendment* (Cambridge: Harvard University Press, 1977), 69–98, 166–92. Scholars who regard Black's reapportionment decisions as anomalous include Yarbrough, *Black and His Critics*, 37–38, 226–32; and G. Edward White, *The American Judicial Tradition: Profiles of Leading American Judges* (New York: Oxford University Press, 1976), 357–58. Ball and Cooper are unaware of the damage that these decisions do to their thesis. See *Of Power and Right*, 188. Silverstein fails to address the issue. See *Constitutional Faiths*.

77. *Wesberry v. Sanders*, 41–42 (Harlan, J., dissenting).

78. *Hadley v. Junior College Dist.*, (see note 76 above).

79. *Reynolds v. Sims*, 589 (Harlan, J., dissenting).

80. Richard Franklin Bensel, *Sectionalism and American Political Development, 1880–1980* (Madison: University of Wisconsin Press, 1984), 256–57; J. Mills Thornton III, "Hugo Black and the Golden Age," *Alabama Law Review* 36 (1985): 904.

81. *Edelman v. California*, 344 U.S. 357, 362 (1953) (Black, J., dissenting) (vague statutes); *Hysler v. Florida*, 315 U.S. 411, 423 (1942) (Black, J., dissenting) (prejudiced testimony); *Alcorta v. Texas*, 355 U.S. 28 (1957) (suppressed evidence); *Thompson v. City of Louisville*, 362 U.S. 199 (1960) (no evidence); *Miller v. Pate*, 386 U.S. 1 (1967) (false evidence). See also *Lanzetta v. New Jersey*, 306 U.S. 451 (1939); *Pyle v. Kansas*, 317 U.S. 213 (1942); Yarbrough, *Black and His Critics*, 61; Roger W. Haigh, "Defining Due Process of Law: The Case of Mr. Justice Hugo L. Black," *South Dakota Law Review* 17 (1972): 18–25.

82. Berger, *Government by Judiciary*, 193–200. Black revealed that he regarded this protection as an element of due process in *Edelman v. California*, 362 (Black, J., dissenting).

83. For a discussion of other areas of constitutional law in which Black's jurisprudence led to conservative results, see Yarbrough, *Black and His Critics*, 206–08. For a discussion of other instances in which Black voted to use discretion for antihierarchical purposes, see note 89 below and accompanying text.

84. See notes 8–10 above and accompanying text.

85. Hugo Black Jr., *My Father: A Remembrance* (New York: Random House, 1975), 243, 182–83.

86. Black, *A Constitutional Faith*, 10, 14, 20, 24, 36, 39, 51 (p. 20 quoted first, p. 10 quoted third); William O. Douglas, "Mr. Justice Black: A Foreword," *Yale Law Journal* 65 (1956): 449. The scholars who would agree with Douglas's statement concerning Black's supposed aversion to judicial activism include Ball and Cooper, *Of Power and Right*; Yarbrough, *Black and His Critics*; and Silverstein, *Constitutional Faiths*. See also Ball, "Black: A Twentieth Century Jeffersonian," 1059. For instances in which Black invoked the framers as support for his decisions and/or charged his brethren with engaging in constitutional revision, see *Griswold v. Connecticut*, 522 (Black, J., dissenting); *Harper v. Virginia State Bd. of Elections*, 383 U.S. 663, 675–76 (1966) (Black, J., dissenting); *Boddie v. Connecticut*, 401 U.S. 371, 393 (1971) (Black, J., dissenting); Black, *A Constitutional Faith*, xvi, 42; Hugo L. Black, "Justice Black and the Bill of Rights," interview by Eric Sevareid and Martin Agronsky, CBS News Special, December 3, 1968, printed in *Southwestern University Law Review* 9 (1977): 938, 940–41, 947–49. See also Gerald T. Dunne, *Hugo Black and the Judicial Revolution* (New York: Simon & Schuster, 1977), 404. For Black's decisions on the poll tax, see *Breedlove v. Suttles*, 302 U.S. 277 (1937); *Butler v. Thompson*, 341 U.S. 937 (1951); *Harper v. Virginia State Bd. of Elections*, 670 (Black, J., dissenting).

Commenting on Black's efforts to limit judicial discretion, Wallace Mendelson maintains that Black "knew what some of his most ardent apologists seemed unable to grasp: if law is indeed a myth, there is no democratic justification whatsoever for a non-elected super-legislature that pretends to be a court." "Hugo Black and Judicial Discretion," *Political Science Quarterly* 85 (1970): 38. In spite of this observation, Mendelson regards the justice's decisions supporting the status quo as anomalies or "surprises." Indeed, focusing upon those instances in which Black ignored the confines of his jurisprudence in order to reach antihierarchical results, Mendelson goes so far as to say that Black was virtually "unhampered by 'rules' " and was instead "inspired by *ad hoc* or cadi justice." Ibid., 34 n. 65, 35 (quoted); Wallace Mendelson, "Mr. Justice Black and the Rule of Law," *Midwest Journal of Political Science* 4 (1960): 250–66; Wallace Mendelson, *Justices Black and Frankfurter: Conflict in the Court* (Chicago: University of Chicago Press, 1961). While I agree that Black's jurisprudence was fundamentally result oriented in that he constructed it to secure important antihierarchical results, it is a mistake to dismiss as mere rhetoric his pronouncements on the importance of judicial fidelity to the intent behind the Constitution. Moreover, contrary to Mendelson, "Hugo Black and Judicial Discretion," 34 n. 65, 38–39, Black's willingness to render decisions supporting the social status quo was not a late development. See the discussion of Black's Fourth Amendment votes in this chapter.

87. Cf. Silverstein, *Constitutional Faiths*, 130.

88. See note 70 above and accompanying text.

89. Black, *A Constitutional Faith*, 53–54 (quoted), 58–61; James Magee, *Mr. Justice Black: Absolutist on the Court* (Charlottesville: University Press of Virginia, 1980), 173–81. For cases in which Black voted to protect demonstrative conduct, see *Schneider v. Irvington*, 308 U.S. 147 (1939); *Milk Wagon Drivers Union v. Meadowmoor*, 299 (Black, J., dissenting); *Martin v. City of Struthers*, 319 U.S. 141 (1943); *Kovacs v. Cooper*, 336 U.S. 77, 98 (1949) (Black, J., dissenting); *Feiner v. New York*, 340 U.S. 315, 321 (1951) (Black, J., dissenting). For cases in which Black declined to protect demonstrative conduct, see *Bell v. Maryland*, 378 U.S. 226, 318 (1964) (Black, J., dissenting); *Cox v. Louisiana*, 379 U.S. 559, 575 (1965) (Black, J., concurring and dissenting); *Brown v. Louisiana*, 383 U.S. 131, 151 (1966) (Black, J., dissenting); *Adderly v. Florida*, 385 U.S. 39 (1966); *Amalgamated Food Employees Union v. Logan Plaza, Inc.*, 391 U.S. 308, 327 (1968) (Black, J., dissenting); *Tinker v. Des Moines Sch. Dist.*, 393 U.S. 503, 515 (1969) (Black, J., dissenting). Snowiss notes that Black's later opinions involving demonstrative conduct did not address the value of the speech interest that the petitioners asserted. "Legacy of Justice Black," 232–33. This did not mean, however, that Black eschewed the use of discretion; he maintained in his contemporary writings that such cases required balancing. Black, *A Constitutional Faith*, 60–61. Presumably, he balanced the interests at issue but emphasized only those aspects of the cases that were dispositive, namely, the state interest in regulating such conduct.

90. Glendon Schubert, *The Constitutional Polity* (Boston: Boston University Press, 1970), 118–29.

91. Yarbrough, *Black and His Critics*, 184 (quoted); A. E. Dick Howard, "Mr. Justice Black: The Negro Protest Movement and the Rule of Law," *Virginia Law Review* 53 (1967): 1030–86; Hugo Black Jr., *My Father*, 243–45. For writings and decisions revealing that Black did not experience a shift toward jurisprudential conservatism in his later years, see Black, *A Constitutional Faith*, 43–53; *Orozco v. Texas*, 394 U.S. 324 (1969); *Schmerber v. California*, 384 U.S. 757, 773 (1966) (Black, J., dissenting); *Gilbert v. California*, 388 U.S. 263, 277 (1967) (Black, J., concurring in part, dissenting in part); *United States v. Wade*, 388 U.S. 218, 243 (1967) (Black, J., dissenting in part, concurring in part).

92. Tony Freyer, "Introduction," in *Justice Hugo Black and Modern America*, ed. Freyer, 1–27 (p. 5 quoted). See also Tony Freyer, *Hugo L. Black and the Dilemma of American Liberalism* (Glenview, Ill.: Scott, Foresman, 1990); Sheldon Hackney, "The Clay County Origins of Mr. Justice Black: The Populist as Insider," *Alabama Law Review* 36 (1985): 835–43.

93. See Chapter 3 above, notes 63–66 and accompanying text.

94. See note 65 above and accompanying text.

95. Stephen L. Wasby, *The Supreme Court in the Federal Judicial System*,

3d ed. (Chicago: Nelson-Hall Publishers, 1988), 170–77; David M. O'Brien, *Storm Center: The Supreme Court in American Politics* (New York: W. W. Norton, 1986), 163–72; Black, *A Constitutional Faith*, 18–20 (quoted); Ball and Cooper, *Of Power and Right*, 152.

96. Samuel P. Hays, *The Response to Industrialism, 1885–1914* (Chicago: University of Chicago Press, 1957), 116–39; Robert H. Wiebe, *The Search for Order, 1877–1920* (New York: Hill & Wang, 1967), 111–32, 206.

6

Felix Frankfurter, Social Interdependence, and Progressive Politics

Shortly before joining the United States Supreme Court, Felix Frankfurter maintained that the use a judge makes of the power of judicial review "is largely determined by two psychological considerations. It depends upon the judge's philosophy, conscious or implicit, regarding the nature of society; that is, on his theory of the clash of interests. This, in turn, will influence his conception of the place of the judge in the American constitutional system."[1] Through intimate involvement in a political movement that was national in scope but had its center in the North, Frankfurter developed a vision of society and politics that would inform his judicial philosophy. He received ample exposure to the social conditions leading to Progressivism, and he took full advantage of the political opportunities afforded him. With the Progressives, he attached enormous significance to the fact of social interdependence and came to believe that the major source of error in an urban-industrial age is the tendency to think abstractly or to isolate a phenomenon or idea from its social context. As a consequence of his fear of abstraction, he developed a strong preference for legislative and administrative, as opposed to judicial, resolutions to social controversies.

The Influence of Stimson, Roosevelt, and Croly

In view of Frankfurter's humble beginnings, few individuals would have prophesied his quick rise to influence and power in Progressive politics. Arriving from Vienna in 1894 at the age of twelve and unable to speak English, the young, Jewish immigrant became a resident of New York's Lower East Side. His assimilation into American society began when his parents placed him in Public School 25. His teacher, a middle-aged Irish woman named Miss Hogan, used corporal punishment to discipline her pupils and insisted that Felix's friends not speak to him in German. Later in life, he remarked, "It was wonderful for me that speaking English was enforced upon my environment in school, all thanks to Miss Hogan."[2]

Frankfurter especially appreciated the opportunities for social advancement that came with his command of the language of his adopted country. This skill, combined with a native intelligence and a desire to succeed, enabled him to enter the City College of New York and complete an intensive five-year program that combined high school and college. He then sought to further his education, this time at the Harvard Law School. He had a halting start but eventually excelled in his legal studies, ending up first in his class and an editor of the *Harvard Law Review*.[3]

After graduating in 1906, Frankfurter worked for a short time in a prestigious Wall Street law firm. While there, he received a call from Henry L. Stimson, United States attorney for the Southern District of New York. Stimson, who had joined Theodore Roosevelt's administration in the president's second term, was staffing his office. He acquired Frankfurter's name after "asking the deans [of Harvard, Yale, Columbia, and Cornell] what promising young men had recently come out of their schools." In view of the fact that, with few exceptions, the prestigious corporate law firms of the Northeast excluded Jews from partnerships, Frankfurter was wise to accept Stimson's offer to become assistant United States attorney.[4] His decision to enter public life proved to be much more than a sensible career move: he obtained access to the highest levels of power and came under the influence of two individuals who would do much to shape his political consciousness.

Both Stimson and Roosevelt shared the middle-class, Progressive concern over the twin threats to stability in an age of interdependence—irresponsible corporate wealth and militant organized labor—and they viewed an active state with a developed administrative apparatus as requisite means to ensure societal health. Roosevelt "sensed the growing frustrations of small businessmen, farmers, middle-class consumers, and industrial workers who properly blamed these new industrial titans for unfair methods of competition, inflation, monopolistic transportation rates, low wages, poor working conditions, and political corruption." He thus supported, among other measures, a law prohibiting corporations from contributing to political parties. He also secured legislation expanding the powers of the Interstate Commerce Commission (ICC) over the nation's railroads, created a Bureau of Corporations to investigate corrupt business practices, and acquired a reputation as a trustbuster with the spectacular prosecution of the Northern Securities Company under the Sherman Antitrust Act.[5]

Anticipating increased resistance from the business community toward his policies and seeking intelligent subordinates who could match in legal sophistication the members of the corporate bar, the president managed to lure Stimson away from the Wall Street firm of Root and Clark. Stimson accepted the federal post with the conviction that his work as United States attorney would prove more fulfilling than his corporate labors, which were "essentially devoted to the making of money." Federal service "was a good deal more worth while," he believed, since it enabled him to combat the circumstance "that whenever the public interest has come into conflict with private interests, private interest was more adequately represented than the public interest."[6]

As assistant United States attorney under Stimson, Frankfurter did not consistently participate in the politics of Progressivism. He devoted considerable time to the prosecution of petty smugglers, illegal gamers, counterfeiters, gunrunners, and importers of illegal immigrants. Four years of service in this post, however, ensured an adequate schooling in the new public philosophy. In numerous instances, he participated in important litigation that advanced the president's Square Deal. In addition to handling various antitrust suits, for example, he helped obtain the conviction of the New York Central Railroad and its traffic manager for transgressing the antirebating provisions of the Elkins Act. (Roosevelt had backed this law to strengthen the regulatory powers of the ICC.) Frankfurter also shared in Stimson's prosecution of the American Sugar Refining Company for corruption of the New York customhouse. The United States attorney and his aides took special satisfaction in the resulting convictions, since this company "had a well-deserved reputation for monopolistic behavior, extorting rebates from railroads, gouging customers, and purchasing politicians." Reflecting on his years under the tutelage of a man who believed that an active state is needed to secure corporate responsibility in an age of interdependence, Frankfurter gratefully acknowledged his indebtedness: "I don't see how a young fellow coming to the bar could possibly have had a more desirable, more deepening, and altogether more precious influence during his formative years than to be junior to Henry L. Stimson."[7]

Frankfurter continued his professional relationship with Stimson well after the two left the United States attorney's office in 1909. He followed Stimson into private practice for a brief time and worked on his mentor's ultimately unsuccessful campaign for the governorship of New York in 1910. The following year, when Stimson accepted President Taft's offer to become secretary of war, Frankfurter moved to the nation's capital to serve as Stimson's assistant. Formally, Frankfurter became the War Department's law officer for the Bureau of Insular Affairs; he had responsibility for legal matters involving waterpower issues and the nation's recently acquired overseas possessions and territories. He willingly accepted his share of the "white man's burden," helping to administer the spoils of the Spanish-American War and of the aggressive nationalism that had been a major component of the politics of Theodore Roosevelt.[8]

Aware of the power of nationalism as a mobilizing force, Stimson's protege found the work of Herbert Croly fascinating. Indeed, Frankfurter regarded *The Promise of American Life*, in which Croly sought to blend patriotism and domestic reform, as "the most powerful single contribution to progressive thinking." Croly accepted the Progressive premise, which followed from the insight concerning the interdependent nature of industrial society, that the widespread unfulfillment of America's promise of individual economic independence and prosperity and the consequent rise of class conflict stemmed from the anticompetitive practices and inflated prices of concentrated wealth. But Croly criticized those Progressive reformers who still paid obeisance to the Jeffersonian-Jacksonian shibboleth "Equal rights to all, special privileges for none." Those reformers sought "the restoration of American democracy to a former condition of purity and excellence" through trustbusting and attacks on the corrupt political machines that served as the local allies of big business. According to Croly, they failed to realize that concentrated power is inevitable in an age of interdependence. The conditions of the pre-industrial order, Croly argued, "cannot be restored," because businesses pursue concentration for greater efficiency and production (and, therefore, profits), while machine politics provide a means to meet the increased social demands that attend urbanism and industrialism.[9]

Yet to say concentrated authority is inevitable, Croly maintained, is not to say political and economic power need assume current forms.

Indeed, shorn of its excesses and properly reconstituted, aggregated power affords a means to end industrial conflict. Croly regarded large corporations as "desirable economic institutions" because of their demonstrated efficiency. He believed, however, that "the solution of the social problem [of class conflict] demands the substitution of a conscious social ideal" for the corporate lodestar of competitive individualism or economic liberty. America's situation requires "the subordination of the individual to the demand of a dominant and constructive national purpose," which he identified as "a morally and socially desirable distribution of wealth." Local machine politics cannot achieve this social ideal, because economic relationships transcend state boundaries in an interdependent social order. Only Hamiltonian means, or the "specialized leadership" of official, national action, can formulate a constructive national purpose. Specifically, Croly desired national supervision of concentrated wealth through a federal incorporation act and a developed administrative apparatus.[10]

The success of Croly's political program depended ultimately upon the leadership of the statesman. This "exceptionally able individual" effectively communicates to the public the importance of adopting measures that administrative expertise deems necessary. Stated more generally, the statesman educates the public that the fulfillment of America's promise demands "that individuals shall love and wish to serve their fellow countrymen, and . . . shall reorganize their country's economic, political, and social institutions and ideas."[11]

In view of Frankfurter's profound respect for Croly's thought and his prior involvement in Roosevelt's administration, it is not surprising that, while still a subordinate of President Taft, he decided to support "unashamedly, though not offensively," the Bull Moose revolt of 1912. Theodore Roosevelt's "New Nationalism" speech of August 1910 contained the substance of this third-party movement. That speech, in turn, bore unmistakably the impress of Croly's *Promise*. Roosevelt now called upon Republicans to abandon the Sherman Antitrust Act. "The way out," the former president argued, lay "not in attempting to prevent such combinations, but in completely controlling them in the interests of the public welfare."[12] This statement marked a departure from his earlier trustbusting feats (in which Stimson and Frankfurter had participated).

Croly's influence must not be overdrawn, however. As president, Roosevelt had for the most part accepted "these big aggregations [as] an inevitable development of modern industrialism"; he had reserved his use of the Sherman Act for combinations that resisted his attempts "to subordinate the big corporation to the public welfare" through regulation. Indeed, Croly acknowledged this use of national administration and leadership: "More than [that of] any other political leader, except Lincoln, [Roosevelt's] devotion to the national and democratic ideas is thorough-going and absolute." The president "exhibited his genuinely national spirit in nothing so clearly as his endeavor to give to men of special ability, training, and eminence a better opportunity to serve the public." Roosevelt appointed such men to office and supplied "them with an administrative machinery which would enable them to use their abilities to the best public advantage." Croly might have made special mention of Roosevelt's resolution of the anthracite strike of 1902, for this was the first time in American history that a president intervened in a major strike to secure arbitration and, through the vehicle of an independent commission, put an end to the conflict.[13]

After Roosevelt's "New Nationalism" speech, Frankfurter and Stimson pressed Taft to adopt the former president's economic program. Taft balked, however, and then initiated a new round of prosecutions under the Sherman Act. These actions greatly disappointed Frankfurter. They also led Roosevelt to begin his independent Bull Moose campaign, which would split the Republican party and clear the way for Woodrow Wilson's victory. Frankfurter became convinced that Taft "totally lack[ed] capacity for effective leadership in a modern democracy." Although "amiable and well-intentioned," the president "lack[ed] vision and decision. He [was] indeed the tragedy of opportunities of greatness unrealized." By contrast, the more Frankfurter studied Theodore Roosevelt's "administration . . . [and] the more [he] contrast[ed] Roosevelt] with Taft, the more permanent [Roosevelt's] labors seem[ed], the bigger his statesmanship."[14]

Wartime Administrator

If Frankfurter dreaded the prospect of Taft's victory at the polls, he was no more confident during the election of 1912 that Wilson's New Freedom could offer the nation effective leadership. "The Democratic party in its traditional ideals of government as to states['] rights, separation of powers, strict construction, etc.," he declared, "is not a fit instrument for working out the social and economic problems of the day." Frankfurter was especially concerned about "Wilson's sneer against government by experts," given that the country was "singularly in need . . . of the deliberateness and truthfulness of really scientific expertness." The candidate's expressed desire to use the Sherman Act to combat artificial mergers also alienated Frankfurter and other Bull Moosers.[15] Ironically, it was Wilson who would provide Frankfurter with several opportunities to participate in a Hamiltonian use of national leadership and administration for the resolution of social conflict.

At the request of the Wilson administration, Frankfurter remained for a time in the War Department to lend his expertise on waterpower matters. But, in 1913, he joined the Harvard Law School faculty to teach in the new area of administrative law. He regarded Cambridge as a better outlet for his talents and reformist impulses. Specifically, Frankfurter thought he could help build the law school into a "source of thought for the guidance of public men and the education of public opinion, as well as a source of trained men for public life." The identification and solution of social problems "require[d] adequate data, and correlated, persistent, prophetic thinking." "[W]e propose, determine, [and] legislate," he lamented, "without knowing enough." In addition, he thought necessary "a jurisprudence to meet the social and industrial needs of the time," lest reform efforts continue to die at the hands of judges who imported the principles of laissez-faire into constitutional language. The task of reforming public thinking "must be assumed by our law schools," what with their proximity to public power. Frankfurter anticipated that Harvard would lead the way in addressing the "economic and sociological" problems of the modern era because Roscoe Pound had recently joined the faculty. Pound's innovative writings on "sociological jurisprudence" emphasized the relevance of the social sciences to legislative and judicial decision making.[16]

Frankfurter also anticipated that his reformist efforts would involve much more than a refashioning of the Harvard law curriculum. Indeed, he planned for his years as a professor to be "not cloistered, but in the very current of the . . . national problems that [were] of greatest appeal to [him]." He succeeded in maintaining a connection to national politics, partly by becoming involved with the *New Republic*, a periodical advancing the principles of the New Nationalism. Frankfurter helped found the magazine in 1914, but, with Harvard beckoning, he declined editor-in-chief Herbert Croly's offer of an editorship. (The refusal greatly disappointed Croly, since he regarded Frankfurter as "the only man [he had] ever met who really [understood] Progressivism as [Croly understood] it.") Still, Frankfurter supplied the magazine with regular contributions, and he was more than willing to offer his advice at editorial conferences.[17]

In addition to nurturing the *New Republic*, Frankfurter hoped that he would aid the cause of reform by sharpening and making available his talent for administration, or, as he put it, his ability to "enlighten public selfishness and harmonize the public will." With Wilson in office, however, he expected that this New Nationalist attribute would be in demand only at the state level.[18]

Frankfurter's hopes rose in 1916 with a discernible change in Wilson's style of governing. Attempting to attract the old Bull Moose vote for the upcoming election, the president pressed Congress for several measures dear to the hearts of New Nationalists, including a suspension of antitrust laws in the export business. After witnessing Wilson's efforts, the editors of the *New Republic* went so far as to say that "there is hardly a shred left of the fabric of his Jeffersonian revival. With every development of his policy he has been approximating to the spirit and creed of a Hamiltonian nationalist." Frankfurter also welcomed these measures, although, along with the editors of the *New Republic*, he had concluded that a constructive nationalism required opposition to German ambitions on the Continent. American involvement in the war, he thought, would pave the way for a league of nations. War would also serve as the vehicle for significant domestic reform, given the national mobilization that a state of emergency would engender. Although the president had not yet called for American participation in the war, he came to support the notion of an international league. Frankfurter and his associates, however, suspected that Wilson's support for the league and his changes in domestic policy represented a temporary political conversion. They nevertheless supported Wilson's reelection, in considerable measure because of their belief in the unworthiness of his opponent, Charles Evans Hughes. In a statement that was disheartening to New Nationalists, Hughes had said that he regarded "the President as the administrative head of the government . . . [, not] the political leader and lawmaker of the nation."[19]

Shortly after the United States entered the war, Frankfurter became convinced of the genuineness of Wilson's nationalism. The president began to employ federal administrative expertise to organize the nation's vast industrial capacity for modern warfare. Although Frankfurter never placed Wilson's statecraft in the same league as Theodore Roosevelt's, now he at least viewed the president as a potential lever for reform rather than an impediment to progress.[20] Frankfurter also appreciated the Wilson administration's asking him to play a significant role in the wartime bureaucracy.

Frankfurter's administrative involvement began in early 1917, when the secretary of war, Newton Baker, asked him to resolve labor-management conflicts in the clothing industry. These conflicts centered on the deterioration of labor standards, which resulted from War Department supply contracts that failed to include worker safeguards. As Baker's principal civilian advisor, Frankfurter drafted a set of model contracts that required an eight-hour day, payment of equal wages for equal work (to protect women and minorities), acceptance of collective bargaining, and discontinuation of employment of children under sixteen. He also obtained an increase in the number of government inspectors charged with enforcing the new labor code of the clothing industry.[21]

Frankfurter became more deeply involved in wartime labor matters when he became secretary and legal counsel to the president's Mediation Commission. The president had established this body in September of 1917 to resolve major strikes threatening the war production program. Specifically, he had created the commission in response to a conflict in the copper mines of Arizona. There, miners who protested poor working conditions, low wages, and discrimination against union members confronted employers who not only refused to accede to the workers' demands but rejected unionism in any form. A division in the ranks of labor complicated the situation. The conservative, pro-war trade unionists of the American Federation of Labor, whom Samuel Gompers led, squared off against radical, antiwar miners, for whom the Socialist Party or the Industrial Workers of the World (IWW) provided leadership. Seeking to use the war to destroy worker organizations, the copper companies accused the miners of being pro-German and requested military assistance to escort strikebreakers and to battle workers. In the absence of clear instructions from the secretary of war, military commanders at times accommodated such requests. In instances when neither the federal nor the state government offered assistance, the mine owners resorted to vigilantism. The worst case took place in Bisbee, where the copper companies forced over one thousand protestors into cattle cars and then dumped them in the deserts of New Mexico without food or water. (The army ultimately rescued the miners and their supporters.)[22]

When the copper crisis became acute, the president sought to form a mediation commission. Frankfurter initially opposed this idea. He believed that resolution of the conflict required attention to the needs of antiwar, as well as conservative, labor elements, yet Wilson refused to deal with the radicals. Ultimately, Frankfurter agreed to serve, lest he have no influence on the negotiations. As it turned out, he came to be a major figure on a commission that included Secretary of Labor William B. Wilson and two representatives each from labor and business. The commission remained in Arizona for nearly two months, in large measure because of the intransigence of the mine owners. These individuals earned Frankfurter's ire: "These old bags, who have fought labor . . . and unions as poison for decades, now wrap themselves in the flag and are confirmed in their old biases and . . . obscurantism by a passionate patriotism. Gee—but it's awful and then they wonder at the fecundity of the IWW." Through hard-nosed tactics (including an occasional disingenuous threat that the government was considering taking over the mines), the commission managed what Frankfurter later characterized as a "rational and sensible settlement." Outwardly, the settlement appeared generous toward the miners. It provided for the rehiring of strikers, prohibited discrimination against union members, and established a grievance resolution procedure. The agreement, however, did not compel the companies to bargain with union representatives. Moreover, it banned strikes for the duration of the war and gave no protection to antiwar laborers. (The settlement specifically excluded "disloyal" strikers.) After the commission departed from Arizona, the labor situation quickly deteriorated. When a local contact informed Frankfurter of these developments, he still held to his nationalist faith and insisted that the situation merely required education and execution.[23]

A mix of successes and failures marked the remainder of Frankfurter's tenure on the Mediation Commission. The greatest disappointment involved the case of Thomas J. Mooney, a labor organizer, whom the state of California had sentenced to death for a San Francisco bombing that killed ten people and wounded forty. With a nationwide anarchist scare providing the backdrop for the case, the state had used perjured testimony to secure Mooney's conviction. Frankfurter wrote the president a report in which he urged Wilson to call for a retrial of Mooney, "whereby guilt or innocence may be put to the test of unquestionable justice." Wilson followed this advice and released the report. Sustained criticism, most notably from Theodore Roosevelt, greeted the commission secretary. The former president, who strongly supported the war and had lost a son in the conflict, charged Frankfurter with defending traitors to democracy and the United States. Frankfurter scolded his political hero for failing to realize the importance of preventing "ignorance or selfishness or prejudice from using the disguise of patriotism for ends alien to the national interest." This advice also would have benefited the governor of California, who, rather than allow a retrial, commuted Mooney's sentence to life imprisonment.[24]

Several commission successes, secured mostly in areas where unions had considerable political influence, mitigated Frankfurter's disappointment over the Mooney affair. While in California, the mediators negotiated settlements of conflicts in the oil fields of the southern portion of the state and in the Pacific-coast telephone industry. In the latter agreement, labor fared much better than it had in Arizona. The commission negotiated a wage increase, greater protection for union members, and limited collective bargaining. The mediators later obtained a similar agreement in Chicago's meatpacking plants. The commission also settled a strike in the spruce industry of the Pacific Northwest. The mediators succeeded in the latter instance in spite of complications stemming from Secretary Baker's decision (which he failed to communicate to the commission) to use soldiers and scabs to recommence production. The apparent lack of coordination among federal officials greatly disturbed Frankfurter; he believed that this incident indicated larger deficiencies in the wartime bureaucracy. "The confusion of authority [and] its haphazardness . . . cannot go on much longer," he said.[25]

Frankfurter had an opportunity to voice his concerns over bureaucratic inefficiencies when Baker asked him to write a report on the War Department's performance, in preparation for congressional hearings. Frankfurter surprised the secretary with his brutal honesty and far-reaching recommendations. He argued that Baker should concentrate solely upon military training and strategy and should leave labor matters and industrial production concerns to separate, expert administrators. The current War Industries Board (WIB), Frankfurter believed, was inadequate for organizing production, since it had little formal authority and could thus function only in an advisory capacity. He was equally critical of current labor policy, which gave responsibility for the adjustment of labor disputes to numerous concurrent and conflicting agencies.[26]

After prodding from Justice Louis Brandeis (whom Frankfurter enlisted in his cause), the president reorganized the WIB; he made it independent of the War Department and invested it with significant power. The board now had authority to commandeer plants, products, and equipment; to regulate prices and compensation; and to decide how best to meet the program needs of various government departments. Wilson also created the War Labor Policies Board (WLPB) to address the chaos in labor policy. He named Frankfurter as chairman, thus ensuring the presence of competence and fortitude on the board. But Frankfurter had to rely on his powers of persuasion to accomplish anything, since the board had no formal authority.[27]

Under Frankfurter's directorship, the WLPB prepared reports on workers' compensation, life insurance, night work by women, enforcement of state labor codes, and profiteering. The board also pursued national wage standards for various industries, so as to avoid the supposed inefficiencies that came with decentralized wage adjustments. Despite opposition from unions that benefited from a competitive market for labor and from industrialists who hoped to maintain low wages, Frankfurter organized joint employer–employee wage boards for a conference that promised greater wage uniformity. The war soon ended, however, and brought an end to the WLPB and its wage conference. The Armistice also undid the progress Frankfurter had made on union demands for an eight-hour day. He had concentrated on reforming the steel industry, a redoubt of anti-union sentiment. And, after considerable resistance, he had secured a "basic" eight-hour day, under which work done in excess of eight hours earned time and a half. Steel executives viewed this settlement as a war measure, however, and promptly returned to the old twelve-hour day with the war's end.[28]

An Enduring Faith in Politics and Administration

The Repudiation of Nationalism

Federal dismantling of the WLPB was part of a return to normalcy in governing that was as rapid as it was complete. There had been some discussion within the WIB of maintaining public supervision of industry after the war. "If the [WIB's] actions during the war had strengthened confidence in government supervision of business, fear of the collapse of the wartime boom, and of the consequent postwar inflation[,] led to early consideration of an extension of the WIB, or some similar agency." Nothing came of these discussions, however, in part because the members of the WIB believed that relaxation of the Sherman Act in a postwar situation was politically infeasible. An absence of executive leadership also contributed to the breakup of the wartime bureaucracy. The labor adjustment boards were particularly vulnerable, since the business community had never fully accepted them.[29]

Frankfurter viewed these developments with considerable apprehension. He had argued that "needless unemployment and misery and [the] inevitable lowering of labor standards" would follow federal abandonment of agencies concerned with production. He had also feared that "reactionary" individuals (that is, persons who "still regard[ed] labor as a commodity") would benefit at the expense of workers if the government dismantled the labor adjustment boards. More specifically, many employers would attempt to use the economic downturn following demobilization to destroy the gains workers had made during the war. As the adjustment boards disjoined and the labor market swelled with returning soldiers, Frankfurter could only stand by and watch. America, he thought, was fast becoming "the most reactionary country in the world."[30]

The outcome of the Versailles Peace Conference had already confirmed this observation for Frankfurter. He thought that the success of Wilson's initial peace formula (which included a removal of trade barriers, the reduction of armaments, self-determination in Central Europe, and a league of nations) depended upon the president's willingness to mobilize those forces on the Continent most receptive to his ideals, namely, left-wing trade unionists, socialists, and intellectuals. Frankfurter advised as much upon his return from a preconference information-gathering trip for Wilson. The president rejected this strategy, however. As the conference progressed, the soundness of Frankfurter's advice became apparent. Herbert Croly noted that the reactionary political forces with whom the President was cooperating had "not the slightest intention of writing anything but a punitive peace." Croly (and Frankfurter) believed that a lasting peace required Allied acceptance "of industrial democracy as the desirable alternative to the tyranny of Bolshevism or the anarchy of unredeemed capitalism." Wilson's "punic peace of annihilation," however, "merely [wrote] the future specifications for revolution and war."[31]

While it would be some time before the rise of fascism in Germany revealed the prescience of Croly's statement, events immediately demonstrated the soundness of Frankfurter's fears on the domestic front. Following demobilization, corporations attempted to slough off wartime regulations and government-sponsored labor agreements. Workers responded with strikes to secure these gains; in 1919, four million laborers joined picket lines in 3,600 confrontations with employers. Without the wartime labor boards, intolerance seemed to be the only remaining form of nationalism. With the Bolshevik victory in the background, strikers, along with communists, socialists, and critics of the economic status quo, became the focus of a massive "red scare." The Wilson administration exacerbated the situation with its Siberian invasion and anticommunist propaganda. Moreover, the government actively suppressed expressions of social discontent, using troops to crush a vast steel strike and to intimidate striking coal miners. Federal intolerance reached a climax with Attorney General A. Mitchell Palmer's infamous raids upon the offices and headquarters of left-wing groups in over thirty cities. The states matched this antiradical paranoia with criminal anarchism laws and "red flag" statutes that prohibited the teaching or the advocacy of economic change through force or violence. Frankfurter himself became a target of antiradical passions. Upon returning to Harvard, he received harsh criticism from Boston conservatives for his supposed leftist activities, including his wartime criticism of the Mooney conviction, his continued sensitivity toward the plight of labor, and his outspoken condemnation of the Palmer raids.[32]

The antiradical hysteria of the postwar era and the punitive nature of the Versailles treaty led many individuals who had viewed nationalism as a positive force for change to undertake a full reexamination of their political faith. The process of reevaluation actually began during the war, with the Wilson administration's suppression of antiwar organizations and periodicals and its use of propaganda to dehumanize the enemy. The administration's promotion and use of the Espionage Act resulted in thousands of convictions, of mostly socialists and antiwar unionists. Wilson's Committee on Public Information fostered an oppressive war psychology by mobilizing journalists, artists, and speakers to convince Americans that Germans were violent beasts and that all opposition to the war was part of a German plot. The editors of the *New Republic* suggested that Wilson's use of methods that were "autocratic and coercive" had made him too fierce a nationalist. Herbert Croly discussed the need to enlist "corporate bodies" as intermediaries to restrain the excesses of nationalism.[33]

With the disappointment of Versailles and the continuation of antiradical hysteria after the war, Croly went beyond his call for efforts to establish rival loyalties to the state: he advocated that Americans abandon nationalism. Conceding that he had failed to anticipate "what the psychology of the American people would be under the strain of fighting a world war," he despaired that "the most vital religion of the present day consists in the worship of the state."[34] By the end of 1922, he counseled against centralization in American political life and advised persons seeking " 'worthy political activity' to turn to their local communities. Local consumer and producer co-operatives, local schools, and local churches, he thought, might stem the trend toward 'national aggrandizement.' Such became the final way toward 'surely good Americanism' for the onetime prophet of the New Nationalism."[35]

Several years before Croly repudiated nationalism, Harold Laski, another associate of the *New Republic*, had put forth a more developed argument for political decentralization. Laski became an intimate of the magazine's staff after Frankfurter secured him an instructorship at Harvard in 1916. In a book dedicated to Frankfurter (and Justice Holmes), Laski remarked that the defining characteristic of modern life is the lack of a shared sense of membership in a social enterprise. He traced the absence of a sense of belonging or oneness to the scale, complexity, and specialization of the urban-industrial age: "Nothing is more simple in the great society than to be lost amongst one's neighbors; nothing is more dangerous to the attainment of the social end." Such rootlessness is cause for concern, since it is only through the conscious fulfillment of a social function or a sharing of responsibility for society's well-being "that the personality of man obtains its realization"; "no man can make his life a thing worthy of himself without the possession of [social] responsibility." Laski looked to decentralized politics as a means to restore a shared sense of purpose in modern life: politics necessarily involves responsibility, while decentralization promotes its democratization.[36]

Laski noted that a commendable desire for efficiency partly explained the recent "fetish of centralization." He maintained, however, that the actual effect of this policy is often abstraction and inefficiency. "The attempt to govern territories so diverse as Arizona and New York by uniform methods would be fraught with disaster," since the social problems involved frequently "are in fact not simple and general, but specialized and local." The incredible volume of business centralized authority undertakes in this situation forces government "to substitute for a real effort to grapple with special problems an attempt to apply [abstract] generalizations that are in fact irrelevant."[37]

Sounding themes similar to those of Croly and Laski, Frankfurter repudiated concentration in economic as well as political life. With the excesses of national authority and corporate resistance to regulation fresh in his mind, he now thought that concentration in industry or government usually portends disaster "because of the obfuscations and the arrogances which power almost invariably generates." Furthermore, he no longer believed as much in the efficiency of corporate bigness or the capacity of federal administration to address many of the nation's social and economic problems in anything other than abstract terms. While he was not "doctrinaire either about the curse of bigness or the blessings of littleness," he contended that "the Lord hasn't created anybody competent to rule wisely the kind of a thing the Chase bank" is. His "years in the government service and all the rest of the years watching its operations intently [had] made [him] less jaunty about devices for running the whole continent from Washington."[38]

Frankfurter conceded that "the national government will necessarily absorb more and more power" in a society where mutual dependencies extend beyond states or regions, but he did not regard the "ultimate organic nature of society" as "a decree of constitutional centralization." In his view, "despite the unifying forces of technology, the States for many purposes remain distinctive communities"; certain relationships remain local, and with the regional or local specialization that attends the nationalization of markets come problems and concerns that are unique to those areas. To entrust centralized authority with matters that are "not obviously of common national concern" would be to lose "a concreteness of interest" and "a localized knowledge of details" that only the states possess. "An extremely complicated society inevitably entails special treatment for distinctive social phenomena."[39]

Frankfurter was well aware that the genealogy of this critique of concentrated power extended beyond his associates at the *New Republic*: "[Louis] Brandeis saw it all with a seer's discernment more than twenty years ago and everything that he prophesied has been vindicated with an almost tragic uncanniness." Echoing Brandeis, Frankfurter now spoke of the importance of "states' responsibilities," or of regarding "the States as organs of legal control in determining most of our social relations." He saw state government as the appropriate vehicle for achieving "cooperative . . . action," or a shared sense of purpose in an industrial social order.[40]

A Predisposition toward Integration

In view of continued conflicts between capital and labor and the harsh suppression of expressions of social discontent, one wonders why Croly, Laski, and Frankfurter continued to believe in the attainability of social harmony. The explanation for this enduring confidence lies in the implications they (and other Progressives) drew from the concept of social interdependence. Interdependence, they thought, affords conditions for the resolution of the problems of an urban-industrial age, even though this social fact was the source of these very problems. As noted, Croly held that mutual dependence leads to social conflict when those who are economically disadvantaged come to view their situation as the product of external circumstance or of the behavior of others. And Laski maintained that increased interdependence fosters the breakdown of a sense of community: economic integration entails specialization, which, in turn, fragments an individual's vision of society and leads to a shrinkage of common experience. As noted in Chapter 3, however, the concept of interdependence entered serious social discourse in this country through the writings of Herbert Spencer, who used an organicist metaphor to illustrate the concept. According to the Progressive sociologist Albion Small, "Not merely in sociology, but in every department of knowledge, the organic concept is the most distinctive modern note." And many individuals who accepted this metaphor believed that the constituent elements of society are predisposed toward harmony or integration in the same way that the parts of a healthy organism tend toward cooperation and concert for the purpose of survival. The social fact of physical integration thus laid the groundwork for the reestablishment of moral integration or a sense of social solidarity; interdependence presents a potentiality, the actualization of which is merely a matter of technique.[41]

It was Croly's belief in a social predisposition toward integration that enabled him, in the first place (in *The Promise of American Life*), to advocate the effectiveness of national expertise and leadership. To suggest, as he did, that the increased empirical knowledge that comes with administration is sufficient to resolve social conflicts is to assume that conflict stems from ignorance of the mutual interests inherent in an interdependent relationship, rather than from permanent class conflict and perennial division over qualitative issues.[42] The belief that physical integration predisposes society toward harmony gave Croly cause not to abandon hope after he had witnessed the excesses of federal power. Rather than adopt a fatalistic view of class conflict, he searched for an alternative to nationalism and political centralization.

Croly's postwar movement toward Laski's politics of decentralization was not entirely a new departure for him. In *Progressive Democracy*, published in 1914, he had already identified individual participation in political and economic decision making as a means to cultivate a sense of social solidarity. In that work, he called for industrial democracy (that is, involvement of workers in managing the workplace), direct primaries, and a limbering of the procedure for amending the Constitution. Borrowing from John Dewey, he also argued that the nation's schools must make individuals aware of their responsibilities in an interdependent social order. In calling for a politics of decentralization, then, Croly merely extended his early belief that " 'the only way to prepare for social life is to engage in social life,' first in school and then as an active citizen.''[43]

If Croly came to see the relevance of political participation for restoring a shared sense of purpose in an organic social order, Laski acknowledged the importance of administrative expertise for achieving the same end. "[T]hrow[ing] the business of judgment upon the individual mind," Laski insisted, "does not mean that we shall not trust the expert. . . ." Given the complexities of specialized technologies and the difficulties involved in identifying sources of conflict and anticipating consequences of proposed remedies, administrative expertise is essential to governmental efforts to address the problems of an interdependent society. Croly and Laski believed that an established division of labor within government would reconcile the seemingly discordant values of participation and expertise: administrators would identify policy options and execute the public will, while accountable officials would assume responsibility for ultimate policy choices.[44]

Frankfurter revealed in his scholarly writings, especially his book *The Public and Its Government*, that his enduring faith in the attainability of social harmony likewise stemmed from a belief in a social predisposition toward integration. The organicist metaphor, from which Progressive theorists derived this social inclination, figured prominently in his work. He wrote with great insight about the sources of the interconnectedness, or organic nature, of society: In the early days of the republic, the "interdependencies of men were relatively narrow"; self-sufficiency characterized the American economy. The "almost magical industrial growth" that followed the Civil War, however, produced a "pervasive economic interdependence." Specifically, the laying of thousands of miles of railroad tracks extended the reach of market forces, pulling "into an articulate body the detached and sprawling members of our great domain." A "vast nervous system of telephones and telegraphs and wireless" heightened interdependence by "electrif[ying] the scattered regions of the country into a self-conscious whole." The specialization that attended market expansion further intensified these mutually dependent, economic relations. Quoting Senator Elihu Root, Frankfurter went so far as to say that this " 'division of labor . . . leaves each individual unable to apply his industry and intelligence except in cooperation with a great number of others whose activity, conjoined to his[,] is necessary to produce any useful result.' " To elucidate the social fact of interdependence, he invoked the organicist metaphor, quoting Justice Holmes: " 'In modern societies every part is related so organically to every other, that what affects any portion must be felt more or less by all the rest.' "[45]

With this organic social theory, Frankfurter could view politics simply as "a process of popular education—[as] the [integrative] task of adjusting the conflicting interests of diverse groups in the community, and bending the hostility and suspicion and ignorance engendered by group interests toward a comprehension of mutual understanding." Like his *New Republic* associates, he came to view active political participation as an integral part of this educative process. His new emphasis upon the value of state politics stemmed in part from his desire "to energize the people of the States"—to foster "the educative process of having the people in each State secure social conditions which are within the[ir] compass." "[T]he process of such an effort," he believed, "would give us a very different body of citizens than we now have," namely, citizens who are aware of their social obligations.[46]

For Frankfurter, the achievement of social harmony through the educative process of state politics seemed probable, if not inevitable. The legislatures of his native Northeast, especially that of Massachusetts, had led the rest of the nation in the development of more active and responsive government. Indeed, even "before 1900, with a few exceptions, Massachusetts had enjoyed in practice if not in form all the democratic innovations which progressives emphasized after 1900. It had, in addition, the most effective corporation laws in the nation, and it led the country in labor legislation." After conducting his own examination of the performances of the legislatures of New York, Connecticut, and Massachusetts in addressing the problems of an urban-industrial age, Frankfurter concluded: "In the unexciting pages of contemporary session laws, one finds that nothing that is human is alien to the legislator. Callings are regulated, conduct is prescribed and proscribed. Private enterprise is subjected to a network of public control. Practically the whole gamut of economic enterprise is under the state's scrutiny by an intricate administrative system of licenses, certificates, permits, orders, awards, and what not. The *Index to State*

Legislation . . . reads like an inventory of all man's secular needs and the means of their fulfillment.''[47]

As this passage demonstrates, Frankfurter, all of whose professional life to this point involved either the practice or study of administration, continued to argue, along with Croly and Laski, that administrative "*expertise* is indispensable" for the achievement of social harmony. Frankfurter made starkly manifest that this Progressive premise had profound implications for the judiciary: His arguments for a developed administrative apparatus included an extended analysis of the perceived inadequacies of what had been the prevailing system for performing the operational tasks of governing. He noted that "the intricate range of problems thrown up by our [interdependent] industrial civilization"—problems involving a "vast body of technical knowledge, more and more beyond the comprehension even of the cultivated"—"make heavy demands upon wisdom and omniscience" in governing. Legislators, "too distracted to acquire mastery of any political problem," have essentially passed responsibility for economic surveillance to the judiciary. But lawmakers are unwise to rely on courts because judicial machinery has proved to be "cumbersome and ineffective." Litigation, he pointed out, is "necessarily a sporadic process, securing at best merely episodic and mutilated settlements." The fact that judges must base their decisions "upon evidence and information limited by the narrow rules of litigation, shaped and intellectually influenced by the fortuitous choice of particular counsel," compounds the abstractness of the process. The doctrine of judicial notice, which permits judges to draw upon common knowledge or information found in reference books, supplements counsels' briefs. But Frankfurter viewed this doctrine as "a tenuous basis for informing the judicial mind."[48]

Judicial invalidation of legislative efforts to respond to the problems of a complex, urban-industrial society, Frankfurter believed, is the most injurious consequence that the institutional deficiencies of the judicial process has spawned. Before laissez-faire became a discredited social philosophy, certain judges saw "[s]imple terms, like 'liberty,' and phrases like 'without due process of law' [as] the instruments for judgment upon the whole domain of economic, social, and industrial life." Oblivious to the social facts that induced economic legislation, courts applied the Constitution's less precise terms "as barriers against piecemeal efforts of adjustment through legislation to a society permeated by the influence of technology, large-scale industry, progressive urbanization, and the general dependence of the individual on economic forces beyond his control.''[49]

"By the pressure of experience," Frankfurter noted, "legislative regulation of economic and social activities turned to administrative instruments." In contrast to a regulatory system dependent upon "the occasional explosion of a lawsuit," a developed administrative apparatus provides "the continuity of study, the slow building up of knowledge, the stimulation of experiments, [and] the initiative and enforcement" that are essential to intelligent adjustments of competing social claims. Administrative agencies are able to provide such continual oversight because they have authority to conduct investigations independent of the claims of litigants (although one responsibility of agencies is to adjudicate complaints). Not confined to rules of evidence designed for an adversary relationship involving only two parties, agencies can take social context into account in executing legislative mandates. This broad authorization for fact gathering takes on added significance when one considers that, besides the executive duty of surveillance, administrators have the quasi-legislative task of translating a general legislative standard into regulations adapted to a myriad of instances. A fact-finding process superior to that of courts helps make for policy that is not abstract. Through the withdrawal of matters from courts and their reassignment to administrative devices partaking "of all three forms of governmental power—legislative, executive, and judicial''—government is able to "move with freedom in modern fields of legislation, with their great complexity and shifting facts, calling for technical knowledge and skill in administration." Frankfurter noted that this "break with the simplicities of the past" had occurred when Congress created the ICC in 1887. But the onetime New Nationalist recalled that Theodore Roosevelt had erected "[a]ctive regulation . . . into a political philosophy [that] has been pursued by all succeeding Presidents.''[50]

Although Frankfurter anticipated that a developed administrative apparatus would greatly improve our system of government, he believed that "even this [was] not enough." He noted that party, as well as court, dominance marked the old system for performing the operational tasks of governing. Partisan staffing of federal offices had led, over time, to a situation in which the public "suffered from too many mediocre lawyers appointed for political considerations." "The theoretical defense of the spoils system could hardly withstand its practical results''; this defense featured "a distorted belief in the simplicity of government" that became wildly anachronistic with an increase in social interdependence. If this nation was to avoid "the terrible mischief of an administrative system based on patronage," he believed, it must learn from the example of the British civil service and its well-compensated, career administrators. He looked forward to a time when American institutions of higher learning would serve as training schools for public servants and when a career in public administration would carry prestige sufficient to attract the nation's most talented persons.[51]

New Deal Advisor

Frankfurter did his utmost to improve the quality of American administration; he used his position and influence as a Harvard professor to populate federal and state bureaucracies with his best students. In 1928, he was pleased to find the newly elected governor of New York, Franklin Roosevelt, receptive to his advice and recommendations. Frankfurter exploited and cultivated this relationship. (The contact between the men actually began in the final years of the Wilson administration, when Roosevelt was assistant secretary of the Navy.) Besides offering advice on executive and judicial appointments, Frankfurter provided suggestions on a range of policy issues. He also sent Roosevelt a copy of *The Public and Its Government*, in the hope that the governor would appreciate Frankfurter's discussion of the importance of administrators in managing an interdependent economy.[52]

When Roosevelt became president in the midst of the depression, Frankfurter once again became influential in national politics. He continued to render invaluable service to Roosevelt as an informal personnel officer. His influence over staffing decisions extended to numerous agencies, including the Departments of Interior, Labor, and Agriculture and, especially, the new Agricultural Adjustment Administration. But reality did not quite correspond with the over-drawn impression of those who complained that Frankfurter had created a "vast, cohesive, personal empire that spread throughout the executive branch, the White House, and the independent regulatory commissions, where hundreds of Harvard Law School graduates . . . jumped instantly to the command of their former professor."[53]

Frankfurter did not limit his service to the New Deal to staffing federal agencies. Although he declined Roosevelt's offer to become solicitor general (because he thought the position would be too confining), he managed to influence national policy as an informal advisor to the president. Initially, he held little sway with the Roosevelt administration. The brain trust, a triumvirate of Columbia University professors (Raymond Moley, Adolph A. Berle Jr., and Rexford Guy Tugwell), was largely responsible for the president's first "hundred days." These men viewed concentrated wealth as an inevitable feature of modern society, and they asserted the need for centralized direction from Washington. No longer believing in the politics of the New Nationalism, Frankfurter attempted unsuccessfully to persuade the president to abandon this legislative tack and to adopt a plan for economic recovery and reform that emphasized significant spending for public works and taxation to curb corporate bigness.[54]

When the policies of the brain trust proved ineffective and encountered Supreme Court opposition, Frankfurter took advantage of the opportunity. He "became a source of almost constant intellectual stimulation" for the president and "placed his personal mark upon more pieces of legislation in 1935 than any other adviser." Frankfurter was a principal author of the Social Security Act (whose unemployment insurance provision featured decentralized administration), the Revenue Act of 1935 (which penalized bigness and discouraged holding companies), and the Public Utility Holding Company Act (which limited the size of corporate properties). At least one observer, marveling over the Harvard professor's policy successes, declared him "the most influential single individual in the United States."[55]

Frankfurter also counseled the president on how best to wage the effort to enlarge the Supreme Court. Before Roosevelt announced the plan, Frankfurter had stated publicly that it "would be self-defeating" to tamper with the Court's size to discipline those justices opposed to the New Deal. He offered nothing but (private) encouragement and advice, however, when the president (consulting neither Congress nor Frankfurter) went forward with the strategy. In correspondence with Roosevelt, Frankfurter now accepted the necessity of significant action to "save the Constitution from the Court and the Court from itself." But he urged Roosevelt to be candid about the plan's rationale: he thought the president should cease using the rhetoric of efficiency and focus on the abuse of judicial authority. Frankfurter revealed the depth of his disagreement with the Court's behavior in a draft letter to Justice Brandeis: "Tampering with the Court is a very serious business. Like any major operation it is justified only by the most compelling considerations. But no student of the Court can be blind to its long course of misbehavior. I do not relish some of the implications of the President's proposal, but neither do I relish victory for the subtler but ultimately deeper evils inevitable in the victory for Hughes and the Butlers and their successors.'' In view of Brandeis's profound differences with the president on this issue, Frankfurter chose not to send the letter.[56]

Roosevelt's efforts to restructure the Court through the regular process of appointment were, of course, much less controversial. After appointing Hugo Black in 1937 and Stanley Reed the following year, the president was able to place Frankfurter on the bench. This opportunity arose with the untimely death of Justice Cardozo in 1938. Initially, the president sought a westerner for the slot. However, certain members of Roosevelt's administration, many Harvard Law School alumni, and countless Frankfurter acquaintances pushed for the Harvard professor's appointment. (Frankfurter himself was deeply, albeit indirectly, involved in the lobbying effort.) Ultimately, Roosevelt relented. He regarded Frankfurter as an eminently qualified nominee who would bring a scholar's breadth to the bench. Frankfurter was also deserving of reward for his counsel on the Court-packing plan, his advice on economic legislation, and his expertise on personnel matters. The Senate concurred in the president's choice, confirming Frankfurter by unanimous voice vote twelve days after Roosevelt announced the nomination. ''For almost a quarter of a century Frankfurter would serve with brilliance, dedication, and persuasiveness, almost—but not quite—equaling the performance of Hugo L. Black in lasting impact and influence.''[57] He would establish his reputation, however, as the jurisprudential opposite of his colleague from Alabama.

Notes

1. Felix Frankfurter, *Mr. Justice Holmes and the Supreme Court* (1938; reprint, Cambridge: Harvard University Press, Belknap Press, 1961), 56.

2. Harlan B. Phillips, ed., *Felix Frankfurter Reminisces* (New York: Reynal, 1960), 4–5 (quoted); Michael E. Parrish, *Felix Frankfurter and His Times: The Reform Years* (New York: Free Press, 1982), 10–13.

3. Phillips, ed., *Felix Frankfurter Reminisces*, 10–19, 26–27; Parrish, *Felix Frankfurter and His Times*, 14–22.

4. Phillips, ed., *Felix Frankfurter Reminisces*, 37–39 (p. 39 quoted); Parrish, *Felix Frankfurter and His Times*, 27; Jerold S. Auerbach, *Unequal Justice: Lawyers and Social Change in Modern America* (New York: Oxford University Press, 1976), 29.

5. Parrish, *Felix Frankfurter and His Times*, 25 (quoted); Richard Hof-

stadter, *The American Political Tradition and the Men Who Made It* (New York: Vintage Books, 1973), 286–99; George Mowry, *Theodore Roosevelt and the Progressive Movement* (Madison: University of Wisconsin Press, 1946).

6. Parrish, *Felix Frankfurter and His Times*, 27; Hofstadter, *Age of Reform*, 162–63 (quoted).

7. Parrish, *Felix Frankfurter and His Times*, 29–32, 34 (p. 30 quoted); Phillips, ed., *Felix Frankfurter Reminisces*, 41–49 (p. 48 quoted).

8. Phillips, ed., *Felix Frankfurter Reminisces*, 50–53; Parrish, *Felix Frankfurter and His Times*, 39–46; Samuel P. Hays, *The Response to Industrialism, 1885–1914* (Chicago: University of Chicago Press, 1957), 163–87.

9. Charles Forcey, *The Crossroads of Liberalism: Croly, Weyl, Lippmann, and the Progressive Era, 1900–1925* (New York: Oxford University Press, 1961), 6 (quoting Frankfurter), 25–32; Herbert Croly, *The Promise of American Life* (1909; reprint, Indianapolis: Bobbs-Merrill, 1975), 1–9, 20–24, 124–25, 149–53, 362 (p. 149 quoted); Archibald MacLeish and E. F. Prichard Jr., eds., *Law and Politics: Occasional Papers of Felix Frankfurter, 1913–1938* (New York: Harcourt, Brace, 1939), 305–13; Phillips, ed., *Felix Frankfurter Reminisces*, 88; R. Jeffrey Lustig, *Corporate Liberalism: The Origins of Modern American Political Theory, 1890–1920* (Berkeley: University of California Press, 1982), 123–24.

10. Croly, *Promise of American Life*, 23, 124, 139, 269, 351–98 (pp. 362, 139, 23, 125 quoted); Lustig, *Corporate Liberalism*, 212–16; Forcey, *Crossroads of Liberalism*, 33–44.

11. Croly, *Promise of American Life*, 439–54 (pp. 449, 439 quoted).

12. Phillips, ed., *Felix Frankfurter Reminisces*, 53–54 (quoted); Parrish, *Felix Frankfurter and His Times*, 56; Forcey, *Crossroads of Liberalism*, 130–34 (quoting Roosevelt, p. 133).

13. Hofstadter, *American Political Tradition*, 292–93 (quoting Roosevelt); James Weinstein, *The Corporate Ideal in the Liberal State: 1900–1918* (Boston: Beacon Press, 1968), 67; Forcey, *Crossroads of Liberalism*, 127–34; Croly, *Promise of American Life*, 170 (quoted); Lustig, *Corporate Liberalism*, 150–51.

14. Joseph P. Lash, ed., *From the Diaries of Felix Frankfurter* (New York: W. W. Norton, 1975), 105–6, 108, 112, 115 n. 1, 116–18 (pp. 112, 116, 117 quoted); Parrish, *Felix Frankfurter and His Times*, 24, 53–55; Weinstein, *Corporate Ideal in the Liberal State*, 83–84, 139–71; Forcey, *Crossroads of Liberalism*, 130–31; Hofstadter, *American Political Tradition*, 301–4; Mark Silverstein, *Constitutional Faiths: Felix Frankfurter, Hugo Black, and the Process of Judicial Decision Making* (Ithaca: Cornell University Press, 1984), 60 n. 23; Phillips, ed., *Felix Frankfurter Reminisces*, 54–55, 64–66, 88.

15. Parrish, *Felix Frankfurter and His Times*, 56 (quoting Frankfurter); Weinstein, *Corporate Ideal in the Liberal State*, 161–66; Lustig, *Corporate Liberalism*, 201–8.

16. Phillips, ed., *Felix Frankfurter Reminisces*, 73–75, 165–68, 80–83 (pp. 80–81 quoted); Parrish, *Felix Frankfurter and His Times*, 57–61.

17. Phillips, ed., *Felix Frankfurter Reminisces*, 82 (quoted), 88–93; Parrish, *Felix Frankfurter and His Times*, 67 (quoting Croly); Forcey, *Crossroads of Liberalism*, 169–217.

18. Phillips, ed., *Felix Frankfurter Reminisces*, 82–84, 167 (p. 82 quoted).

19. Forcey, *Crossroads of Liberalism*, 221–63 (editors quoted, p. 255; Hughes quoted, p. 261); Parrish, *Felix Frankfurter and His Times*, 78–80, 82; James T. Kloppenberg, *Uncertain Victory: Social Democracy and Progressivism in European and American Thought, 1870–1920* (New York: Oxford University Press, 1986), 363–64.

20. Weinstein, *Corporate Ideal in the Liberal State*, 216–20; Phillips, ed., *Felix Frankfurter Reminisces*, 67–69, 72–73, 75–76, 130.

21. Phillips, ed., *Felix Frankfurter Reminisces*, 113–15; Parrish, *Felix Frankfurter and His Times*, 84–85.

22. Phillips, ed., *Felix Frankfurter Reminisces*, 119, 135–36; Parrish, *Felix Frankfurter and His Times*, 87–90.

23. Parrish, *Felix Frankfurter and His Times*, 91–95 (Frankfurter quoted, p. 93); Phillips, ed., *Felix Frankfurter Reminisces*, 115–21 (p. 120 quoted).

24. Phillips, ed., *Felix Frankfurter Reminisces*, 130–35 (p. 132 quoted); Parrish, *Felix Frankfurter and His Times*, 97–100 (Frankfurter quoted, p. 99).

25. Parrish, *Felix Frankfurter and His Times*, 95–97, 101 (Frankfurter quoted); Phillips, ed., *Felix Frankfurter Reminisces*, 121–29.

26. Parrish, *Felix Frankfurter and His Times*, 102–04.

27. Ibid., 104–7; Weinstein, *Corporate Ideal in the Liberal State*, 214–28; Stephen Skowronek, *Building a New American State: The Expansion of Administrative Capacities, 1877–1920* (New York: Cambridge University Press, 1982), 234–41.

28. Parrish, *Felix Frankfurter and His Times*, 108–14; Weinstein, *Corporate Ideal in the Liberal State*, 228–29; Phillips, ed., *Felix Frankfurter Reminisces*, 139–42.

29. Weinstein, *Corporate Ideal in the Liberal State*, 230–33.

30. As quoted in Parrish, *Felix Frankfurter and His Times*, 116–17.

31. Ibid., 114–15; Forcey, *Crossroads of Liberalism*, 285, 289, 290–91 (Croly quoted); Phillips, ed., *Felix Frankfurter Reminisces*, 163–64.

32. Parrish, *Felix Frankfurter and His Times*, 118–28; Phillips, ed., *Felix Frankfurter Reminisces*, 168–77; Robert K. Murray, *Red Scare: A Study in National Hysteria, 1919–1920* (Minneapolis: University of Minnesota Press, 1955); William Preston, *Aliens and Dissenters: Federal Suppression of Radicals, 1903–1933* (Cambridge: Harvard University Press, 1963).

33. Weinstein, *Corporate Ideal in the Liberal State*, 214–17, 233–47; Forcey, *Crossroads of Liberalism*, 288, 282 (editor and Croly quoted, respectively).

34. Forcey, *Crossroads of Liberalism*, 301 (Croly quoted); Kloppenberg, *Uncertain Victory*, 370–73.

35. Forcey, *Crossroads of Liberalism*, 301–2. Cf. Kloppenberg, *Uncertain Victory*, 391–92.

36. Forcey, *Crossroads of Liberalism*, 90, 230; Harold J. Laski, *Authority in the Modern State* (1919; reprint, New York: Archon Books, 1968), 89–109 (pp. 108, 107, 91 quoted); Harold J. Laski, *A Grammar of Politics* (New Haven: Yale University Press, 1925), 241–91; Kloppenberg, *Uncertain Victory*, 405.

37. Laski, *Authority in the Modern State*, 69–81, 90–91 (pp. 91, 75, 76, 78 quoted).

38. As quoted in Parrish, *Felix Frankfurter and His Times*, 208, 210.

39. Philip B. Kurland, ed., *Felix Frankfurter on the Supreme Court: Extrajudicial Essays on the Court and the Constitution* (Cambridge: Harvard University Press, Belknap Press, 1970), 260, 255 (quoted); Felix Frankfurter, *The Public and Its Government* (New Haven: Yale University Press, 1930), 48–49, 66, 72, 74, 121–22.

40. Parrish, *Felix Frankfurter and His Times*, 208 (Frankfurter quoted); Felix Frankfurter to Herbert Croly, 8 January 1923, Papers of Felix Frankfurter, Library of Congress, Manuscript Division (hereafter cited as FFP), Box 50.

41. Quandt, *From the Small Town to the Great Community*, 17–20, 23–25, 27 (Small quoted), 86–87; Cynthia Eagle Russett, *The Concept of Equilibrium in American Social Thought* (New Haven: Yale University Press, 1966), 59–61, 80–82; Boskoff, "From Social Thought to Sociological Theory," 11–14; Chapter 3 above, notes 48–53 and accompanying text.

42. Lustig, *Corporate Liberalism*, 136–38, 143, 151–53, 170, 175.

43. Herbert Croly, *Progressive Democracy* (New York: Macmillan, 1914); Kloppenberg, *Uncertain Victory*, 358, 376 (quoted), 383, 402, 406–8, 413; Forcey, *Crossroads of Liberalism*, 155–57; Quandt, *From the Small Town to the Great Community*, 82–84, 95, 97–101, 149–57.

44. Laski, *Authority in the Modern State*, 108 (quoted); Kloppenberg, *Uncertain Victory*, 383–86, 390–91; Quandt, *From the Small Town to the Great Community*, 137–49.

45. Frankfurter, *Public and Its Government*, 15, 23, 32–33; Frankfurter, *Mr. Justice Holmes and the Supreme Court*, 74, 103. See also ibid., 62, 95–96; MacLeish and Prichard, eds., *Law and Politics*, 347; Kurland, ed., *Felix Frankfurter on the Supreme Court*, 37, 260, 296.

46. Frankfurter, *Public and Its Government*, 161 (quoted); Felix Frankfurter to Herbert Croly, 8 January 1923, FFP, Box 50 (quoted); Philip Elman, ed., *Of Law and Men: Papers and Addresses of Felix Frankfurter, 1939–1956* (New York: Harcourt, Brace, 1956), 362; Max Freedman, ed., *Roosevelt and Frankfurter: Their Correspondence, 1928–1945* (Boston: Little, Brown, 1967), 39.

47. Richard M. Abrams, *Conservatism in a Progressive Era: Massachusetts Politics, 1900–1912* (Cambridge: Harvard University Press, 1964), 2–3 (quoted); Morton Keller, *Affairs of State: Public Life in Late Nineteenth Century America* (Cambridge: Harvard University Press, Belknap Press, 1977), 322, 329, 479, 526, 537; Geoffrey Blodgett, *The Gentle Reformers: Massachusetts Democrats in the Cleveland Era* (Cambridge: Harvard University Press, 1966); Frankfurter, *Public and Its Government*, 10–31, 83, 85, 113–14 (p. 29 quoted).

48. Frankfurter, *Public and Its Government*, 161, 127, 35, 149 (emphasis in original); Felix Frankfurter and James M. Landis, "The Compact Clause of the Constitution: A Study in Interstate Adjustments," *Yale Law Journal* 34 (1925): 707; Kurland, ed., *Felix Frankfurter on the Supreme Court*, 553, 189. See also ibid., 187–90; MacLeish and Prichard, eds., *Law and Politics*, 217.

49. Kurland, ed., *Felix Frankfurter on the Supreme Court*, 151; Frankfurter, *Mr. Justice Holmes and the Supreme Court*, 62.

50. Frankfurter, *Public and Its Government*, 149, 72–73, 87–88, 78, 25–26. See also ibid., 83–86; Felix Frankfurter, "The Task of Administrative Law," *University of Pennsylvania Law Review* 75 (1927): 614–19.

51. Frankfurter, *Public and Its Government*, 112, 114, 149–50, 147, 142. See also ibid., 136–45, 163–64; MacLeish and Prichard, eds., *Law and Politics*, 241–42.

52. Parrish, *Felix Frankfurter and His Times*, 199–202.

53. Ibid., 199–203, 220–30 (pp. 228–29 quoted); MacLeish and Prichard, eds., *Law and Politics*, 238–49; G. Edward White, "Felix Frankfurter, the Old Boy Network, and the New Deal: The Placement of Elite Lawyers in Public Service in the 1930s," *Arkansas Law Review* 39 (1986): 631–67.

54. Parrish, *Felix Frankfurter and His Times*, 202–19.

55. Ibid., 220–37, 243–51, 263 (pp. 246, 220–21 quoted).

56. MacLeish and Prichard, eds., *Law and Politics*, 28; Freedman, ed., *Roosevelt and Frankfurter: Their Correspondence*, 380–81; Felix Frankfurter to Louis Brandeis, 26 March 1937, FFP, Box 28. See also Parrish, *Felix Frankfurter and His Times*, 268, 270; Nelson Lloyd Dawson, *Louis D. Brandeis, Felix Frankfurter, and the New Deal* (Hamden, Conn.: Archon Books, 1980), 139–53.

57. Abraham, *Justices and Presidents*, 217–19 (p. 217 quoted); Parrish, *Felix Frankfurter and His Times*, 273–78.

7

The Passive Jurisprudence of Justice Frankfurter

"In No Instance Is This Court the Primary Protector of Liberty"

Even before becoming a member of the United States Supreme Court, Felix Frankfurter had articulated the major outlines and aims of his constitutional jurisprudence. Indeed, his writings on the role of the judiciary were central to his Progressivism. His judicial philosophy was the logical outgrowth of a view of society and politics that emphasized the danger of abstract thinking in an age of interdependence and regarded the judiciary as prone to abstraction. Frankfurter sought to reduce radically the Court's influence in American life by reassigning the task of balancing competing constitutional claims to institutions he believed to be better equipped to account for the relatedness of the urban-industrial age.

The concept of justiciability marked the starting point of Frankfurter's jurisprudence. Before the Court renders a decision, he insisted, the record must present "a *case*—a live, concrete, present controversy between litigants"; the Court's "judgment upon a constitutional issue can be invoked only when inextricably entangled with a living and ripe lawsuit." Attentiveness to justiciability forces judges, in deciding whether to prohibit governmental action, to contemplate the specific consequences that would attend such an exercise of judicial power. Put another way, justiciability compels the Court "to rely more on the impact of reality than on abstract unfolding." By contrast, constitutional decision making that is "unrelated to actualities" leads necessarily to "dialectics" and "sterile conclusions."[1]

Present actualities would not be relevant, of course, if judges were to view constitutional limitations as absolute, or as stated in terms that preclude judicial consideration of matters of time and circumstance. Frankfurter provided an excellent measure of the depth of his Progressive-inspired fear of abstraction (and of his distance from his colleague Hugo Black) when he argued that the "most important, single sentence in American Constitutional Law" is "John Marshall's . . . utterance that 'it is a *constitution* we are expounding.' " This sentence—"the background against which [Marshall] projected every inquiry as to specific power *or specific limitation*"—counsels that the Constitution is "not a detached document inviting scholastic dialectics." Rather, it is a document "designed for the unknown future" and is thus "bounded with outlines not sharp and contemporary, but flexible and prophetic." "[T]he difficulties that government encounters from law," Frankfurter insisted, "do not inhere in the Constitution. They are due to the judges who interpret [and misconstrue] it." "The Constitution of the United States," he elaborated, "is not a printed finality but a dynamic process." "The great judges are those to whom the Constitution is not primarily a text for interpretation but the means of ordering the life of a progressive people."[2]

While fidelity to the concept of justiciability and an appreciation of the Constitution's amplitude are necessary elements of judicial statecraft, they are not sufficient, in Frankfurter's view. Believing that judicial decisions are inherently abstract, he felt compelled to move beyond admonitions against constitutional dialectics and promote the virtual withdrawal of the judiciary from constitutional decision making: "In sitting in judgment upon the attempts of others to meet the perplexities of society, it makes all the difference how aware one is of the . . . organic relation of abstractly unrelated transactions." The "restricted nature of the judicial process," however, renders the Court singularly unqualified to weigh most competing constitutional claims; such issues are usually "enmeshed in larger public issues beyond the Court's reach of investigation." The process of social adjustment must thus fall increasingly *"to the legislature as interests and activities in society become more and more interdependent.* The considerations which thus prompt legislation and the intricate, dubious materials out of which laws are written bring into sharp focus the *duty of deference to legislative determinations* demanded from the revisory process called adjudicative." In short, judicial statesmanship involves, "*above all*, the humility not to set up [one's] own judgment against the conscientious efforts of those whose primary duty is to govern"; it demands the indulgence of "every presumption of validity on behalf of challenged powers." Specifically, the Court "may interpose its veto only when there is no reasonable doubt about the constitutional transgressions."[3]

Like many other Progressives, Frankfurter drew upon James Bradley Thayer in maintaining that the Court's role in constitutional matters is to invalidate only those laws that no rational person could regard as constitutional. Indeed, he viewed Thayer as "the great master of constitutional law." He also identified the piece in which Thayer articulated the rational-basis standard as "the most important single essay" on the subject of "the place of the judiciary . . . in relation to constitutional questions."[4]

While Hugo Black denounced Thayer's standard (or, at least, its blanket application) as approximating "legislative omnipotence," Frankfurter defended the standard because he, like Thayer, repudiated judicial hegemony over the resolution of constitutional controversies. In rejecting judicial supremacy, Frankfurter borrowed Holmes's observation that "legislatures are ultimate guardians of the liberties and welfare of the people in quite as great a degree as the courts." "In no instance," Frankfurter argued, "is this Court the primary protector of . . . liberty."[5]

Frankfurter's integrative conception of society inspired his confidence that the constitutional oath administered to legislators provides sufficient cause to disregard the suspicion of political majorities that informs the notion of judicial supremacy. He revealed his belief in the importance of political participation for achieving social integration when he contended that a mischievous consequence of exercises of judicial review is a "general weakening of the sense of legislative responsibility" to adhere to constitutional strictures. He spoke optimistically of "the gain of having experience demonstrate the fallacy of a law after the Supreme Court has sustained its constitutionality." And he took the supposed higher regard for liberties exhibited in England, a country with no tradition of judicial review, as evidence that social integration and judicial review are, to some degree, mutually exclusive. Viewing politics freed of judicial interference as integrative and judicial decision making as inherently abstract, he endorsed Ernst Freund's statement that " 'gross miscarriages of justice are probably less frequent in legislation than they are in the judicial determination of controversies.' " Not surprisingly, then, judicial retrenchment from the legislative arena became for Frankfurter a moral, as well as a professional, obligation.[6]

Frankfurter advocated a nominal judicial presence in the administrative realm also. He conceded that "administrative law is inextricably bound up with constitutional law," in view of "the danger of arbitrary conduct in the administrative application of legal standards." But he did not regard judicial review as the primary means of preventing bureaucratic abuses of power.

> Ultimate protection is to be found in the people themselves, their zeal for liberty, their respect for one another and for the common good—a truth so obviously accepted that its demands in practice are usually overlooked. But safeguards must also be institutionalized through machinery and processes. These safeguards largely depend on a highly professionalized civil service, an adequate technique of administrative application of legal standards, a flexible, appropriate and economical procedure . . . , easy access to public scrutiny, and a constant play of criticism by an informed and spirited bar.[7]

In cases involving constitutional claims against administrative determinations, Frankfurter believed, the judiciary should not deviate from the role it assumes in the legislative arena; in either realm, judges should merely police the perimeters of rational policy. After joining the Court, Frankfurter employed the rational-basis test in his opinion for the Court in a case involving a Fourteenth Amendment challenge to an oil proration order of the Texas Railroad Commission.

> A controversy like this always calls for [a] fresh reminder that *courts must not substitute their notions of expediency and fairness for those which have guided the agencies to whom the formulation and execution of policy have been entrusted.* . . . Certainly in a domain of knowledge still shifting and growing, and in a field where judgment is therefore necessarily beset by the necessity of inferences bordering on conjecture even for those learned in the art, it would be presumptuous for courts, on the basis of conflicting expert testimony, to deem the view of the administrative tribunal, acting under legislative authority, offensive to the Fourteenth Amendment.[8]

In a statement revealing the extraordinary degree of deference that the rational-basis standard prescribes, he noted that the Court must accept the agency's judgment "even in the face of convincing proof that a different result would have been better."[9]

One might argue, with regard to judicial review of administrative determinations, that Frankfurter exceeded Thayer's counsel of deference. Thayer, after all, limited his analysis to the relationship between the judicial and legislative branches. Frankfurter might have responded, however, that Thayer wrote before the appearance in this country of a developed administrative apparatus. (Congress had created the ICC only six years before Thayer published his influential essay.) Moreover, one has reason to believe that Thayer would have concurred with Frankfurter. Federal and state legislators are not alone in their legal obligation to support the Constitution; Article 6 of that document requires that "all executive and judicial Officers, both of the United States and of the several States, shall be bound by Oath or Affirmation . . . to support this Constitution."

Frankfurter was also deferential toward administrators in nonconstitutional cases, specifically, controversies over the meaning of empowering statutes and the validity of administrative findings of fact. Judges inclined to limit their review in constitutional cases might justify a more active role in nonconstitutional contexts by noting the comparative ease with which legislators are able to correct judicial errors. Frankfurter argued, however, that the availability, as well as the scope, of judicial review (constitutional issues apart) depends entirely upon legislative mandate. Shortly before his appointment, the Court had affirmed the availability of judicial review of administrative findings in the absence of express congressional authorization. When the Court ruled similarly in 1944, Frankfurter dissented forcefully:

> Except in those rare instances . . . when a judicial trial becomes a constitutional requirement . . . , whether judicial review is available at all, and, if so, who may evoke it, under what circumstances, in what manner, and to what end, are questions that depend for their answer upon the particular enactment under which judicial review is claimed. . . . There is no such thing as a common law of judicial review in federal courts. . . . [T]he manner in which Congress has distributed responsibility for the enforcement of its laws between courts and administrative agencies runs a gamut all the way from authorizing a judicial trial *de novo* of a claim determined by the administrative agency to denying all judicial review and making administrative action definitive.[10]

In the absence of statutory review provisions, then, Frankfurter believed that administrative orders are final (unreviewable) even though they may lack supporting evidence and contravene the will of the legislature. By contrast, Justice Black regarded "[s]uch a sweeping contention for administrative finality [as] out of harmony with the general legislative pattern of administrative and judicial relationships."[11]

In instances where Congress provided for judicial oversight, Frankfurter refused to join "the ranks of those seeking to broaden the scope
of review over agency action" through broad notions of statutory
interpretation or resort to doctrines heightening judicial scrutiny of
administrative findings of fact. He believed that an uncomplicated
understanding of statutory interpretation, which reserves to the judiciary all matters of law no matter how esoteric or technical the
concepts involved, would thrust federal courts into fields beyond their
capacities. In reviewing a decision of the Tax Court, for example,
he observed:

> [T]he construction of documents has for historic reasons been deemed to
> be a question of law in the sense that the meaning is to be given by judges
> and not by laymen. But this crude division between what is "law" and
> what is "fact" is not relevant to the proper demarcation of functions as
> between the Tax Court and the reviewing courts. To hold that the Circuit
> Court of Appeals, and eventually this Court, must make an independent
> examination of the meaning of every word of tax legislation, no matter
> whether the words express accounting, business or other conceptions
> peculiarly within the special competence of the Tax Court, is to sacrifice
> the effectiveness of the judicial scheme designed by Congress especially
> for tax litigation to an abstract notion of "law" derived from the merely
> historic function of courts generally to construe documents, including leg-
> islation.[12]

He preferred to leave the interpretation of complex, specialized concepts to those possessing appropriate expertise.[13]

Another way in which Frankfurter limited the scope of judicial
review over agency action was to adhere strictly to the usual legislative
requirement for finality of administrative findings, namely, the existence of "substantial evidence." The substantial evidence rule requires that "as long as the court [can] find that some evidence in the
record support[s] the administrative finding (the testimony of one
witness, for instance), and even though the preponderance of the
evidence [is] contrary (the testimony of fifty other witnesses), the
court ha[s] to affirm." Some of Frankfurter's colleagues sought to
expand the scope of review through resort to the jurisdictional-fact
doctrine: the notion that judges "have a special responsibility for the
finding of facts upon which the jurisdiction of an administrative tribunal
depend[s]." Rejecting this doctrine, Frankfurter argued that "[a]naly-
sis is not furthered by speaking of . . . findings as 'jurisdictional' and
not even when—to adapt a famous phrase—jurisdictional is softened

by a *quasi.* 'Jurisdiction' competes with 'right' as one of the most deceptive of legal pitfalls.''[14]

A study of Supreme Court review of National Labor Relations Board (NLRB) orders covering the period 1941–45 revealed the effect of the jurisprudential differences among Frankfurter and some of his brethren: "[I]t is clear that the Board's string of victories [in seventeen out of twenty-one cases] has not been due solely to the Supreme Court's general attitude toward administrative agencies. For a majority of the members of the Court—and particularly Justices Black, Douglas, Murphy, and Rutledge, the Justices who have been the most unwilling to set aside anything which the Labor Board has done—have during these same four terms of court shown considerably less reluctance to reverse the [ICC], an administrative agency at present out of favor in so-called liberal circles.'' Specifically, Black voted to sustain the NLRB in twenty of twenty-one cases; he upheld the ICC in only two of fifteen. By contrast, Frankfurter voted to sustain the NLRB in sixteen out of twenty-one cases, while he supported the ICC in thirteen out of sixteen.[15]

Congressional passage of a directive for expanded judicial review represented the only instance in which Frankfurter would set aside his usual deference toward administrative directives. He did not allow his preference for administration to thwart the legislative will. In *Universal Camera Corp. v. NLRB*, for example, the Court sought to determine whether the Taft-Hartley Act, passed in 1947, had expanded the scope of review of NLRB orders. The court of appeals had held that the act's ambiguous new language—" 'substantial evidence *on the record considered as a whole*' ''—merely codified the traditional substantial-evidence rule. However, the "Act, passed over President Harry S. Truman's veto by the first Republican-controlled Congress since the New Deal, was the product of a decade of conservative attacks on the pro-labor ideology of the Labor Board. More than any other New Deal administrative agency, the Labor Board had become a lightening rod for conservative skepticism about claims to administrative expertise.'' Conservatives, indeed, "hoped both to reduce judicial deference to claims of agency expertise and to re-legalize the process of administrative regulation.'' In overturning the lower court's ruling, Frankfurter (the Court's spokesman) took account of the circumstances surrounding the law's passage:

The legislative history of these Acts demonstrates a purpose to impose a responsibility which has not always been recognized. Of course, it is a statute[,] and not a committee report, which we are interpreting. But the fair interpretation of a statute is often "the art of proliferating a purpose" . . . revealed more by the demonstrable forces that produced it than by its precise phrasing. The adoption in these statutes of the judicially-constructed "substantial evidence" test was a response to pressures for stricter and more uniform practice, not a reflection of approval of all existing practices. To find the change so elusive that it cannot be precisely defined does not mean it may be ignored.[16]

The implications of this ruling were profound, since the Administrative Procedure Act of 1946, which had extended review to "[a]ny person suffering legal wrong because of *any agency action*," also contained the revised substantial-evidence test.[17]

In view of *Universal Camera*, it is tempting to conclude that an increased skepticism concerning the Progressive notion of administrative expertise, which had appeared in academic and political circles after the Second World War, affected Frankfurter.[18] His willingness to expand the scope of review at the insistence of Congress, however, did not indicate a loss of faith in administration. Recall that when he denied the permissibility of judicial review in the absence of a legislative mandate, he still defended the right of Congress, should it see fit, to authorize even *de novo* review of agency findings.

Frankfurter made a similar argument in his earlier testimonial to administrative expertise, *The Public and Its Government*, where he conceded that the "expert should be on tap, but not on top." As noted in the preceding chapter, he was primarily concerned in that work with releasing administration from legislative restraints. ("In this country we have been so anxious to avoid the dangers of having the expert on top that we suffer from a strong reluctance to have him on tap.") But he also made a point of saying that he was "far from suggesting that the conquest of science calls for a new type of oligarchy, namely, government by experts." To resolve the tension between accountability and expertise, he adopted the same division of labor Croly and Laski had endorsed: "[W]hile expert administrators may sift out issues, elucidate them, bring the light of fact and experience to bear upon them, the final determinations of large policy must be made by the direct representatives of the public and not by the experts."[19] Determining the degree to which administration should be subject to judicial oversight would qualify as a most important exercise of policy.

Frankfurter's consistent willingness to show deference to the constitutional determinations of elected and appointed officials was the clearest indication of his continued preference for legislative and administrative, over judicial, resolutions of social controversies. Congress cannot control directly the standard of review used in such cases, and Frankfurter never repudiated Thayer's rational-basis test. Indeed, he remained unmoved even in the face of arguments asserting the centrality of the First Amendment's freedoms to democratic government.[20]

"Limits There Are Even to This Essential Condition of a Free Society"

A Flirtation with Heightened Review

Frankfurter's passivity in First Amendment cases surprised many people. In his scholarly writings on Justices Holmes and Brandeis, he had expressed views consistent with what jurists would later call the "preferred freedoms" doctrine: the belief that First Amendment rights (as opposed to economic liberties) are fundamental to democratic government and that legislation infringing upon these liberties should be presumed unconstitutional. (Recall the discussion of this doctrine in chapter 5 above.) In his book on Justice Holmes, he said that "social development is an effective process of trial and error only if there is the fullest possible opportunity for the free play of the mind. [Holmes] therefore attributed very different legal significance to those liberties which history has attested as the indispensable conditions of a free society from that which he attached to liberties which derived merely from shifting economic arrangements." Similarly, he wrote of Brandeis's teachings:

> Truth and knowledge can function and flourish only if error may freely be exposed. And error will go unchallenged if dogma, no matter how widely accepted or dearly held, may not be questioned. Man must be allowed to challenge it by speech or by pen, not merely by silent thought. Thought, like other instincts, will atrophy unless formally exercised. If men cannot speak or write freely, they will soon cease to think freely. Limits there are, of course, even to this essential condition of a free society. But they do not go beyond the minimum requirements of an imminent and substantial threat to the very society which makes individual freedom significant.[21]

Yet it is apparent that Frankfurter was not entirely comfortable with a heightened standard of review in First Amendment cases; he praised

Holmes and Brandeis as much for their attention to social context as for their recognition of the special nature of the freedoms of the First Amendment. In the same way that Holmes and Brandeis eschewed abstraction in cases involving economic liberties, he noted, they refused (as much as the process of judicial fact-finding would allow) to divorce their free speech opinions from the realities of life. "[Holmes] did not erect [even the freedom of speech] into a dogma of absolute validity[,] nor did he enforce it to doctrinaire limits." Brandeis likewise "refused to make freedom of speech an absolute." "[H]is opinions reveal consciousness of a world for which no absolute is adequate. It is a world of more or less, of give and take, of live and let live. Interests clash, but no single one must yield. Self-willed power must be guarded against, but government cannot be paralyzed. And even liberty has its bounds." "Facts, not catchwords, are [Brandeis's] sovereigns."[22]

Frankfurter's insight into the causes and consequences of economic interdependence, and his marked concern over the dangers of abstract thinking in the modern age, enabled him to recognize that the move toward interdependence increased the complexity of (and, therefore, the potential for judicial abstraction with respect to) nonproprietarian, as well as proprietarian, relations. A city dweller for most of his life, he was no stranger to the closeness and, therefore, the complications of urban living. In *The Public and Its Government*, he had discussed how advances in communications technology attended the move toward interdependence and heightened the relatedness of life. And in the same and other works, he had noted the differentiation or heterogeneity (and thus the divergent values and lifestyles) of an interdependent social order. Although differentiation heightens societal complexity, Frankfurter believed, the social division of labor provides a means to understand and address the perplexities, noneconomic as well as economic, of an urban-industrial age: he viewed the development of expertise in governance and the social sciences as a very fortunate consequence of the process of social differentiation.[23] Possessing an abiding faith in administrative and scientific expertise, he had only to be confronted with the task of ruling on First Amendment issues to embrace the same deferential standard of review that he had advocated for use in cases involving economic liberties.

Proponent of Deference

Very early in his tenure, Frankfurter revealed that his fear of judicial abstraction outweighed his belief in the need for a heightened standard of review in First Amendment cases. Indeed, his opinion for the Court in *Minersville School District v. Gobitis* serves as a primer for his earlier scholarly writings on judicial abstraction and on the role of the Court in an interdependent social order.[24] The case involved a constitutional challenge to the decision of a local school board to require the children of Jehovah's Witnesses to participate in a daily flag-salute ceremony. The Witnesses argued that their religion forbids involvement in such ceremonies (because the act of saluting the flag constitutes worship of a graven image) and that the First Amendment's free-exercise-of-religion clause precludes governmental efforts to compel participation.

In his majority opinion, Frankfurter noted that the Court had the unenviable task of "reconcil[ing] two rights in order to prevent either from destroying the other." "[E]very possible leeway should be given to the claims of religious faith," he argued, "because in safeguarding conscience we are dealing with interests so subtle and so dear." Yet "the manifold character of man's relations may bring his conception of religious duty into conflict with the secular interests of his fellow man." In *Gobitis*, the Court was "dealing with an interest inferior to none in the hierarchy of legal values. National unity is the basis of national security." In deciding "whether the legislatures of the various states and the authorities in a thousand counties and school districts of this country are barred from determining the appropriateness of various means to evoke that unifying sentiment without which there can ultimately be no liberties, civil or religious," Frankfurter expressed a profound fear of judicial abstraction:

> To stigmatize legislative judgment in providing for this universal gesture of respect for the symbol of our national life in the setting of the common school as a lawless inroad on that freedom of conscience which the Constitution protects, would amount to no less than the pronouncement of pedagogical and psychological dogma in a field where courts possess no marked and certainly no controlling competence. The influences which help toward a common feeling for the common country are manifold. Some may seem harsh and others no doubt are foolish. Surely, however, the end is legitimate. And the effective means for its attainment are still so uncertain and so unauthenticated by science as to preclude us from putting the widely prevalent belief in flag-saluting beyond the pale of legislative power. . . .
>
> The wisdom of training children in patriotic impulses by those compulsions which necessarily pervade so much of the educational process is not for our independent judgment. . . . [T]he courtroom is not the arena

for debating issues of educational policy. It is not our province to
choose among competing considerations in the subtle process of securing
effective loyalty to the traditional ideals of democracy, while respecting
at the same time individual idiosyncracies among a people so diversified
in racial origins and religious allegiances. So to hold would in effect make
us the school board for the country. That authority has not been given to
this Court, nor should we assume it.[25]

Frankfurter noted that social scientists were uncertain about "the
best way to train children for their place in society"; he maintained,
nevertheless, that the Court should defer on this matter to legislative
and administrative judgment. Echoing Thayer, he opined that the
Court must sustain governmental action, "[e]xcept where the trans-
gression of constitutional liberty is too plain for argument." Here,
officials might rationally believe that a mandatory flag salute law
does not violate the First Amendment. As in his scholarly writings,
Frankfurter defended judicial deference by rejecting the notion of
judicial supremacy: "Judicial review . . . is a fundamental part of our
constitutional scheme. But to the legislature no less than to courts is
committed the guardianship of deeply-cherished liberties."[26]

Drawing upon his writings once more, Frankfurter complemented
his discussion of the dangers of judicial abstraction with commentary
concerning the value of decentralized politics for achieving social
integration. He suggested that, should the flag-salute regulation prove
ill advised, the political process would correct itself: "Where all
the effective means of inducing political changes are left free from
interference, education in the abandonment of foolish legislation is
itself a training in liberty. To fight out the wise use of legislative
authority in the forum of public opinion and before legislative assemblies rather than to transfer such a contest to the judicial arena serves to
vindicate the self-confidence of a free people." Judicial deference thus
strengthens societal regard for individual liberties. "[S]o long as the
remedial channels of the democratic process remain open and unobstructed . . . , personal freedom is best maintained . . . when it is
ingrained in a people's habits and not enforced against popular policy
by the coercion of adjudicated law."[27]

Only Justice Stone dissented. He was "not persuaded that [the
Court] should refrain from passing upon the legislative judgment 'as
long as the remedial channels of the democratic process remain open
and unobstructed.' " In sharp contrast to Frankfurter, he expressed
skepticism concerning both the motives behind the flag-salute require-

ment and the integrative nature of society and politics: "History teaches us that there have been but few infringements of personal liberty by the state which have not been directed, as they are here, in the name of righteousness and the public good, and few which have not been directed, as they are now, at politically helpless minorities." Stone objected to the school district's attempt "to coerce these children to express a sentiment which, as they interpret it, they do not entertain, and which violates their deepest religious convictions." And he showed little fear of judicial abstraction in suggesting that "there are other ways to teach loyalty and patriotism which are the sources of national unity, than by compelling the pupil to affirm that which he does not believe and by commanding a form of affirmance which violates his religious convictions."[28]

Stone argued that precedent supported his rejection of Frankfurter's deferential standard of review. He suggested that footnote 4 of his own opinion for the Court in *United States v. Carolene Products Co.* had called for heightened judicial scrutiny in cases like the present one. In that footnote, which served an important part in the development of the "preferred freedoms" doctrine, he had said:

> There may be narrower scope for operation of the presumption of constitutionality when legislation appears on its face to be within a specific prohibition of the Constitution, such as those of the first ten amendments, which are deemed equally specific when held to be embraced within the Fourteenth.
>
> It is unnecessary to consider now whether legislation which restricts those political processes which can ordinarily be expected to bring about repeal of undesirable legislation, is to be subjected to more exacting judicial scrutiny under the general prohibitions of the Fourteenth Amendment than are most other types of legislation. . . .
>
> Nor need we enquire whether similar considerations enter into review of statutes directed at particular religious . . . or national . . . or racial minorities . . . ; whether prejudice against discrete and insular minorities may be a special condition, which tends seriously to curtail the operation of those political processes ordinarily to be relied upon to protect minorities, and which may call for a correspondingly more searching judicial inquiry.[29]

Applying these ideas to the facts of *Gobitis*, Stone concluded that the Jehovah's Witnesses are "such a small minority entertaining in good faith a religious belief, which is such a departure from the usual course of human conduct, that most persons are disposed to regard it with little toleration or concern." To relegate the balancing of the interests at stake to the political process would thus amount to "the surrender of the constitutional protection of the liberty of small minorities to the popular will."[30]

Before the Court announced *Gobitis*, Frankfurter had attempted to persuade Stone to join the majority. In a memorandum, Frankfurter had emphasized the similarities in their opinions: "I am aware of the important distinction which you skillfully adumbrated in your footnote 4 (particularly the second paragraph of it) in the *Carolene Products Co.* case. I agree with that distinction; I regard it as basic. I have taken over that distinction in its central aspect, however inadequately, in the present opinion by insisting on the importance of keeping open all those channels of free expression by which undesirable legislation may be removed, and keeping unobstructed all forms of protest against what are deemed invasions of conscience." Frankfurter was disingenuous to suggest that he agreed with the philosophy of footnote 4. Stone believed that an open political process is a necessary, rather than a sufficient, jurisprudential aim. In contrast to Frankfurter, he emphasized the points of paragraphs 1 and 3 of his footnote, namely, the need for judicial protection of the Bill of Rights and of minorities. Frankfurter did not overlook this jurisprudential difference. In an unsuccessful attempt to persuade Stone to repudiate heightened judicial scrutiny, he stressed the danger of judicial abstraction: "What weighs with me strongly in this case is my anxiety that, while we lean in the direction of the libertarian aspect, we do not exercise our judicial power unduly, and as though we ourselves were legislators[,] by holding with too tight a rein the organs of popular government. In other words, I want to avoid the mistake comparable to that made by those whom we criticized when dealing with the control of property."[31]

Frankfurter revealed the depth of his commitment to judicial deference in First Amendment cases when in 1943 the Court overruled *Gobitis* in response to another challenge from Jehovah's Witnesses. Scholars had roundly criticized *Gobitis*, and several justices had begun to have second thoughts about the ruling. Indeed, Justices Black, Douglas, and Murphy went so far as to indicate formally their willingness to overrule it. In a short dissent to a 1942 decision sustaining municipal license taxes on booksellers as applied to Jehovah's Witnesses, the three men reflected: "This case is but another step in the direction which *Minersville School District v. Gobitis* . . . took against the same religious minority, and is a logical extension of the principles upon which that decision rested. Since we joined in the opinion in the

Gobitis case, we think this is an appropriate occasion to state that we now believe that it also was wrongly decided." They noted that "our democratic form of government, functioning under the historic Bill of Rights, has a high responsibility to accommodate itself to the religious views of minorities, however unpopular and unorthodox those views may be."[32]

In *West Virginia State Board of Education v. Barnette*, Black, Douglas, and Murphy helped form a majority to declare compulsory flag-salute laws unconstitutional. In his opinion for the Court, Justice Jackson departed somewhat from Stone's *Gobitis* dissent and invoked the free speech (as opposed to the free exercise) clause of the First Amendment: a compulsory flag salute "requires affirmation of a belief and an attitude of mind." Government cannot force individuals to express beliefs without violating the freedom of speech. "To sustain the compulsory flag salute, we are required to say that a Bill of Rights which guards the individual's right to speak his own mind, left it open to public authorities to compel him to utter what is not in his mind."[33]

In an impassioned dissent, Frankfurter reiterated the jurisprudential considerations that had motivated him in *Gobitis*. He began with a very personal statement of belief in judicial deference:

> One who belongs to the most vilified and persecuted minority in history is not likely to be insensible to the freedoms guaranteed by our Constitution. Were my purely personal attitude relevant I should wholeheartedly associate myself with the general libertarian views in the Court's opinion, representing as they do the thought and action of a lifetime. But as judges we are neither Jew nor Gentile, Catholic nor agnostic. . . . It can never be emphasized too much that one's own opinion about the wisdom or evil of a law should be excluded altogether when one is doing one's duty on the bench. The only opinion of our own even looking in that direction that is material is our opinion whether legislators *could in reason* have enacted such a law.[34]

Once again, he supported his call for deference with a discussion of the danger of judicial abstraction:

> Conscientious scruples, all would admit, cannot stand against every legislative compulsion to do positive acts in conflict with such scruples. We have been told that such compulsions override religious scruples only as to major concerns of the state. But the determinations of what is major and what is minor itself raises questions of policy. For the way in which men equally guided by reason appraise importance goes to the very heart

of policy. Judges should be very diffident in setting their judgment against that of a state in determining what is and what is not a major concern, what means are appropriate to proper ends, and what is the total social cost in striking the balance of imponderables.[35]

As in *Gobitis*, Frankfurter argued that the Court had no reason to reject deference and thus risk abstraction, because effective means of inducing political change were present already in the normal course of electoral and interest-group politics: "All channels of affirmative free expression are open to both children and parents." Undoubtedly, the Jehovah's Witnesses were less sanguine about the prospects for change in the law and found less than inspiring the justice's extended quotation of Thayer's statement on the virtues of judicial modesty under a democratic form of government.[36]

One scholar suggests that Frankfurter's disavowal of what would become known as the "preferred freedoms" doctrine was not inevitable: "[U]nder different conditions, [the justice] quite conceivably could have elaborated Holmes's doctrine of clear-and-present-danger into a truly First-Amendment-protective doctrine, as his opponents later did." Had someone other than Stone (for whom Frankfurter had little regard) been the author of the *Carolene Products* footnote and "had the issue not been first raised in such dramatic form in the *Gobitis* case" (which evoked "[Frankfurter's] patriotism" and "his devotion to the symbols of American life"), Frankfurter might have accepted the heightened standard of review that he had acknowledged in his writings on Holmes and Brandeis. "But in the context of the *Gobitis* case, and with Stone representing the opposition, such an outcome was impossible for [him]." Frankfurter's failure to weigh economic and civil liberties differently in *Gobitis* "boxed him into a corner" from which he could not escape in subsequent cases.[37]

This argument is problematic, however. Frankfurter had demonstrated earlier, with his wartime criticism of the Mooney conviction, that he did not view patriotism and the protection of individual liberties as mutually exclusive. Yet, even if one assumes that *Gobitis* accorded with his patriotic sentiments, it is doubtful that these impulses and his dislike of Stone fully explain his rejection of a heightened standard of review in First Amendment cases. It is telling that in post-*Gobitis* free speech cases, which involved neither patriotic considerations nor Stone's immediate influence, Frankfurter continued to fret over the danger of judicial abstraction. Indeed, considering his scholarly treatment of the danger of abstraction in nonproprietarian rights controversies, and given his belief in the integrative nature of society and politics, it would have been peculiar had he *not* resorted to the same deferential standard of review that he regarded as appropriate for economic liberty cases. Rather than box himself into a corner in *Gobitis*, then, his opinion served to declare the relevance of his writings on judicial abstraction to the nonproprietarian rights questions that came to dominate the Court's docket. He would work in subsequent opinions to stem the Court's move toward a heightened standard of review in First Amendment cases (and toward what he viewed as certain judicial abstraction).

Frankfurter commenced this effort in *Bridges v. California*. Recall that this case involved a state judge's contempt citation of a local labor leader whose writings had supposedly interfered with the administration of justice. Speaking for the majority, Justice Black maintained, not only that the "clear and present danger" test was the relevant standard for decision, but that this "working principle [requires] that the substantive evil must be extremely serious and the degree of imminence extremely high before utterances can be punished." The Court held that, while interference with the maintenance of the orderly and fair administration of justice is a serious substantive evil, the charge that Bridges's statements even *tended* to interfere with justice (which was all the state required for contempt) was an exaggeration.[38]

In his dissent, Frankfurter suggested that the Court improperly applied the "clear and present danger" test; contrary to the original purpose of that standard, the majority had made an abstraction of the First Amendment by neglecting the circumstances surrounding the controversy. "Rights must be judged in their context and not *in vacuo*." He conceded that "freedom of expression . . . is indispensable to the democratic process" because it "alone assures the unfolding of truth." But the justices had to realize that "[f]ree speech is not so absolute or irrational a conception as to imply paralysis of the means for effective protection of all the freedoms secured by the Bill of Rights." "Freedom of expression can hardly carry implications that nullify the guarantees of impartial trials." The "clear and present danger" test, Frankfurter believed, in no way encourages judges to lose sight of these considerations. "The phrase 'clear and present danger' is merely a justification for curbing utterance where that is warranted by the substantive evil to be prevented." As Justice Brandeis said, "[the test] 'is a rule of reason. . . . Like many other rules for human conduct, it can be applied correctly only by the exercise of good judgment.' " Frankfurter interpreted Brandeis's statement to mean that First Amendment controversies are "to be solved not by short-hand phrases but by consideration of the circumstances of the particular case." He chided the majority for failing to realize that "[the Court's] duty is not ended with the recitation of phrases that are a short-hand of a complicated historic process."[39]

While the existence of the "clear and present danger" test might tempt some judges to substitute rhetoric for informed judgment, such an occurrence is not inevitable, nor did it happen in *Bridges.* Justice Black predicated his ruling upon an examination of the facts before the Court. Frankfurter may have thought Black could have provided a more detailed treatment of the surrounding circumstances. But the disparaging tone of Frankfurter's dissent was due most likely to his disagreement with the majority's standard of review. To insist that the state demonstrate an "extremely high degree of imminence" of an "extremely serious evil"—a requirement that followed from the majority's implicit weighting of the First Amendment claim—is necessarily to scrutinize carefully the determination of the local judge. By contrast, Frankfurter suggested that the Court should merely ascertain whether "the state court was *out of bounds* in concluding that [a person's] conduct offends the free course of justice."[40]

Frankfurter was loath to exceed the rational-basis test, because of the danger of judicial abstraction. As in the flag-salute cases, he expressed great doubt about the Court's capacity to acquire enough information to balance adequately the conflicting interests in the case: "We are, after all, sitting over three thousand miles away from a great state, without intimate knowledge of its habits and its needs, in a matter which does not cut across the affirmative powers of the national government. Some play of policy must be left open to the states in the task of accommodating individual rights and the overriding public well-being which makes those rights possible. How are we to know whether an easy-going or stiffer view of what affects the actual administration of justice is appropriate to local circumstances?"[41]

As a majority of the Court continued to move toward the "preferred freedoms" doctrine, Frankfurter became increasingly strident in his dissents. In *Martin v. City of Struthers*, the Court struck down as a violation of the freedoms of speech and press a municipal ordinance against ringing the door bell or otherwise summoning the occupants of any residence in order to distribute handbills, circulars, or other advertisements. A Jehovah's Witness who had distributed an announcement of a religious meeting challenged the ordinance. Speaking for the majority, Black noted that "[d]oor to door distribution of circulars is essential to the poorly financed causes of little people.'' He then argued that ''[t]he dangers of distribution can so easily be controlled by traditional legal methods [i.e., the law of trespass], leaving to each householder the full right to decide whether he will receive strangers as visitors, that stringent prohibition can serve no purpose but that forbidden by the Constitution, the naked restriction of the dissemination of ideas.''[42]

In his dissent, Frankfurter once again scolded the Court for engaging in abstraction. ''The Constitution cannot be applied in disregard of the external circumstances in which men live and move and have their being.'' ''Therefore, neither the First nor the Fourteenth Amendment is to be treated by judges as though it were a mathematical abstraction, an absolute having no relation to the lives of men.'' He lectured his brethren on the complexities of life in an urban-industrial age: ''The habits and security of life in sparsely settled rural communities, or even in those few cities which a hundred and fifty years ago had a population of a few thousand, cannot be made the basis of judgment for determining the area of allowable self-protection by present-day industrial communities. The lack of privacy and the hazards to peace of mind and body caused by people living not in individual houses but crowded together in large human beehives, as they so widely do, are facts of modern living which cannot be ignored.''[43]

In keeping with his profound skepticism concerning the ability of the litigation process to inform the judicial mind, Frankfurter argued that the justices must do more than acknowledge the complexity of the situation before them. He insisted that the Court relegate the balancing of competing social claims to the legislature. In response to the majority's objection that ''the ordinance before us merely penalizes the distribution of 'literature,' '' he counseled deference:

> To be sure, the prohibition of this ordinance is within a small circle. But it is not our business to require legislatures to extend the area of prohibition or regulation beyond the demands of revealed abuses. And the greatest leeway must be given to the legislative judgment of what those demands are. The right to legislate implies the right to classify. We should not, however unwittingly, slip into the judgment seat of legislatures. I myself cannot say that those in whose keeping is the peace of the City of Struthers and the right of privacy of its home dwellers could not single out, in *circumstances of which they may have knowledge and I certainly have not*, this class of canvassers as the particular source of mischief.[44]

When the assumption underpinning the Court's decisions in *Bridges* and *Martin*—that a heightened standard of review is warranted in cases involving the freedoms of the First Amendment—became an explicit constitutional philosophy, Frankfurter took the lead in challenging this new "preferred freedoms" doctrine. In *Kovacs v. Cooper*, for example, the Court held that a local ordinance forbidding the use of "sound trucks" on the public streets did not violate the First Amendment. In a plurality opinion, Justice Reed stated that the "preferred position of freedom of speech in a society that cherishes liberty for all does not require legislators to be insensible to claims by citizens to comfort and convenience."[45]

Frankfurter concurred in the ruling. But he felt compelled to comment on Reed's reference to the "preferred position" of freedom of speech, a phrase that, according to Frankfurter, had "uncritically crept into some recent opinions of [the] Court." He worried that judicial reference to this standard would lead to abstraction or the disregard of the "admonition most to be observed in exercising the Court's reviewing power over legislation, 'that it is *a constitution* we are expounding.' " Frankfurter took the arguments of the dissenters as proof of the Court's drift from its constitutional obligation to consider the circumstances prompting governmental action. The dissenters, he said, engaged in "sterile argumentation [that] treats society as though it consisted of bloodless categories."[46]

Justice Black, however, *did* consider the circumstances of the case in his dissent. He observed: "The record reflects not even a shadow of evidence to prove that the noise was either 'loud or raucous,' unless these words of the ordinance refer to any noise coming from an amplifier, whatever its volume or tone."[47]

Had Frankfurter acknowledged this statement, he would have been no less disparaging toward Black or the "preferred freedoms" concept. For Frankfurter abhorred any doctrine or standard that precludes deference to the decisions of local officials. The preferred position of freedom of speech, he believed, is "a mischievous phrase, if it carries the thought, which it may subtly imply, that any law touching communication is infected with presumptive invalidity." A presumption of invalidity necessarily involves heightened judicial scrutiny of the conclusions of legislators concerning the need for the curtailment of speech. Frankfurter argued, by contrast, that it was not "for [the] Court to devise the terms on which sound trucks should be allowed to operate, if at all. These are matters for the legislative judgment controlled by public opinion." Rather than "supervise the limits the legislatures may impose in safeguarding the steadily narrowing opportunities for serenity and reflection," the Court should merely watch for actions that are unconstitutional beyond reason, such as the prescription of "what ideas may be noisily expressed and what may not be." He rejected a less deferential standard of review because of the inability of the judicial process to cope with the complexities of modern communication technology: "The various forms of modern so-called 'mass communications' raise issues that were not implied in the means of communication known or contemplated by Franklin and Jefferson and Madison. . . . Movies have created problems not presented by the circulation of books, pamphlets, or newspapers, and so the movies have been constitutionally regulated. . . . Broadcasting in turn has produced its brood of complicated problems hardly to be solved by an easy formula about the preferred position of free speech."[48]

Frankfurter also sought in his opinion to dissociate Justice Holmes's name from the concept of "preferred freedoms." He noted that the "ideas now governing the constitutional protection of freedom of speech derive essentially from the opinions of Mr. Justice Holmes." And he conceded that "Holmes was far more ready to find legislative invasion where free inquiry was involved than in the debatable area of economics." But Frankfurter "object[ed] to summarizing this line of thought by the phrase 'the preferred position of freedom of speech' [because] it expresses a complicated process of constitutional adjudication by a deceptive formula."[49]

Without a fuller argument, the conclusion that Holmes did not view legislation infringing upon speech as presumptively invalid did not seem to follow from Frankfurter's observations in *Kovacs* or from his scholarly writings on Holmes. Six years earlier, however, in his dissent in *West Virginia State Board of Education v. Barnette*, the second flag-salute case, Frankfurter had explained why he thought Holmes never supported a general presumption of invalidity. In an argument that was not at all apparent in his pre-*Barnette* writings on Holmes, he had said that the justice meant to limit a heightened standard of review to the particular circumstances in which he designed and used the "clear and present danger" test. Holmes was concerned with "inducement of insubordination in the military and naval forces of the United States and obstruction of enlistment while the country was at war." Frankfurter objected to "tak[ing] a felicitous phrase [and, more generally, a heightened standard of review] out of the context of the particular situation where it arose and for which it was adapted."[50]

Frankfurter made the narrowness of his conception of judicial re-

view most evident in *Dennis v. United States*, where the Court moved
away from the "preferred freedoms" doctrine. Recall that the Court
participated in the federal government's efforts to combat the Communist Party in this country by weakening the protection that the "clear
and present danger" test afforded. Chief Justice Vinson subordinated
the requirement of a "present" or "imminent" danger to a "probable"
one, which effectively meant that the standard would serve to justify
convictions.[51]

For Frankfurter, even this reduced level of scrutiny—the mere
balancing of the government's security interest against the individual's
interest in speech, with no special weight accorded the latter—
permitted too pronounced a judicial role. Although he agreed that the
Communists' convictions should be sustained, he rejected the Court's
use of the "clear and present danger" test. "Bearing in mind that Mr.
Justice Holmes regarded questions under the First Amendment as
questions of 'proximity and degree,' " he argued, "it would be a
distortion, indeed a mockery, of his reasoning to compare the 'puny
anonymities' . . . to which he was addressing himself [when he
formulated the "clear and present danger" test] . . . with the setting of
events in this case in 1950." Frankfurter may have thought that a
diluted "clear and present danger" test was less pernicious than the
interpretation the Court gave the test under the "preferred freedoms"
doctrine. Still, he believed that the *Dennis* facts demanded a standard
that did not permit the justices to weigh for themselves the interests
involved. "Primary responsibility for adjusting the interests which
compete in the situation before us of necessity belongs to Congress,"
he explained. "Free-speech cases are not an exception to the principle
that we are not legislators, that direct policy-making is not our province." Echoing Thayer, he argued that the Court must "attach great
significance to the determination of the legislature" and "set aside the
judgment of those whose duty it is to legislate . . . [only] if there is no
reasonable basis for it." Here, Frankfurter found "ample justification
for a legislative judgment that the conspiracy . . . before [the Court
was] a substantial threat to national order and security."[52]

Once again, Frankfurter revealed that a fear of judicial abstraction
informed his efforts to relegate the balancing of competing social
claims to the legislature. He expressed profound reservations about
the ability of the litigation process to provide sufficient information to
the Court: "[Judicial] judgment is best informed, and therefore most
dependable, within narrow limits." To him, *Dennis* presented anything
but a narrowly circumscribed controversy. "To make validity of legis-

lation depend on judicial reading of events still in the womb of time—a forecast, that is, of the outcome of forces at best appreciated only with knowledge of the topmost secrets of nations—is to charge the judiciary with duties beyond its equipment."[53] So, while Hugo Black rejected the "clear and present danger" test because it does not guarantee strong protection for the freedoms of speech and press (as *Dennis* demonstrated), Frankfurter avoided its use because he believed that the balancing process inhering in the standard, even when the test involves only low-level scrutiny of legislative determinations, exceeds judicial capabilities.

Frankfurter ended his concurring opinion with an apology: "In finding that Congress has acted within its power, a judge does not remotely imply that he favors the implications that lie beneath the legal issues." He then quoted George Kennan: " 'The worst thing that our Communists could do to us, and the thing we have most to fear from their activities, is that we should become [intolerant] like them.' " Frankfurter looked forward to the legislature's retraction of the law, observing "that in sustaining the power of Congress in a case like this nothing irrevocable is done. The democratic process at all events is not impaired or restricted."[54] Surely, these comments gave slight comfort to the Communists who were headed to prison. But Frankfurter's remarks demonstrated the profound implications of social interdependence for his thought: This social phenomenon inspired within him such fear of judicial abstraction that he refused to act on his convictions. At the same time, interdependence gave him such faith in the integrative nature of politics that he thought even the most reviled of political pariahs would ultimately receive justice at the hands of their oppressors.

"Standards of Justice Not Authoritatively Formulated Anywhere"

Deference to Local Knowledge

The fear of judicial abstraction that informed Frankfurter's First Amendment decisions also affected his performance in Fourteenth Amendment cases, specifically, his approach to the doctrine of incorporation. His understanding of the Court's usual vehicle for applying the provisions of the Bill of Rights against the states—the due process clause of the Fourteenth Amendment—informed his position on this issue. In interpreting the due process clause, he responded largely to the Court's use of that provision during the early part of the century.

As noted in chapter 6, Frankfurter profoundly regretted judicial importation of the doctrine of laissez-faire into the Fourteenth Amendment; he recoiled at the Court's erection of "abstract conceptions concerning 'liberty of contract' . . . [and due process of law] into constitutional dogmas." His predecessors on the Court, he believed, failed to appreciate the danger of abstract notions of rights and were unaware that the state cases before them involved matters exceeding judicial capabilities.

> The veto power of the Supreme Court over the social-economic legislation of the States, when exercised by a narrow conception of . . . due process . . . , presents undue centralization in its most destructive and least responsible form. The most destructive, because it stops experiment at its source, preventing an increase of social knowledge by the only scientific method available, namely, the test of trial and error. The least responsible, because it so often turns on the fortuitous circumstances which determine a majority decision, and shelters the fallible judgment of individual Justices, in matters of fact and opinion not peculiarly within the special competence of judges, behind the impersonal authority of the Constitution.[55]

Judicial judgment proved fallible because the litigation process failed to alert the Court to the unique circumstances of distinctive communities constituting an interdependent social order. "At almost every point of legislative activity," he noted, "the Supreme Court imposed its veto against State action in matters confessedly of local concern, dealing solely with local situations and expressing remedies derived from local experience."[56]

Initially, Frankfurter went so far as to maintain that "the due process clauses ought to go": "[N]o nine men are wise enough and good enough to be entrusted with the power which the unlimited provisions of the due process clauses confer." In time, he saw the inevitability and the wisdom of retaining clauses that, he believed, constitutionalized "general intimations of fairness and reason" in government's dealings with individuals. He insisted, however, that judges not employ this constitutional generality "to defeat life by formal logic." The due process clauses were

> not intended to shut off remedies, however tentative, for the moral and economic waste, the friction of classes, urban congestion, the relaxation of individual responsibility, the subtler forms of corruption, and the

abuses of power which have followed in the wake of a highly developed laissez faire industrialism.

Particularly, the States should not be hampered in dealing with evils at their points of pressure. Legislation is essentially ad hoc. To expect uniformity in law where there is diversity in fact is to bar effective legislation. An extremely complicated society inevitably entails special treatment for distinctive social phenomena. If legislation is to deal with realities, it must address itself to important variations in the needs, opportunities, and coercive power of the different elements in the State.[57]

To minimize the danger of judicial abstraction under the due process clause of the Fourteenth Amendment, Frankfurter sought to relegate the balancing of social interests to the states. To ensure that "facts, not general principles or well-worn phrases, [are] the determinants" of decisions, the appropriate course for a flawed judiciary is to show a marked "regard for local needs and local habits" and great "deference to local knowledge." Like Thayer, he thought the Court must exercise "the *utmost tolerance* and detachment" when reviewing the reasonableness of the policy choices of the states.[58]

Frankfurter continued to counsel judicial deference when, after his appointment, the Court's docket featured demands for the procedural protections of the Bill of Rights, rather than claims of economic liberty. In a letter to Justice Black in 1943, he discussed his view of the "*narrow scope* of the Court's power to strike down political action" under the Fourteenth Amendment:

My starting point is, of course, the democratic faith on which this country is founded—the right of a democracy to make mistakes and correct its errors by the organs that reflect the popular will—which regards the Court as a qualification of the democratic principle and *desire[s] to restrict the play of this undemocratic feature to its narrowest limits*. I am aware that men who have power can exercise [it] and too often do—to enforce their own will, to make their will, or if you like their notions of policy, the measure of what is right. But I am also aware of *the forces of tradition and the habits of discipline whereby men entrusted with power remain within the limited framework of their professed power. More particularly, the history of this Court emboldens me to believe that men need not be supermen to observe the conditions under which judicial review of political authority—that's what judicial review of legislation really amounts to—is ultimately maintainable in a democratic society.* When men who had such background and relation to so-called property interests as did, for instance, Waite, Bradley, Moody, Holmes, Brandeis, and Cardozo, showed *how scrupulously they did not write their private notions of policy into the Constitution*, then I am not prepared to say that all that a court does when it adjudicates in these constitutional controversies is an elaborate pretense, and that judges in fact merely translate their private convictions into decisions and call it the law and the Constitution.[59]

This letter was a not-so-subtle effort to spell out for Black the (supposed) advantages of a concept of due process informed by Thayer's insights. By restricting the power of review to "its narrowest limits," Frankfurter believed, the rational-basis test precludes subordination of the policy choices of state officials to the uninformed policy preferences of judges. Furthermore, a standard that merely demands deference obviates the need for judges to possess the qualities of "supermen."[60]

Frankfurter grounded his continued reluctance to interfere with state actions in the same belief that explained his passivity in First Amendment controversies: the move toward interdependence, he thought, complicated noneconomic, as well as economic, relations. Just as property controversies became more involved in an age of interdependence, issues of criminal law and procedure (as well as speech and press) grew in complexity. Specifically, the specialization or heterogeneity that accompanied social interdependence made for local or regional variations in types and severity (not to mention volume) of criminal behavior. And varying circumstances require uneven responses from the states. Frankfurter thus viewed judicial efforts to impose a uniform system of justice on the country as a pernicious form of judicial abstraction; application of the provisions of the Bill of Rights against the states fails to account for the particular circumstances of distinctive communities. Armed with an interpretation of due process that prohibits only governmental actions no rational person could regard as fair, Frankfurter became a vocal opponent of the doctrines of total and selective incorporation.

Incorporation Opponent

When Black first explicitly endorsed total incorporation, in *Betts v. Brady*, Frankfurter chose not to make his response public. He joined Justice Roberts, who, speaking for the majority, declined to apply against the states the Sixth Amendment right to counsel. Roberts stated that due process "formulates a concept less rigid and more fluid than those envisaged in other specific and particular provisions of the

Bill of Rights''; it prohibits only "a denial of fundamental fairness, [that is, actions] shocking to the universal sense of justice." Justice Murphy's notes indicate that when Black argued in conference that the framers of the Fourteenth Amendment "intended to make applicable to the states the Bill of Rights," Frankfurter responded that the amendment "did not incorporate the first 10. If it did you would uproot all the structure of the states."[61]

In *Malinski v. New York*, Frankfurter publicly expressed his desire to maintain the diversity of state legal systems. He joined his brethren who voided a murder conviction tainted by a coerced confession, but he was dissatisfied with the Court's avoidance of a detailed treatment of the Fourteenth Amendment. In his concurring opinion, he made a point of saying that due process does not incorporate the provisions of the Bill of Rights: "Unlike the limitations of the Bill of Rights upon the use of criminal penalties by federal authority, the Fourteenth Amendment placed no specific restriction upon the administration of their criminal law by the states."[62]

Frankfurter then expressed the fear of abstraction informing his assertion: "In reviewing a state criminal conviction we must be deeply mindful of the responsibilities of the States for the enforcement of criminal laws, and exercise with due humility our merely negative function in subjecting convictions from state courts to the very narrow scrutiny which the Due Process Clause of the Fourteenth Amendment authorizes." Reiterating what he had said during deliberations in *Betts*, he maintained that a construction of due process that

> makes of it a summary of the specific provisions of the Bill of Rights would tear up by the roots much of the fabric of law in the several States. Thus, it would require all the States to prosecute serious crimes through the grand jury system long ago abandoned by many of them, . . . to try such crimes by a jury of twelve which some of the States have seen fit to modify or abandon, . . . to enforce the privilege against self-incrimination with the technical requirements prevailing in the federal courts when States, consistently with fundamental notions of justice, have seen fit to make other arrangements, . . . and to have jury trials "In Suits at common law, where the value in controversy shall exceed twenty dollars."[63]

If "an alert deference to the judgment of the state court under review" precludes incorporation of the procedural requirements of the Bill of Rights, this case demonstrated that, in Frankfurter's mind, such deference does not imply judicial abdication. Frankfurter's phraseology suggested that no reasonable person could regard the officers' treatment of the defendant as fair:

> I cannot escape agreement with the Chief Judge of the New York Court of Appeals and two of his associates that there was not in this case a fair trial of issues vital to the determination of guilt or innocence. Considering the circumstances of Malinski's detention, the long and continuous questioning, the willful and wrongful delay in his arraignment and the opportunity that that gives for securing, by extortion, confessions such as were here introduced in evidence, the flagrant justification by the prosecutor of this illegality as a necessary police procedure, inevitably calculated to excite the jury—all these in combination are so below the standards by which the criminal law, especially in a capital case, should be enforced as to fall short of due process of law.[64]

Although Frankfurter's conception of due process did not imply judicial abdication, his concurring opinion in the macabre case *Francis v. Resweber* revealed that the conception was very narrow. The case involved Willie Francis's claim to the protections of the double jeopardy provision of the Fifth Amendment and the cruel-and-unusual punishment provision of the Eighth Amendment against the efforts of the state of Louisiana to execute him for the crime of murder. The state had attempted to kill him by electrocution (even subjecting him to a current of electricity) but had failed because the electric chair malfunctioned. In a plurality opinion, Justice Reed rejected Francis's plea for protection, despite assuming (purely for purposes of argument) that violations of the relevant elements of the Fifth and Eighth Amendments would contravene the due process clause of the Fourteenth Amendment. Reed found that the state had violated neither provision.[65]

Frankfurter explained, in a memorandum to his brethren, why he could not join Reed's opinion:

> In order that there be an opinion of the Court, I had hoped to join brother Reed's opinion in addition to expressing my own views. The reason I cannot do so, inter alia, is that I do not think we should decide the case even on the assumption that the Fifth Amendment as to double jeopardy is the measure of due process in the Fourteenth Amendment. I do not see why we should make an assumption which is contrary to the whole tenor of [the *Palko* decision]. It makes for nothing but confusion in the consideration of constitutional cases under the Due Process Clause to cite cases that construe the scope of the double jeopardy provision of the Fifth Amendment.[66]

Once again, Frankfurter's opposition to incorporation stemmed from a fear of judicial abstraction. To impose the provisions of the Bill of Rights on the states, he thought, is to assume the relevance of eighteenth century procedures to the more complicated and varied problems confronting the states in the twentieth century. In his concurring opinion, he argued that, under the doctrine of incorporation, "the States would be confined in the enforcement of their criminal codes by those views for safeguarding the rights of the individual which were deemed necessary in the eighteenth century. Some of those safeguards have perduring validity. Some grew out of transient experience or formulated remedies which time might well improve. The Fourteenth Amendment did not mean to imprison the States into the limited experience of the eighteenth century."[67]

Frankfurter emphasized that the due process clause of the Fourteenth Amendment "expresses a demand for civilized standards which are not defined by the specifically enumerated guarantees of the Bill of Rights. They neither contain the particularities of the first eight amendments nor are they confined to them." Due process, in short, "has its own independent function." Explaining his earlier acceptance of the application of portions of the First Amendment against the states (as seen in the preceding section), he said that insofar as the due process clause of the Fourteenth Amendment requires the states to observe any of the provisions of the Bill of Rights, it does so because, as Justice Cardozo held in *Palko v. Connecticut*, those provisions " 'have been found to be implied in the concept of ordered liberty.' " The states, however, are usually free to enforce their own notions of fairness; as Cardozo stated in an opinion preceding *Palko*, the Court's role is the very narrow one of invalidating only policies or forms of behavior that offend " 'some principle of justice so rooted in the traditions and conscience of our people as to be ranked as fundamental.' "[68] In short, a state might very well violate a particular provision of the Bill of Rights without violating the concept of due process.

In the case of Willie Francis, Frankfurter believed that Louisiana's failure to mitigate the death sentence after the "innocent misadventure" of the first attempt did not offend a principle of justice "rooted in the traditions and conscience of our people." Revealing that he predicated his interpretation of Cardozo's language—and, therefore, of due process—upon the rational-basis test, he concluded that the state had treated Francis "by a mode about which opinion [over its fairness] is fairly divided," rather than "in a manner that violates standards of decency more or less universally accepted.'' Just as Thayer counseled judges to put aside personal values in favor of policing the perimeters of rational policy, Frankfurter thought the Court must avoid interfering in this case, "no matter how strong one's personal feeling of revulsion against a State's insistence on its pound of flesh.'' Although he believed Louisiana's actions to have been barbaric, he could not rid himself of the conviction that holding the state in violation of the due process clause would amount to "enforcing [his] private view rather than that consensus of society's opinion which, for purposes of due process, is the standard enjoined by the Constitution.'' Since he could not say "that it would be 'repugnant to the conscience of mankind' . . . for Louisiana to exercise the power on which she here stands," he felt compelled to remain passive.[69]

Because Frankfurter believed in the "independent potency" of the due process clause, he responded predictably to Justice Black's detailed defense of the doctrine of total incorporation in *Adamson v. California.* Frankfurter agreed with the majority's ruling that the Fifth Amendment privilege against self-incrimination does not apply against the states through the Fourteenth Amendment and that a state practice of permitting judges and prosecutors to comment adversely on the defendant's refusal to testify on his own behalf does not violate the concept of due process. But he felt compelled to write a concurring opinion attacking any notion of incorporation. He assailed Black's historical argument, stressing the improbability that the states would have agreed to a massive restructuring of their justice systems. In sharp contrast to Black, he lauded Justice Moody's opinion in *Twining v. New Jersey*: "The *Twining* case [which rejected any connection between the clauses of the Fourteenth Amendment and the provisions of the Bill of Rights] shows the judicial process at its best.''[70]

Frankfurter supported his historical critique of Black's opinion with a discussion of the policy implications of total incorporation. Once again, he feared that application of the provisions of the Bill of Rights against the states would be an exercise in abstraction. "A construction which gives to due process no independent function but turns it into a summary of the specific provisions of the Bill of Rights would . . . tear up by the roots much of the fabric of law in the several States." He conceded that "[s]ome of these [provisions] are enduring reflections of experience with human nature," but argued that others "express the restricted views of Eighteenth-Century England regarding the best methods for the ascertainment of facts." The Court had to be "mindful of the relation of our federal system to a progressively democratic society and therefore duly regardful of the scope of authority that was left to the States even after the Civil War.'' Besides interfering with the efforts of states to address contemporary problems that the framers could not foresee, a concept of due process restricted to the provisions of the Bill of Rights fails to account for the likelihood that the framers did not anticipate all forms of abuse of power. Black's view of due process ''would deprive the States of opportunity for reforms in legal process designed for extending the area of freedom. It would assume that no other abuses would reveal themselves in the course of time than those which had become manifest in 1791.''[71]

Total incorporation represented for Frankfurter the worst form of abstraction in Fourteenth Amendment adjudication (next to substantive economic due process), but he was also critical of the doctrine of selective incorporation. ''There is suggested merely a selective incorporation of the first eight Amendments into the Fourteenth Amendment. Some are in and some are out, but we are left in the dark as to which are in and which are out. Nor are we given the calculus for determining which go in and which stay out.'' If the only rationale supporting the doctrine is ''that those provisions of the first eight Amendments are incorporated which commend themselves to individual justices as indispensable to the dignity and happiness of a free man, we are thrown back to a merely subjective test.''[72]

Frankfurter's criticism of selective incorporation may seem puzzling, in view of both his acceptance of the incorporation of portions of the First Amendment and his frequent references to Cardozo's language in *Palko*. The Court used Cardozo's language in the late 1940s and in the 1960s to apply selectively provisions of the Bill of Rights against the states. (In his *Adamson* dissent, Justice Black also identified *Palko* with the doctrine of selective incorporation.) Frankfurter's charge of subjectivity and his effort to distance himself from the selective approach to incorporation, however, rested upon his rejection of the view that Cardozo had intended anything approximating the application of numerous provisions of the Bill of Rights against the states. Recall that Frankfurter read Cardozo's language in light of the rational-basis test. He thus believed Cardozo's reference to elements of the First Amendment (as examples of provisions that are ''implicit in the concept of ordered liberty'') to be well-nigh exhaustive, rather than suggestive. (A person could believe rationally in the fairness of a justice system that does not afford most of the protections contained in the Bill of Rights.) Since Frankfurter interpreted *Palko* to support his own position, he felt justified in branding selective incorporation as standardless.[73]

To say Frankfurter viewed selective incorporation as subjective is not to say he saw the application of his own conception of due process as entirely objective. He conceded in *Rochin v. California* (among other cases) that "judgment [concerning the import of due process] is bound to fall differently at different times and differently at the same time through different judges." Indeed, he illustrated the potential for such subjectivity in this very case. *Rochin* presented a due process challenge to a narcotics conviction police obtained through questionable methods. The arresting officers had illegally entered the defendant's home and later had had an emetic forced down the man's throat in order to retrieve an illegal substance. Frankfurter spoke for the Court: "This is conduct that shocks the conscience. Illegally breaking into the privacy of the petitioner, the struggle to open his mouth and remove what was there, the forcible extraction of his stomach's contents—this course of proceeding by agents of government to obtain evidence is bound to offend even hardened sensibilities. They are methods too close to the rack and screw to permit of constitutional differentiation."[74] The problem with Frankfurter's argument, if one regards rationality as the measure of constitutionality, is that only the illegal entry of the police was relevant to a finding of unconstitutionality. Arguably, the officers' behavior after the break-in would not "offend even hardened sensibilities." Had the police entered the premises legally, a rational person could regard their subsequent treatment of Rochin as "fair": they had information that he was selling narcotics, saw him put the capsules into his mouth after being questioned about them, had the emetic administered in a hospital, and in fact recovered morphine.

In spite of the potential for judicial misapplication, Frankfurter's deferential conception of due process was not entirely subjective. With considerable justification, he asserted in *Rochin* that the "vague contours of the Due Process Clause do not leave judges at large" or permit them to "draw on merely personal and private notions and disregard the limits that bind judges in their judicial function." As he demonstrated in *Francis* (among other cases), it is possible for judges to put to one side their personal objections to governmental action when they think that a rational person could believe in the fairness or constitutionality of the challenged behavior. To the extent that judges draw inspiration from James Bradley Thayer rather than the *Lochner* majority, then, Justice Black was mistaken to suggest that Frankfurter's due process standard "license[s] this Court to roam at large in the broad expanses of policy and morals and to trespass, all too freely, on the legislative domain of the States as well as the Federal Government."[75]

A Faith in Judicial Power?

An Allowance of Discretion

While Frankfurter remained passive in most constitutional matters, he was anything but reserved in certain contexts. In federal cases involving the Fourth Amendment prohibition of unreasonable searches and seizures, for example, he proved libertarian in his voting. Indeed, of the fifteen instances during his judicial tenure in which defendants raised Fourth Amendment claims against the federal government, he voted in every case, save one, to sustain the constitutional challenge and exclude evidence allegedly obtained illegally.[76] In articulating his operating principle for search and seizure conflicts, he revealed that his votes in these cases were departures from his Thayerian jurisprudence, rather than responses to patently unreasonable police conduct. "[W]ith minor and severely confined exceptions, inferentially a part of the [Fourth] Amendment," he declared, "every search and seizure is unreasonable when made without a magistrate's authority expressed through a validly issued warrant." Frankfurter's statement notwithstanding, law enforcement officers might believe reasonably (as did Hugo Black) that there is no near-essential connection between the constitutionality of a search and the possession of a warrant. And Thayer's principles of interpretation would require of judges great deference to an officer's determination of the permissibility of a warrantless search. After all, policemen, as well as legislators, take an oath to support the Constitution.[77]

A rational person might also think (again, as did Hugo Black) that the explicit reference in the Fourth Amendment to "persons, houses, papers, and effects" precludes extending protection against unreasonable searches and seizures to evidence obtained through electronic surveillance. Here, too, Frankfurter's position conflicted with the major tenets of his jurisprudence. "[W]iretapping," he said, "is within the clear scope of the prohibition of the Fourth Amendment." Criminal prosecution "should not be deemed a dirty game in which 'the dirty business' of criminals is outwitted by 'the dirty business' of law officers. The contrast between morality professed by society and immorality practiced on its behalf makes for contempt of law."[78]

Another area in which Frankfurter was noticeably lacking in deference was the First Amendment's prohibition of laws respecting an establishment of religion. He regarded transportation-reimbursement programs (where states provide reimbursement to parents for transportation expenses incurred in sending their children to parochial or private school) and released-time programs (where states excuse students from their secular classes once weekly for the purpose of receiving religious instruction) as a violation of that provision. Aside from the question of whether Frankfurter's application of the establishment clause against the states was consonant with his narrow conception of the Fourteenth Amendment due process clause, one wonders how he could have found unreasonable the belief that such programs, if nondiscriminatory, do not constitute laws respecting an establishment of religion. One might reasonably contend that the First Amendment forbids only governmental preference of one religion over another, not impartial assistance to all religions. Although Frankfurter detected discrimination in the operation of the programs at issue in the cases before the Court, he could not explain away his decisions in this manner. Confounding those conditioned to hear echoes of (and, frequently, explicit references to) Thayer in his opinions, he maintained that the establishment clause "is a requirement to abstain from fusing functions of Government and of religious sects, not merely to treat them all equally."[79]

Before concluding that Frankfurter's opinions in search-and-seizure and establishment-clause controversies were anomalous departures from a jurisprudence based upon a fear of judicial power, one must consider the argument that these decisions were actually the most obvious manifestations of a judicial philosophy informed by *a profound faith in judicial power*. Consider that, unlike legal positivists (who truly distrust the judicial resolution of social controversies), Frankfurter scrupulously avoided a legalistic approach to decision making. He called instead for a degree of judicial discretion. Deriding Justice Black's efforts to define due process in terms of the provisions of the Bill of Rights, he said that such an approach to constitutional interpretation "could only be on the assumption that we cannot trust five members of the highest court of the land to exercise a judgment of whether or not a thing does offend fundamental decency because that would vest too much discretion in a majority of the Court, who, one would suppose, are disciplined by the responsibility of their office and the great tradition of the history of this Court." Similarly, he assailed legalistic approaches to free speech controversies with the argument that the "demands of free speech in a democratic society . . . are better served by candid and informed weighing of the competing interests, within the confines of the judicial process, than by announcing dogmas too inflexible for the non-Euclidian problems to be solved." If he allowed for discretion in these contexts, one scholar argues, he would logically view a constitutionally imposed reasonableness standard, like that contained in the Fourth Amendment, as a "source of judicial power" or "a broad mandate for judicial protection of privacy."[80]

Scholars who suggest that Frankfurter possessed a faith in judicial power emphasize the broader social context in which he developed his jurisprudence. Rather than focus on the social fact of increased interdependence, they stress the significance of the spread of totalitarianism in Europe during the 1930s. Frankfurter revealed the jurisprudential relevance of totalitarianism when he replaced his early view that the "due process clauses ought to go" with the belief that "[d]ue process is perhaps the most majestic concept in our whole constitutional system." He changed his view of due process in response to the "brutal conception of society [inhering in European fascism] at the very heart of which is disdain of what we mean by law." The very notion of due process, he came to believe, rebels "against the tyrannical conception of Germany and other Fascist countries that you can put a man in jail [merely] because he is a 'bad' man or because he has violated some undefined general purpose." Viewed against this background, Frankfurter's allowance of judicial discretion would seem to suggest that he extended to the judiciary his Progressive confidence in public power. In the words of one scholar, Frankfurter saw judges, "restrained neither by rigid rules nor constitutional absolutes," as responsible for "the disinterested application of [constitutional] principle to new situations as well as the disinterested accommodation of conflicting principles." While the courts would not use the Constitution to hinder social progress, they would assume responsibility for ensuring, in contradistinction to totalitarian regimes, that government pursues social and economic change in accordance with enduring principles of liberty.[81]

The Approximation of Legislative Supremacy

Frankfurter's extensive critique of the process of judicial decision making, a critique he reiterated throughout his tenure on the bench, complicates the view that he had confidence in judicial power. One might argue that his observations on the inadequacies of the judicial process were merely admonitions to judges who, through discretionary standards, would direct the progress of society. But he obviously intended the critique to be more than cautionary: The judicial judgment he allowed was merely that of Thayer's rational-basis test and was thus very narrow in scope. Moreover, he justified this standard with the argument that the Court is not primarily responsible for enforcing constitutional limitations. Defenders of the view that Frankfurter possessed a faith in judicial power argue that these elements of his jurisprudence merely ensured that he would not employ "judicial power as a means of foreclosing the future."[82] But he achieved this objective simply by emphasizing the Constitution's amplitude and the importance of the concept of justiciability. His use of Thayer's rational-basis standard did much more than reinforce the point that the Constitution allows for consideration of matters of time and circumstance; it effectively assigned the disposition of constitutional questions to the other branches of government. Frankfurter, in short, sought to relieve courts of the task of balancing competing social claims—he sought to relegate judges to policing the perimeters of rational policy.

One proponent of the view that Frankfurter had faith in judicial power finds significant the fact that "balancing did take place" in Frankfurter's opinions. This scholar fails to realize that balancing performed merely to assess the rationality of governmental action is in no way equivalent to weighing for oneself the conflicting interests in a case. Time and again, after examining the conflict before the Court, Frankfurter insisted that a legislative judgment may not "be overturned merely because the Court would have made a different choice between the competing interests had the initial legislative judgment been for it to make."[83]

Still, Frankfurter refused to move beyond the rational-basis test and, in the manner of the positivists, restrain judicial judgment through rigid rules. His decision to preserve a degree of discretion, however, does not suggest that he trusted judicial authority. Quite the contrary. As Justice Black revealed, legalism in a constitutional context works against the principle that nonjudicial bodies provide superior forums for resolving social conflicts: the eradication of discretion forces the exercise of judicial review in many instances. In short, the discretion inherent in Thayer's standard suggests anything but a confidence in judicial power; the reasonable-doubt test represents the only means by which the judiciary can approximate legislative and administrative supremacy under a constitutional scheme in which judges possess the power of review.

Although Frankfurter distrusted judicial power, he did not begrudge the Court its influence under Thayer's standard: "The Supreme Court is indispensable to the effective workings of our federal government. If it did not exist, we should have to create it." He believed that government (on rare occasions) is capable of reprehensible conduct. For this reason, he had a firm belief in the importance of judicial review and even recognized the need for a conception of due process unconnected to the provisions of the Bill of Rights. But it is one thing to acknowledge the need for review and quite another to possess a faith in judicial power. Frankfurter sought to limit exercises of judicial review to situations in which the injustice is so apparent that virtually no danger exists that an abstract judicial ruling will result in the invalidation of a necessary policy or practice. He also sought to reduce the incidence of review to the point that it would not interfere with the process of social integration. (The spread of totalitarianism never compromised his faith in the integrative nature of democratic politics.) So, while Frankfurter did not desire "an abdication of the judicial function," the conclusion is inescapable that he based his jurisprudence upon fears rather than hopes.[84]

We are thus forced to consider once again why, in search-and-seizure and establishment-of-religion controversies, Frankfurter abandoned his customary deference toward the decisions of nonjudicial officers. One might proffer the explanation that, at least in Fourth Amendment cases, he lost his faith in politics. More specifically, he found jurisprudentially significant the point that social miscreants (as opposed to individuals participating in a network of interdependent social relationships) usually invoke Fourth Amendment rights. The Court, he argued, "should be more exacting in observing the prohibition of unreasonable search and seizure than the requirement of freedom of speech, for the simple reason that the latter has strongly organized forces in its support—the press, the movie interests, publishers, etc., etc., while there is no such organized constituency on the alert against unreasonable search and seizure." The Fourth Amendment "is normally invoked by those accused of crime[,] and criminals notoriously have few friends." That provision is thus likely "to be encroached upon . . . in a short-sighted desire to protect society against crime."[85] Frankfurter, however, regarded this consideration as at most a necessary, rather than a sufficient, condition to warrant departing from Thayer's teaching, for he was not as aggressive in protecting other rights that are usually invoked by those accused of crimes.[86]

An argument that emphasizes Frankfurter's strong personal commitment to the Fourth Amendment and his experiences in complying with the amendment's provisions as a prosecutor provides the soundest explanation for his behavior in this area of the law. In a telling passage in one of his opinions, he recalled: "The third degree, search without warrant, wiretapping and the like, were not tolerated in what was probably the most successful administration in our time of the busiest United States Attorney's office. This experience under Henry L. Stimson in the Southern District of New York, compared with happenings elsewhere, doubtless planted in me a deep conviction that these short-cuts in the detection and prosecution of crime are as self-defeating as they are immoral." He later confessed that his opinions in search-and-seizure cases reflected "a bias derived from having served under a United States Attorney who observed [the Fourth Amendment's] standards and [still] won his cases." The experience of complying with these standards effaced his fear of judicial abstraction.[87]

Frankfurter's lack of deference in establishment clause controversies likewise stemmed from his inability to put aside a strong personal value. In this area of the law, the ideal of the public school as a unifying force in American social life informed his opinions. He never forgot the Irish schoolmarm whose lessons in English and self-discipline were instrumental in his own assimilation and professional success, nor did he undervalue Croly's teaching regarding the importance of the public school for cultivating within American society a sense of solidarity. Because he regarded "the public school as a symbol of our secular unity" and "perhaps the most powerful agency for promoting cohesion among a heterogeneous democratic people," he thought that the institution "must be kept scrupulously free from entanglement in the strife of sects." And again: "In no activity of the State is it more vital to keep out divisive forces than in its schools." The principle of separation of church and state "is one of the vital reliances of our Constitutional system for assuring unities among our people stronger than our diversities. It is the Court's duty to enforce this principle to its full integrity."[88] Convinced that, in this context, judicial quiescence actually impedes social integration, he was willing to risk judicial abstraction by challenging legislative determinations regarding the necessity of public aid to religious institutions.

Frankfurter's understanding of the function of American public schools also makes more intelligible his decisions in the flag-salute cases. His passivity in these instances reflected, not only his fear of judicial abstraction and his faith in politics, but also his belief that classrooms should not serve as forums for sectarian strife. (He did not regard as relevant the fact that the sectarianism in these cases involved claims of the free exercise of religion, as opposed to governmental sponsorship of faith.) As a Jew, he was predisposed to accept the Jehovah's Witnesses' claim to religious liberty. But his belief that sectarian displays in an educational setting hinder social integration lessened the angst he felt when, to avoid judicial abstraction, he resorted to Thayer's deferential standard of review. Indeed, his aversion to sectarianism stoked the fire of his impassioned dissent in the second flag-salute case. There, he said: "It never would have occurred to [the leaders of the American Revolution] to write into the Constitution the subordination of the general civil authority of the state to sectarian scruples."[89]

If the second flag-salute case prompted one of Frankfurter's most significant dissents, it also occasioned one of Justice Robert H. Jackson's most memorable decisions. Recall that Jackson's majority opinion was the target of Frankfurter's wrath. Although the level of discord the two justices exhibited here did not characterize their relations in most cases (indeed, they voted together with relative frequency), it suggested much more than a disagreement of limited scope and duration. The flag-salute controversy signaled major jurisprudential differences between these men. One will find the source of these differences in the contrast that Jackson's traditional legal background presented to Frankfurter's Progressive past.

Notes

1. Philip B. Kurland, ed., *Felix Frankfurter on the Supreme Court: Extrajudicial Essays on the Court and the Constitution* (Cambridge: Harvard University Press, Belknap Press, 1970), 263, 451–52 (quoted; emphasis in original); Alexander M. Bickel, *The Least Dangerous Branch: The Supreme Court at the Bar of Politics*, 2d ed. (New Haven: Yale University Press, 1986), 115–16 (Frankfurter quoted). See the discussion of the concept of justiciability in chapter 5 above, note 95 and accompanying text.

2. Harlan B. Phillips, ed., *Felix Frankfurter Reminisces* (New York: Reynal, 1960), 166; Felix Frankfurter, *The Public and Its Government* (New Haven: Yale University Press, 1930), 75 (emphasis in original); Kurland, ed., *Felix Frankfurter on the Supreme Court*, 24–25 (emphasis added); Felix

Frankfurter, *Mr. Justice Holmes and the Supreme Court* (1938; reprint, Cambridge: Harvard University Press, Belknap Press, 1961), 23, 96; Frankfurter, *Public and Its Government*, 75, 79, 76.

3. Frankfurter, *Mr. Justice Holmes and the Supreme Court*, 21, 30–31, 60, 95 (p. 95 quoted first, pp. 30–31 quoted fourth; emphasis added); Kurland, ed., *Felix Frankfurter on the Supreme Court*, 5–7, 193, 205, 216, 263, 288, 296, 454 (p. 263 quoted second and third, p. 296 quoted fifth, p. 454 quoted sixth and seventh; emphasis added); Frankfurter, *Public and Its Government*, 50–51.

4. Kurland, ed., *Felix Frankfurter on the Supreme Court*, 252 (quoted); Phillips, ed., *Felix Frankfurter Reminisces*, 299–301 (pp. 301, 300 quoted second and third); Frankfurter, *Public and Its Government*, 74–75. See the discussion of Thayer in chapter 3 above, notes 64–66 and accompanying text.

5. Hugo L. Black, "The Bill of Rights," *New York University Law Review* 35 (1960): 866, 878; Frankfurter, *Public and Its Government*, 76; *West Virginia State Bd. of Educ. v. Barnette*, 319 U.S. 624, 648 (1943) (Frankfurter, J., dissenting). See also Kurland, ed., *Felix Frankfurter on the Supreme Court*, 269, 296; Frankfurter, *Mr. Justice Holmes and the Supreme Court*, 28.

6. Kurland, ed., *Felix Frankfurter on the Supreme Court*, 7, 164, 215, 266–67, 296, 455 (pp. 455, 7, 296 quoted); Phillips, ed., *Felix Frankfurter Reminisces*, 299–301; Frankfurter, *Mr. Justice Holmes and the Supreme Court*, 86, 106; Frankfurter, *Public and Its Government*, 48, 59.

7. Felix Frankfurter, "The Task of Administrative Law," *University of Pennsylvania Law Review* 75 (1927): 618 (quoted); Frankfurter, *Public and Its Government*, 157–62.

8. *Railroad Comm'n v. Rowan & Nichols Oil Co.*, 310 U.S. 573, 580–82, 584 (1940) (emphasis added). See also *Railroad Comm'n v. Rowan & Nichols Oil Co.*, 311 U.S. 570, 576–77 (1941).

9. *Railroad Comm'n v. Rowan & Nichols Oil Co.*, 310 U.S. at 584.

10. *Shields v. Utah Idaho Cent. R. R.*, 305 U.S. 177 (1938); *Stark v. Wickard*, 321 U.S. 288, 312-13 (1944) (Frankfurter, J., dissenting). See also Louis L. Jaffe, "The Judicial Universe of Mr. Justice Frankfurter," *Harvard Law Review* 62 (1949): 372–73; Wallace Mendelson, "Mr. Justice Frankfurter on Administrative Law," *Journal of Politics* 19 (1957): 445–50; Bernard Schwartz, "The Administrative World of Mr. Justice Frankfurter," *Yale Law Journal* 59 (1950): 1246–56.

11. *United States v. ICC*, 337 U.S. 426, 433–34 (1949).

12. Schwartz, "Administrative World of Mr. Justice Frankfurter," 1256; *Trust of Bingham v. Commissioner*, 325 U.S. 365, 380 (1945) (Frankfurter, J., concurring).

13. *Trust of Bingham v. Commissioner*, 379, 380–81 (Frankfurter, J., concurring); Schwartz, "Administrative World of Mr. Justice Frankfurter," 1258–61; Mendelson, "Mr. Justice Frankfurter on Administrative Law," 450–52.

14. William C. Chase, *The American Law School and the Rise of Adminis-*

trative Government (Madison: University of Wisconsin Press, 1982), 129–30; Mendelson, "Mr. Justice Frankfurter on Administrative Law," 451; *City of Yonkers v. United States*, 320 U.S. 685, 695 (1944) (Frankfurter, J., dissenting). See also Alfred C. Aman Jr. and William T. Mayton, *Administrative Law* (St. Paul: West Publishing, 1993), 460; *Estep v. United States*, 327 U.S. 114, 142 (1946) (Frankfurter, J., concurring); Schwartz, "Administrative World of Mr. Justice Frankfurter," 1261.

15. E. Merrick Dodd, "The Supreme Court and Organized Labor, 1941– 1945," *Harvard Law Review* 58 (1945): 1066–67 (quoted); Mendelson, *Justices Black and Frankfurter*, 36–41; Mendelson, "Mr. Justice Frankfurter on Administrative Law," 458–59; Chase, *Law School and Rise of Administrative Government*, 103–5, 106–16, 134, 141–44.

16. *NLRB v. Universal Camera Corp.*, 179 F. 2d 749, 751–52 (2d Cir. 1950) (quoted; emphasis added); Morton J. Horwitz, *The Transformation of American Law, 1870–1960* (New York: Oxford University Press, 1992), 230–40 (p. 235 quoted second and third); *Universal Camera Corp. v. NLRB*, 340 U.S. 474, 489–90 (1951) (quoted fourth); Chase, *Law School and Rise of Administrative Government*, 147–58. See also *Heikkila v. Barber*, 345 U.S. 229, 238 (1953) (Frankfurter, J., dissenting).

17. Mendelson, "Mr. Justice Frankfurter on Administrative Law," 449 (Act quoted; emphasis added); *Universal Camera Corp. v. NLRB*, 487; Horwitz, *Transformation of American Law, 1870–1960*, 236.

18. See, e.g., Horwitz, *Transformation of American Law, 1870–1960*, 230–40. See also Chase, *Law School and Rise of Administrative Government*, 147–61; *SEC v. Chenery Corp.*, 332 U.S. 194, 216–17 (1947) (Jackson, J., dissenting) (Frankfurter joined Jackson's dissent); Jaffe, "Judicial Universe of Mr. Justice Frankfurter," 375–76.

19. Frankfurter, *Public and Its Government*, 161–62, 157, 159–60. See the discussion of Croly and Laski in chapter 6 above, notes 41–44 and accompanying text.

20. See, e.g., *Beauharnais v. Illinois*, 343 U.S. 250, 261–63, 267 (1952).

21. Frankfurter, *Mr. Justice Holmes and the Supreme Court*, 22; Kurland, ed., *Felix Frankfurter on the Supreme Court*, 265. See chapter 5 above, note 16 and accompanying text.

22. Frankfurter, *Mr. Justice Holmes and the Supreme Court*, 22–23; Kurland, ed., *Felix Frankfurter on the Supreme Court*, 265, 268, 267.

23. See chapter 6 above, notes 45–51 and accompanying text.

24. *Minersville Sch. Dist. v. Gobitis*, 310 U.S. 586 (1940).

25. Ibid., 594, 593, 595, 597, 597–98.

26. Ibid., 598, 599, 600.

27. Ibid., 600, 599.

28. Ibid., 605–6, 604, 601, 603–4 (Stone, J., dissenting).

29. Ibid., 606 (Stone J., dissenting); *United States v. Carolene Prod. Co.*, 304 U.S. 144, 152 n. 4 (1938) (quoted); Henry J. Abraham, *Freedom and the*

Court: Civil Rights and Liberties in the United States, 5th ed. (New York: Oxford University Press, 1988), 21–28.

30. *Minersville Sch. Dist. v. Gobitis*, 606 (Stone, J., dissenting).

31. Felix Frankfurter to Harlan F. Stone, 27 May 1940, Papers of Felix Frankfurter, Library of Congress, Manuscript Division (hereafter cited as FFP), Box 105 (underline in original).

32. Alpheus Mason, *Harlan Fiske Stone: Pillar of the Law* (New York: Viking Press, 1956), 532; *Jones v. Opelika*, 316 U.S. 584, 623–24 (1984) (Black, Douglas & Murphy, JJ., dissenting) (quoted).

33. *West Virginia State Bd. of Educ. v. Barnette*, 633–34.

34. Ibid., 647, 661–62 (Frankfurter, J., dissenting) (emphasis added).

35. Ibid., 652 (Frankfurter, J., dissenting).

36. Ibid., 664, 667–70 (Frankfurter, J., dissenting).

37. H. N. Hirsch, *The Enigma of Felix Frankfurter* (New York: Basic Books, 1981), 151–52.

38. *Bridges v. California*, 314 U.S. 252, 263, 273 (1941).

39. Ibid., 303, 293, 282, 284, 295–96 (Frankfurter, J., dissenting) (italics in original).

40. Ibid., 268–75; ibid., 300 (Frankfurter, J., dissenting) (emphasis added).

41. Ibid., 294 (Frankfurter, J., dissenting). See also *Craig v. Harney*, 331 U.S. 367, 391–93 (1947) (Frankfurter, J., dissenting).

42. *Martin v. City of Struthers*, 319 U.S. 141, 146–47 (1943).

43. Ibid., 152–53 (Frankfurter, J., dissenting).

44. Ibid., 153–54 (Frankfurter, J., dissenting) (emphasis added). See also *Saia v. New York*, 334 U.S. 558, 563–64 (1948) (Frankfurter, J., dissenting).

45. *Kovacs v. Cooper*, 336 U.S. 77, 88 (1949).

46. Ibid., 90, 96 (Frankfurter, J., concurring) (emphasis in original).

47. Ibid., 98 (Black, J., dissenting).

48. Ibid., 90, 97, 96 (Frankfurter, J., concurring).

49. Ibid., 95–96 (Frankfurter, J., concurring).

50. *West Virginia State Bd. of Educ. v. Barnette*, 663 (Frankfurter, J., dissenting). See also *Dennis v. United States*, 341 U.S. 494, 526–27, 542–44 (1951) (Frankfurter, J., concurring).

51. *Dennis v. United States*, 510.

52. Ibid., 543, 525, 539, 541, 525, 542 (Frankfurter, J., concurring). See also ibid., 540 (Frankfurter, J., concurring); David M. O'Brien, *The Public's Right to Know: The Supreme Court and the First Amendment* (New York: Praeger, 1981), 80–87.

53. *Dennis v. United States*, 525, 551 (Frankfurter, J., concurring).

54. Ibid., 553, 555, 552 (Frankfurter, J., concurring).

55. Frankfurter, *Mr. Justice Holmes and the Supreme Court*, 62 (quoted), 151; Frankfurter, *Public and Its Government*, 44–45, 50–51; Kurland, ed., *Felix Frankfurter on the Supreme Court*, 255–56 (quoted); chapter 6 above, note 49 and accompanying text.

56. Kurland, ed., *Felix Frankfurter on the Supreme Court*, 181, 214 (quoted); Frankfurter, *Public and its Government*, 46–47.

57. Kurland, ed., *Felix Frankfurter on the Supreme Court*, 166–67, 254, 32, 254–55.

58. Ibid., 3, 32 (quoted first and second); Archibald MacLeish and E. F. Prichard Jr., eds., *Law and Politics: Occasional Papers of Felix Frankfurter, 1913–1938* (New York: Harcourt, Brace, 1939), 35, 255–56, 263–64 (p. 35 quoted third; emphasis added); Frankfurter, *Public and Its Government*, 48–49.

59. As quoted in Mark Silverstein, *Constitutional Faiths: Felix Frankfurter, Hugo Black, and the Process of Judicial Decision Making* (Ithaca: Cornell University Press, 1984), 152–53 (my emphasis).

60. Silverstein mistakenly reads Frankfurter's letter as a statement of faith in judicial power. Ibid. He fails to see that the justice's use of discretion indicated a distrust of the judicial resolution of constitutional conflicts. See notes 80–84 below and accompanying text.

61. *Betts v. Brady*, 316 U.S. 455, 462 (1942); Tinsley E. Yarbrough, *Mr. Justice Black and His Critics* (Durham: Duke University Press, 1988), 87–88 (Murphy's notes quoted).

62. *Malinski v. New York*, 324 U.S. 401, 414, 413 (1945) (Frankfurter, J., concurring).

63. Ibid., 418, 415–16 (Frankfurter, J., concurring).

64. Ibid., 417–18 (Frankfurter, J., concurring).

65. *Francis v. Resweber*, 329 U.S. 459, 462–64 (1947).

66. Felix Frankfurter, "Memorandum for the Conference, No. 142— Louisiana v. Resweber," 11 January 1947, *Papers of Robert H. Jackson*, Library of Congress, Manuscript Division (hereafter cited as RHJP), Box 138.

67. *Francis v. Resweber*, 468 (Frankfurter, J., concurring).

68. Ibid., 468–69 (Frankfurter, J., concurring), quoting *Palko v. Connecticut*, 302 U.S. 319, 324–25 (1937), and *Snyder v. Massachusetts*, 291 U.S. 97, 105 (1934).

69. *Francis v. Resweber*, 469–72 (Frankfurter, J., concurring). See also Felix Frankfurter to Harold Burton, 13 December 1946, RHJP, Box 138.

70. *Adamson v. California*, 332 U.S. 46, 59 (1947) (Frankfurter, J., concurring).

71. Ibid., 67, 63, 62 (Frankfurter, J., concurring). Recall Black's efforts to avoid the conservative implications of his conception of due process. See chapter 5 above, notes 81–82 and accompanying text.

72. *Adamson v. California*, 65 (Frankfurter, J., concurring).

73. Abraham, *Freedom and the Court*, 72–108; *Adamson v. California*, 85–86, 89 (Black, J., dissenting); ibid., 65 (Frankfurter, J., concurring). In *Wolf v. Colorado*, 338 U.S. 25 (1949), Frankfurter agreed that the Fourth Amendment's prohibition of unreasonable searches and seizures applies against the states through the Fourteenth Amendment. In his opinion for the

Court, however, he denied that the federal exclusionary rule (i.e., the rule making illegally obtained evidence inadmissible in court) also applies against the states:

> The security of one's privacy against arbitrary intrusion by the police—which is at the core of the Fourth Amendment—is basic to a free society. It is therefore implicit in "the concept of ordered liberty" and as such enforceable against the States through the Due Process Clause. . . .
>
> Accordingly, we have no hesitation in saying that were a State affirmatively to sanction such police incursion into privacy it would run counter to the guaranty of the Fourteenth Amendment. But the ways of enforcing such a basic right raises questions of a different order. How such arbitrary conduct should be checked, what remedies against it should be afforded, the means by which the right should be made effective, are all questions that are not to be so dogmatically answered as to preclude the varying solutions which spring from an allowable range of judgment on issues not susceptible of quantitative solution. . . . Granted that in practice the exclusion of evidence may be an effective way of deterring unreasonable searches, it is not for this Court to condemn as falling below the minimal standards assured by the Due Process Clause a State's reliance upon other methods which, if consistently enforced, would be equally effective.

Wolf v. Colorado, 27–28. Note the concern with judicial abstraction in this passage. Frankfurter dissented when, in *Mapp v. Ohio*, 367 U.S. 643 (1961), the Court applied the exclusionary rule against the states.

74. *Rochin v. California*, 342 U.S. 165, 170, 172 (1952). See also *Haley v. Ohio*, 332 U.S. 596, 604–5 (1948) (Frankfurter, J., joining in reversal of judgment).

75. *Rochin v. California*, 170; *Adamson v. California*, 90 (Black, J., dissenting). See also ibid., 67–68 (Frankfurter, J., concurring); *Haley v. Ohio*, 602–3.

76. Silverstein, *Constitutional Faiths*, 213. For cases in which Frankfurter voted against the federal government under the Fourth Amendment, see *Harris v. United States*, 331 U.S. 145, 155 (1947) (Frankfurter, J., dissenting); *Johnson v. United States*, 333 U.S. 10 (1948); *McDonald v. United States*, 335 U.S. 451, 461 (1948); *Brinegar v. United States*, 338 U.S. 160, 188 (1949); *United States v. Rabinowitz*, 339 U.S. 56, 68 (1950) (Frankfurter, J., dissenting); *On Lee v. United States*, 343 U.S. 747, 758 (1952) (Frankfurter, J., dissenting). See also Felix Frankfurter to Sherman Minton, 25 January 1950, FFP, Box 84.

77. *Harris v. United States*, 162 (Frankfurter, J., dissenting). For Black's approach to the Fourth Amendment, see chapter 5 above, notes 64–66 and accompanying text.

78. *On Lee v. United States*, 758–62 (Frankfurter, J., dissenting). Five years after Frankfurter left the bench, the Court accepted his position on this issue. See *Katz v. United States*, 389 U.S. 347 (1967), which overruled *Olmstead v. United States*, 277 U.S. 438 (1928).

79. *Everson v. Board of Educ.*, 330 U.S. 1, 18 (1947) (Jackson, J., dissenting) (Frankfurter joined Jackson's dissent); *McCollum v. Board of Educ.*, 333 U.S. 203, 212, 227 (quoted) (1948) (Frankfurter, J., separate opinion).

80. Joseph P. Lash, ed., *From the Diaries of Felix Frankfurter* (New York: W. W. Norton, 1975), 242–43; *Dennis v. United States*, 524–25 (Frankfurter, J., concurring); Silverstein, *Constitutional Faiths*, 214. For a discussion of positivism, see chapter 5 above, notes 72–73 and accompanying text.

81. *Joint Anti-Fascist Refugee Comm. v. McGrath*, 341 U.S. 123, 174 (1951) (Frankfurter, J., concurring) (quoted first and second); Felix Frankfurter to Max Lerner, 3 March 1943, FFP, Box 76 (quoted third and fourth); Silverstein, *Constitutional Faiths*, 15, 70–71, 74–76, 129 n. 2 (pp. 15, 129 n. 2 quoted fifth and sixth); Gary J. Jacobsohn, *Pragmatism, Statesmanship, and the Supreme Court* (Ithaca: Cornell University Press, 1977), 120, 131, 141. For a discussion of the impact of totalitarianism upon legal and political thought, see Edward A. Purcell Jr., *The Crisis of Democratic Theory: Scientific Naturalism and the Problem of Value* (Lexington: University Press of Kentucky, 1973), 117–38.

82. Jacobsohn, *Pragmatism, Statesmanship, and the Supreme Court*, 125 (quoted), 131; Silverstein, *Constitutional Faiths*, 145–46, 180–81.

83. Silverstein, *Constitutional Faiths*, 200; *Dennis v. United States*, 540 (Frankfurter, J., concurring). See also *Minersville Sch. Dist. v. Gobitis*, 598; *West Virginia State Bd. of Educ. v. Barnette*, 647, 652 (Frankfurter, J., dissenting); *Francis v. Resweber*, 470–71 (Frankfurter, J., concurring).

84. Kurland, ed., *Felix Frankfurter on the Supreme Court*, 295; *West Virginia State Bd. of Educ. v. Barnette*, 667 (Frankfurter, J., dissenting). Frankfurter overstated the case when he said that his judicial philosophy reserved to the Court "a great and stately jurisdiction." Phillips, ed., *Felix Frankfurter Reminisces*, 301.

85. Felix Frankfurter to Zechariah Chafee Jr., 25 October 1955, FFP, Box 42; Felix Frankfurter to Frank Murphy, 15 February 1947, FFP, Box 86.

86. See Helen Shirley Thomas, *Felix Frankfurter: Scholar on the Bench* (Baltimore: Johns Hopkins University Press, 1960), 138–42.

87. *On Lee v. United States*, 761 (Frankfurter, J., dissenting); Phillips, ed., *Felix Frankfurter Reminisces*, 49. One should also note that Justices Holmes and Brandeis, both of whom Frankfurter admired greatly, believed firmly that the Fourth Amendment concept of a "search" should not be confined to actual physical entry. See *Olmstead v. United States*, 469 (Holmes, J., dissenting).

88. *McCollum v. Board of Educ.*, 216–17, 231 (Frankfurter, J., separate opinion).

89. *West Virginia State Bd. of Educ. v. Barnette*, 653 (Frankfurter, J., dissenting).

8

Robert H. Jackson and Traditional Legal Assumptions in the Modern Age

If a fear of political oppression dominated Hugo Black's thinking, while a fear of judicial abstraction characterized that of Felix Frankfurter, both sentiments appeared in Robert Jackson's thought. Yet one can link neither element of Jackson's thinking with the political movements industrialism inspired. In contrast to Black, Jackson did not acquire his distrust of political power through exposure to Populism. Rather, he shared in the court-centered thought patterns of the pre-industrial legal community. He was the last member of the Court to learn his law as an apprentice, and, in his professional life prior to government service, he exemplified the mainstay of the nineteenth-century legal community: the generalist country lawyer. In contrast to Frankfurter, he did not acquire his mistrust of the judicial process through involvement in Progressive politics. This element of Jackson's thought stemmed primarily from his awareness of the interdependent nature of an urban-industrial age and from his efforts as a government attorney to defend the New Deal before the federal judiciary. With such conflicted thought, he defended vigorously the concept of judicial supremacy at the same time as he provided detailed arguments concerning the defects of the process of judicial fact-finding.

Apprentice in the Law

Jackson was born in 1892 on a small farm in Spring Creek, Pennsylvania. He spent approximately the next four decades living in or around Jamestown, New York. During that time, he remained fairly sheltered

from the harsh and disruptive effects of industrialization. He described
his rural hometown as "a somewhat isolated community" and "somewhat parochial . . . by reason of its physical location." Although steel
communities surrounded the people of Jamestown, he said, "we didn't
think of ourselves or our rights as being in any way affected by
what went on in some of those steel towns. We thought ourselves
independent of such conditions, and were happy in the thought." Put
another way, "the interdependence of communities was not so apparent [then] . . . , particularly not before the First World War." Even
during the depression, Jamestown residents found the effects of interdependence relatively imperceptible. Because the town's "farmer[s]
. . . raised most of [their] own food," he explained, they "didn't suffer
to the extent that the one-crop farms . . . suffered" when the depression brought declining national and international markets for agricultural products.[1]

In view of the absence of a sense of interdependence, one should not
be surprised that Jackson's discussions of the character of Jamestown
residents emphasized the core value of nineteenth-century social
thought, namely, the ethic of self-mastery or self-reliance. He described his townsmen as "a very independent, self-sufficient people."

> Everybody was expected to work. The only person who was not re-
> spected was the one who did not work. . . . Everybody lived on very
> much the same level. It was really a democratic existence and a very
> individualistic one. Nobody asked favors except on the basis of repay-
> ment and there was a strong desire to avoid real poverty. Pauperism was
> regarded as sort of a moral judgment that one had wasted his opportunity.
> In that kind of society it often was true. To an unfortunate individual
> there was utmost kindness, but if one was a pauper that was probably his
> own fault. He either drank, or gambled, or was lazy, or something evil.
> Poverty, as such, attracted no sympathy and little help. The way of the
> poor was hard, but so was the way of the not poor.[2]

While Jackson admired Jamestown residents for their individualism
and self-reliance, he reserved special praise for his progenitors. Of
course, the Jacksons and the Houghwouts were "hard-working people
and very independent." But their stoutheartedness was notable even
among a self-reliant people. "They were all independent of the community life, in a sense." They "never looked to others for support or
even companionship." "They went to various social occasions," but
Jackson "always felt [that they exhibited] a certain detachment from
other people, a certain self-reliance and self-dependence in them that

did not care very much what other people thought, or did, or said. They were going their own way. . . . They looked to their own acres and left everybody to take care of theirs. They were individualists of the strongest kind. . . . They were self-sufficient and self-reliant, believed it was up to them to take care of themselves, sought no help and taught, insofar as they consciously taught anything, thrift, industry, and self-reliance."[3]

Jackson described his grandmother as "a very independent woman in thought and action" and his mother as "very individualistic, very self-sufficient." His father, a farmer by trade, was "an intense individualist. What he did was his affair; what the community did was its affair." Jackson surmised that had his father lived to see the income tax, "he would have told the United States that it was none of their God-damn business how much money he made. He didn't want anything to do with the government and didn't want them to have anything to do with him." Acknowledging the influence of his forbears generally and his father specifically, Jackson remarked: "In spirit, my father and . . . I are much closer to the frontier than most. . . . [The frontier tradition] has always been strong with me because of my association with these older people [of Jamestown]."[4]

Jackson's relatives exhibited (and contributed to) their independence by remaining "sturdy and uncompromising Democrats" in an area that was "overwhelmingly Republican." Although his "people were never sympathetic with the South in the sense of either favoring slavery or favoring disunion," "[t]hey were invariably Democrats, and remained so all during the Civil War." As such, the Jacksons had "no political preferment and . . . there was no political course open to [them]." Still, Jamestown Republicans tolerated their Democratic neighbors. The Jacksons were "so much a minority" that they presented no threat to Republican control. Moreover, these Democrats were not given to ostentatious political displays, for, as Jackson said, "[n]one of [his] people [had] ever been fanatics on any subject."[5]

Jackson applied this last observation to religious matters as well. He recalled that, while his forebears "knew their Bible and . . . were [thus] not free of religious feeling, they were free of religious organization." "They supported religious institutions, but . . . their attitude was one of toleration rather than of adherence." Jackson's parents "had no religious affiliations and never tried to teach [their son] anything about religion except the most elemental things." They found particularly offensive the "silly exhibitions of emotionalism" that frequently characterized camp meetings and revivals in the area.

Collectively, Jackson's relatives "were pretty practical people who were not carried away by either religious emotions or any other."[6]

With regard to his earliest political and religious influences, then, Jackson "came from people too busy making a living, to work life's annoyances up into a philosophy." Like his progenitors, he preferred an approach to life that "is practical, hard-headed and concrete," as opposed to one based upon "pernicious abstraction." The "distinguishing ideology [of such an approach] is that it has no 'ideology' except to get results."[7]

Although Jackson's relatives were practical people, they were not unconcerned with matters of the intellect. Jackson noted that the people of Jamestown generally acquired a degree of "intellectual independence" through involvement in that nineteenth-century institution of self-improvement and self-culture, the Chautauqua. The Jacksons in particular "were great readers and a literate people," despite having "little formal education." They "all had and read books, which few families in the community did." Jackson recalled that these books "were sometimes read to [him] by [his] grandmother and created a certain interest in the printed word." His high-school principal, Milton J. Fletcher, and English teacher, Mary R. Willard, nurtured this intellectual curiosity. Jackson described Fletcher as a "scholarly man" and "a powerful influence." He remembered Willard as the person who brought him into "contact with the best in literature." Her "influence would be hard to overestimate."[8]

Jackson was indebted to his high-school mentors for more than their contributions to his intellectual development. Without their guidance and encouragement, he may not have followed through on his long-standing ambition to become a lawyer. He "had been interested in [the law] from earliest times." Local trials "attracted a great deal of attention" in Jamestown before the advent of radio and television, and the young Jackson was often in attendance. Besides finding entertainment, he "acquired a rough familiarity with the [legal] process" and a desire to emulate the attorneys arguing before him. His father, however, was "dead-set against" his aspirations; his mother refused to become involved in the matter. With the support of his high-school preceptors, he would join the bar in spite of his father's protestations.[9]

Upon graduating from high school in 1910, Jackson immediately acted upon his career goal. He became a legal apprentice in the office of two local attorneys, Frank Mott and Benjamin Dean. Mott was related by marriage to Jackson's mother, and his tendency to live beyond his means accounted for the elder Jackson's strong dislike of lawyers. With a love of books and a penchant for political conversation, Mott would have an influence upon Jackson that "was all in the same direction as that of Mary Willard."[10]

Dean was also "a very strong influence in [Jackson's] life." Indeed, he was most responsible for shaping the young man's legal thought. Unlike most masters in the traditional system of legal education, Dean was learned and conscientious. Jackson described him as "a very industrious, scholarly lawyer" who "had great acquaintance with the literature of the law." Dean made his protege study in the office, feeding him a steady diet of readings from the oracle of the common law, Blackstone, and from the "American Blackstone," James Kent. (Recall from Chapter 2 that Kent's *Commentaries* contained a defense of the doctrine of judicial supremacy, as well as a treatment of common-law principles.) Instructed in the method of the common law, Jackson shed his layman's view that law is "something of a code with definite principles . . . that were invariable." He learned that while the common-law mind strives for continuity—and he was trained in the use of "digests, encyclopedias and texts to find answers to a client's particular problem"—it also allows for adaptation of principles to meet particular circumstances. He found himself dealing "with the uncertainties, the lack of codification, the fact that law existed in decision, unwritten law, and custom."[11]

After one year as an apprentice, Jackson "decided that [he] ought to go to a law school, not having had any college." He entered Albany Law School, intending to complete a two-year program of instruction in one year. As a student, he led a bookish existence. But he characterized Albany as "a practical school"; "its courses were designed as equipment for the New York bar [examination] rather than for legal philosophy, jurisprudence and legal theory." One would think that a young man with a practical bent would have embraced this curriculum, but Jackson found his law professors uninspiring. He valued more the time he spent out of class, listening to arguments before the New York Court of Appeals. Indeed, he chose Albany in large measure because its proximity to the appellate courts of New York enabled him to observe law in concrete circumstances. He thought that, in Albany, he "would learn more that was not in the books . . . than in any other place"; "that opportunity was really one of the most important assets of the school."[12]

Jackson completed the program of study at Albany in one year, as he had planned. But he had to return to the office of Mott and Dean because the state required, as preparation for the bar, three years of either office work or law school instruction, or any combination thereof. In addition to resuming his schooling under Dean's watchful eye, Jackson found that he "had a source of education . . . , somewhat like the [British] Inns of Court," in "the lawyers [of the area who] gathered and discussed cases." Listening to their conversations, he imbibed the concerns and advice of those who were preoccupied with the relation between law and circumstance.[13]

These concerns soon became material to Jackson, for "Mott turned many small things over to [him upon his return from law school,] and [he] was . . . trying cases almost as though [he] was admitted to the bar, so far as justice court and city court were concerned." Jackson "began to learn how to deal with clients, witnesses and adversaries and how to investigate facts and law." In short, "he accumulated experience in the matters on which he would first be put to test in his profession."[14]

Country Lawyer

The challenge of professional independence came sooner than Jackson had expected. In the final year of Jackson's apprenticeship, Mott abandoned his law practice to become secretary of the New York Public Service Commission. Jackson assumed the burden of his master's caseload and litigated conflicts "of all sorts, many for goods sold, or breach of contract." Recalling the pressures of his situation, he said that "there was more at stake [in these cases] than the money involved." The conflicts "were apt to involve rather leading men of the community as adversaries. . . . Their prestige in the community, in a sense, was at stake—their word, their honor."[15]

Jackson learned quickly that in order to win at trial he had "to organize and present materials, not to satisfy professors, but to convince farmers and carpenters and laborers and miscellaneous humanity in the jury box." When litigating, he thus emphasized the circumstances of the particular case over any concern with continuity in the law. "The law, as a science or a philosophy, cut very little figure in those trials. . . . *It was the facts that counted.*" Lay jurors "weren't interested in technicalities or fine [legal] distinctions," and the "justice of the peace was not a lawyer" and "knew little law generally." "[J]ustice court," in short, "was a rough, natural justice court, rather than a sophisticated or learned tribunal."[16]

Jackson also discovered that the manner in which he appealed "to people's sense of natural justice" was just as important as his command of the circumstances of the particular case. He thus "learned to speak, not merely so he could be understood by persons of education, but so he could not be misunderstood by those without it." He found courtroom eloquence essential, not only to win the immediate case, but also to attract future clients.

> A young lawyer that went into [a case] had to take care of himself and put on a good show. If he didn't, he didn't get any more business in that section. His client usually was bitter at the adversary and expected a lawyer to protect his prestige as well as win his case. . . . [If a] young lawyer got off some witty remarks at his adversary, if he got out of a hole that the group could see was being dug for him, [then he] got business. It was a rough and tumble training by which a man quickly proved his mettle. Word went around that he did a good job or that he didn't. Often these remarks had very little relation to real legal ability, but it was of prime importance that a lawyer hold his own in a rough and tumble debating contest.[17]

Evidently, Jackson impressed many people because he soon built a very successful and diverse practice. He "took contract litigations, commercial litigations, promissory note cases, a good deal of will and estate work and a whole host of other things." Among his larger clients, he counted the Home Telephone Company, the International Railway, the Warren and Jamestown Street Railway Company, and the Pennsylvania Gas Company. He also handled cases for farmers, labor organizations, and small merchants and manufacturers. Given the size of his community, he could not specialize in the law. Yet, even if he had had that option, his "wish always was to keep [his] practise [*sic*] broad and diversified . . . and to depend upon many rather than a few clients." He "never wanted to get in a position . . . where the failure of one client . . . would seriously affect [his income]."[18]

With a legal education acquired primarily through office training, and with a practice that fit the standard of the nineteenth-century legal community (i.e., the generalist country lawyer), Jackson possessed a thoroughly traditional legal background. He revealed a strong commitment to the idea of the paradigmatic independent practitioner when, soon after he began practicing law, the state of New York abolished the apprenticeship system. He greatly regretted this development and called for the reinstatement of the office-training option. As an active member of local, state, and national bar associations, he had available forums for his proposal. He served as president of the Jamestown Bar

Association in the early 1920s and later became vice-president of the New York State Bar Association. In the latter capacity, he joined the effort to toughen entry requirements to the profession, ostensibly to improve the quality of legal services. "The legal profession is overloaded," he asserted, and "[e]xcessive competition among lawyers is . . . bad for society. A man having but little business is more tempted to advise unnecessary litigation, refuse compromises, solicit employment or bring 'strike' lawsuits, than one better occupied." At a time when "scientific" law schools were well on their way to becoming the dominant method of legal instruction, he advocated as a means of restricting entry to the profession an institution that was becoming anachronistic: "Perhaps there should be a year or more of probation during which an applicant, after the success in his [bar] examinations, should serve an apprenticeship under older members of the bar. . . . It is only by sustained observation in the actual stress and strain of practice that we can judge what pressure a character will withstand and whether one has the adaptability to the art of law practice."[19]

Jackson made his attachment to the legal culture of the pre-industrial age even more apparent in his response to changes in the composition of the bar. With the appearance of the attorney who specializes in corporate matters and responds to the demands of big business, he voiced concern that lawyers no longer commanded the respect that accompanied professional independence and detachment:

> The public questions our disinterestedness, and our intellectual integrity and our independence as a class. Does a lawyer have any unpurchasable convictions on any subject, especially if he has, or hopes for, clients who have an interest in that subject? Does he lead an independent mental life or is he nourished solely by retainers? . . . Perhaps explanation of the loss of prestige of the bar lies largely in the loss of independence by the lawyer. In the early days of the Republic, the counselor was a dominating factor in his community. The rise of the banker, the industrialist and the press had not yet subordinated him. He might be retained, but he was likely to govern the policy of the client in the affairs committed to his hands. Nothing has so much accelerated the decline of the bar as the tendency of lawyers to have jobs instead of practices. At least half of the business in court is only nominally in the control of the attorney and the real control is in an insurance claim agent or a corporation executive. When our lawyers become salaried servants, like office boys, it marks the end of the pleasing fiction that we are officers of the court.[20]

At times, Jackson seemed to acknowledge the inevitability of the shift toward legal specialization and the datedness of the country lawyer prototype. For example: "I fear that nothing can save the family lawyer or general practitioner from being buried in the same fossil strata as the tandem bicycle. The whole profession is carried along upon the economic tide[,] and professions . . . must perform their functions in society or move toward the scrap heap." But he continued to exhibit a nostalgic, restorationist impulse, clinging "to the hope that the . . . scornful estimate of the lawyer as 'the mouth-piece', will no longer find confirmation in the public attitude of the bar." He deplored "the narrow lawyer" and pined for a resurgence of the "sturdy and independent general practitioners [whose welfare] means much to the future good order of a democratic society."[21]

The impact of industrialism upon the judicial process disturbed Jackson even more than the disappearance of the country lawyer. Specifically, he worried about "the increasing tendency to substitute the administrative method for litigation and the administrative tribunal for the court." "The development of a body of administrative law in this country as a substitute for, or supplement to, the common law," he lamented, "has passed almost unnoticed by the bar associations." He found this situation puzzling, since the shift toward administrative decision making suggested not only a loss of prestige (and business) for the legal profession in civil matters but also an "even more threatening . . . [prospect] in the field of government and public law." "[B]y [virtue of] membership in the legal profession," he explained, attorneys tend to possess a "traditional set of values." They are committed to "the supremacy of an independent judiciary" or "the maintenance of the judicial branch as a corrective force in our [consti-tutional] system." Legislative transference of responsibility from courts to agencies, however, means that, unless individuals appeal administrative directives, we do not benefit from the "judicial depart-ment's wisdom and neutral views."[22]

"If we are to continue to have government by adjudication," Jack-son argued, advocates of the judicial process must remedy the institu-tional inadequacies of courts that prompted legislators to create admin-istrative bodies. In particular, judicial judgments must "be rendered in *the same era* that raised the questions and in the light of conditions of that era." At present, courts are "severely and needlessly handi-capped by a load of delays, costs, formality, technicality and uncer-tainty, which win [the judicial process] nothing but public suspicion and hostility." He believed that "[r]esponsibility for training our legal system down to fighting weight and sweating out its excess cost and formality and speeding it up so as to have a fair chance to compete for its life is definitely that of the organized bar."[23]

Jackson did not seek to dismantle bureaucratic institutions at any cost. He believed that inattention to the disruptions attending industrialization would lead to evils more serious than those appertaining to the administrative process. "Not even the most ardent champion of judicial supremacy" would call for a halt to governmental efforts to address economic problems "while the judicial view was slowly made available through the tedious and often devious process of private litigation." "Legislation, and administration, cannot await the interminable delays of the courts. Congress and the executive departments are compelled to outrun the judiciary."[24]

Early on, Jackson saw the need for governmental attention to economic matters. Jamestown's relative isolation did not prevent him from learning about the problems of industrialization. Upon resuming his apprenticeship after finishing law school, he served as head of the Woodrow Wilson Club and worked to secure the nomination of the former president of Princeton. Jackson "was very strong for Wilson . . . [and] the New Freedom," since the program "seemed . . . not only sound but essential to our times." He "took the need for a Federal Reserve System on faith in Wilson and his arguments for it" but "was a believer in the Wilsonian philosophy of maintaining competition and in the Louis Brandeis philosophy of the curse of bigness."[25] It was the restorationist element in Wilson's Progressive politics, then, that most attracted the young lawyer, whose personal and professional background stressed the traditional values of self-reliance and professional independence. He regarded as essential governmental efforts to combat forms of economic domination that frustrate self-reliant individuals' attempts to define their own material existence.

Jackson did not oppose all aggregations of power. While he resisted corporate influence, he "always favored labor's right to organize." "[T]hough often requested to do so," he recalled, "I never . . . sought a labor injunction [in my practice]." Indeed, he represented labor unions in litigation "and went to the Central Labor Council [of Jamestown] and spoke on various local problems from time to time." He denied that his "thoughts on labor's right to organize were at variance with [his] individualist background":

> It must be remembered that at that time the union was battling against what appeared to be a much more dominating threat to individualists.

The employer group was organized into a manufacturers' association which was powerful. In those days the blacklist was used. The association could blacklist a man for asking for higher wages or stirring up the wage problem. The individual workman[,] I felt, and still feel, had almost no chance to survive or to get a decent wage against the power of the employer represented by an aggregation of capital and an aggregation of employers in a manufacturers' association. It seemed to me that the independence of the working class of people was pretty much at stake in their ability to organize.[26]

Jackson acknowledged that his willingness to represent labor stemmed more from a desire "to put [his] professional goods on the market" than an attempt to help "soften the harsh blows of society on the individual." ("[A] great deal of that philosophy of the profession as a social force," he said, "didn't begin to take shape until after the First World War.") And he noted that a "lawyer lost no caste at the bar by taking an unpopular case"; Jamestown lawyers did not attribute radical motives to individuals who represented labor in court. Yet Jackson was part of a group of young lawyers whose expressed views on "the shortcomings of the industrial system, the needs of labor, and the struggle that was going on in the economic world" earned them a "radical [reputation] in the eyes of the conservatives" of the Jamestown bar. The conservatives, of course, did not look favorably upon Jackson's support of Wilson. But they saved their harshest criticism for the "radicals" of the bar—those so-called traitors to Republicanism who enlisted in the Bull Moose campaign.[27]

Following Wilson's election, Jackson presided over the distribution of the spoils of victory in his county. (He had become a member of the Democratic state committee at the tender age of twenty-one.) He found himself "getting into fights over . . . little post office jobs which didn't have any importance to anything that [he] was interested in in a larger way." The fact that the county's Democrats "had no . . . Congressman of [their] own to whom [they] could turn" for help in securing appointments complicated Jackson's task as patronage chief. Fortunately, he had earlier made the acquaintance (through Frank Mott) of Franklin D. Roosevelt, who was now Wilson's secretary of the Navy. "Through Roosevelt[, Jackson] succeeded in getting [Democratic] postmasters appointed in every place where there was a vacancy."[28]

In spite of these accomplishments, Jackson soon retired from organization politics. He disliked its quarrelsome nature and was concerned about the amount of time he had to spend away from his law practice.[29] Although brief and unpleasant, this episode in his professional life was of great moment, for he developed an acquaintance with the person who would ultimately place him on the Supreme Court.

New Deal Lawyer

Initial Misgivings

Despite having established a working relationship with Roosevelt, Jackson revealed no burning desire to tie his political fortunes to those of the ambitious New York politician. As governor, Roosevelt offered Jackson a position on the New York Public Service Commission. Jackson declined, preferring to remain in private practice.[30]

Even after Roosevelt became president, Jackson "had no thought of asking [for], or being offered, a position" in the administration. When Harry Hopkins approached Jackson about becoming general counsel to the Works Progress Administration (WPA), Jackson "told Hopkins [that he] wouldn't consider any full-time job." Jackson refused to agree to realistic terms of employment in part because he believed that the WPA smacked too much of "getting something for nothing"; the agency offended his belief in the principle of self-help. More generally, he was reluctant to become involved in the New Deal because he rejected the philosophy underpinning the National Recovery Administration (NRA). Instead of the view of the president's influential brain trust concerning the inevitability of concentrated wealth and the need for centralized direction from Washington, Jackson adhered to "the basic philosophy of the anti-trust laws"; he "agreed with the Wilsonian doctrine [of breaking up economic power] rather than with the Theodore Rooseveltian philosophy of control of big business." He also had a more powerful, practical reason to decline involvement in the New Deal: he desired to continue a law practice that was as lucrative (earning him "about $30,000 in the net during the depression year") as it was stimulating.[31]

For similar reasons, Jackson hesitated when next the secretary of the Treasury, Henry Morgenthau, approached him about becoming assistant general counsel for the Bureau of Internal Revenue. This time, Jackson overcame his reluctance because Morgenthau accommodated his concerns about his law practice. Jackson must have been surprised when the Treasury secretary proposed the part-time status that Hopkins had earlier rejected. Jackson accepted the offer in 1934, believing that he would spend only four days a week in Washington for only six months. Yet this time commitment seems a significant sacrifice on Jackson's part, particularly in view of his reservations over the direction of the New Deal. The sacrifice was more apparent than real, however; he thought that experience as a government attorney would make him "a more useful man [i.e., lawyer] in the community."[32]

As one suspicious of the philosophy of the early New Deal, Jackson suffered no illusions about his standing with those who were most responsible for this philosophy. As he put it: "I was never strictly a New Dealer in the sense of belonging to the crowd of young college men that came to Washington and formed a sort of clique. I wasn't a member of the so-called 'brain trust.' I never even went to college. Neither was I one of the political group, for I never had served in the political national committee, run for office, had a political following or any of that sort of thing. I was pretty much outside of all those groups and yet friendly with many of the members of all of them."[33]

Jackson made his differences with the more influential members of Roosevelt's team almost conspicuous. In public addresses, he betrayed his allegiance to an irrecoverable America. Commenting on the "steady centralization of wealth and business control" that occurred before the depression, he noted plaintively that "[o]ne by one the clients of the country and small city lawyer disappeared." He found this occurrence especially troubling because the " 'country lawyers' from whom we used to get our statesmen have largely disappeared" as well. To the proliferation of administrative bodies, he gave grudging acceptance. He believed that the "litigation method has failed in such fields as rate regulation, anti-trust regulation, protection of minority stock holders, and protection of creditors through receiverships." But he still held out hope that there might "be some method by which the speed, informality and low cost of administrative decisions can be combined with judicial neutrality." Finally, his explicit mentioning of the Interstate Commerce Commission, the Federal Trade Commission, and the Federal Securities Commission as examples of the "effort of the law to . . . reduce the area of economic and social anarchy and lawless irresponsibility" was telling in its omission of the president's NRA.[34]

Ideological scruples aside, Jackson found his new situation interesting and agreeable. Indeed, he "was [soon] giving all [of his] time to the administration and letting things run themselves in Jamestown." He indicated a shift in professional priorities when he decided to dissolve his hometown law office. By this point, he expected to remain in Washington well beyond the six-month stay he had anticipated.[35]

Antitrust Proponent

If Jackson harbored doubts about committing all of his time to an administration that he believed was "heading in the wrong direction," events soon eased his discomfort. In 1936, he transferred from the tax division of the Department of Justice (having moved there from the Bureau of Internal Revenue in 1935) to its antitrust division. He "was entirely happy in the tax division." But he could not forgo the opportunity to become assistant attorney general in charge of antitrust matters, because the Supreme Court had recently declared unconstitutional the legislation behind the NRA. Upon accepting the position, he immediately engaged the attorney general, Homer Cummings, in a long conversation over "the prospect and the necessity for a revival of the anti-trust philosophy following the collapse of the NRA." Jackson thought "it . . . essential . . . that the department become . . . more aggressive in asserting the old anti-trust philosophy," which had fallen into desuetude during the early New Deal. The new assistant attorney general convinced his superior on this score, whereupon Cummings "put [the antitrust] problem in [Jackson's] lap without restraint or instructions, and expected [him] to work it out."[36]

Jackson found that the attorney general's approval was not sufficient to change federal policy. Many others within the administration were still "devoted to the proposition that industry cooperation under the eye of a government regulator" was the appropriate strategy for dealing with concentrated economic power. These people "favored [a] revival of some sort of NRA" that would pass constitutional muster. The president, Jackson noted, "was torn between the Theodore Roosevelt theory of regulated business and the Wilsonian-Brandeis theory of free competition and retention of the smaller units." Simply put, "there was rather a state of bafflement and of confusion in the administration about the anti-trust laws" at the time Jackson accepted his new position.[37]

Dissatisfied with such ambiguity, Jackson and several other antitrust proponents attempted to force the issue by engaging in "some speech-making on the subject." In a series of addresses made without explicit presidential approval, Jackson sought to "tear the veil of pious pretense off from what was really going on in the economy, which was a very rapid concentration of power and wealth." He "advocated a stringent enforcement of the anti-trust laws" after pointing out "the use that [large industries] were making of their economic power under [the NRA's] cover of unity, appeasement, good will, and other platitudes." On one occasion, he declared:

> Now, if American business were wise, it would agree that fair enforcement of a policy against monopoly is all to the good. The American people will not permanently tolerate monopoly. Every business man knows that, for he himself is against monopoly except his own. Anti-trust complaints originate almost entirely with business men against business men.
>
> Yet business as a whole has been plunging headlong down the road that leads to government control. Merger, consolidation, concentration, and the crushing of small competitors go on apace. Though they complain bitterly against "government interference" and "regimentation," they drive in a direction that leaves no alternative. They are asking for the medicine they dislike, and the lawyers and judges are writing their prescriptions.[38]

In attempting "to stir up enough feeling and sentiment to support the president in turning the [pro-NRA] group down," Jackson conceded that he and his associates "created a sort of panic among the business interests" and incurred "the heavy expense of creating enemies" within the administration. He had little respect for his critics on either end of the political spectrum, however. He thought both "groups lack[ed] imagination and constructive thinking." "[T]he great difficulty with the conservative class in this country," he complained, "is that they've lost their guts." No longer "an individualist," the American businessman now wants "organization" and "mass support." "The same thing is more or less true of the liberals," he argued. "Instead of an old-fashioned liberalism," contemporary liberals "have tended to collectivism"; they "are not individualists anymore."[39]

While Jackson differed with the brain trust over policy regarding aggregations of economic power, he disagreed with his immediate superiors over the rationale that would explain the president's plan to enlarge the Supreme Court. "The Attorney General, Homer Cummings[;] the Solicitor General, Stanley Reed[;] and a small group of assistants had been the salesmen of the plan to the President," he said. Jackson "had a vague notion that something was generating along the line of dealing with the judiciary, but . . . [he] had been in on none of the conferences, knew nothing about the proposal and was as surprised as anybody at its nature." His "initial impressions of the plan['s rationale] were not particularly good. It didn't seem to deal with the problem that was in the minds of most of the people—the kind of decision that the Court had been making. It dealt with the number of decisions. It argued as to the dispositions of *certioraris*, as to which there certainly had been no great public dissatisfaction and very little public understanding. It wss [*sic*] dry, statistical, [and] rather uninspiring.''[40]

Shortly after Roosevelt announced the plan, Jackson took a trip to Jamestown and upstate New York. While there, he discussed the proposal with friends and acquaintances. Upon his return, he "addressed a letter . . . to the President telling him rather bluntly that . . . support was not increasing for the court reform, but was decreasing, and that this was due to the terms in which the problem had been approached." "It seemed to [Jackson] . . . that instead of talking about the cases the Court did not take, [proponents of the plan] should talk about the cases that [the Court] did take, and how [it] had gone out of [its] way in a number of cases to prohibit Congress from ever enacting a law on such subjects as railroad retirement, and to hold that no act could ever be passed by either the state or nation dealing with the subject of minimum wage and hours and matters of that kind. [Jackson] suggested to the President that the people were unquestionably ready to support him if they understood that the fight was one to make the Court 'a contemporary and non-partisan institution.' " He told Roosevelt that people "didn't understand calendar congestion" and "that 'nobody ever yet went into a fight over a set of statistics.' "[41]

Because of these concerns, Jackson hesitated when Henry Ashurst, chairman of the Senate Judiciary Committee, asked him to testify with the attorney general on the president's Court plan. In discussing the matter with Roosevelt, Jackson "made clear . . . that [his viewpoint] did not, in all respects, correspond with that of the Attorney General." "The President thought that that didn't matter" and told Jackson to "go and give the plan whatever support [he] could."[42]

In defending the plan before the committee, Attorney General Cummings emphasized "the presence on the Federal bench of aged or infirm judges" and the "crowded condition of the Federal dockets, the delays in the lower courts, and the heavy burden imposed upon the Supreme Court." By contrast, Jackson stressed that it "is a responsibility of Congress to see that the Court is an instrumentality in the maintenance of a just and constitutional government, and that it does not become an instrumentality for the defeat of constitutional government." "The industrialization of society and the movement toward city dwelling, foreign political and economic dislocations, together with depression and distress," he testified, "have generated an unrest which has put the whole complicated Federal system under severe strain. The ability of a federated form of Government to withstand these pressures is greatly impaired by any dissension between branches that were intended to be cooperating and coordinate."[43]

The president disappointed Jackson by not requiring the members of the administration to abandon the efficiency rationale for the Court plan. But Roosevelt pleased the assistant attorney general by abandoning the philosophy of the NRA. Jackson had to savor vicariously the triumph of antitrust policy. For, by the time Roosevelt called for such a policy change in April of 1938 (in a message to Congress that Jackson helped craft), he had named Jackson solicitor general of the United States.[44]

Solicitor General and Attorney General

The opportunity to serve as solicitor general arose when the President elevated Stanley Reed, solicitor general from 1935 until 1938, to the Supreme Court. Roosevelt did not have to spend much time deciding upon Reed's successor. Jackson "had argued a number of cases in the Supreme Court as Assistant Attorney General, both in the tax division and the anti-trust division," and "Justice Brandeis had sent a very favorable comment on [his] work to the President." Roosevelt "had great respect for Brandeis," and "[t]hat was . . . enough to cinch the matter . . . in his mind."[45]

The new solicitor general "entered upon the most enjoyable period of [his] whole official life." Not only was Jackson "[c]oming back to the practice of law [full time]," which he compared to "coming home after being out in a bad storm," but his new office was "the highest prize that could come to a lawyer." He relished the thought of assuming "the foremost place in the legal profession," serving as the "chief spokesman in court for the . . . [federal] government." He also enjoyed the intimacy that he developed with the justices. (He became particularly close to Frankfurter.) And he appreciated the praise of these same individuals. (Justice Brandeis once remarked, "Jackson should be Solicitor General for Life.") The fact that the Court had recently altered its standard of review regarding social and economic legislation (no longer placing on the government the burden of proof for the constitutionality of such laws) must have made the position even more attractive to him.[46]

Although Jackson did not have the unenviable task of defending the administration before a hostile tribunal, he thought the recent struggle between the courts and the elected branches to be of such moment that he undertook the task of chronicling this protracted conflict. He later published this account as *The Struggle for Judicial Supremacy.* The book, he said, "was written with the approval and at the suggestion of President Roosevelt, because we had found that the earlier struggles between the executive and the Court were poorly recorded." Not so incidentally, the work portrayed the failed effort to enlarge the Court in a very positive light.[47]

Jackson noted in his book that public displeasure with the Court had preceded the New Deal. Among other things, he mentioned the Court's use in the early part of the century of a substantive notion of due process to invalidate wage-and-hour legislation in the states. He also drew attention to certain late-nineteenth-century decisions that especially troubled his traditional sensibilities. Specifically, he criticized the Court's evisceration of federal antitrust laws through misinterpretation and the unwarranted extension of these laws to labor organizations: "A failure to enforce the antitrust laws against the real offenders would have been bad enough, but they were turned to strengthen the forces bearing down upon labor as it tried to find through self-organization and with legislative aid the voice with which to bargain on equal terms with the masters of industry."[48]

In his discussion of the federal judiciary's attack on the New Deal, Jackson drew upon personal experience, noting, among other things, the invalidation by the Court of Appeals for the First Circuit of both the unemployment-compensation and the old-age-benefit provisions of the Social Security Act. In arguing one of these cases before that court, he had contended that "[t]hese laws represented the most forward step of the Administration in its effort to forestall further crises in unemployment and to end the neglect of the aged." The appeals court, he recalled, had no appreciation of the problems being addressed. One of the judges went so far as to suggest during oral argument that "there was no hardship in his town" when, in fact, "his town was suffering from extensive unemployment."[49]

Upon appeal, the Supreme Court, having altered its standard of review in cases involving social and economic legislation, reversed the lower court and upheld the provisions of the Social Security Act. In Jackson's view, the Court had shifted the burden of proof to those challenging the government only after the president had threatened to enlarge the Court's membership. The justices never understood and accepted fully the need for such legislation. The federal judiciary's unawareness of the context surrounding legislative responses to industrialization profoundly disturbed Jackson. His reading of social conditions before and during his years as a public servant had given him an understanding of the complex, interdependent nature of an urban-industrial order. "The difficulty was that this group of judges . . . were applying the standards of their youth to the legislation of an entirely different period. They thought they were applying the Constitution, but they really were misapplying it . . . because what is reasonable [under the concept of due process] also has to depend on the environment and the circumstances. They were not open to conviction on the facts. They were not open to conviction that conditions had changed. They were striking down a good deal of legislation on the basis of what conditions were when they were brought up on the frontier."[50]

Jackson did not attribute the shortsightedness of the judiciary to stupidity, intellectual laxity, or malevolence. Rather, having observed and dealt with the judiciary during the New Deal, he broadened his critique of the judicial process beyond his initial concern with the slow pace of litigation. "Judicial justice is well adapted to ensure that established legislative rules are fairly and equitably applied to individual cases," he concluded. "But it is inherently ill suited, and never can be suited, to devising or enacting rules of general social policy." Sounding themes similar to those of Frankfurter and the Progressives, he maintained that the litigation technique suffers from certain practical weaknesses "when it is used to review far-flung economic and social conditions which vex modern government." Judicial decision making, he believed, is inherently abstract, since the litigation process must, of necessity, focus upon only a portion of the information that the legislature utilizes.

> Justices . . . cannot know the conditions in every industry or the experiences in every social layer of our national life. No form of lawsuit has yet been devised suitable to inform them adequately, with judicial standards of proof, of the factors in our mass problems. To follow the effects of a minimum-wage policy, for example, through our business and social structure or to establish the effects of the Social Security Act on the general welfare by legal testimony and exhibits would produce a mass that would be incomprehensible and exhausting.
>
> The vice of the litigation process in broad constitutional questions is that since we cannot expand the lawsuit to include an era, a people, and a continent, we simply cut down the problem to the scope of a lawsuit. The cases we have recited demonstrate how the broad and impersonal

policy that moved Congress became subjected to the procedures of a very narrow, individual, and legalistic controversy.[51]

Jackson noted that the "deficiencies of this lawsuit method appear clearly when we look to the make-up of the information that it provides for the judges." The Court's primary source of information is the lawyers appearing before it: "If the views of the scientist, the laborer, the business man, the social worker, the economist, the legislator, or the government executive reach the Court, it is only through the lawyer, in spite of the fact that the effect of the decision may be far greater in other fields than in jurisprudence. Thus government by lawsuit leads to a final decision guided by the learning and limited by the understanding of a single profession—the law." Not surprisingly, Jackson argued, attorneys lack the "capacity to furnish single-handed the rounded and comprehensive wisdom to govern all society." Indeed, an attorney's "preparations will be superficial as compared with those of the men who have specialized in the theory or the administration of the questioned Act." "At best, [a lawyer's] presentation of economic and social backgrounds is elementary and amateurish—and generally apologetically relegated to an appendix." And "[m]ost Justices have little time for supplemental reading." In view of his belief that "the conventional 'case' or 'controversy' procedure is inadequate to collect, summarize, and interpret the experience and reason of our [interdependent] society," Jackson thought that judicial adjustments of competing social interests are likely to be uninformed, imprudent, and perhaps dangerous.[52]

Unlike Frankfurter, Jackson did not move from a critique of the process of judicial fact-finding to a rejection of the concept of judicial supremacy. His traditional sensibilities remained in tension with his contemporary observations, as he revealed in an extended defense of the view that the Court should serve as the ultimate arbiter of constitutional boundaries.

[Alexander Hamilton regarded a] life-tenure judiciary during good behavior . . . as one of the "modern improvements in the practice of Government" because it was an "excellent barrier to the encroachments and oppressions of the representative body." He saw it as a "safeguard against the effects of occasional ill humors in the society" and as "mitigating the severity, and confining the operation" of "unjust and partial laws." Hamilton's use of the polite language of the creditor class of his day hardly concealed his fear of the debtor class and its influence in lawmaking. More than any other of his time he wanted a check on

Congress, and better than any other he estimated the effects of the judiciary as such.[53]

Jackson noted that, over time, the Court had fulfilled Hamilton's hopes and "established its ascendancy over the entire government as a source of constitutional doctrine." Although recently the Court "had used that supremacy to cripple other departments of government and to disable the nation from adopting [essential] social or economic policies," Jackson argued as follows:

> Some arbiter is almost indispensable when power is granted among many states and the nation and is also balanced between different branches, as the legislative and executive, and when written and fundamental limitations on all governmental agencies, such as the Bill of Rights, are set up for protection of the citizen. Each unit cannot be left to judge the limits of its own power.
>
> In some federations conflict of power between the several parts of government is treated as a political question to be settled by vote of the national legislature. . . . No doubt it was the hope of obtaining greater consistency and neutrality of decision that led our forefathers to entrust the keeping of the equilibrium of the Federal Union to a court rather than to Congress. . . .
>
> Thus was cast upon the Supreme Court the duty of being, within its proper jurisdiction, the voice of the Constitution speaking the final word in composing conflicts within our complicated political system. No greater task has challenged the vision and statesmanship of any little group of men calling themselves a court.[54]

Jackson published these observations in 1940, when he became attorney general. He had served not quite two years as the nation's chief litigator. Although moving to the foremost position in the Department of Justice (and thus to membership in the president's cabinet) brought him a significant increase in prestige, he did not look back upon his service in this post as fondly as he recalled his time as solicitor general. "The Attorney General is [the Solicitor General's] superior in the political hierarchy, but the Attorney General has no opportunity to be a lawyer. He has to spend most of his time on administrative matters" and at times seems to be "a managing clerk of a law office."[55]

Jackson tired quickly of the post's more tedious and frustrating aspects. He regarded the patronage system (particularly as it applied to federal judgeships) as "a very regrettable thing," since it interfered with his efforts to place the most competent and deserving people in federal positions. He found bothersome the tendency of senators to "insist that it is their right to see the Attorney General personally[,] and many of them at any time that it's convenient to them." Finally, he viewed as very unpleasant the responsibility of handling such details as complaints concerning the behavior of Department of Justice personnel, arguments between divisions over the assignment of cases, and, especially, quarrels over garage space. In short, it is possible that he found this post more nettlesome than his earlier stint as a local patronage officer for the Wilson administration.[56]

Nevertheless, the attorney generalship held a certain interest for Jackson, since America's increasing involvement in the European conflict presented him with some challenging legal questions. Specifically, he had the responsibility of justifying to the international community the 1940 destroyer-for-bases exchange with Britain and the Lend-Lease Act of 1941. (He also had to explain the former measure to a United States Congress suspicious of any unilateral presidential actions.) He undertook this task because some nations had voiced concern that America had violated the international obligation of nonbelligerent states to treat warring nations impartially.[57]

Even with such questions of international law to occupy him, Jackson found foreign affairs less stimulating than domestic governance. Yet the war's effect on domestic policy troubled him greatly. As American entrance into the conflict became imminent, the administration de-emphasized antitrust actions and engaged in "a policy of surveillance and spying on people that [Jackson found] distasteful," although he "recognized the necessity" for such action. With "antitrust policy and . . . civil liberties . . . moving in a direction that [he] didn't like," he was especially grateful when, in 1941, the president chose him to be his seventh Supreme Court nominee.[58]

Jackson's appointment came about with the retirement of Chief Justice Hughes. When the retirement was announced, Jackson recalled, the president said to him: "I've always felt, and we've had some talk, that I'd like to see you chief justice. If I thought that now was the time, I would appoint you chief justice. But I have doubts about whether now is the time." For political and practical reasons, Roosevelt decided to nominate Justice Stone, a Republican, for the position. In a letter to the president, Justice Frankfurter revealed the political considerations informing the choice.

> On personal grounds I'd prefer Bob [Jackson]. While I've known Stone longer and our relations are excellent and happy, I feel closer friendship

with Bob. But from the national interest I am bound to say that there is no reason for preferring Bob to Stone—quite the contrary. Stone is senior and qualified professionally to be C.J. But for me the decisive consideration, considering the fact that Stone is qualified, is that Bob is of your personal and political family, as it were, while Stone is a Republican. . . . [W]hen war does come, the country should feel you are a national, the Nation's President, and not a partisan President. Few things would contribute as much to confidence in you as a national and not a partisan President than for you to name a Republican, who has the profession's confidence, as Chief Justice.[59]

For practical reasons, Hughes also advised Roosevelt to appoint Stone. The chief justice was "very strongly of the opinion that what [the president] ought to do [was] to promote from within the Court someone who knows the detail of the job."[60]

As the person who would fill Stone's vacated slot, Jackson good-naturedly accepted Roosevelt's decision. He comforted himself with the thought that "associate justice of the Supreme Court is a long ways from the farm in Spring Creek." The Judiciary Committee unanimously approved him, and the whole Senate confirmed him, with only one dissenting vote.[61] The former solicitor general now joined the justices before whom he had once argued the government's cases. He would regard Frankfurter as his closest friend and ally on the Court. But Jackson's traditional sensibilities would on numerous occasions distance him from his Progressive colleague.

Notes

1. Robert H. Jackson, Oral History, 196, 154, 172–73, Papers of Robert H. Jackson, Library of Congress, Manuscript Division (hereafter cited as RHJP), Box 190. See also ibid., 150–51.

2. Ibid., 196, 25–26.

3. Ibid., 36a, 16a, 29a, 37a. See also ibid., 13, 19, 184.

4. Ibid., 29a, 22, 19–20.

5. Ibid., 4, 34, 5, 6a, 6, 38–39, 6. See also ibid., 36a, 45–47.

6. Ibid., 15, 6–7, 22, 7–8, 6. See also ibid., 20a, 16.

7. As quoted in William L. Ransom, "Associate Justice Robert H. Jackson," *American Bar Association Journal* 27 (1941): 481.

8. Jackson, Oral History, 196a-196b, 15, 19a, 21a, 47–49, RHJP, Box 190. See also John G. Cawelti, *Apostles of the Self-Made Man* (Chicago: University of Chicago Press, 1965), 95, 174–75.

9. Jackson, Oral History, 51–52, 43, 48, RHJP, Box 190. See also ibid., 63–64.

10. Ibid., 50–51.

11. Ibid., 53–54 (quoted); Robert H. Jackson, "The Advocate: Guardian of Our Traditional Liberties," *American Bar Association Journal* 36 (1950): 607–8.

12. Jackson, Oral History, 55–56, RHJP, Box 190.

13. Ibid., 56, 58.

14. Ibid., 56–57; Jackson, "Advocate," 698. See also ibid., 610.

15. Jackson, Oral History, 67, 105, RHJP, Box 190.

16. Jackson, "Advocate," 698; Jackson, Oral History, 106–07, 59–60, 106, RHJP, Box 190 (emphasis added).

17. Jackson, "Advocate," 698 (quoted second); Jackson, Oral History, 107, 60, RHJP, Box 190 (quoted first and third). See also ibid., 63–64.

18. Jackson, Oral History, 57, 69–79, 107–35, 157, RHJP, Box 190 (pp. 112, 134–35 quoted).

19. Ibid., 67, 140, 158; Robert H. Jackson, "Bar Associations Viewed by New Vice President," *New York State Bar Association Bulletin* (February 1931): 108, 111 (quoted); Robert H. Jackson, "The Future of the Bar," 2–5, RHJP, Box 54; Jackson, "Advocate," 610–99.

20. Robert H. Jackson, "The Lawyer: Leader or Mouthpiece?" *Journal of the American Judicature Society* 28 (1934): 71–73.

21. Jackson, "Future of the Bar," 5, RHJP, Box 54; Jackson, "Lawyer: Leader or Mouthpiece?" 75; Jackson, "Bar Associations Viewed," 106.

22. Jackson, "Lawyer: Leader or Mouthpiece?" 73–75.

23. Ibid., 74–75 (emphasis in original).

24. Ibid., 74 (quoted); Jackson, Oral History, 136–39, RHJP, Box 190; Robert H. Jackson, "The Bar and the New Deal," *American Bar Association Journal* 21 (1935): 95–96; Robert H. Jackson, "It's Up to Us," *Commentator* (December 1937): 45.

25. Jackson, Oral History, 80–81, RHJP, Box 190. See also ibid., 429–30.

26. Ibid., 75–76.

27. Ibid., 78–79, 152, 77.

28. Ibid., 86–93 (pp. 93, 90 quoted).

29. Ibid., 93.

30. Ibid., 129.

31. Ibid., 209–10, 429–30, 213. See also ibid., 135.

32. Ibid., 210–14 (p. 212 quoted).

33. Ibid., 350.

34. Jackson, "Bar and the New Deal," 94–96 (quoted); Jackson, Oral History, 533, RHJP, Box 190; Jackson, "Lawyer: Leader or Mouthpiece?" 73–75; Jerold S. Auerbach, *Unequal Justice: Lawyers and Social Change in Modern America* (New York: Oxford University Press, 1976), 174–76.

35. Jackson, Oral History, 214, RHJP, Box 190.

36. Ibid., 373, 426–27, 435, 427–28. See also ibid., 520–21. The Supreme Court declared the NRA legislation unconstitutional in *Schechter Poultry Corp. v. United States*, 295 U.S. 495 (1935).

37. Jackson, Oral History, 431, 435, RHJP, Box 190.

38. Ibid., 522–23; Jackson, "It's Up to Us," 46.

39. Jackson, Oral History, 530, 527, 529, 531–32, RHJP, Box 190. See also Jackson, "It's Up to Us," 46–47.

40. Jackson, Oral History, 378, 377, RHJP, Box 190.

41. Ibid., 379–80. See also Robert H. Jackson, *The Struggle for Judicial Supremacy: A Study of a Crisis in American Power Politics* (New York: Knopf, 1941), 189.

42. Jackson, Oral History, 380–81, RHJP, Box 190.

43. Senate Committee on the Judiciary, *A Bill to Reorganize the Judicial Branch of the Government: Hearings on S. 1392*, 75th Cong., 1st sess., 1937, pt. 1: 4, 8, 39, 51. Jackson recalled: "I had nothing to do with the organization of the lobbying or pressure side of the [Court] struggle. I didn't at any time go to any of the Senators to persuade them individually as to their votes. After giving my testimony, I took no part in the struggle. . . . I had no place on the strategy board. I had presented my views and was not persuading individual Senators or trying to put material in their hands." Jackson, Oral History, 384, RHJP, Box 190.

44. Jackson, Oral History, 533–39, RHJP, Box 190; Alan Brinkley, "The New Deal and the Idea of the State," in *The Rise of the New Deal Order, 1930–1980*, ed. Steve Fraser and Gary Gerstle (Princeton: Princeton University Press, 1989), 87–92.

45. Jackson, Oral History, 577, RHJP, Box 190.

46. Ibid., 581, 564, 563, 970; Henry J. Abraham, *Justices and Presidents: A Political History of Appointments to the Supreme Court*, 2d ed. (New York: Oxford University Press, 1985), 232 (Brandeis quoted). With regard to the Court's deferential approach to social and economic legislation, see *West Coast Hotel v. Parrish*, 300 U.S. 379 (1937); Henry J. Abraham, *Freedom and the Court: Civil Rights and Liberties in the United States*, 5th ed. (New York: Oxford University Press, 1988), 11–14; Robert H. Jackson, "Back to the Constitution," *American Bar Association Journal* 25 (1939): 745–49; Jackson, *Struggle for Judicial Supremacy*, 197–285.

47. Jackson, Oral History, 386 (quoted), 571–72, RHJP, Box 190; Jackson, *Struggle for Judicial Supremacy*, 86–196.

48. Jackson, *Struggle for Judicial Supremacy*, 48–68 (p. 63 quoted); Jackson, "It's Up to Us," 43–48.

49. Jackson, *Struggle for Judicial Supremacy*, 221; Jackson, Oral History, 586–87, RHJP, Box 190.

50. Jackson, *Struggle for Judicial Supremacy*, vi, xiv, 191–96, 221–34; Jackson, Oral History, 390–92, RHJP, Box 190 (p. 390 quoted).

51. Jackson, Oral History, 383, RHJP, Box 190; Jackson, *Struggle for Judicial Supremacy*, 288, 291, 298–99 (quoted).

52. Jackson, *Struggle for Judicial Supremacy*, 299, 291–92, 300–01, 298. See also Jackson, Oral History, 390, RHJP, Box 190.

53. Jackson, *Struggle for Judicial Supremacy*, 8.

54. Ibid., x–xi, 10–11. See also ibid., 311–13; Robert H. Jackson, *The Supreme Court in the American System of Government* (New York: Harper & Row, 1955), 23, 26–27, 61–80.

55. Jackson, Oral History, 564–65, 963, RHJP, Boxes 190, 191.

56. Ibid., 729, 731–33, 737–38, RHJP, Box 191 (pp. 733, 737–38 quoted); Robert H. Jackson, "Progress in Federal Judicial Administration," *Journal of the American Judicature Society* 23 (1939): 60.

57. See Jeffrey D. Hockett, "Justice Robert H. Jackson, the Supreme Court, and the Nuremberg Trial," in *The Supreme Court Review*, ed. Gerhard Casper, Dennis J. Hutchinson, and David A. Strauss (Chicago: University of Chicago Press, 1990), 275–76; Jackson, Oral History, 785–818, RHJP, Box 191.

58. Jackson, Oral History, 965–66, 968–78, RHJP, Box 191 (pp. 965–66 quoted).

59. Ibid., 969–70 (quoted), 977; Abraham, *Justices and Presidents*, 230 (Frankfurter quoted).

60. Jackson, Oral History, 969 (quoted), 977, RHJP, Box 191; Abraham, *Justices and Presidents*, 230.

61. Jackson, Oral History, 970–71 (quoted), RHJP, Box 191; Abraham, *Justices and Presidents*, 231–32.

9

The Pragmatic Jurisprudence of Justice Jackson

"We Act in These Matters Not by Authority of Our Competence but by Force of Our Commissions"

Early in his judicial tenure, Jackson distinguished himself through the eloquence and force of his prose. His facility of expression, honed by the "rough and tumble training" of his days as a country lawyer, would place him in the company of the greatest stylists ever to serve on the Court, including Oliver Wendell Holmes and Benjamin Cardozo. Jackson's beautiful language in the celebrated second flag-salute case was indicative of his formidable talent: "Those who begin coercive elimination of dissent soon find themselves exterminating dissenters. Compulsory unification of opinion achieves only the unanimity of the graveyard. . . . If there is any fixed star in our constitutional constellation, it is that no official, high or petty, can prescribe what shall be orthodox in politics, nationalism, religion, or other matters of opinion or force citizens to confess by word or act their faith therein."[1]

This opinion served as more than an index of Jackson's skill as a rhetorician; it also illustrated a more substantive aspect of his traditional legal background, namely, his acceptance of the concept of judicial supremacy. Because he believed courts to be the primary guardians of constitutional boundaries and limitations, he necessarily rejected the demand, articulated in Frankfurter's powerful dissent, that the Court apply Thayer's rational-basis standard in determining the constitutionality of West Virginia's flag-salute law. Jackson took note of the assumptions underlying Frankfurter's demand: "that it is committed to the legislatures as well as the courts to guard cherished

241

liberties and that it is appropriate to 'fight out the wise use of legislative authority in the forum of public opinion and before legislative assemblies rather than to transfer such a contest to the judicial arena,' since all the 'effective means of inducing political changes are left free.' " But he dismissed these arguments, maintaining that the "very purpose of a Bill of Rights was to withdraw certain subjects from the vicissitudes of political controversy, to place them beyond the reach of majorities and officials and to establish them as legal principles *to be applied by courts.* One's right to life, liberty, and property, to free speech, a free press, freedom of worship and assembly, and other fundamental rights may not be submitted to vote; they depend on the outcome of no elections."[2]

Jackson sought to preserve a vigorous role for the Court, unencumbered by Thayer's standard, because of a concern fundamental to any student of James Kent: the tendency of political majorities to overstate their interests and to neglect the concerns of minorities. Unlike Frankfurter, Jackson did not conclude that an interdependent social order is necessarily integrative. "[S]mall and local authority," Jackson stated, "may feel less a sense of responsibility to the Constitution" than judges who are not directly accountable to majorities. In this case, the Court justly interposed its veto against "officially disciplined uniformity for which history indicated a disappointing and disastrous end." Jackson disparaged the state's apparent belief "that patriotism will not flourish if patriotic ceremonies are voluntary and spontaneous instead of a compulsory routine." To his mind, the school board made "an unflattering estimate of the appeal of our institutions to free minds."[3]

Recall, however, that Frankfurter believed that the Court was not competent to evaluate the need for a flag-salute law, what with the institutional inadequacies of the judicial process. Jackson conceded that "the task of translating the majestic generalities of the Bill of Rights . . . into concrete restraints on officials dealing with the problems of the twentieth century, is one to disturb self-confidence." But, in a passage that illuminated brilliantly the relative weight he accorded to the dangers of judicial abstraction and majority oppression, he opined: "[O]ur duty to apply the Bill of Rights to assertions of authority [does not] depend upon our possession of marked competence in the field where the invasion of rights occurs. . . . [W]e act in these matters not by authority of our competence but by force of our commissions. We cannot, because of modest estimates of our competence in such specialties as public education, withhold the judgment that history authenticates as the function of this Court when liberty is infringed."[4]

Indeed, Jackson thought that "[c]onstitutional litigation is so important to the preservation of [constitutional equilibriums] . . . that no effort should be spared to make it modern, systematic, expeditious, and simple." He made this statement in *The Struggle for Judicial Supremacy*, where (as noted in the preceding Chapter) he defended the Court's role as constitutional guardian, even though he detailed the deficiencies of the process of judicial fact-finding. In that work, he also spoke against a judicial preoccupation with the doctrine of justiciability. (Recall that the elements of this doctrine serve, in part, to ensure that the Court does not address abstract legal questions.) Specifically, Jackson remarked upon Frankfurter's readiness to avoid the disposition of constitutional controversies when they do not satisfy the doctrines of adverseness, standing, ripeness, and nonmootness. "Mr. Frankfurter thought this prolonged uncertainty less harmful than 'the mischief of premature judicial intervention.' " But Jackson wondered whether it was necessary to "choose between 'premature judicial intervention' on the one hand and 'technical doctrines for postponing if not avoiding constitutional adjudication' on the other." Answering himself with another question, he asked: "Should we not at least try to lay inevitable constitutional controversies to early rest?"[5]

Although Jackson advocated a significant role for the Court, he heeded the danger of judicial abstraction. He showed a respect similar to that of Frankfurter for the supposedly well-grounded determinations of administrators. His lack of deference to the compulsory flag-salute requirement of the West Virginia State Board of Education revealed that he differed with Frankfurter over the appropriate standard of review for administrative actions raising constitutional questions. (Recall that, before joining the Court, Jackson had voiced concern over the threat administrators present to constitutional guarantees.) But in nonconstitutional contexts, Jackson matched his colleague's efforts to minimize the judicial presence in the administrative realm. He agreed with Frankfurter that "[u]nless Congress has chosen to give the courts oversight of a determination by [administrators], the courts have not the power of oversight where . . . the Constitution does not require it." He also accepted Frankfurter's view that the Court should not assume, in those instances where Congress provides for judicial oversight, that all questions of law, no matter how esoteric or technical, are appropriate matters for judicial consideration. Finally, like Frankfurter, he rejected the attempts of some of his brethren to heighten judicial scrutiny of administrative findings of fact through resort to the jurisdictional-fact doctrine.[6]

Jackson did express concern that "judges more and more are called on to affirm and enforce executive or administrative orders without inquiry as to their factual foundation or justice and are increasingly refused access to sources of evidence." And, with Frankfurter, he sought to promote some degree of accountability by insisting that administrators at least furnish a rationale for their decisions. In other words, he thought that where Congress provides for review but requires deference to administrative determinations of fact, courts can test the legality of administrative directives only if agencies relate their decisions to empowering legislation. The possession of expertise does not liberate administrators from their obligation to adhere to law. As he dissented in *SEC v. Chenery Corp.*: "[A]dministrative experience is of weight in judicial review only to this point—it is a persuasive reason for deference to the [Securities and Exchange] Commission in the exercise of its discretionary powers under and within the law. It cannot be invoked to support action outside of the law. And what action is, and what is not, within the law must be determined by courts, *when authorized to review*, no matter how much deference is due to the agency's fact finding. Surely an administrative agency is not a law unto itself."[7]

To require administrators to root their decisions in law is not, however, to display contempt for administration. Jackson (and Frankfurter) still gave full play to administrative expertise. Jackson "always felt that regulation was necessary; that the administrative process, while it had obvious defects and difficulties, was an absolutely essential thing to complete our legal system." He would only engage in heightened review of the factual conclusions of administrators when Congress demanded as much of judges and (as noted) when cases involved constitutional issues.[8]

Even in constitutional cases, Jackson displayed concern over judicial abstraction. Like Frankfurter, he wanted the justices to appreciate the Constitution's amplitude, that is, its allowance of considerations of time and circumstance. Also like his colleague, he drew inspiration from Chief Justice John Marshall in discussing the document's scope: "The powers of government conferred by the Framers were meant to be construed and applied in no parochial or petty sense; they were meant to be applied with courage and vision, for, as Marshall reminded his contemporaries in speaking of the 'necessary and proper' clause, it is a Constitution 'intended to endure for ages to come, and consequently, to be adapted to the various crises of human affairs.' " Jackson upbraided the anti–New Deal Court for having "*narrowed* the scope of the great clauses of the Constitution granting powers to Congress. It seriously contracted the interstate commerce power and it read startling exemptions into the taxing power." The Court also deserved censure, he believed, for having "[s]imultaneously . . . *expanded* the scope of clauses which limited the power of the Congress, such as the 'due process clause'." While the Court was "strict and niggardly in construing *powers* of government," it was "liberal to the point of extravagance in construing *limitations*—even inventing such limitations as 'freedom of contract' where none existed in the Constitution."[9]

Beyond the insight that the Constitution should not be viewed abstractly, Jackson believed that the Court could expect little guidance from the framers. "From the very beginning," he said in an address he gave as attorney general, "the duties of the Court required it, by interpretation of the Constitution, to settle doubts which the framers themselves had been unable to resolve. . . . [C]ontroversies so delicate that the framers would have risked their unity if an answer had been forced were bequeathed to this Court." On subjects where evidence of constitutional intent exists, he later commented: "Just what our forefathers did envision, or would have envisioned had they foreseen modern conditions, must be divined from materials almost as enigmatic as the dreams Joseph was called upon to interpret for Pharaoh. A century and a half of partisan debate and scholarly speculation yields no net result but only supplies more or less apt quotations from respected sources on each side of any question."[10]

To permit effective, democratic governance without abdicating the Court's guardianship role, Jackson thought judges must weigh for themselves the contending interests before them (instead of merely asking whether a rational person could defend the constitutionality of the law or directive at issue), yet be observant of the particular circumstances surrounding each controversy. Indeed, he expected judges to be scrupulous in their attention to social and political context. If the Court, because of its institutional inadequacies, could not avoid abstraction entirely, it could certainly refrain from exacerbating the problem. Jackson reserved his highest praise for Justice Brandeis, who "mastered completely the facts of his case, respecting facts for the stubborn things that they are," and who made a point of saying " 'that because of varying conditions there must be much constant inquiry into facts.' "[11]

In essence, Jackson extended the method of the common law to constitutional matters, making use of a judicial technique that emphasizes the adaptation of legal principles (in this case, constitutional principles) to meet "the endless variation of the facts of cases." He acknowledged as much: "In extending the litigation process to constitutional issues," Americans "have put a burden upon the techniques of the common law which they were not evolved [in England] to carry." Yet he believed that the Court must choose among interpretive methods (lest it abdicate its historic function) and should use one that had been time tested. "What has been of most permanent importance to the lawyer is not substantive doctrine but the common-law method and habit of thought which leaves a large measure of discretion to judges and gives intellectual satisfaction to the advocate." This method demands that judges have the "vision of a prophet," for they are involved in the important task of reworking law "to adapt it to contemporary needs." Failure to take this role seriously leads to a situation in which judges view law abstractly, "as an end in itself, as a thing apart from life, to be logical and symmetrical and harmonious in itself, [but] aloof from the experience of illogical people."[12] Integration of this aspect of the common-law method into a constitutional jurisprudence was natural for one who, not only had studied the method as a legal apprentice, but also had revered his progenitors for their practicality as much as their independence and who, as a country lawyer, had emphasized the particular circumstances of cases over general, legal principles.

Like any dedicated student of the common law, Jackson had, in addition to his respect for legal flexibility, considerable regard for the value of legal continuity. He sought to avoid a "wilderness of single instances" in the law. Judges must have "a profound appreciation of the continuity between the law of today and that of the past." Jackson could not

> believe that any person who at all values the judicial process or distinguishes its method and philosophy from those of the political and legislative process would abandon or substantially impair the rule of *stare decisis*. Unless the assumption is substantially true that cases will be disposed of by application of known principles and previously disclosed courses of reasoning, our common-law process would become the most intolerable kind of *ex post facto* judicial law-making. Moderation in change is all that makes judicial participation in the evolution of law tolerable. Either judges must be fettered to mere application of a legisla-

tive code with a minimum of discretion, as in continental systems, or they must formulate and adhere to some voluntary principles that will impart stability and predictability to judicial discretion.[13]

Yet Jackson emphasized that in constitutional contexts, where the Court reviews governmental responses to the economic and social conditions of an interdependent society, "the practice of *stare decisis* has only limited application." In private law, precedents "are a force for stability and predictability, but in constitutional law they are the most powerful influence in forming and supporting reactionary opinions. The judge who can take refuge in a precedent does not need to justify his decision to the reason. He may 'reluctantly feel himself bound' by a doctrine, supported by a respected historical name, that he would not be able to justify to contemporary opinion or under modern conditions." Because of the shortcomings of the judicial process in addressing complex social problems, the Court's "[constitutional] decisions must be tentative and subject to judicial cancellation if experience fails to verify them."[14]

"Let Us State Some Facts Which the Court Omits"

A Rejection of Judicial Deference

If the second flag-salute case had proved to be an isolated use of judicial power on Jackson's part, one would be justified in concluding that he did not believe that judicial responsiveness to circumstances and a capacity to admit error were adequate to deal with the problem of judicial abstraction. Two years before that decision, however, he had sided with the majority in *Bridges v. California*, which, as noted earlier, had held as violative of the First Amendment a contempt citation of a local labor leader for his writings. Jackson accepted Justice Black's libertarian interpretation of the "clear and present danger" test, as well as Black's treatment of the circumstances surrounding the case. He did not find compelling Justice Frankfurter's plea for a low level of scrutiny of the state court's action. Although he must have sympathized with Frankfurter's discussion of the Court's limitations in fact gathering, he put these concerns aside in the interest of protecting the free press claim.[15]

In the year following the second flag-salute case, the Court in *United States v. Ballard* examined the constitutionality of a federal mail-fraud conviction of a religious leader. Specifically, a jury found that Guy

Ballard, in soliciting funds for his religious organization, had claimed in bad faith to be the medium for St. Germain and to have the supernatural ability to heal the sick. In his opinion for the Court, Justice Douglas said that a conviction the government obtains through examination of the sincerity (as opposed to the truth) of a person's religious beliefs passes constitutional muster. But the majority remanded the case for review of other points Ballard had raised but the appeals court had not addressed. It seems the district court had asked the jury to rule on only part of the matters contained in the indictment, and Ballard claimed that this deviation amounted to the denial of a fair trial.[16]

Justices Frankfurter and Roberts joined Justice Stone's dissent, but not because they thought the conviction violated the First Amendment. Like the majority, they were "not prepared to say that the constitutional guaranty of freedom of religion affords immunity from criminal prosecution for the fraudulent procurement of money by false statements as to one's religious experiences, more than it renders polygamy or libel immune from criminal prosecution." But there was, in their view, "no legally sufficient reason" for disturbing the conviction. The district court's limitation of the issues for trial, they thought, was anything but prejudicial to the respondent. Moreover, Ballard had raised no objection at trial.[17]

Jackson alone refused to accept the constitutionality of convictions based on findings of religious beliefs held in bad faith. Initially, he voted to dissent only in part from Douglas's opinion. The Court had split evenly between those who sought to remand the case for further proceedings and those who wanted to affirm the convictions outright. So as "to avoid equal division of the Court [and sustainment of the conviction,] and as the lesser of alternative errors[, Jackson at first voted to] join in the result reached in the opinion of Mr. Justice Douglas." However, he expressed strong disagreement with Douglas on the constitutional issue.[18]

When Douglas managed to attract another vote, Jackson had no reason to join in any aspect of Douglas's opinion. Ever suspicious of majorities, Jackson warned in dissent that "[p]rosecutions of this character easily could degenerate into religious persecution." Those of unorthodox persuasions, he argued, are particularly vulnerable to charges of bad faith: "If religious liberty includes, as it must, the right to communicate such experiences to others, it seems to me an impossible task for juries to separate fancied from true clairvoyance. Such experiences, like some tones and colors, have existence for one, but none at all for another. They cannot be verified to the minds of those whose field of consciousness does not include religious insight. When one comes to trial which turns on any aspect of religious belief or representation, unbelievers among his judges are likely not to understand and are almost certain not to believe him.'' Jackson admonished that "[s]uch inquiries [into the genuineness of a person's religious conviction] may discomfort orthodox as well as unconventional religious teachers, for even the most regular of them are sometimes accused of taking their orthodoxy with a grain of salt.''[19]

Because of "the danger of such prosecutions,'' or the potential for oppression when government makes misrepresentation of religious experience or belief subject to prosecution, Jackson "would dismiss the indictment and have done with this business of judicially examining other people's faiths.'' Although he saw in Ballard's teachings "nothing but humbug, untainted by any trace of truth,'' he maintained that "the price of freedom of religion or of speech or of the press is that we must put up with, and even pay for, a good deal of rubbish.''[20]

In an earlier version of his dissent, Jackson had expressed concern that the Court's decision might do more than harm religious freedom. The Court risked public disillusionment with law, he warned, because its decision in *Ballard* slighted a very important claim of religious liberty, while recent pronouncements protective of religion (to be discussed later in this Chapter) made "trifles of first [amendment] principles.'' He continued: "But what prosecution of these [*sic*] kind does to religion is as nothing to the way they will demoralize the law. If the Ballard or the 'I Am' cult have the same rights as Jehovah's Witnesses, their case comes to this: A state has no right to tax their 'high constitutional privilege' of making money by disseminating their doctrines . . . and a state may not protect the homes of citizens who do not want to be converted and solicited from being subjected to this 'spread of intelligence', but the colporteurs may be tried and sent to jail for their state of mind in representing their experiences or beliefs. That one can find this in the Constitution is as incredible to me as that the Ballards chum with St. Germain.''[21]

The following year, Jackson again acted on his belief in the importance of adjudication for the maintenance of constitutional equilibriums. In *Thomas v. Collins*, the Court examined a Texas statute that required labor organizers to register with the state before making a public speech to encourage union memberships. In a plurality opinion, Justice Rutledge held that the statute, as applied in this case, imposed an unconstitutional prior restraint upon free speech. He conceded that states can regulate the solicitation of organization memberships, as opposed to the encouragment of memberships generally through speech. But he reserved judgment on whether the Court would have sustained the state's restriction of the labor leader in this case. After making a speech on the benefits of union membership, the labor official *had* attempted to enlist an individual from his audience. But the state had sought and received a court order restraining the official, Rutledge noted, before having any indication that he intended to do anything other than speak.[22]

Jackson "concur[red] in the opinion of Mr. Justice Rutledge that this case falls in the category of a public speech, rather than that of practicing a vocation as solicitor." He noted that "Texas did not wait to see what Thomas would say or do." Thus, he could not "escape the impression that the injunction sought before [the labor organizer] had reached the state was an effort to forestall him from speaking at all and that the contempt is based in part at least on the fact that he did make a public labor speech."[23]

Revealing his mistrust of government, Jackson observed that "[m]odern inroads on [free speech] rights come from associating the speaking with some other factor which the state may regulate so as to bring the whole within official control." Thus, "speech admittedly otherwise beyond the reach of the states is attempted to be brought within [their] licensing system by associating it with 'solicitation.' Speech of employers otherwise beyond the reach of the Federal Government is brought within the Labor Board's power to suppress by associating it with 'coercion' or 'domination.' Speech of political malcontents is sought to be reached by associating it with some variety of 'sedition.' " Jackson conceded that "[w]hether in a particular case the association or characterization is a proven and valid one often is difficult to resolve." But, in sharp contrast to Frankfurter (who dissented in this case), he argued that it is the Court's task to balance the conflicting claims: "If this Court may not or does not in proper cases inquire whether speech or publication is properly condemned by association, its claim to guardianship of free speech and press is but a hollow one." For the following reason, the Court must scrutinize state efforts to restrict speech through licensing:

> [I]t cannot be the duty, because it is not the right, of the state to protect the public against false doctrine. The very purpose of the First Amendment is to foreclose public authority from assuming a guardianship of the public mind through regulating the press, speech, and religion. In

this field every person must be his own watchman for truth, because the forefathers did not trust any government to separate the true from the false for us. [Here, Jackson cited the second flag-salute case.] Nor would I. Very many are the interests which the state may protect against the practice of an occupation, very few are those it may assume to protect against the practice of propagandizing by speech or press. These are thereby left great range of freedom.[24]

Disagreements over "Preferred Freedoms"

While Jackson's concern with oppressive majorities sometimes distanced him from Frankfurter, his concern with judicial abstraction at times separated him from his colleagues who adhered to the "preferred freedoms" concept. In *Saia v. New York*, for example, the Court struck down a Lockport, New York, ordinance that forbade individuals to use sound-amplifying devices in public places without first obtaining permission from the chief of police. Saia, a Jehovah's Witness minister, had received permission to use loudspeaking equipment in a city park. When the permit expired, however, the chief of police refused to issue a renewal, claiming that other park users had complained of the noise. Justice Douglas spoke for the majority: "Courts must balance the various community interests in passing on the constitutionality of local regulations of the character involved here. But in that process they should be mindful to keep the freedoms of the First Amendment in a preferred position." Heeding this obligation, Douglas noted that "[l]oud speakers are today indispensable instruments of effective public speech. The sound truck has become an accepted method of political campaigning. It is the way people are reached." "When a city allows an official to ban [loudspeakers] in his uncontrolled discretion," he concluded, "it sanctions a device for suppression of free communication of ideas."[25]

Jackson dissented from Douglas's opinion, which seemed to him "neither judicious nor sound." "[M]ore than the ordinance in question menace[d] free speech by regulating use of loud-speakers," Jackson argued, the Court's decision "endanger[ed] the great right of free speech by making it ridiculous and obnoxious." Indeed, "this [was] not [even] a free speech issue. Lockport ha[d] in no way denied or restricted the free use, even in its park, of all the [faculties] for speech with which nature ha[d] endowed the appellant." Since the case was, in fact, a due process controversy, Jackson "disagree[d] entirely" with Douglas's contention that it was the Court's task to balance the contending interests before the Court. "It is for the local communities to balance their own interests—that is politics—and what courts should keep out of." As will be seen in the next section, Jackson believed that the vagueness of the concept of due process warrants only judicial deference to the actions of government. Therefore, he could "only repeat the words of Mr. Justice Holmes, disregarded in his time and even less heeded now: 'I cannot believe that the [Fourteenth] Amendment was intended to give us *carte blanche* to embody our economic or moral beliefs in its prohibitions.' "[26]

"[E]ven if this were a civil liberties case," Jackson continued, "I should agree with Chief Justice Hughes . . . : 'Civil liberties, as guaranteed by the Constitution, imply the existence of an organized society maintaining public order without which liberty itself would be lost in the excesses of unrestrained abuses.' " Jackson devoted much of his opinion to articulating a balance he thought accorded with Hughes's insight. Revealing his common-law sensibilities, he remarked: "Let us state some facts which the Court omits." He noted that the "scene of action in this case [was] an area . . . [of a city park] set apart for the people's recreation." Saia was "demand[ing] even more than the right to speak and hold a meeting in this area . . . reserved for other and quite inconsistent purposes"; Saia had "set up a sound truck so as to flood this area with amplified lectures on religious subjects." "He [had] located his car, on which loud-speakers were mounted, either in the park itself, [which was] not open to vehicles, or in the street close by. The microphone for the speaker [had been] located some little distance from the car and in the park, and electric wires [had been] strung, in one or more instances apparently across the sidewalk, from one to the other. So that what the Court [was] holding, [was] that the Constitution of the United States forbids a city to require a permit for a private person to erect, in its streets, parks and public places, a temporary public address system, which certainly has potentialities of annoyance and even injury to park patrons if carelessly handled."[27]

Jackson argued that the state must be able to control "apparatus which, when put to unregulated proselyting, propaganda and commercial uses, can render life unbearable." In a draft opinion, he remarked, "[T]he peace and good order and proper use of a family park is getting very little consideration in the [Court's] balances because we are hysterical lest somebody shut off political discussion." The Court should realize that "[n]o right is absolute and the right of free speech is considered by all who have given it temperate and philosophical consideration to end when it becomes a public nuisance." "It seems to me," he concluded in his final opinion, "that society has the right to control, as to place, time and volume, the use of loud-speaking devices for any purpose, provided its regulations are not unduly arbitrary, capricious or discriminatory." In response to the majority's concerns about the discretion allowed Lockport's police chief, he noted, "There is not the slightest evidence of discrimination or prejudice against [Saia] because of his religion or his ideas." If the police were ever to differentiate between permit applicants on the basis of speakers' views, the Court could "deal with that when, and if, it arises."[28]

In *Kovacs v. Cooper*, Jackson broadened his view of the extent to which states could legislate against the use of sound-amplification devices. He concurred in the Court's ruling that an ordinance *forbidding the use* on the public streets of a "sound truck" or any instrument which emits "loud and raucous noises" does not violate the First Amendment. He joined the Court's judgment because he believed "that operation of mechanical sound-amplifying devices conflicts with quiet enjoyment of home and park and with safe and legitimate use of street and market place, and that it is constitutionally subject to regulation or prohibition by the state or municipal authority. . . . Freedom of speech for Kovacs does not . . . include freedom to use sound amplifiers to drown out the natural speech of others."[29]

Although Jackson had paid scrupulous attention to the circumstances surrounding *Saia*, he was impervious to Justice Black's argument that the record contained no evidence to suggest that the noise of Kovac's sound truck was either "loud or raucous." Nor did he find persuasive Black's testimonial to the value of amplified speech in a democratic society (although he did not join Frankfurter's diatribe against the "preferred freedoms" concept). Revealing his Populist sensibilities, the Alabamian said:

> There are many people who have ideas that they wish to disseminate but who do not have enough money to own or control publishing plants, newspapers, radios, moving picture studios, or chains of show places. . . .
>
> It is of particular importance in a government where people elect their officials that the fullest opportunity be afforded candidates to express and voters to hear their views. It is of equal importance that criticism of governmental action not be limited to criticisms by press, radio, and moving pictures. In no way except public speaking can the desirable objective of widespread public discussion be assured. . . . And it is an

obvious fact that public speaking today without sound amplifiers is a
wholly inadequate way to reach the people on a large scale.[30]

Finally, Jackson failed to respond even to Black's observation that
"ordinances can be drawn which adequately protect a community
from unreasonable use of public speaking devices without absolutely
denying to the community's citizens all information that may be
disseminated or received through this new avenue for trade in ideas."[31]
Apparently, Jackson believed that sound-amplification devices are
inherently grating and that the invalidation of ordinances prohibiting
such devices amounts to judicial abstraction.

Although Jackson did not support the First Amendment claim in this
case, he had abandoned neither his suspicion of government nor his
common law concern with context. He agreed with Black's observation that "the result of today's opinion in upholding this statutory
prohibition of amplifiers would surely not be reached by [the] Court if
such channels of communication as the press, radio, or moving pic-
tures were similarly attacked." On a circulated copy of Black's opinion, he wrote: "[I] agree[, and such decisions] should not be
[reached]." In his concurrence, he noted: "The moving picture screen,
the radio, the newspaper, the handbill, the sound truck and the street
corner orator have differing natures, values, abuses, and dangers.
Each, in my view, is a law unto itself, and all we are dealing with now
is the sound truck." He did "not agree [with Justice Reed's assertion
in the plurality opinion] that, if [the Court] sustain[s] regulations or
prohibitions of sound trucks, they must therefore be valid if applied to
other methods of 'communication of ideas.' "[32]

Perhaps Jackson's sharpest disagreement with his colleagues who
identified with the "preferred freedoms" concept occurred in *Terminiello v. Chicago*, where the Court reversed Arthur Terminiello's
conviction for breach of the peace. Terminiello, who had come to
Chicago to address the Christian Veterans of America, preached an
anticommunist, anti-Semitic message that attracted a large group of
left-wing protestors and prompted several disturbances both inside and
outside the building. The Court overturned the conviction and held
that the ordinance at issue, which prohibited speech that merely "stirs
the public to anger, invites dispute, [or] brings about a condition
of unrest," seriously invaded the province of speech that the First
Amendment protects. In his opinion for the majority, Justice Douglas
said that free speech "may indeed best serve its high purpose when it
induces a condition of unrest, creates dissatisfaction with conditions
as they are or even stirs people to anger."[33]

In a scathing dissent, Jackson reproached the Court for deciding the case "by reiterating generalized approbations of freedom of speech with which, in the abstract, no one will disagree." The majority, he complained, failed to consider the circumstances surrounding the case and judged Terminiello's speech "as if he had spoken to persons as dispassionate as empty benches, or like a modern Demosthenes practicing his Philippics on a lonely seashore." The local court that tried Terminiello did not indulge in theory; "[i]t was dealing with a riot and with a speech that provoked a hostile mob and incited a friendly one, and threatened violence between the two." Jackson sought to "bring [the Court's] deliberations down to earth by a long recital of facts." He devoted nine pages of his twenty-four-page opinion to recounting passages from Terminiello's speech that seemed especially provocative or incendiary. Among other things, he emphasized Terminiello's condemnation of "Zionist Jews"; these statements had incited members of the audience to say " 'Kill the Jews,' 'Dirty Kikes,' and much more of ugly tenor." In Jackson's view, this was "the specific and concrete kind of anger, unrest and alarm, coupled with that of the mob outside, that the trial court charged the jury might find to be a breach of peace induced by Terminiello." Since "the evidence prove[d] beyond dispute that danger of rioting and violence in response to the speech was clear, present and immediate," and since it did "not appear that the motive in punishing [Terminiello was] to silence the ideology he expressed as offensive to the State's policy or as untrue," Jackson was "unable to see that the local authorities [had] transgressed the Federal Constitution."[34]

"We Have No Such Supervisory Power Over State Courts"

A Desire For Principled Decision Making

The tension in Jackson's constitutional jurisprudence between a concern with judicial abstraction and a fear of majority oppression was evident, not only in his First Amendment opinions, but also in his Fourteenth Amendment decisions. He illustrated the concern with abstraction in his treatment of the concept of due process. As one who had participated in battles with a Court that had used a substantive notion of due process to frustrate the responses of state legislatures and of the United States Congress to "the excesses and . . . oppressions of a rising industrial economy," Jackson argued for a retrenchment of judicial authority in this area of the law. In *The Struggle for Judicial Supremacy*, he noted that early in the nation's history an "important restraint [upon judicial power] was that the guarantee of due process was then a guarantee of regularity of procedure and had not been expanded to a test of reasonableness of legislative policy." Judicial development of a substantive notion of due process "carried the Court into realms of fact and of policy for which it ha[d] no adequate procedure." Although Jackson thought the Court had strayed from the traditional understanding of due process, he did not call upon the justices to repudiate the substantive interpretation. Rather, he thought the substantive concept acceptable, and perhaps beneficial, so long as courts employ the rational-basis standard. Judges must understand that "it is an awesome thing to strike down an act of the legislature approved by the Chief Executive, and that power so uncontrolled is not to be used save where the occasion is clear beyond fair debate."[35]

Jackson's advocacy of judicial deference may seem peculiar, given that he feared oppressive government as much as judicial abstraction. One must recall, however, that he was instinctively wary of unprincipled decision making. As a student of the common law, he sought stability, as well as flexibility, in the law. (Courts must "adhere to some voluntary principles that will impart stability and predictability to judicial discretion.") In his study of judicial supremacy, he drew a distinction between the "clear and explicit terms of the Constitution, such as the specific prohibitions of the Bill of Rights," and the document's "vague" provisions, such as the due process clauses. While the Court need not (indeed, should not) employ the rational-basis test in cases involving explicit constitutional principles, he argued, it should move beyond an appreciation of the context of cases and adhere to that formula when consulting the Constitution's vague provisions. When a law is "question[ed] under the *due process* clause, . . . if a rational basis is perceived it of course is not the Court's function to balance the reasons."[36]

When, in the 1930s, the Court's docket shifted away from suits presenting claims of economic liberty and toward cases involving demands for procedural justice in the face of hostile state action, Jackson would reveal this same understanding of due process. Consider *Ashcraft v. Tennessee*, where the Court invalidated a murder conviction. The suspect had confessed to the crime, but only after police held him incommunicado for thirty-six hours. During this time, the officers deprived the suspect of sleep and interrogated him without respite. When the Court heard this case, the rule against the admissibility of coerced confessions, even at the federal level, existed independently of the Fifth Amendment privilege against self-incrimination. (The Court had yet to apply the latter provision against the states.) But case law established that state use of an involuntary confession to convict an accused would violate due process. Speaking for the *Ashcraft* majority, Justice Black held that "a situation such as that here shown by uncontradicted evidence is so inherently coercive that its very existence is irreconcilable with the possession of mental freedom by a lone suspect against whom its full coercive force is brought to bear."[37]

Jackson dissented vigorously. Echoing Frankfurter (who joined his dissent), Jackson argued that the possibility of judicial abstraction is not limited to cases involving economic liberties. "The use of the due process clause to disable the States in protection of society from crime," he said, "is quite as dangerous and delicate a use of federal judicial power as to use it to disable them from social or economic exploitation." "The burden of protecting society from most crimes against persons and property falls upon the State. Different States have different crime problems and [they should have] some freedom to vary procedures according to their own ideas."[38]

Jackson regarded Black's opinion as a regrettable example of judicial abstraction.

> Always heretofore the ultimate question has been whether the confessor was in possession of his own will and self-control at the time of confession. . . .
> But the Court refuses in this case to be guided by this test. It rejects the finding of the Tennessee courts and says it must make an "independent examination" of the circumstances. Then it says that it will not "resolve any of the disputed questions of fact" relating to the circumstances of the confession. Instead of finding as a fact that Ashcraft's freedom of will was impaired, it substitutes the doctrine that the situation was "inherently coercive." It thus reaches on a *part* of the evidence in the case a conclusion which I shall demonstrate it could not properly reach on *all* the evidence.[39]

In Jackson's view, the evidence demonstrated "that despite the 'inherent coerciveness' of the circumstances of [Ashcraft's] examination, the confession when made was deliberate, free, and voluntary in the sense in which that term is used in criminal law." Jackson placed great emphasis upon the fact that, after the confession, Ashcraft's physician had examined the accused and had testified that "Ashcraft appeared normal," had "said he had been treated all right," and had even admitted to the crime.[40]

Revealing his preference for principled decision making, Jackson was not content (as he was in First Amendment cases) simply to balance the conflicting interests at issue. "We must bear in mind," he pointed out, "that this case does not come here from a lower federal court over whose conduct we may assert a general supervisory power." The Court has "no such supervisory power over state courts. [The justices] may not lay down rules of evidence for them nor revise their decisions merely because [they] feel more confidence in [their] wisdom and rectitude." State actions should have "the benefit of a presumption of regularity and legality" and should fall only when no rational person could regard them as fair. To overturn Ashcraft's conviction, the Court must find that "the individual will of the . . . confessor had been overcome by torture, mob violence, fraud, trickery, threats, or promises." While the majority may have thought the evidence suggested that the suspect's confession was involuntary, at the very least (and this was all that was necessary to sustain the conviction), the courts below could *reasonably believe* from the testimony of the physician that Ashcraft had not suffered impairment of his free will.[41]

At the end of his opinion, Jackson made explicit his discomfort with the concept of due process. "The warning words of Mr. Justice Holmes in his dissenting opinion in *Baldwin v. Missouri*," he remarked, "seem to us appropriate reading for now." There, Holmes (in disparaging the Court's use of due process in economic liberty cases) had said he saw "hardly any limit but the sky to the invalidating of [state actions under the due process clause] if they happen to strike a majority of [the] Court as for any reason undesirable." Jackson shared Holmes's disbelief "that the [Fourteenth] Amendment was intended to give [the justices] *carte blanche* to embody [their] economic or moral beliefs in its prohibitions."[42]

When Jackson first circulated his opinion, Frankfurter suggested the following passage for incorporation or paraphrase:

Were we called upon to do so, we could as readily as do the other members of the Court disapprove police methods in ferreting out crime which this case illustrates. But many things in the administration of criminal justice in the forty-eight States that we privately disapprove of does not make them unconstitutional. It cannot be too often repeated that before this Court can deny to the States the power of dealing with strictly local matters [the States] must offend deep-seated notions of our democratic society so clearly that fair-minded men can hardly differ about them. . . . This is especially pertinent regarding the administration of criminal justice. We ought to exercise the utmost self-restraint against writing as a court of criminal appeals for prosecutions in the state courts even though we profess not to be. The Constitution has denied us that power.[43]

Frankfurter commented: "Some such thing as the foregoing may be redundant but I do not believe it would be superfluous."[44] Apparently regarding the passage as unnecessary, Jackson declined to include it. Nevertheless, Frankfurter found Jackson's references to deference (most of which appeared in the initial draft) sufficient to check the impulse to write separately.

For different reasons, then, the two men advocated judicial use of a reasonableness standard. Unlike Frankfurter, Jackson did not regard the possibility of judicial abstraction as sufficient grounds for resorting to deference. Rather, *the absence of explicit constitutional principle* prompted him merely to police the perimeters of rational policy.

Although in agreement with Frankfurter on the appropriate standard for use in due process cases, Jackson at times disagreed with his colleague on the proper application of that standard. A seemingly minor disagreement between the two men in *Rochin v. California* revealed the potential for more significant conflict. Recall that the Court sustained a due process challenge to a conviction police had obtained after illegally entering the petitioner's home and forcibly extracting illicit drugs from his stomach.[45] In a draft opinion for the Court, Frankfurter had stated that "[i]nvoluntary verbal confessions are not constitutionally obnoxious because of their unreliability." Rather, "[c]oerced confessions offend the community's sense of fair play and decency."[46]

Jackson drafted a concurring opinion: "I agree with the result and, generally, with the opinion. But I do not wish to be committed to the proposition that involuntary confessions are not constitutionally objectionable because of their unreliability." In contrast to Frankfurter, he believed "that unreliability is the basic reason for their exclusion." (Indeed, he went so far as to say: "If a sound beating of a suspect was [a] dependable way of getting the truth [out] of him I doubt that we would find it so reprehensible.") He continued:

The point probably has little bearing on this case. But it may be important in those cases where it is proposed to extend the constitutional exclusion to the results of mere interrogation of an accused without threats, violence or other impairments of the confessor's volition except that he is under arrest, reasonable detention and interrogation. In such cases [e.g., *Ashcraft v. Tennessee*] I have differed with some of my colleagues, one of the reasons being that I do not think the same incredibility inheres in the results of all such examination as [it] does in all cases of torture. Hence, I decline to join in what seems to be a burning of bridges, although some of my colleagues have already crossed them—perhaps without realizing that they were bridges.[47]

Frankfurter wrote to Jackson, "To enable me to have a Court could you not, as a matter of conscience . . . [,] *join* the opinion but with the reservation you are making[?]" (Had Frankfurter not been afraid of losing a vote, he might have noted the peculiar nature of Jackson's decision to overturn Rochin's conviction on the basis of the officers' conduct after the illegal break-in. After all, the evidence the police obtained was reliable.) Jackson eventually joined the opinion and even agreed not to write separately, but only after Frankfurter changed the offending sentence to read: "Use of involuntary verbal confessions in State criminal trials is constitutionally obnoxious *not only because of their unreliability*."[48]

In *Irvine v. California*, Jackson made public his differences with Frankfurter on this issue. There, the Court sustained a gambling conviction the state had secured with incriminating statements obtained through a concealed microphone. Officers entered the petitioner's home without a search warrant (and without his knowledge) to install the microphone, and, on two other occasions, they returned to reposition the device. In a plurality opinion, Jackson sought to distinguish *Rochin*: "That case involved, among other things, an illegal search of the defendant's person. But it also presented an element totally lacking here—coercion . . . , applied by a physical assault upon his person to compel submission to the use of a stomach pump. . . . However obnoxious are the facts in the case before us, they do not involve coercion, violence or brutality to the person, but rather a trespass to property, plus eavesdropping."[49]

Frankfurter dissented and took issue with Jackson's interpretation of *Rochin*. He conceded that "[t]here was lacking here physical violence, even to the restricted extent employed in *Rochin*."

[However, w]e have here . . . a more powerful and offensive control over the Irvines' life than a single, limited physical trespass. Certainly the conduct of the police here went far beyond a bare search and seizure.

The police devised means to hear every word that was said in the Irvine household for more than a month. Those affirming the conviction find that this conduct, in its entirety, is "almost incredible if it were not admitted." Surely the Court does not propose to announce a new absolute, namely, that even the most reprehensible means for securing a conviction will not taint a verdict so long as the body of the accused was not touched by State officials. . . .

The underlying reasoning of *Rochin* rejected the notion that States may secure a conviction by any form of skulduggery so long as it does not involve physical violence.[50]

Selective Incorporation Proponent

Jackson may have displayed in his due process decisions, not only a fear of judicial abstraction, but also a mistrust of unprincipled decision making that prompted him, at times, to be even more reserved than Frankfurter.[51] Yet, Jackson exhibited a fear of oppressive government that his Progressive colleague did not possess. He found the case law surrounding the doctrine of incorporation to be sufficiently principled to indulge somewhat his belief in the importance of adjudication for the preservation of individual liberty.

Jackson did not immediately distinguish himself from Frankfurter in the Court's battles over incorporation. In *Betts v. Brady* (where Black, in dissent, first explicitly endorsed the doctrine of total incorporation), Jackson and Frankfurter joined Justice Roberts's majority opinion. Recall that Roberts refused to apply against the states the Sixth Amendment right to counsel. He said that due process "formulates a concept less rigid and more fluid than those envisaged in other specific and particular provisions of the Bill of Rights"; the concept forbids only "a denial of fundamental fairness, [that is, actions] shocking to the universal sense of justice."[52]

In *Malinski v. New York*, Jackson and Frankfurter disagreed on the Court's decision to void a murder conviction. Frankfurter joined the judgment that police had coerced the petitioner's confession, and he provided an excursus on the independent potency of due process. Jackson joined Chief Justice Stone's dissent, which maintained the lawfulness of the conviction. But Stone announced: "We agree that the controlling principles upon which this Court reviews on constitutional grounds a state court conviction for crime, are *as stated in the opinion of Mr. Justice Frankfurter.*"[53]

Jackson's differences with Frankfurter over incorporation emerged in the Court's deliberations on *Francis v. Resweber*. As we have noted, the Court allowed Louisiana to proceed with the execution of Willie Francis, although the state had failed in its first attempt to kill him. In a draft opinion for the Court, Justice Reed had rejected Francis's claim to the protections of the double jeopardy provision of the Fifth Amendment and the cruel and unusual provision of the Eighth Amendment. He stressed the independent potency of due process and concluded that the execution of Francis would not "offend this nation's conception of justice."[54]

Black drafted a concurring opinion in which he objected vigorously to Reed's conception of due process. He could not "agree that the due process clause of the Fourteenth Amendment, or that Amendment itself, empowers [the] Court to strike down every state law, or state executive action, or state court judgment under state law, which may 'offend national standards of decency in the treatment of criminals.' If the due process clause means that, [the justices] must measure the validity of every state and federal criminal law by [their] conception of 'national standard of decency' without the guidance of constitutional language. Conduct believed 'decent' by millions of people may be believed 'indecent' by million[s] of others." Anticipating his opinion in *Adamson v. California*, he provided a brief historical defense of total incorporation.[55]

Apparently not expecting his brethren to embrace this doctrine, Black put forth an alternative argument. "While the Bill of Rights was held inapplicable to the States prior to the Fourteenth Amendment, since its adoption [the] Court has held that it made certain selected Bill of Rights safeguards applicable to the States." Citing Jackson's flag-salute opinion as support, he noted that the "First Amendment, safeguarding freedom of speech, press and religion, has been literally and emphatically applied to the States in its very terms." Black then said: "There is no good reason that I can perceive, nor is there any good reason suggested in any of the opinions in this case, why the process, heretofore followed, of selecting the provisions of the Bill of Rights to be applied to the States, should discriminate against the constitutional protections against cruel and unusual punishment and double jeopardy." He "agree[d] with Mr. Justice Reed that [the] Court [could not] under the Constitution hold that Louisiana authorities [were] barred from electrocuting the petitioner after a prior unsuccessful attempt to electrocute him [had] failed because of a mechanical accident." But "the only basis for decision should be consideration of whether the Eighth Amendment's prohibition against cruel and unusual punishment, and the Fifth Amendment's ban against double jeopardy, have been made applicable to the States by the Fourteenth, and if so, whether Louisiana's execution of petitioner would violate either of them."[56]

Much to Frankfurter's dismay (and, no doubt, Black's amusement), Jackson circulated a concurring opinion that echoed Black's statements on the nebulousness of due process:

> [N]othing demonstrates the lack of fixed standards of due process which this Court has recently invoked to direct the conduct of state courts in criminal cases more than the opinions in this case which wage a battle over the catchword "decency."
>
> The writer for the Court, guided by "national standards of decency," arrives at a conclusion which permits what to another is "repugnant to a civilized sense of justice," "inhuman and barbarous" and violates the "first principles of humanitarianism." A third proposes "elementary standards of decency" which brings him to a result exactly opposite the one reached by those who use as [a] guide "national standards of decency." A fourth identifies "national standards of decency" with "mystic natural law" and rejects the whole philosophy, but still comes out with the same result as those who use it. While I should not want to be thought less zealous for decency, either national or elementary, than my colleagues, I doubt if the word or concept affords either an objective or intelligible test of due process. If it is to be useful at all, it must mean that there is a judicial decency as there has long been recognized to be a "judicial discretion," a disciplined and impersonal decency which expresses society's will and the policy of the law—a quite different thing from personal bias or dislike. . . . But . . . the courts of the country must be pretty well confused about what they must do to avoid having conviction upset here on unpredictable and incomprehensive application of such vague standards as "decency."[57]

At this point, Jackson attached a footnote: "The term ['decency'] was used, but I think in a limited sense, in [Frankfurter's concurrence in] the *Malinski* case, . . . in which opinion was so individual that five opinions were required. The length to which the individualism of our standards of due process may carry us has classic illustration in that case."[58]

These comments so disturbed Frankfurter that he wrote a lengthy handwritten memo, attempting to convince Jackson of the laxity of his argument.[59] With regard to Jackson's discussion of the multiple opinions, and thus the supposed confusion, that *Malinski* had generated, Frankfurter said:

I venture to call your attention to [Stone's dissent in *Malinski*,] . . . where the C. J. said[:] "*We* agree that the controlling principles upon which this Court reviews on constitutional grounds a state court conviction for crime, are as stated in the opinion of Mr. Justice Frankfurter" (italics supplied).

"We" = Mr. Chief Justice Stone
          Mr. Justice Roberts
          Mr. Justice Reed
          Mr. Justice Jackson
                                                    _____
                                                              4

"as stated in the
opinion of
Mr. Justice Frankfurter["] = 1
. . .   _____

          Total   5

After noting the degree of consensus present in *Malinski*, Frankfurter attempted to defend the objectivity of the standard upon which the justices had agreed. "*You* wouldn't say," he told Jackson, "that a conviction under a state law that called for quartering and gibbeting, after public branding, *ala The Scarlet Letter*, of an adulterer would not, under modern precedents[,] be offensive to 'due process.[']'" And referring to a hypothetical situation Jackson had mentioned in his opinion, Frankfurter asserted: "[A] law—a statute—saying that a state may have five (5) efforts at execution would surely call for the determination here whether that's consonant with 'due process.'" He ended on a conciliatory note: "I'd like to salvage much of your opinion. . . . [But I would like] to change the figure—not to throw out [the] 'due process' baby with some of our brethren's hogwash."[60]

Frankfurter appreciated those portions of Jackson's draft opinion, such as the following exerpts, that suggested a very limited conception of due process: "If I am at liberty, in the name of due process, to vote my personal sense of 'decency,' I not only would refuse to send Willie Francis back to the electric chair, but I would not have sent him there in the first place. If my will were law, it would never permit execution of any death sentence. This is not because I am sentimental about criminals, but I have doubts of the moral right of society to extinguish a human life, and even greater doubts about the wisdom of doing so." "But judges are servants, not masters, of society and it is society's laws that should govern judges." In this case, Jackson was "unable to cite any constitutional backing for [his] prejudice against executing Francis and, hence, must vote to leave the case to Louisiana's own law and sense of decency.''[61]

Jackson also pleased Frankfurter with a note of thanks for his editorial assistance. Jackson conceded that his analysis of *Malinski* was "terrible." And he drew a distinction between the word " 'decency' [which] means different things to different people" and "[a] judicial decency, meaning a disciplined and informal search for things the law holds indecent." Acknowledging Frankfurter's assistance in clarifying the concept of due process, he remarked: "Our only escape from drivel is to swat it [out] now and then." (Jackson revealed in subsequent opinions that, with Frankfurter, he would continue to employ the rational-basis test in due process controversies.)[62]

Yet Jackson revealed a significant jurisprudential difference with Frankfurter when Reed circulated a revised version of his opinion. To retain Black's vote, Reed abandoned discussion of the independent potency of due process and assumed, "but without so deciding, that violation of the principles of the Fifth and Eighth Amendments, as to double jeopardy and cruel and unusual punishment, would be violative of the due process clause of the Fourteenth Amendment." After underlining this sentence on his copy, Frankfurter addressed the following marginalia to Jackson: "Dear Bob: I respectfully suggest that this is the way things not 'decided' are, by a process of penetration, found to be decided next time. How much better and wiser [to follow?] Cardozo in *Palko* . . . where it was held that 'double jeopardy['] of [the] Fifth Am't does *NOT* bind [the] States.''[63]

By joining Reed's opinion, as opposed to Frankfurter's statement on the independent potency of due process, Jackson signaled his acceptance of selective incorporation. True, Reed did not formally incorporate any constitutional provisions. But there were several reasons for Jackson—had he opposed incorporation—not to join an opinion that hypothetically incorporated provisions of the Bill of Rights. First, Black joined the plurality opinion only after Reed agreed to stop just short of endorsing selective incorporation, and the Alabamian had already publicly endorsed total incorporation.[64] Had Jackson been opposed to selective incorporation, he would have been wise to avoid associating with Black and any opinion approximating incorporation. Second, recall that, in a draft opinion for this case, Black had identified Jackson with the doctrine of selective incorporation. Although Black had suppressed the opinion in which this statement appeared, *Francis* provided Jackson with an opportunity to take preemptive measures against such an interpretation of his decisions. Third, any true proponent of an independent notion of due process would have heeded Frankfurter's warning that a hypothetical incorporation would eventually become reality. Fourth, for Jackson, there were no disincentives associated with joining Frankfurter's opinion. Jackson felt no pressure to maintain a majority opinion, since Reed only spoke for a plurality.

In *Francis*, Jackson merely returned to an earlier position. In 1942, he had stated: "That specification of activities that cannot be touched by the central government constitutes our Bill of Rights—the Bill of Rights which can be invoked when civil liberties are invaded. Originally, these limitations were applied only to the central government, but of late years, mainly by the force of the Fourteenth Amendment, they are applied to states as well. So we now have a certain area of policy in which neither state nor federal government can legislate." Apparently, Jackson had not finalized his position on this issue upon joining the Court, since the publication of this passage coincided with his decision to join Justice Roberts's decision in *Betts v. Brady*.[65]

Events after *Francis* revealed that Jackson was no longer indecisive on the issue of incorporation. In his dissent in *Everson v. Board of Ewing Township*, he expressed agreement with applying the establishment clause of the First Amendment against the states, although he disagreed with the majority about the meaning of that provision. Frankfurter also accepted the application of the establishment clause against the states.[66] But after the Court ruled in *Adamson v. California* later in the term,[67] only Frankfurter had to contend with reconciling the incorporation of that portion of the First Amendment with an independent conception of due process.

In *Adamson*, Jackson joined Justice Reed who, speaking for the majority, declined to incorporate the Fifth Amendment right against self-incrimination. Tellingly, Jackson did not join Frankfurter, whose concurring opinion stressed the independent potency of the due process clause and disparaged any notion of incorporation, selective as well as total. Had Jackson rejected selective incorporation, he would have felt compelled to join Frankfurter (even though doing so would have left Reed with a plurality), for Reed clearly left open the possibility of future applications of provisions of the Bill of Rights against the states. Reed stated: "The due process clause of the Fourteenth Amendment . . . does not draw *all* the rights of the federal Bill of Rights under its protection. That contention was made and rejected in *Palko v. Connecticut*." But he also noted that "*Palko* held that such provisions of the Bill of Rights as were 'implicit in the concept of ordered liberty' . . . became secure from state interference by the clause.'' Jackson joined Reed, then, because he believed that future cases might reveal that certain of the protections contained in the Bill of Rights are "of the essence of a scheme of ordered liberty" or are so important "that neither liberty nor justice would exist if they were sacrificed" on the state level.[68]

Sharing Black's fear of oppressive majorities, Jackson was inclined to apply provisions of the Bill of Rights against the states. Yet, it is understandable that he would not embrace total incorporation, for he also shared Frankfurter's fear of judicial abstraction. The selective application of provisions of the Bill of Rights against the states would seem the likely recourse for someone so torn.

As one steeped in the method of the common law, Jackson demanded a principled manner of selecting among constitutional provisions. He (and Reed) found such a principle in *Palko*. Benjamin Cardozo, one of the greatest common-law judges in our nation's history, formulated the *Palko* standard: "implicit in the concept of ordered liberty." He induced the principle from past cases, in part to rationalize or explain the Court's pre-*Palko* incorporation of certain provisions of the Bill of Rights. Like any common-law judge, he also sought to afford guidance in future cases, leaving open the possibility that unforeseen circumstances might reveal the indispensability of a provision in the Bill of Rights to a system of liberty and justice.[69] As one who distrusted political majorities and who possessed a common-law sensitivity to a changing and complex reality, Jackson did not share Frankfurter's confidence that Cardozo regarded the concept of due process and the provisions of the Bill of Rights as, for all intents and purposes, mutually exclusive. Yet, as one who considered judicial abstraction to be a serious threat in the modern age, he appreciated Cardozo's effort to incorporate only those provisions without which "neither liberty nor justice would exist."

The Nuremberg Trial as a Determinant?

An Apparent Shift

To some students of Jackson's career, the argument of this chapter would seem vulnerable, since it does not attribute significance to the political event the justice regarded as "the most satisfying and gratifying experience" of his life and for which he is perhaps best remem-

bered: his service as United States chief of counsel at the Nuremberg
War Crimes Trial from June of 1945 until October the following year.
One might argue against attributing the pragmatic character of his
decisions (at least his free speech decisions) to his use of the decision-
making methods of an earlier era in American law to resolve a tension
between a traditional fear of majority oppression and a fear of abstract
thinking in an interdependent society. His jurisprudence, the argument
would go, was pragmatic in appearance only: he underwent a profound
jurisprudential change from a marked, early concern with the protection of constitutional liberties to a Nuremberg-inspired constitutional
conservatism. In the words of one scholar:

> Jackson was brilliant at Nurnberg, yet he returned from the trials a
> different man: the once libertarian judicial activist, who had so often sided
> with Black, Douglas, Murphy, and Rutledge, had become profoundly
> cautious, a markedly narrow interpreter of the Bill of Rights. He now
> more often than not sided with the Frankfurter wing of the Court. . . .
> This intriguing metamorphosis may well have resulted from his Nurnberg
> experiences—his firsthand perception of the melancholy events resulting
> in the destruction of the Weimar Republic and the rise of Nazism. It was
> his conclusive judgment that one of the major contributory factors was
> the failure of the Weimar government to crack down on radical dissenters
> and extremist groups.[70]

This argument seems tenable. The free speech decisions discussed
earlier, in which Jackson was attentive to the circumstances supposedly
justifying legislative abridgments of liberty, followed the Nuremberg trial,
while his eloquent opinions supporting free speech claims preceded that
event. Furthermore, Jackson's writings on Nuremberg and certain of his
later free speech opinions reveal that, indeed, he believed the event had
important implications for liberty in this country.

Jackson listed as one accomplishment of the Nuremberg trial the lesson
it provided to nations concerned with maintaining the conditions essential
to freedom, for Nuremberg illuminated the methods Hitler had used to
obtain power. The trial, Jackson said, demonstrated that the Nazis should
not be thought of in terms of the unstructured organizations referred to
in this country as political parties. They did not acquire control of the
German state through conventional or republican means. Instead, they
employed various forms of fraud, intimidation, and sabotage to seize
power. For example, the SA (or *Die Sturmabteilungen*), a voluntary
organization of young, fanatical Nazis, practiced violent interference with
elections, the breaking up of opposition meetings, and the terrorization
of adversaries. The members of the SA "boasted that their task was
to make the Nazi Party 'master of the streets.' " The SD (or *Der
Sicherheitsdienst*), a component of the SA, violated the secrecy of

elections in order to identify those opposed to the Nazis. Finally, the burning of the Reichstag building in February of 1933, less than a month after Hitler became chancellor, helped solidify Nazi power. Hitler claimed that this act of arson was the beginning of a communist revolution, and he exploited the resulting hysteria to subdue his political enemies and lobby for dictatorial power to meet the crisis. The regrettable destruction of German freedom and the tragedy that followed in the wake of Hitler's international aggression might have been averted, Jackson believed, had it not been for the "complacency and tolerance as well as the impotence of the Weimar Republic towards the growing organization of Nazi power." The German experience, he thought, revealed the importance of controlling such aggregations of power in their incipient stages.[71]

Jackson revealed the impress of Nuremberg in his *Terminiello* dissent. As noted earlier, he berated the majority in this case for failing to appreciate the riotous situation confronting local officials. But he also sought to put the case in context for his brethren by lecturing them on recent European history: The conflict between the anti-Semite, Terminiello, and his fierce opponents

> was not an isolated, spontaneous and unintended collision of political, racial or ideological adversaries. It was a local manifestation of a world-wide and standing conflict between two organized groups of revolutionary fanatics, each of which has imported to this country the strong-arm techniques developed in the struggle by which their kind has devastated Europe. Increasingly, American citizens have to cope with it. One faction organizes a mass meeting, the other organizes pickets to harass it; each organizes squads to counteract the other's pickets; parade is met with counterparade. Each of the mass demonstrations has the potentiality, and more than a few the purpose, of disorder and violence. This technique appeals not to reason but to fears and mob spirit; each is a show of force designed to bully adversaries and to overawe the indifferent. [The Court] need not resort to speculation as to the purposes for which these tactics are calculated nor as to their consequences. Recent European history demonstrates both.[72]

Jackson ended his dissent with the ominous warning that "if the Court does not temper its doctrinaire logic with a little practical wisdom, it will convert the constitutional Bill of Rights into a suicide pact."[73]

Jackson also revealed the influence of Nuremberg in *Kunz v. New York*. In that case, the Court protected a Baptist minister who had publicly denounced Jews and Catholics while in areas of the city that these groups inhabited. The Court held as a prior restraint on the exercise of First Amendment rights an ordinance that prohibited individuals from conducting public worship meetings on the street without first obtaining a permit from the police commissioner. Speaking for the majority, Chief Justice Vinson said that "New York cannot vest restraining control over the right to speak on religious subjects in an administrative official where there are no appropriate standards to guide his action."[74]

In a biting dissent, Jackson berated the Court for its naivete: "Jews, many of whose families perished in extermination furnaces of Dachau and Auschwitz, are more than tolerant if they pass off lightly [Kunz's] suggestion that unbelievers in Christ should have all been burned." He elaborated:

> Is it not reasonable that the City protect the dignity of these persons against fanatics who take possession of its streets to hurl into its crowds defamatory epithets that hurt like rocks?
> If any two subjects are intrinsically incendiary and divisive, they are race and religion. Racial fears and hatreds have been at the root of the most terrible riots that have disgraced American civilization. They are ugly possibilities that overhang every great American city. The "consecrated hatreds of sect" account for more than a few of the world's bloody disorders. These are the explosives which the Court says Kunz may play with in the public streets, and the community must not only tolerate but aid him. I find no such doctrine in the Constitution.[75]

The tone of these opinions was striking in comparison with that of Jackson's opinion in the second flag-salute case, which contained, not only a paean to the guarantees of the First Amendment (with which this Chapter opened), but also an apparent affirmation of the "preferred freedoms" concept. The "freedoms of speech and press, of assembly, and of worship," Jackson had said, "may not be infringed on such slender grounds" as is allowed in property rights cases, where the legislature has only to demonstrate a rational basis for enacting the law. First Amendment freedoms "are susceptible of restriction only to prevent grave and immediate danger to interests which the State may lawfully protect."[76]

If anyone doubted that Jackson now rejected this doctrine, they soon became convinced of this fact. Shortly after *Terminiello*, in *Brinegar v. United States*, he repudiated the notion of "preferred freedoms" in these explicit terms: "We cannot give some constitutional rights a preferred position without relegating others to a deferred position; we can establish no firsts without establishing seconds." The significance of this statement did not escape Jackson's law clerk, who asked: "Is anything here inconsistent with your *Barnette* flag salute case . . . where you say First Amendment freedom cannot be infringed on as slender grounds as claims under due process of the 14th [Amendment]?"[77]

What all of this discussion might suggest, then, is that Jackson's scrupulous attention to the circumstances surrounding cases was a manifestation, not of his traditional legal background, but of his Nuremberg experience. His new-found emphasis upon context, in short, may have served merely to rationalize governmental efforts to curtail liberty.

The Consistency of Jackson's Thought

Jackson would have denied that his decisions betrayed a jurisprudential shift. He maintained in *Brinegar* that he was never an adherent of the "preferred freedoms" concept, citing as evidence his pre-Nuremberg opinion in *Murdock v. Pennsylvania*. There, he had dissented from the Court's invalidation of a license-tax ordinance the state had construed to apply to religious colporteurs (in this case, Jehovah's Witnesses). The Court had held that such a restriction on itinerant evangelism is a violation of the freedoms of press, speech, and religion, which "are in a preferred position."[78] Jackson's *Murdock* opinion served as a response to two related cases, each involving Jehovah's Witnesses. In the first case, *Martin v. City of Struthers*, he dissented from the Court's ruling that an ordinance forbidding any person to summon the occupants of any residence for the purpose of giving them handbills is a denial of free speech and press. In the second case, *Douglas v. City of Jeannette*, he concurred in the ruling that an ordinance prohibiting individuals from soliciting orders for merchandise without first procuring a license from city authorities and paying a license tax does not violate the First Amendment.[79]

Referring to *Douglas*—the only one of the three cases to provide "a comprehensive story of the broad plan of campaign employed by Jehovah's Witnesses and its full impact on a living community"— Jackson lamented that "the facts of this case are passed over as irrelevant to the theory on which the Court would decide its particular issue." (In a draft opinion, he said: "I think the Court in the fervent transcendentalism of its opinions overlooks the very earthy problems of local authorities trying vainly to keep the peace of their communities.") In language that matched the tone of his post-Nuremberg rulings, he warned: "Unless we are to reach judgments as did Plato's men who were chained in a cave so that they saw nothing but shadows, we should consider the facts of the *Douglas* case at least as a hypothesis to test the validity of the conclusions in the other cases."[80]

At this point, Jackson proceeded, over the space of seven pages, to illuminate the Witnesses' aggressive door-to-door proselytizing tactics that generated many citizen complaints; to examine the national structure of that religious organization; and to explicate the provocative nature of the Witnesses' literature and statements. His dissents in *Murdock* and *Martin*—"induced in no small part by the facts cited"— suggested that the Court's rulings in favor of the speech claims of the Witnesses were "at odds with the realities of life in those communities where the householder himself drops whatever he may be doing to answer the summons to the door and is apt to have positive religious convictions of his own." In *Martin*, he noted, the Court acknowledged the speech claims of the Witnesses and concluded that the ordinance " 'submits the distributer to criminal punishment for annoying the person on whom he calls, even though the recipient of the literature distributed is in fact glad to receive it.' " Jackson retorted that "the hospitable householder thus thrown in the balance with the Witness to make weight against the city ordinance is wholly hypothetical and the assumption is contrary to the evidence [i.e., the citizen complaints] we have recited." And in a statement noteworthy for its failure to place the burden of proof on the government (as the "preferred freedoms" concept requires), he remarked: "There is not a syllable of evidence that [the amount of the license tax at issue in *Murdock*] exceeds the cost to the community of policing this activity."[81]

Admonishing the Court, Jackson argued that the "real task of determining the extent of [the Witnesses'] rights on balance with the rights of others is not met by pronouncement of general propositions [concerning the importance of First Amendment freedoms] with which there is no disagreement." He conceded that the "First Amendment grew out of an experience which taught that society cannot trust the conscience of a majority to keep its religious zeal within the limits that a free society can tolerate." But he did "not think [the amendment] any more intended to leave the conscience of a minority to fix its limits." Freedom "comes of hard-headed fixing of those limits by neutral authority with an eye to the widest freedom to proselyte compatible with the freedom of those subject to proselyting pressures." In a draft of his opinion, he had said that "[r]eligious liberty includes a great deal of latitude in proselyting, but . . . it does not mean freedom to provoke religious brawls." In another pre-Nuremberg case, he argued that "the limits [on religious practices] begin to operate whenever [these] activities begin to affect or collide with the liberties of others or of the public."[82]

If Jackson's claim—that *Murdock* demonstrated his disagreement with the "preferred freedoms" concept—is to be convincing, one must still reconcile that decision with the second flag-salute case, which the Court decided the following month. Because Jackson spoke for a majority in the latter case, it is possible that he added the passage affirming the "preferred freedoms" concept at the behest of another. In fact, a memorandum in his case file demonstrates that the passage was one of several "changes [that] were discussed in conference." This memorandum, however, does not prove that he was not the author of the passage. Moreover, he once said, while reflecting upon the opinion-writing process, that he "[did not] think there would be many instances in which any justice would allow a compromise that made him say something he didn't agree with, [although he] might omit something that he would say if he were speaking for himself." And one must also note that Jackson maintained, in *The Struggle for Judicial Supremacy* (which he wrote shortly before joining the Court), that "[t]he presumption of validity which attaches in general to legislative acts is frankly reversed in the case of interferences with free speech and free assembly, and for a perfectly cogent reason. Ordinarily, legislation whose basis in economic wisdom is uncertain can be redressed by the processes of the ballot box or the pressures of opinion. But when the channels of opinion and of peaceful persuasion are corrupted or clogged, these political correctives can no longer be relied on, and the democratic system is threatened at its most vital point. In that event the Court, by intervening, restores the processes of democratic government; it does not disrupt them."[83]

If Jackson's *Murdock* opinion did not demonstrate that the concept of "preferred freedoms" was alien to his constitutional jurisprudence, it proved conclusively that he did not regard the concept as precluding judicial consideration of matters of time and circumstance. Indeed, this and other conservative opinions on free speech claims, which he wrote prior to Nuremberg, revealed that one could not predict his position in First Amendment cases with any degree of accuracy relying simply on the knowledge that he apparently accepted the notion of "preferred freedoms." Although he may have placed the burden of proof on the government in such cases (which would mean he misspoke in *Murdock*), the burden was not insurmountable, and he was always attentive to the circumstances surrounding cases. Even Jackson's celebrated tribute to the First Amendment in the second flag-salute case—a passage many view as one of the finest statements of the "preferred freedoms" concept—followed a discussion of context. "The freedom asserted by these appellees," he said, did "not bring them into collision with rights asserted by any other individual." The Jehovah's Witnesses' refusal "to participate in the [flag] ceremony [did] not interfere with or deny the rights of others to do so." Had there been such a conflict, or had the Witnesses not been "peaceable and orderly," he would have allowed the state "to determine when the rights of one end and those of another begin."[84]

Since Jackson evidently did not believe that the notion of "preferred freedoms" affords sufficient guidance to judges in First Amendment cases, one must search elsewhere for a statement of the principles that informed his decisions. In a passage reminiscent of a nineteenth-century treatise writer's efforts to articulate guiding principles generalized from past cases, Jackson once offered an account of his free speech opinions (each of which this chapter addressed):

> I adhere to the views I have heretofore expressed, whether the Court agreed, *West Virginia Board of Education v. Barnette* [the second flag-salute case], . . . or disagreed, see dissenting opinion in *United States v. Ballard*. . . , that our Constitution excludes both general and local governments from the realm of opinions and ideas, beliefs and doubts, heresy and orthodoxy, political, religious or scientific. The right to speak out or to publish, also is protected when it does not clearly and presently threaten some injury to society which the Government has a right to protect. Separate opinion, *Thomas v. Collins*. . . . But I have protested the degradation of these constitutional liberties to immunize and approve mob movements, whether these mobs be religious or political, radical or conservative, liberal or illiberal, *Douglas v. City of Jeannette* . . . ; *Terminiello v. Chicago* . . . , or to authorize pressure groups to use amplifying devices to drown out the natural voice and destroy the peace of other individuals. *Saia v. People of New York* . . . ; *Kovacs v. Cooper.* . . . And I have pointed out that men cannot enjoy their right to personal freedom if fanatical masses, whatever their mission, can strangle individual thoughts and invade personal privacy. *Martin v. Struthers.* . . . A catalogue of rights was placed in our Constitution, in my view, to protect the individual in his individuality, and neither statutes which put those rights at the mercy of officials nor judicial decisions which put them at the mercy of the mob are consistent with its text or its spirit.[85]

At Once a Noisome and Liberalizing Influence

While Jackson's post-Nuremberg repudiation of the "preferred freedoms" concept did not represent a fundamental shift in his constitutional jurisprudence, it most certainly signified a change in tone. He revealed this change in his off-the-bench writings as well. In his Godkin lectures, which he wrote at the end of his career, he denounced a "cult of libertarian judicial activists [that] now assails the Court almost as bitterly for renouncing power as the earlier 'liberals' once did for assuming too much power." He attempted in this not-so-subtle state- ment to distance himself from the Court's most devoted free speech advocates, principally Justices Black and Douglas. He saw rejection of the "preferred freedoms" concept as another way to avoid being identified with justices whom he thought substituted general or abstract propositions concerning free speech for a careful consideration of the circumstances surrounding First Amendment cases. Although he had been critical of his brethren all along on this score, the lessons of Nuremberg, especially the need to be solicitous of the efforts of local officials to deal with social conflict and expressions of dissent, prompted him to disparage his colleagues in his writings and opinions and to reject their organizing principle.[86]

To say that Jackson's rejection of "preferred freedoms" did not represent a *fundamental* change in his jurisprudence is not to say that Nuremberg inspired *no* change or only a change in tone. For he demonstrated a renewed respect for federalism when he modified his position on incorporation. The first signs of change appeared in *Terminiello*, where he expressed doubt concerning the legitimacy of the selective-incorporation doctrine. He asked the Court to "recall that [its] application of the First Amendment to [the states] rests entirely on authority which the Court has voted to itself." He also noted that, for years, the Court had denied that the Fourteenth Amendment incorporates the First. However, he concluded he had "no quarrel" with the Court's later application of the First Amend- ment against the states. Ultimately, he rested his opinion on his interpretation of the free speech guarantee. Apparently, he felt com- pelled to remain consistent with his opinion in the second flag-salute case (which he cited), where he had said that the "test of legislation which collides with the Fourteenth Amendment, because it also col- lides with the principles of the First, is much more definite than the test when only the Fourteenth is involved."[87]

Jackson revealed no desire for consistency when the Court sustained an attempt by Illinois authorities to punish Joseph Beauharnais for violating a group-libel law. (The accused had distributed racist leaflets on Chicago streets.) Jackson dissented from the decision because he believed that the manner in which authorities had applied the statute violated due process. (The state had required no proof of injury to any person or group.) But he agreed that group-libel statutes are permissible; they "represent a commendable desire to reduce sinister abuses of our freedoms of expression—abuses which I have had occasion to learn can tear apart a society, brutalize its dominant elements, and persecute, even to extermination, its minorities." In contrast to the majority, however, Jackson argued that the reason this sort of legislation does not violate the Constitution is that the First Amendment does not apply against the states in its entirety. He explicitly rejected the argument that the Fourteenth Amendment incorporates the provisions of the First, because, in his view, the history of criminal libel demonstrates otherwise. More than forty state constitutions, which extended protection to speech and press, he noted, "reserve[d] a responsibility for their abuse and implicitly or explicitly recognize[d] validity of criminal libel laws." One can assume "that the men who sponsored the Fourteenth Amendment in Congress, and those who ratified it in the State Legislatures, knew of such provisions then in many of their State Constitutions," and one would be unreasonable to believe they were consciously canceling them, as the incorporation of the First Amendment would require. (Federal courts had always reserved the issue of libel to the states.) Jackson believed that Justices Holmes and Brandeis had articulated the "wise and historically correct view of the Fourteenth Amendment." They had argued that, while " '[t]he general principle of free speech' " inheres in the Fourteenth Amendment, " 'a somewhat larger latitude of interpretation than is allowed to Congress' " should be accorded to the states.[88]

Jackson acknowledged this change in his Fourteenth Amendment jurisprudence with an apology: "Whence we are to derive metes and bounds out of the state power is a subject to the confusion of which, I regret to say, I have contributed—comforted in the acknowledgement, however, by recalling that this Amendment is so enigmatic and abstruse that judges more experienced than I have had to reverse themselves as to its effect on state power." He might also have repeated his argument for relaxing the principle of *stare decisis* in constitutional cases—that the Court's rulings in these contexts are often flawed—because his change of heart was the product more of his conviction that the Court's position on incorporation was unwise than of his view that it contradicted constitutional history. Recall that Jackson was not one to believe that historical analysis provides definitive answers to constitutional controversies. Furthermore, he conceded that he was "more inclined to [preserve the federal form of government] since the

Second World War than [he] was before, because of the post-mortem examination of the Hitler regime, which took place at Nuremberg.''[89]

Jackson's Nuremberg experience affected, not only his attitude toward incorporation, but also his First Amendment jurisprudence, at least with respect to seditious speech. As noted earlier, Nuremberg was not responsible for the justice's marked concern with the circumstances of cases. But it *was* the cause of his adopting an approach toward seditious speech that was even more deferential toward legislatures than the approach Frankfurter took. Jackson revealed this jurisprudential change in *Dennis v. United States*. There, as we have seen, the Court weakened the protection afforded by the "clear and present danger" test and thus participated in the United States government's effort to combat the Communist Party. In his plurality opinion, Chief Justice Vinson subordinated the requirement of a "present" or "imminent" danger to a "probable" one. Jackson concurred in the decision to sustain the Communists' convictions under the conspiracy provisions of the Smith Act but refused to apply the Court's revised version of the "clear and present danger" test. He probably based this refusal on the principle that had guided him at Nuremberg, namely, that courts should not participate in the perversion of law. (Jackson worked diligently at Nuremberg to quell criticism that the proceedings against the Nazis were political.) The Court's evisceration of the "clear and present danger" test essentially politicized the proceedings, and only Jackson seemed aware of the damage that a domestic political trial would cause to legal values and judicial prestige.[90]

But Jackson did not ask the Court to apply properly the "clear and present danger" test. The implications of requiring the existence of an imminent danger before the state would be permitted to suppress radical speech disturbed him. The Court fashioned this test, he argued, when the primary forces viewed "as antagonists in the struggle between liberty and authority were the Government on the one hand and the individual citizen on the other." The political situation had been complicated in recent times "by the intervention between the state and the citizen of permanently organized, well-financed, semisecret highly disciplined political organizations." Employing the "clear and present danger" test would mean "that the Communist plotting is protected during its period of incubation; [that] its preliminary stages of organization and preparation are immune from the law; [and that] the Government can move only after imminent action is manifest, when it would, of course, be too late." Drawing upon his belief, acquired at Nuremberg, that government must curb radical organiza-

tions in their early stages, he argued that the Court should resort to
the controversial doctrine of conspiracy. The Nuremberg prosecution
team had used this doctrine against individuals who may not have
actually participated in international crimes but whose cooperation the
Nazis found vital. Jackson acknowledged that criminal conspiracy is
"a dragnet device capable of perversion into an instrument of injustice
in the hands of a partisan or compliant judiciary." But he contended
that this doctrine "has an established place in our system of law."
Since the federal government had used the doctrine to frustrate concerted action that disturbs interstate commerce, the Court would be
unreasonable not to apply it to those attempting to undermine our
government.[91]

So, while Nuremberg impressed upon Jackson the dangers that
judicial involvement in the distortion of law for political purposes
presents to legal values and judicial prestige, his analysis of the
destruction of German liberty inured him to the perils associated with
a legal doctrine that permits government to punish individuals for
having done nothing more than agree to assemble and discuss radical
politics. Among the justices, only he was willing to accept at face value
the conspiracy provisions of the Smith Act and not insist on the
demonstration of a danger, or at least a rational belief that a danger
existed, as Frankfurter would have it. Conviction of the Communists
through use of the conspiracy doctrine would not have compensated
for the harm done to liberal or constitutional values. Elimination of
the Communist Party would not have lessened the Soviet threat
appreciably, if at all. By contrast, the "history of the law of conspiracy
. . . is such as to inspire only misgivings."[92]

Acknowledgment of Jackson's increased conservatism in limited
areas of the law should not lead one to overlook the fact that his study
of Nazi methods of maintaining power had a liberalizing influence in
other areas of his constitutional jurisprudence. He noted that the Nazis
had employed several means to perfect control over German society,
including formation of the Gestapo, whose role was to detect opposition. The Nazis did not level charges against those whom they suspected or disliked, nor did they present evidence against these supposed enemies of the state. Instead, they employed the techniques of
secret arrest and indefinite detention. In short, the "German people
were in the hands of the police, the police were in the hands of the
Nazi Party and the Party was in the hands of a ring of evil men." This
highly centralized system of coercion existed "outside of and [was]
immune to any law, with party-controlled concentration camps and

firing squads [administering] privately decreed sanctions.'' The Nazis seized property, deprived individuals of liberty, and even took away life itself ''[w]ithout responsibility to any law and without warrant from any court.''[93]

These insights occasioned a heightened appreciation, on Jackson's part, of the Constitution's procedural guarantees. Many of these provisions, he noted, are discredited ''as 'technicalities' which irritate by causing delays and permitting escapes from what [public opinion] regards as justice. But by and large, sober second thought sustains most of them as essential safeguards of fair law enforcement and worth whatever delays or escapes they cost.''[94]

This principle guided him in *Shaughnessy v. Mezei*, where the Court sustained the attorney general's order, based ostensibly on national security grounds, to exclude an alien without a hearing. In his dissent, Jackson noted that the communists' conspiratorial techniques of infiltration tempt government to confine suspects on secret information secretly judged, and he conceded that he was not one to discount the communist threat. ''But my apprehensions about the security of our form of government,'' he said, ''are about equally aroused by those who will not see the danger in anything else.'' Here, the government's detention of Mezei had ''unmistakable overtones of the [Nazis'] 'protective custody' '' against which the arrested could claim no judicial or other hearing. Just as Nazi ''concentration camps [had been] populated with victims of summary executive detention for secret reasons,'' this practice, ''once established with the best of intentions, [would] drift into oppression of the disadvantaged in this country as it has elsewhere.'' In Jackson's view, ''[p]rocedural fairness and regularity are of the indispensable essence of liberty.'' And ''the most scrupulous observance of due process, including the right to know a charge, to be confronted with the accuser, to cross-examine informers and to produce evidence in one's behalf, is especially necessary where the occasion of detention is fear of future misconduct rather than crimes committed.''[95]

In a draft opinion, Jackson had stated even more passionately his belief in the importance of procedural justice:

> [T]he simplicity of my origins and the mediocrity of my attainments leaves me still believing that something in the mysterious order of the universe . . . gives a man, just because he is a human being, certain dignities and personal immunities which no man and no government can trample or invade without setting in motion forces of retribution. I have

seen it—and may God have mercy on this country if ever our people cease to believe it.

Such I think was the concept carried into the Fifth Amendment of the Constitution of the United States which provides that no person shall be deprived of life, liberty or property without due process of law. This asks no status except that conferred by possession of a human personality to claim in this country whatever immunities that amendment recognizes.[96]

Jackson's Fourth Amendment opinions (at least those involving the federal government), like his opinions on procedural justice, also revealed Nuremberg's liberalizing effect. They disclosed his belief that the prohibition against unreasonable searches and seizures (and the attendant requirement of particularity in search warrants) is one of the most important procedural safeguards against arbitrary government. In Jackson's words: "Among deprivation of rights, none is so effective in cowing a population, crushing the spirit of the individual and putting terror in every heart [as is deprivation of Fourth Amendment freedoms]. Unconstitutional search and seizure is one of the first and most effective weapons in the arsenal of every arbitrary government." Requiring officers to have some valid basis in law for intrusions, he believed, is "one of the most fundamental distinctions between our form of government, where officers are under the law, and the police state where they are the law."[97]

One should note that the former passage appeared in the opinion in which Jackson repudiated the "preferred freedoms" concept, namely, in his dissent in *Brinegar v. United States*. As we have seen, in *Brinegar*, Jackson justified his position with the statement: "We cannot give some constitutional rights a preferred position without relegating others to a deferred position."[98] Thus, he renounced "preferred freedoms" as much to secure a constitutional provision he regarded as second to none in importance as to distance himself from the Court's most aggressive free speech advocates.

A careful examination of Jackson's opinions, then, reveals that, apart from influencing him to change the tone of his free speech opinions and to modify his approach to incorporation and seditious speech, Nuremberg did not serve as a determinant in his constitutional jurisprudence. He was fundamentally the same justice upon returning from his service as "America's Advocate"[99] as he had been before accepting the assignment. He never became a "markedly narrow interpreter of the Bill of Rights" in the manner of Frankfurter, nor was he ever a "libertarian judicial activist." The pragmatic character of his free speech votes, which stemmed from his attentiveness to the circumstances of the cases before him, was apparent from the outset. And he possessed, and acted upon, a traditional belief in judicial supremacy throughout his judicial tenure.

Toward the end of his career, Jackson did say: "[T]here's a great deal in Judge [Learned] Hand's viewpoint that the existence of the Bill of Rights in the form that we have it, enforced in the form that we have it, makes people tend to sleep on their own liberties on the assumption that the Court is the watchdog. It might very well be that in the long run the British system by which liberties are defended in Parliament is stronger than our system by which they're defended in court." Yet Jackson could not bring himself to accept fully these arguments, which were at the center of Frankfurter's, as well as Hand's, jurisprudence. Indeed, to Hand's view that "the Bill of Rights should . . . be regarded as a political admonition, rather than as legal doctrine," Jackson responded with the statement: "It's hard to see how minority rights can be very well protected except by making them legal rights, rather than political principles." And again: "[Without judicial review,] the majority would override everything. . . . I suppose that men would be sent to jail for not convicting themselves, for not confessing crimes before Congressional committees, if [the Court] didn't constantly reiterate that the Bill of Rights says that no man shall be required to be a witness against himself. I don't know how far 'search and seizure' would be carried if there wasn't a Court which can limit it. Freedom of speech, freedom of press are all protected. While the Court doesn't go so far in protecting some of those things as extremists would have us go, there is a certain amount of security for liberties in the existence of the Court."[100]

One should also note that Jackson returned, in his Godkin lectures, to a theme about which he had written some thirteen years earlier, in *The Struggle for Judicial Supremacy*. The task of a justice, he declared, is "to maintain the great system of balances upon which our free government is based." For the "Supreme Court, whatever its defects, is still the most detached, dispassionate, and trustworthy custodian that our system affords for the translation of abstract into concrete constitutional commands."[101]

Notes

1. *West Virginia State Bd. of Educ. v. Barnette*, 319 U.S. 624, 641–42 (1943). See also Richard A. Posner, *Cardozo: A Study in Reputation* (Chicago:

University of Chicago Press, 1990), 140–41; Henry J. Abraham, *Justices and Presidents: A Political History of Appointments to the Supreme Court*, 2d ed. (New York: Oxford University Press, 1985), 233–34.

2. *West Virginia State Bd. of Educ. v. Barnette*, 638 (emphasis added).

3. Ibid., 637, 641.

4. Ibid., 639–40.

5. Robert H. Jackson, *The Struggle for Judicial Supremacy: A Study of a Crisis in American Power Politics* (New York: Knopf, 1941), 302, 305–06. See also ibid., 309. Cf. Robert H. Jackson, *The Supreme Court in the American System of Government* (New York: Harper & Row, 1955), 11–12, 61–62.

6. *United States v. ICC*, 337 U.S. 426, 449 (1949) (Frankfurter, J., dissenting) (quoted); *Trust of Bingham v. Commissioner*, 325 U.S. 365, 379–81 (1945) (Frankfurter, J., concurring); *City of Yonkers v. United States*, 320 U.S. 685, 695 (1944) (Frankfurter, J., dissenting). See Chapter 7 above, notes 10–14 and accompanying text. Jackson joined Frankfurter's opinion in each of these cases. For cases (other than the second flag-salute controversy) in which Jackson differed with Frankfurter over the appropriate standard of review for administrative actions raising constitutional questions, see *Bowles v. United States*, 319 U.S. 33, 36 (1943) (Jackson, J., dissenting); *Joint Anti-Fascist Refugee Comm. v. McGrath*, 341 U.S. 123, 183 (1951) (Jackson, J., concurring).

7. Robert H. Jackson, "The Advocate: Guardian of Our Traditional Liberties," *American Bar Association Journal* 36 (1950): 607; *SEC v. Chenery Corp.*, 332 U.S. 194, 215 (1947) (Jackson, J., dissenting) (emphasis added; Frankfurter joined Jackson's dissent). See also *Federal Power Comm'n v. Hope Natural Gas Co.*, 320 U.S. 591, 625–28 (1944) (Frankfurter, J., dissenting); ibid., 645–46 (Jackson, J., dissenting); Jackson, *Supreme Court in the American System*, 44–46, 51.

8. Robert H. Jackson, Oral History, 136–37 (quoted), Papers of Robert H. Jackson, Library of Congress, Manuscript Division (hereafter cited as RHJP), Box 190; Jackson, *Supreme Court in the American System*, 44–45, 46, 51. Jackson joined Frankfurter's majority opinion in *Universal Camera Corp. v. NLRB*, 340 U.S. 474 (1951).

9. Robert H. Jackson, "Back to the Constitution," *American Bar Association Journal* 25 (1939): 748; Jackson, *Struggle for Judicial Supremacy*, xii–xiii (emphasis in original).

10. Robert H. Jackson, "Address of the Honorable Robert H. Jackson, Attorney General of the United States," *American Bar Association Journal* 26 (1940): 204; *Youngstown Sheet & Tube Co. v. Sawyer*, 343 U.S. 579, 634–35 (1952) (Jackson, J., concurring).

11. Robert H. Jackson, "The Law Is a Rule for Men to Live By," *Vital Speeches of the Day* 9 (1943): 666.

12. Ibid., 665; Robert H. Jackson, "The Genesis of an American Legal Profession: A Review of 150 Years of Change," *American Bar Association*

Journal 38 (1952): 617; Robert H. Jackson, "Advocacy before the Supreme Court: Suggestions for Effective Case Presentations," *American Bar Association Journal* 37 (1951): 864; Robert H. Jackson, "The Product of the Present-Day Law School," *California Law Review* 27 (1939): 638. See also Jackson, "Advocate," 608; Robert H. Jackson, "The Meaning of Statutes: What Congress Says or What the Court Says," *American Bar Association Journal* 34 (1948): 536.

13. Robert H. Jackson, "Decisional Law and Stare Decisis," *American Bar Association Journal* 30 (1944): 334 (quoted first and third); Jackson, "Advocacy before the Supreme Court," 864 (quoted); Jackson, "Meaning of Statutes," 535–36; Jackson, Oral History, 168, RHJP, Box 190; Jackson, "Law Is a Rule," 665.

14. Robert H. Jackson, "The Task of Maintaining Our Liberties: The Role of the Judiciary," *American Bar Association Journal* 39 (1953): 962 (quoted first and third); Jackson, *Struggle for Judicial Supremacy*, 291–98 (p. 295 quoted).

15. *Bridges v. California*, 314 U.S. 252 (1941). Frankfurter said that Jackson had "told [him] on more than one occasion . . . [that] he really couldn't understand why he [had gone] with the majority in [*Bridges*] and why he [had] even allowed himself to be dissuaded not to write one of his usual separate opinions." Felix Frankfurter to Walter Murphy, 9 March 1960, RHJP, Box 5. I was unable to substantiate Frankfurter's claim. Its veracity, however, would not harm my argument that Jackson's pragmatism resulted from his use of the method of the common law to resolve a tension in his thought between a fear of majority oppression and a fear of judicial abstraction.

16. *United States v. Ballard*, 322 U.S. 78, 88 (1944).

17. Ibid., 88–89, 92 (Stone, C.J., dissenting).

18. Robert H. Jackson, handwritten addendum to memorandum on *United States v. Ballard*, 13 April 1944, RHJP, Box 134.

19. *United States v. Ballard*, 95, 93 (Jackson, J., dissenting).

20. Ibid., 92, 95 (Jackson, J., dissenting).

21. Robert H. Jackson, typewritten memorandum on *United States v. Ballard*, 24 March 1944, 1, 5, RHJP, Box 134. For a discussion of the decisions Jackson believed made "trifles" of First Amendment principles, see notes 78–82 below and accompanying text.

22. *Thomas v. Collins*, 323 U.S. 516, 540–42 (1945).

23. Ibid., 548 (Jackson, J., concurring).

24. Ibid., 547, 545 (Jackson, J., concurring).

25. *Saia v. New York*, 334 U.S. 558, 561–62 (1948).

26. Ibid., 566, 568, 571–72 (Jackson, J., dissenting). See also Robert H. Jackson, untitled memorandum, 1 June 1948, 5, RHJP, Box 147.

27. *Saia v. New York*, 572, 566–67 (Jackson, J., dissenting).

28. Ibid., 569–71 (Jackson, J., dissenting); Jackson, untitled memorandum, 1 June 1948, 6, 1, RHJP, Box 147 (quoted second and third).

29. *Kovacs v. Cooper*, 336 U.S. 77, 97 (1949) (Jackson, J., concurring).

30. Ibid., 98, 102–03 (Black, J., dissenting).

31. Ibid., 104 (Black, J., dissenting).

32. Ibid., 102 (Black, J., dissenting); Robert H. Jackson, note handwritten on memorandum from Hugo L. Black on *Kovacs v. Cooper*, headed "No return," 5, RHJP, Box 148; *Kovacs v. Cooper*, 97 (Jackson, J., concurring).

33. *Terminiello v. Chicago*, 337 U.S. 1, 5, 4 (1949).

34. Ibid., 13–14, 20, 22, 26, 25 (Jackson, J., dissenting).

35. Jackson, "Back to the Constitution," 745; Jackson, *Struggle for Judicial Supremacy*, 289–90, 323–24. See also ibid., 23, 34–35, 283–85, 290.

36. Jackson, "Decisional Law and Stare Decisis," 334; Jackson, *Struggle for Judicial Supremacy*, 319; Robert H. Jackson to Harlan F. Stone, 25 May 1942, RHJP, Box 125 (emphasis in original).

37. *Ashcraft v. Tennessee*, 322 U.S. 143, 154 (1944). The Court applied the Fifth Amendment privilege against self-incrimination against the states in 1964. *Malloy v. Hogan*, 378 U.S. 1 (1964); *Murphy v. Waterfront Comm'n*, 378 U.S. 52 (1964).

38. *Ashcraft v. Tennessee*, 174, 158 (Jackson, J., dissenting).

39. Ibid., 162 (Jackson, J., dissenting) (emphasis in original).

40. Ibid., 163–64, 166–67 (Jackson, J., dissenting).

41. Ibid., 158, 156, 157, 166–67 (Jackson, J., dissenting).

42. Ibid., 174 (Jackson, J., dissenting); *Baldwin v. Missouri*, 281 U.S. 586, 595 (1930) (Holmes, J., dissenting). For an opinion in which Jackson identified state action that violated the notion of a "fair trial," see *Shepherd v. Florida*, 341 U.S. 50 (1951).

43. Felix Frankfurter to Robert H. Jackson, 7 April 1944, RHJP, Box 131.

44. Ibid.

45. *Rochin v. California*, 342 U.S. 165 (1952).

46. This portion of Felix Frankfurter's draft opinion is related in his letter to Robert H. Jackson, 29 December 1951, RHJP, Box 173.

47. Robert H. Jackson, memorandum on *Rochin v. California*, 21 December 1951, RHJP, Box 173; Robert H. Jackson, typewritten memorandum on *Rochin v. California*, 26 December 1951, RHJP, Box 173 (quoted second and fourth); Robert H. Jackson's note handwritten on Frankfurter's memorandum on *Rochin v. California*, 4 December 1951, RHJP, Box 173.

48. Felix Frankfurter, note handwritten on Jackson's memorandum on *Rochin v. California*, 21 December 1951 (underline in original), RHJP, Box 173; Felix Frankfurter to Robert H. Jackson, 29 December 1951 (emphasis added), RHJP, Box 173. The revised sentence appears in the final opinion at 342 U.S. at 173.

49. *Irvine v. California*, 347 U.S. 128, 133 (1954).

50. Ibid., 145–46 (Frankfurter, J., dissenting).

51. See also *Haley v. Ohio*, 332 U.S. 596 (1948).

52. *Betts v. Brady*, 316 U.S. 455, 462 (1942).

53. *Malinski v. New York*, 324 U.S. 401, 438 (1945) (Stone, C.J., dissenting) (emphasis added).

54. *Francis v. Resweber*, 329 U.S. 459 (1947); Tinsley E. Yarbrough, *Mr. Justice Black and His Critics* (Durham: Duke University Press, 1988), 92 (Reed quoted).

55. Hugo L. Black, typewritten memorandum on *Francis v. Resweber*, January 1947, 2–3, RHJP, Box 138.

56. Ibid., 2–3, 1. Recall that Black's constitutional jurisprudence had conservative implications. See Chapter 5 above, notes 61–69 and accompanying text.

57. Robert H. Jackson, memorandum on *Francis v. Resweber*, headed "Corrected, Circulated 12/20/46," 2–3, RHJP, Box 138.

58. Ibid., 3 n. 1.

59. Felix Frankfurter, undated, handwritten memorandum on *Francis v. Resweber* (underline in original), RHJP, Box 138.

60. Ibid. (underline in original).

61. Jackson, memorandum on *Francis v. Resweber*, headed "Corrected, Circulated 12/20/46," 1, 4, RHJP, Box 138.

62. Robert H. Jackson, undated desk note on *Francis v. Resweber*, RHJP, Box 138. With regard to Jackson's subsequent opinions, recall the discussion of *Rochin v. California* and *Irvine v. California*, notes 45–50 above and accompanying text.

63. Felix Frankfurter, note handwritten on Reed's memorandum on *Francis v. Resweber*, January 1947, 2–3 (underline in original), RHJP, Box 138.

64. See *Betts v. Brady*, 474 (Black, J., dissenting).

65. Robert H. Jackson, "Statecraft under a Written Constitution," 1942, 55, RHJP, Box 55.

66. *Everson v. Board of Ewing Township*, 330 U.S. 1, 24 (1947) (Jackson, J., dissenting). Frankfurter joined Jackson's dissent.

67. *Adamson v. California*, 332 U.S. 46 (1947).

68. Ibid., 53–54 (emphasis added); *Palko v. Connecticut*, 302 U.S. 319, 325–26 (1937) (quoted third and fourth).

69. *Palko v. Connecticut*, 324–25; Posner, *Cardozo*; Jackson, Oral History, 992, RHJP, Box 191; Wallace Mendelson, "Mr. Justice Black and the Rule of Law," *Midwest Journal of Political Science* 4 (1960): 254.

70. Jackson, Oral History, 1475–76, RHJP, Box 191; Abraham, *Justices and Presidents*, 233. See also Eugene C. Gerhart, *America's Advocate: Robert H. Jackson* (New York: Bobbs-Merrill, 1958). Jackson's Fourteenth Amendment decisions discussed in the preceding section do not suggest a Nuremberg influence: Supposedly, Nuremberg made him more inclined to support the efforts of states to maintain order. See notes 71–77 below and accompanying text. But his deferential ruling in *Ashcraft v. Tennessee* occurred prior to the war crimes trial (see notes 37–44 above and accompanying text), while his acceptance of selective incorporation occurred after the event (see notes 51–69

above and accompanying text). To say the major outlines of his Fourteenth Amendment decisions do not reveal a Nuremberg-inspired change, however, is not to say Nuremberg had no effect on this area of his jurisprudence. See notes 87–89 below and accompanying text.

71. Jackson, Oral History, 1469–71, RHJP, Box 191; Robert H. Jackson, "Justice Jackson's Final Report to the President Concerning the Nurnberg War Crimes Trial," *Temple Law Quarterly* 20 (1946): 342–44; Robert H. Jackson, *The Nurnberg Case* (New York: Knopf, 1947), 38–46, 95–99, 104 (pp. 41, 104 quoted).

72. *Terminiello v. Chicago*, 337 U.S. 1, 23 (1949) (Jackson, J., dissenting).

73. Ibid., 37 (Jackson, J., dissenting).

74. *Kunz v. New York*, 340 U.S. 290, 295 (1951).

75. Ibid., 299, 314 (Jackson, J., dissenting).

76. *West Virginia State Bd. of Educ. v. Barnette*, 639 (1943).

77. *Brinegar v. United States*, 338 U.S. 160, 180 (1949) (Jackson, J., dissenting); law clerk's undated memorandum, headed "Two questions occur to me" (underline in original), RHJP, Box 149.

78. *Brinegar v. United States*, 180 (Jackson, J., dissenting), citing *Murdock v. Pennsylvania*, 319 U.S. 105, 166 (1943) (Jackson, J., dissenting).

79. *Martin v. City of Struthers*, 319 U.S. 141, 166 (1943) (Jackson, J., dissenting); *Douglas v. City of Jeannette*, 319 U.S. 157, 166 (1943) (Jackson, J., concurring).

80. *Murdock v. Pennsylvania* and *Martin v. City of Struthers*, 166 (Jackson, J., dissenting) (quoted first, second, and fourth); Robert H. Jackson, undated, typewritten memorandum on *Murdock v. Pennsylvania*, 8, RHJP, Box 127.

81. *Murdock v. Pennsylvania* and *Martin v. City of Struthers*, 167–74, 176–77 (Jackson, J., dissenting).

82. Ibid., 178–80 (Jackson, J., dissenting); Robert H. Jackson, undated, typewritten memorandum on *Murdock v. Pennsylvania*, 10, RHJP, Box 127; *Prince v. Massachusetts*, 321 U.S. 158, 177 (1943) (Jackson, J., separate opinion).

83. Robert H. Jackson, memorandum, headed "No. 591—West Virginia Bd. of Education v. Barnette," 12 June 1943, RHJP, Box 127; Jackson, Oral History, 988, RHJP, Box 191; Jackson, *Struggle for Judicial Supremacy*, 284–85. See also ibid., 319, 323–24; Jackson, "Statecraft under a Written Constitution," 1942, 63–65, RHJP, Box 55.

84. *West Virginia State Bd. of Educ. v. Barnette*, 630. This interpretation of Jackson's decisions diverges from the approach I take in "Justice Robert H. Jackson, the Supreme Court, and the Nuremberg Trial," in *The Supreme Court Review*, ed. Gerhard Casper, Dennis J. Hutchinson, and David A. Strauss (Chicago: University of Chicago Press, 1990), 289–91. (There, I suggest that he abandoned the "preferred freedoms" concept before Nuremberg.) For pre-Nuremberg cases (other than *Murdock*) in which Jackson took a conservative stance on free speech claims, see *Jones v. Opelika*, 316 U.S. 584 (1942); *Prince v. Massachusetts*, 176 (Jackson, J., separate opinion).

85. *American Communications Ass'n v. Douds*, 339 U.S. 382, 443–44 (1950) (Jackson, J., concurring in part and dissenting in part). Jackson's common-law preference for legal continuity accounted for this effort to save his pragmatic rulings from seeming to be a collection of single instances. Recall, however, that he believed *stare decisis* to be of only limited application in constitutional controversies because the deficiencies of the judicial process make that process susceptive to abstraction in these contexts. See notes 13–14 above and accompanying text. He thus thought that all constitutional rulings, including his own, should be regarded as tentative and subject to reversal. As he said in an unpublished opinion from another pre-Nuremberg case, where he joined a ruling sustaining municipal license taxes on religious booksellers:

> If the regulations imposed by these ordinances shall appear to be producing the dire results that are predicted [by the dissenters], the break-down of civil liberties, the destruction of the right of free speech, free press, and free worship, I shall unhesitatingly in the light of such trend, change my view. It is undeniable that our rules interpreting the points at which rights conflict and[,] where they do[,] which one must give way must be revised from time to time. That is why we should beware of laying down absolute rights which circumstances and time may prove are not so absolute, after all. And if it should become necessary to revise my views I shall prove that I am then right by declaring that I have theretofore been wrong. I would not be without precedent.

Robert H. Jackson, undated, typewritten memorandum on *Jones v. Opelika*, 4, RHJP, Box 123.

86. Jackson, *Supreme Court in the American System*, 57–58. The dissonance between Jackson, Black, and Douglas also stemmed from an enduring conflict of personalities and from Jackson's belief that his colleagues (Black, especially) derailed his bid to become chief justice after Harlan Stone's death in 1946. Hockett, "Justice Jackson, the Supreme Court, and the Nuremberg Trial," 278–86; Dennis J. Hutchinson, "The Black-Jackson Feud," in *The Supreme Court Review*, ed. Philip B. Kurland, Gerhard Casper, and Dennis J. Hutchinson (Chicago: University of Chicago Press, 1988), 203–43; Robert H. Jackson, undated memorandum headed "The Black Controversy," RHJP, Box 26; Chapter 10 below, notes 3–7 and accompanying text.

87. *Terminiello v. Chicago*, 28–29 (Jackson, J., dissenting); *West Virginia State Bd. of Educ. v. Barnette*, 639.

88. *Beauharnais v. Illinois*, 343 U.S. 250, 304, 292, 293, 291 (1952) (Jackson, J., dissenting) (emphasis omitted). In his reference to Holmes and Brandeis, Jackson is quoting from *Gitlow v. New York*, 268 U.S. 652, 672 (1925) (Holmes, J., dissenting).

89. *Beauharnais v. Illinois*, 288 (Jackson, J., dissenting); Jackson, Oral History, 573, RHJP, Box 190. See also Jackson, *Supreme Court in the American System*, 65–72.

90. *Dennis v. United States*, 341 U.S. 494, 568 (1951) (Jackson, J., concurring); Hockett, "Justice Jackson, The Supreme Court, and the Nuremberg Trial," 259–78, 296; Judith N. Shklar, *Legalism: Law, Morals, and Political Trials* (Cambridge: Harvard University Press, 1986), 217–19.

91. *Dennis v. United States*, 577, 570, 572 (Jackson, J., concurring) (quoted); Hockett, "Justice Jackson, the Supreme Court, and the Nuremberg Trial," 269–70. See also *American Communications Ass'n v. Douds*, 424–30 (Jackson, J., concurring in part and dissenting in part).

92. Shklar, *Legalism*, 215, 218.

93. Jackson, *The Nurnberg Case*, 42, 46, 96.

94. Robert H. Jackson, "Wartime Security and Liberty under Law," *Buffalo Law Review* 1 (1951): 105–6.

95. *Shaughnessy v. Mezei*, 345 U.S. 206, 227, 225–26, 224–25 (1952) (Jackson, J., dissenting).

96. Robert H. Jackson, typewritten memorandum on *Shaughnessy v. Mezei*, 27 January 1953, 4–5, RHJP, Box 180.

97. *Brinegar v. United States*, 183 (Jackson, J., dissenting); *Johnson v. United States*, 333 U.S. 10, 17 (1948). See also *Harris v. United States*, 331 U.S. 145, 195 (1947) (Jackson, J., dissenting); *McDonald v. United States*, 335 U.S. 451, 457 (1948) (Jackson, J., concurring). Jackson joined Frankfurter's majority opinion in *Wolf v. Colorado*, 338 U.S. 25 (1949). While the Court held in that case that the Fourth Amendment prohibition of unreasonable searches and seizures applies against the states through the Fourteenth Amendment, it refused to extend the federal exclusionary rule (i.e., the rule that illegally obtained evidence is not admissible in court) to the state level. See also *Irvine v. California*, 347 U.S. 128, 132–37 (1954). The *Wolf* ruling accorded with Jackson's post-Nuremberg approach to incorporation. See notes 87–89 above and accompanying text.

98. *Brinegar v. United States*, 180 (Jackson, J., dissenting).

99. I take the appellation from Eugene Gerhart's book on Jackson's involvement at Nuremberg. *America's Advocate*, (see note 70 above).

100. Jackson, Oral History, 396, 993, 395, RHJP, Boxes 190, 191.

101. Jackson, *Supreme Court in the American System*, 61, 23. See also ibid., 26–27, 62–80.

10

Conclusion

The New Deal Justices and the Process of Judicial Decision Making

This study of the constitutional jurisprudence of Hugo Black, Felix Frankfurter, and Robert Jackson has established a strong connection between the justices' ideological backgrounds and their judicial performances. Each man verified Benjamin Cardozo's observation that the "great tides and currents which engulf the rest of men do not turn aside in their course and pass the judges by."[1] This book does not deny that the broader psychologies of judges and the interactions among members of a court are relevant to models of judicial behavior.[2] Yet it refutes the arguments of certain scholars who examined the interpersonal dealings among the New Deal justices, dealings that obscured jurisprudential similarities between Black and Jackson and jurisprudential differences between Frankfurter and Jackson.

The personality clash between Black and Jackson that detracted from their shared belief in judicial supremacy (and from Jackson's differences with Frankfurter over this issue) commenced shortly after Jackson joined the Court. The new justice took umbrage at what he viewed as Black's partisan treatment of cases. In particular, he objected to Black's alleged attempt to force the early release of a ruling on the Fair Labor Standards Act. (The decision would have affected a labor dispute that had begun during the Court's deliberations on the case.) Although the alleged effort failed, Jackson commented that Black's "sinister manipulation" of the timing of the decision was "indefensible and could not be condoned." The discord this incident (and others) generated "created [such] uneasiness in [Jackson's] mind" that he said he even considered resigning from the bench.[3]

The public learned of the conflict between Black and Jackson after

the death of Harlan Stone in 1945. When the president identified
Jackson as a possible successor to the chief justice, articles appeared
saying that two justices threatened to resign if Truman promoted
Jackson. One piece suggested that a ''blood feud'' between Black
and Jackson prompted the threatened resignations. Jackson made the
conflict public when he became convinced that Black had been the
source of the story about the feud and had lobbied successfully against
his candidacy for the chief justiceship. Jackson said he felt compelled
to respond to the report because it was slanted and trivialized his
differences with Black.[4]

This conflict, which reached its climax while Jackson was at Nuremberg, contributed to his decision to distance himself from his more
liberal colleagues. Jackson would criticize Black and Douglas in his off-
the-bench writings and repudiate the ''preferred freedoms'' concept.
(Recall that his long-standing conviction, reinforced after Nuremberg,
that Black and Douglas paid insufficient attention to the circumstances
surrounding cases was the other reason for these actions.)[5]

Some scholars subscribed to Jackson's characterization of a divided
Court; they spoke of fairly sharp alignments between Jackson and
Frankfurter, on the one hand, and Black and Douglas, on the other.[6]
While the justices' voting patterns generally supported the notion of a
bifurcated Court, scholars neglected the jurisprudential significance of
votes that deviated from the model. One commentator (who mentioned
the Black-Jackson feud when he articulated the Court's alignments)
observed that ''Jackson [had] often differed from Frankfurter on
specific cases,'' yet erroneously concluded that Jackson was in ''agreement with [Frankfurter] on the function of the Court.''[7] The animosity
between Black and Jackson blinded that scholar and others to the fact
that voting discrepancies between Jackson and Frankfurter indicated
profound jurisprudential differences between the latter two. Stated in
the alternative, these voting differences suggested shared jurisprudential premises between Jackson and Black. An understanding of the
contrasting ideological backgrounds of Jackson and Frankfurter would
have alerted that scholar to the fact that instances of agreement
between the two evidenced similar conclusions arrived at through
divergent means, rather than a shared understanding of the function of
the Court.

While scholarly attention to the clash of personalities on the New
Deal Court detracted from Jackson's jurisprudential similarities with
Black and his differences with Frankfurter, scholarly inattention to the
cultural context in which American judges operate also distorted our

understanding of at least one New Deal justice. When the Progressives deprived judges of the rationalization that interpretation of legal language and precedent is a purely deductive process, the social expectation remained that judges would render decisions according to objective, legal criteria. As Justice Jackson once observed: "In this country we've built up a considerable tradition that the judge doesn't make law, he discovers it. Our decisions, therefore, are [supposed to be] not legislation, but revelation."[8] A judge's values—most importantly, his or her perception of the nature of society and politics—largely determine the selection of a strategy for meeting this expectation in constitutional contexts. (Those judges who ignore the expectation imperil their credibility as constitutional authorities.) A judge's jurisprudence and performance, then, are in considerable measure functions of the *interplay* between personal attributes and perceived social expectations for the judiciary.[9]

Scholarly disregard of this cultural context contributed to the mistaken notion that Black's Populist background could have inspired within him a fear of judicial discretion, rather than a desire to use the Court for antihierarchical purposes.[10] Students of the justice failed to realize that his method of constitutional interpretation, which resulted periodically in conservative rulings, did even more than help to secure important antihierarchical rights against the evisceration that occurred with discretionary standards. His efforts to tie judicial decision making to the language of the constitutional text and the intent behind the document's provisions also served to deflect criticism from a jurisprudence that increased enormously the antihierarchical impact of the Court under the provisions of the First and Fourteenth Amendments. Invoking constitutional language and intent and, especially, rendering periodic decisions at odds with his liberal colleagues, he was able to disavow credibly any desire to remake the Constitution. Unlike Justice Douglas, for example, he could say, with ample evidence to support him, that "[a]lthough some people have urged that this Court should amend the Constitution by interpretation to keep it abreast of modern times, I have never believed that lifetime judges in our system have any such legislative power."[11] Among the more liberal New Deal justices, Black alone recognized that the wisest interpretive strategy for a result-oriented jurist whose politics require exercises of review is one that allows for a demonstration of fidelity to the norm of self-denial while it provides for significant use of judicial power.

Black was not the only New Deal justice whose constitutional jurisprudence reflected an interplay between personal political values and perceived social expectations for the judiciary. One should also regard Frankfurter's passivity in constitutional controversies as a product of these variables. While Frankfurter's personal values influenced his jurisprudence, he did not invariably desire the statist or conservative results that the rational basis standard prescribed in cases involving nonproprietarian rights, for he had revealed strong libertarian propensities before joining the Court. In setting aside his libertarian convictions in constitutional controversies, he paid homage to the ideal of a non-policy-making judiciary. As he wrote in one case, "[O]ne's own opinion about the wisdom or evil of a law should be excluded altogether when one is doing one's duty on the bench."[12]

Yet, while Frankfurter may have practiced a certain asceticism when rendering decisions on constitutional claims directed against flag-salute laws, anticommunist legislation, or the imposition of the death penalty, he was not nearly as self-abnegating as his rhetoric suggested. He drew upon other personal values rooted in his social and political thought: his fear of judicial abstraction in an interdependent social order and his belief in the integrative nature of society and politics consistently informed his votes. Indeed, had he rendered decisions in a political culture that permitted judicial policy making under the Constitution, in all likelihood he still would have sought to relegate decision making to political institutions he regarded as less insulated from the complexities of an organic society.

Of the three justices examined in this study, it is ironic that the one with a traditional background experienced the most difficulty reconciling his jurisprudence with the traditional expectation that judges are not to be lawmakers. Jackson availed himself of the advantages of the rational-basis standard in due process contexts (for, as a student of the common law, he shied away from principles that afford judges little guidance). Deference under the due process clauses permitted him (as it did Frankfurter) to say, without seeming disingenuous, that justices should not "revise [the] decisions [of public officials] merely because [justices] feel more confidence in [their own] wisdom and rectitude."[13]

Yet Jackson's traditional fear of political majorities prevented him from using Thayer's standard in cases involving what he regarded as the less abstract provisions of the Constitution. Aware of the corrosive insights of Progressive jurists, Jackson never would have claimed that even the Constitution's more precise terms preclude exercises of judicial discretion. (He conceded, "[I]t's very difficult [in constitutional matters] to draw the line as to where your views of good policy end and your views of law begin.") And he did not share Black's confidence that historical analysis could consistently afford answers to judges in these contexts. The most likely technique for Jackson to employ in establishing credible boundaries around constitutional decision making—the common-law doctrine of *stare decisis*—was a casualty, not only of Progressive jurisprudence, but also of the modern element in his social and political thought. Although he worked to save his pragmatic votes from appearing a series of isolated instances, he believed that the peculiarly modern problem of judicial abstraction made strict adherence to precedent a dangerous practice in an interdependent social order. In areas of law beyond due process, then, his bow to society's expectations for the judiciary could only take the form of a feeble apology—that his "philosophy has been and continues to be that [the Court] . . . cannot and should not try to seize the initiative in shaping the policy of the law."[14]

A Legacy of Enduring Questions

The benefits of scholarly investigation into the constitutional jurisprudence of these New Deal justices extend beyond insights acquired into the process of judicial decision making. Examination of the underpinnings of the justices' interpretive models also contributes significantly to the normative dimension of constitutional adjudication. The legacy of the New Deal for the modern era of constitutional law is, of course, *not* a uniform concept or ideal of justice. For Black, Frankfurter, and Jackson revealed that even the more progressive elements of the New Deal coalition were hardly of one mind on issues of nonproprietarian rights. But the virtue of this jurisprudential diversity is that the proponent of each model of adjudication afforded provocative and thoughtful treatments of considerations that are central to the issue of the Court's appropriate role under the Constitution.

The justices all reflected on the nature of American society and politics, with a view to determining the need for a judicial corrective to democratic government. Of the three men, Black believed most strongly that the Court should serve a corrective function. The pervasiveness of social and political hierarchy, he thought, obliges judges to provide a haven for victims of political oppression. Defenders of the view that Black's Populist background inspired within him a fear of judicial discretion disagree with this assessment. They argue, instead, that *faith in democracy* was the lodestar of his constitutional jurisprudence.[15] Logic, however, does not support the argument that such confidence would inform the jurisprudence of a Populist jurist. The insurgent agrarians of the nineteenth century suffered electoral fraud and corruption at the hands of Bourbon Democrats. Populism reflected the conviction among yeomen that the political process was captive to great industrial and financial interests and existed merely to maintain the social status quo. If Black possessed a faith in democracy, it was a faith that self-rule is possible *so long as government is under the guardianship of an independent judiciary, a judiciary bound to preserve avenues external to established national and state political institutions for the expression of social discontent.*

Jackson's perception of the nature of society and politics resembled that of his Alabamian colleague. He did not share Black's personal attachment to the political and social thought of the Populists. But Jackson's steeping in the thought of nineteenth-century treatise writers fostered within him a mistrust of political power; the student of James Kent was always suspicious of the designs of majoritarian institutions. He never abandoned his belief that judges should exercise independent judgment when evaluating constitutional challenges to legislative and executive authority. Merely to police the perimeters of rational policy (as Frankfurter would have it) would be to relegate the maintenance of constitutional boundaries to branches of government singularly unqualified to perform such a role.

Unlike Black and Jackson, Frankfurter did not temper his faith in democracy with statements concerning the need for a judicial corrective. He read enormous political significance into the fact of social interdependence, or the organic nature of an industrial social order. He believed that the constituent elements of an interdependent society are predisposed toward harmony in the same way the parts of a healthy organism tend toward integration for the purpose of survival. His consistent refusal to sustain constitutional challenges to the decisions of legislative and administrative authorities reflected, not an insensitivity to the plight of minorities, but a conviction that the attainment of justice through the normal course of interest-group politics is only a matter of time and effort.

Frankfurter devoted an equal amount of attention to another consideration that bears heavily upon the Court's proper role under the Constitution, namely, the capacity of the judiciary to address constitutional problems of the modern age. He defended his call for judicial deference to legislative and administrative determinations with the argument that an active judicial role under the Constitution is dangerous, as well as unnecessary. American methods for informing the judicial mind, he believed, are vestiges of the pre-industrial age and thus fail to summarize the experience and knowledge of an interdependent culture. Judicial policy making, in short, is necessarily abstract.

Jackson concurred with Frankfurter's critique of the process of judicial fact-finding, although he rejected his colleague's response to the problem. As noted, Jackson thought that the threat of political oppression precludes judicial deference as a technique for minimizing the threat of judicial abstraction. Still, he argued that judges must be scrupulous in their attention to the context of the situation before them and sensitive to the possibility of error in their rulings.

Black's indifference to the problem of judicial abstraction distanced him, not only from Frankfurter, his jurisprudential adversary, but also from Jackson, a fellow champion of judicial supremacy. Black did not base this indifference upon a belief in the institutional soundness of judicial machinery. (Indeed, he occasionally remarked upon the shortcomings of the judicial process in addressing constitutional controversies.)[16] Rather, he regarded political hierarchy or oppression as a more significant danger than judicial abstraction, and he was very much alive to the antihierarchical impact of absolute or abstract conceptions of nonproprietarian rights.

While the New Deal justices illuminated considerations or questions central to the issue of the Court's appropriate role in constitutional controversies, current scholarship in political science and public law reveals that the intractability of these questions rivals their importance. Pluralist and critical pluralist scholars continue to debate the nature of American society and politics.[17] Pluralism originated in the scholarly attempt to account for the failure of ideological mass movements (primarily, fascism and communism) to make serious inroads in this country.[18] Pluralists argue, generally, that the comparatively moderate, incremental change that characterizes American politics is a consequence of a pluralistic culture in which individuals possess membership in numerous, diverse and overlapping interest groups. These groups have several points of access to government and, because the resources required for political mobilization are dispersed throughout society, are able to organize effectively to achieve political ends. Even the interests of groups with relatively few resources receive political consideration, the argument runs, because politicians view these groups as potentially significant in a reelection bid.

Pluralist arguments became the object of sustained academic criticism during the 1960s. Some scholars, responding to pervasive social instability and conservative governmental policies on civil rights, poverty, and the war against communism, challenged the view that politics is as accessible and fluid as pluralist theory suggests. Critical pluralists question a theory that denies the existence of economic and social stratification in this country, and they argue that politics favors those individuals and groups fortunate enough to possess economic power. The skewing of policy toward powerful interests and away from a more comprehensive public good, these theorists maintain, becomes more pronounced as the size of the political arena decreases. For these reasons, critical pluralists tend to support the nationalization of policy issues and an increased federal judicial presence in American politics.[19]

While the controversy over the nature of society and politics may remain unresolved, contemporary constitutional doctrine under portions of the First and Fourteenth Amendments approximates the jurisprudential recommendations of Black and the critical pluralists. Case law does not support an absolutist interpretation of the concept of free speech and press, nor does it sanction total application of the provisions of the Bill of Rights against the states. Yet the direction of the Court's decisions in these areas of the law has been decidedly toward Black's model of adjudication and away from that of Frankfurter.[20] One should note the delicious irony present in the fact that the jurisprudence of the southerner and Populist, Black, has prevailed in a nation dominated by northern industrial complexity.

This irony has been anything but lost on critics of the modern judiciary. These scholars voice concern, in the manner of Frankfurter and Jackson, that courts are not competent to speak to the issues in which they have become involved. Admittedly, certain of these issues—judicial administration of state mental hospitals under the concept of due process, for example[21]—are beyond the purview of Black's constitutional jurisprudence. But the antihierarchical thrust of contemporary constitutional doctrine in First and Fourteenth Amendment cases accords generally with Black's view of the role of judicial power. One critic of the direction of constitutional law frets that while "[j]udges may be performing new roles, . . . they continue to act very much within the framework of an old process, a process that evolved, not to devise new programs or to oversee administration, but to decide [individual, isolated] controversies. The constraints of the process operate to limit the range of what can reasonably be expected from courts."[22] In short, that critic and others believe that judicial decision making in modern constitutional controversies is inherently abstract. Echoing the arguments of Frankfurter and Jackson, they identify several causes of judicial abstraction: the inability of judges to give sustained attention to a policy area (because courts have no authority to seek out cases); the establishment of social policy on the basis of the unique factual situation before the court, rather than general social context (because of a narrow fact-finding process); and the failure of judges to monitor rulings for unanticipated consequences (given the absence of adequate oversight mechanisms).[23]

Unlike Black, supporters of contemporary constitutional doctrine are not content to rest their case for an increased judicial presence in American politics on the argument that judicial passivity would relegate constitutional decision making to an arena that is often unjust. These scholars also suggest that the courts are, in fact, competent to address the issues before them. "[D]espite its well rehearsed inadequacies," one scholar asserts, "the judiciary may have some important institutional advantages for the tasks it is assuming": Courts have the capacity to acquire adequate information because a judge "can and does employ experts and amici to inform himself on aspects of the case not adequately developed by the parties."[24] Furthermore, the argument runs, courts are able to provide adequate oversight because judges can move beyond traditional prohibitory relief and fashion ongoing, remedial decrees under their equity powers.[25]

An examination of the thought of Justices Black, Frankfurter, and Jackson will not help resolve the ongoing debates over the nature of society and politics and the institutional competence of the judiciary. After all, these men spent most of their professional lives as public servants, not as academicians. Only Frankfurter devoted a portion of his years to professional scholarship, and his conclusions on these issues were as controversial as those of his nonacademic brethren.

Yet the arguments of the three men are relevant to anyone striving to articulate an appropriate role for the Court under the Constitution. Black's jurisprudence, while certainly a source of intellectual sustenance for scholars who support an active judiciary, is perhaps more useful as a standard against which those favoring judicial passivity might test their assumptions and experiences. Similarly, Frankfurter's jurisprudence is more valuable as a challenge to arguments informing the view that courts should serve a corrective function than as a source of inspiration for proponents of a modest judicial role. Jackson's jurisprudence obliges followers of both Black and Frankfurter to reexamine their premises because Jackson alone raised the vexing possibility that the judiciary is at once the branch of government most qualified to correct the inadequacies of the political process and the one least able to make needed adjustments among competing social claims. In short, these New Deal justices, perhaps more than any group of individuals in the history of the Court, served notice through their writings and opinions that an incorrect choice in the matter of the Court's constitutional role could have consequences of the profoundest sort.

Notes

1. Benjamin N. Cardozo, *The Nature of the Judicial Process* (New Haven: Yale University Press, 1921), 168.

2. See H. N. Hirsch, *The Enigma of Felix Frankfurter* (New York: Basic Books, 1981); J. Woodford Howard Jr., "On the Fluidity of Judicial Choice," *American Political Science Review* 62 (1968): 43–56.

3. Robert H. Jackson, undated memorandum headed "The Black Controversy," 35–37, Papers of Robert H. Jackson, Library of Congress, Manuscript Division (hereafter cited as RHJP), Box 26; Robert H. Jackson, memorandum headed "To President Truman Only from Justice Jackson," 7 June 1946, 4, RHJP, Box 26. See also Jackson, Oral History, 1412–32, RHJP, Box 191; Dennis J. Hutchinson, "The Black-Jackson Feud," in *The Supreme Court Review*, ed. Philip B. Kurland, Gerhard Casper, and Dennis J. Hutchinson (Chicago: University of Chicago Press, 1988), 208–09, 229–38.

4. Jeffrey D. Hockett, "Justice Robert H. Jackson, the Supreme Court, and the Nuremberg Trial," in *The Supreme Court Review*, ed. Gerhard Casper, Dennis J. Hutchinson, and David A. Strauss (Chicago: University of Chicago Press, 1990), 278–86; Hutchinson, "Black-Jackson Feud," 214–22.

5. See Chapter 9 above, notes 25–34, 86, and accompanying text.

6. See, e.g., Arthur M. Schlesinger Jr., "The Supreme Court: 1947," *Fortune* (January 1947): 73–212; Eugene C. Gerhart, "A Decade of Mr. Justice Jackson," *New York University Law Review* 28 (1953): 969–70.

7. Schlesinger, "Supreme Court: 1947," 76.

8. Jackson, Oral History, 993, RHJP, Box 191.

9. To relate these observations to social science literature on judicial decision making, this study illustrates well the concept of judicial role orientation. See James L. Gibson, "Judges' Role Orientations, Attitudes, and Decisions: An Interactive Model," *American Political Science Review* 72 (1978): 911–24; James L. Gibson, "The Role Concept in Judicial Research," *Law and Policy Quarterly* 3 (1981): 291–311. This concept provides a corrective to simplistic models of judicial behavior, which depict rulings purely as products of the personal attributes and values of judges. Role-orientation literature allows for the mediation of the relationship between attitudes and behavior by intervening situational variables. Put another way, "[j]udges' role orientations are their beliefs about the kind of behavior proper for a judge" or "about what

variables can properly be allowed to influence their behavior." And role-orientations "reflect what [judges] think they ought to do tempered by what they think others think they should do." Gibson, "Judges' Role Orientations," 918, 917 & n. 11 (quoted); Gibson, "The Role Concept," 293. Holders of judicial office, in contending with the social expectations that they be neutral or nonpartisan and that they render decisions according to objective, legal criteria may—indeed, it is expected that they will—at times decide cases contrary to their personal values or to the positions they would take were they not judges.

10. Ironically, Silverstein mistakenly concludes that Black feared judicial discretion. Silverstein's use of the concept of judicial role orientation should have alerted him to the possibility that a variable external to the justice's values could have explained his conservative rulings. See note 9 above; Mark Silverstein, *Constitutional Faiths: Felix Frankfurter, Hugo Black, and the Process of Judicial Decision Making* (Ithaca: Cornell University Press, 1984), 15–16, 20.

11. *McGautha v. California*, 402 U.S. 183, 226 (1971) (Black, J., separate opinion). Compare Douglas's opinion for the Court with Black's dissent in *Griswold v. Connecticut*, 381 U.S. 479 (1965).

12. *West Virginia State Bd. of Educ. v. Barnette*, 319 U.S. 624, 647 (1943) (Frankfurter, J., dissenting).

13. *Ashcraft v. Tennessee*, 322 U.S. 143, 158 (1944) (Jackson, J., dissenting).

14. Jackson, Oral History, 985, RHJP, Box 191; Robert H. Jackson, *The Supreme Court in the American System of Government* (New York: Harper & Row, 1955), 79.

15. See Howard Ball and Phillip J. Cooper, *Of Power and Right: Hugo Black, William O. Douglas, and America's Constitutional Revolution* (New York: Oxford University Press, 1992), 319.

16. See Chapter 5 above, note 65 and accompanying text.

17. Major pluralist works include Robert Dahl, *Pluralist Democracy in the United States: Conflict and Consent* (Chicago: Rand McNally, 1967); and David B. Truman, *The Governmental Process: Political Interests and Public Opinion* (New York: Knopf, 1951). Major critical pluralist works include Theodore J. Lowi, *The End of Liberalism: Ideology, Policy, and the Crisis of Public Authority* (New York: W. W. Norton, 1969); and Grant McConnell, *Private Power and American Democracy* (New York: Knopf, 1967).

18. Edward A. Purcell Jr., *The Crisis of Democratic Theory: Scientific Naturalism and the Problem of Value* (Lexington: University Press of Kentucky, 1973), 117–38, 197–217, 235–66.

19. See Lowi, *End of Liberalism*, 287–314.

20. Henry J. Abraham, *Freedom and the Court: Civil Rights and Liberties in the United States*, 5th ed. (New York: Oxford University Press, 1988), 38–117, 194–276.

21. See *Wyatt v. Stickney*, 344 F. Supp. 373 (Middle District, Alabama, 1972).

22. Donald L. Horowitz, "The Courts as Guardians of the Public Interest," *Public Administration Review* 37 (1977): 151.

23. Ibid., 151–53.

24. Abraham Chayes, "The Role of the Judge in Public Law Litigation," *Harvard Law Review* 89 (1976): 1307, 1312. See also Frank M. Johnson Jr., "Judicial Activism Is a Duty—Not an Intrusion," in *Views from the Bench: The Judiciary and Constitutional Politics*, ed. Mark W. Cannon and David M. O'Brien (Chatham, N.J.: Chatham House Publishers, 1985), 281.

25. Johnson, "Judicial Activism Is a Duty," 279–84.

Bibliography

Collections

Black, Hugo L. Papers. Library of Congress, Manuscript Division. Washington, D.C.

Frankfurter, Felix. Papers. Library of Congress, Manuscript Division. Washington, D.C.

Jackson, Robert H. Papers. Library of Congress, Manuscript Division. Washington, D.C.

Articles and Books

Abel, Richard L. *American Lawyers*. New York: Oxford University Press, 1989.

Abraham, Henry J. *Freedom and the Court: Civil Rights and Liberties in the United States*. 5th ed. New York: Oxford University Press, 1988.

————. *The Judicial Process: An Introductory Analysis of the Courts of the United States, England, and France*. 5th ed. New York: Oxford University Press, 1986.

————. *Justices and Presidents: A Political History of Appointments to the Supreme Court*. 2d ed. New York: Oxford University Press, 1985.

Abrams, Richard M. *Conservatism in a Progressive Era: Massachusetts Politics, 1900–1912*. Cambridge: Harvard University Press, 1964.

Aman, Alfred C., Jr., and William T. Mayton. *Administrative Law*. St. Paul: West Publishing, 1993.

Auerbach, Jerold S. *Unequal Justice: Lawyers and Social Change in Modern America*. New York: Oxford University Press, 1976.

Ball, Howard. "Hugo L. Black: A Twentieth Century Jeffersonian." *Southwestern University Law Review* 9 (1977): 1049–68.

————. "Justice Hugo Black: A Magnificent Product of the South." In

Justice Hugo Black and Modern America, edited by Tony Freyer, 31–74. Tuscaloosa: University of Alabama Press, 1990.

———. *The Vision and the Dream of Justice Hugo L. Black: An Examination of a Judicial Philosophy*. Tuscaloosa: University of Alabama Press, 1975.

Ball, Howard, and Phillip J. Cooper. *Of Power and Right: Hugo Black, William O. Douglas, and America's Constitutional Revolution*. New York: Oxford University Press, 1992.

Barnett, Vincent M., Jr. "Mr. Justice Jackson and the Supreme Court." *Western Political Quarterly* 1 (1948): 223–42.

Bensel, Richard Franklin. *Sectionalism and American Political Development, 1880–1980*. Madison: University of Wisconsin Press, 1984.

———. *Yankee Leviathan: The Origins of Central State Authority in America, 1859–1877*. New York: Cambridge University Press, 1990.

Berger, Raoul. *Government by Judiciary: The Transformation of the Fourteenth Amendment*. Cambridge: Harvard University Press, 1977.

Berman, Daniel M. "Hugo L. Black: The Early Years." *Catholic University Law Review* 8 (1959): 103–16.

Bickel, Alexander M. "Justice Frankfurter at Seventy-Five." *New Republic* 137 (18 November 1957): 7–9.

———. *The Least Dangerous Branch: The Supreme Court at the Bar of Politics*. 2d ed. New Haven: Yale University Press, 1986.

Black, Hugo L. "The Bill of Rights." *New York University Law Review* 35 (1960): 865–81.

———. *A Constitutional Faith*. New York: Knopf, 1968.

———. "Justice Black and the Bill of Rights." Interview by Eric Sevareid and Martin Agronsky. 3 December 1968. CBS News Special. Printed in *Southwestern University Law Review* 9 (1977): 937–51.

———. "Justice Black and First Amendment 'Absolutes': A Public Interview." Interview by Edmond Cahn. *New York University Law Review* 37 (1962): 549–63.

———. "Reminiscences." *Alabama Law Review* 18 (1965): 3–11.

Black, Hugo L., and Elizabeth Black. *Mr. Justice and Mrs. Black: The Memoirs of Hugo L. Black and Elizabeth Black*. New York: Random House, 1986.

Black, Hugo, Jr. *My Father: A Remembrance*. New York: Random House, 1975.

Bledstein, Burton J. *The Culture of Professionalism: The Middle Class and the Development of Higher Education in America*. New York: W. W. Norton, 1978.

Blodgett, Geoffrey. *The Gentle Reformers: Massachusetts Democrats in the Cleveland Era*. Cambridge: Harvard University Press, 1966.

Bloomfield, Maxwell. *American Lawyers in a Changing Society, 1776–1876*. Cambridge: Harvard University Press, 1976.

———. "Law vs. Politics: The Self-Image of the American Bar (1830–1860)." *American Journal of Legal History* 12 (1968): 306–23.

Boskoff, Alvin. "From Social Thought to Sociological Theory." In *Modern Sociological Theory: In Continuity and Change*, edited by Howard Becker and Alvin Boskoff, 3–32. New York: Holt, Rinehart & Winston, 1957.

Brinkley, Alan. "The New Deal and the Idea of the State." In *The Rise of the New Deal Order, 1930–1980*, edited by Steve Fraser and Gary Gerstle, 85–121. Princeton: Princeton University Press, 1989.

Cardozo, Benjamin N. *The Nature of the Judicial Process*. New Haven: Yale University Press, 1921.

Cawelti, John G. *Apostles of the Self-Made Man*. Chicago: University of Chicago Press, 1965.

Ceaser, James W. *Presidential Selection: Theory and Development*. Princeton: Princeton University Press, 1979.

Chafee, Zechariah, Jr. *Free Speech in the United States*. Cambridge: Harvard University Press, 1941.

Chase, William C. *The American Law School and the Rise of Administrative Government*. Madison: University of Wisconsin Press, 1982.

Chayes, Abraham. "The Role of the Judge in Public Law Litigation." *Harvard Law Review* 89 (1976): 1281–316.

Cook, Charles M. *The American Codification Movement: A Study of Antebellum Legal Reform*. Westport, Conn.: Greenwood Press, 1981.

Cooley, Charles Horton. *Social Process*. New York: Charles Scribner's Sons, 1926.

Corwin, Edward S. "Freedom of Speech and Press under the First Amendment: A Resume." *Yale Law Journal* 30 (1920): 48–55.

Croly, Herbert. *Progressive Democracy*. New York: Macmillan, 1914.

———. *The Promise of American Life*. 1909. Reprint, Indianapolis: Bobbs-Merrill, 1975.

Dahl, Robert. *Pluralist Democracy in the United States: Conflict and Consent*. Chicago: Rand McNally, 1967.

Dawson, Nelson Lloyd. *Louis D. Brandeis, Felix Frankfurter, and the New Deal*. Hamden, Conn.: Archon Books, 1980.

Dewey, John. *The Public and Its Problems*. 1927. Reprint, Chicago: Athens Press, 1954.

Dodd, E. Merrick. "The Supreme Court and Organized Labor, 1941–1945." *Harvard Law Review* 58 (1945): 1018–71.

Douglas, William O. "Mr. Justice Black: A Forward." *Yale Law Journal* 65 (1956): 449–50.

Dunne, Gerald T. *Hugo Black and the Judicial Revolution*. New York: Simon & Schuster, 1977.

Durr, Clifford J. "Hugo Black, Southerner: The Southern Background." *American University Law Review* 10 (1961): 27–35.

Ellis, Richard E. *The Jeffersonian Crisis: Courts and Politics in the Young Republic*. New York: W. W. Norton, 1971.

Elman, Philip, ed. *Of Law and Men: Papers and Addresses of Felix Frankfurter, 1939–1956*. New York: Harcourt, Brace, 1956.

Emerson, Thomas I. *Toward a General Theory of the First Amendment.* New York: Random House, 1966.

Fairman, Charles. "Associate Justice of the Supreme Court." *Columbia Law Review* 55 (1955): 445–87.

———. "Does the Fourteenth Amendment Incorporate the Bill of Rights? The Original Understanding." *Stanford Law Review* 2 (1949): 5–139.

Faulkner, Robert Kenneth. *The Jurisprudence of John Marshall.* Princeton: Princeton University Press, 1968.

Forcey, Charles. *The Crossroads of Liberalism: Croly, Weyl, Lippmann, and the Progressive Era, 1900–1925.* New York: Oxford University Press, 1961.

Frank, John P. *Mr. Justice Black: The Man and His Opinions.* New York: Knopf, 1949.

Frankfurter, Felix. *Mr. Justice Holmes and the Supreme Court.* 1938. Reprint. Cambridge: Harvard University Press, Belknap Press, 1961.

———. "Mr. Justice Jackson." *Harvard Law Review* 68 (1955): 937–39.

———. *The Public and Its Government.* New Haven: Yale University Press, 1930.

———. "The Task of Administrative Law." *University of Pennsylvania Law Review* 75 (1927): 614–21.

Frankfurter, Felix, and James M. Landis. "The Compact Clause of the Constitution: A Study in Interstate Adjustments." *Yale Law Journal* 34 (1925): 685–758.

Freedman, Max, ed. *Roosevelt and Frankfurter: Their Correspondence, 1928–1945.* Boston: Little, Brown, 1967.

Freund, Paul A. "Individual and Commonwealth in the Thought of Mr. Justice Jackson." *Stanford Law Review* 8 (1955): 9–25.

Freyer, Tony. *Hugo L. Black and the Dilemma of American Liberalism.* Glenview, Ill.: Scott, Foresman, 1990.

———, ed. *Justice Hugo Black and Modern America.* Tuscaloosa: University of Alabama Press, 1990.

Friedman, Lawrence. *A History of American Law.* 2d ed. New York: Simon & Schuster, 1985.

Gabin, Sanford Byron. *Judicial Review and the Reasonable Doubt Test.* London: Kennikat Press, 1980.

Gerhart, Eugene C. *America's Advocate: Robert H. Jackson.* New York: Bobbs-Merrill, 1958.

———. "A Decade of Mr. Justice Jackson." *New York University Law Review* 28 (1953): 927–74.

Gibson, James L. "Judges' Role Orientations, Attitudes, and Decisions: An Interactive Model." *American Political Science Review* 72 (1978): 911–24.

———. "The Role Concept in Judicial Research." *Law and Policy Quarterly* 3 (1981): 291–311.

Going, Allen Johnston. *Bourbon Democracy in Alabama: 1874–1890.* Tuscaloosa: University of Alabama Press, 1951.

Goodwyn, Lawrence. *Democratic Promise: The Populist Moment in America*. New York: Oxford University Press, 1976.

Gordon, Robert W. "Historicism in Legal Scholarship." *Yale Law Journal* 90 (1981): 1017–56.

———. "Legal Thought and Legal Practice in the Age of American Enterprise, 1870–1920." In *Professions and Professional Ideologies in America*, edited by Gerald L. Geison, 70–139. Chapel Hill: University of North Carolina Press, 1983.

———. Review of *Tort Law in America: An Intellectual History*, by G. Edward White. *Harvard Law Review* 94 (1981): 903–18.

Hackney, Sheldon. "The Clay County Origins of Mr. Justice Black: The Populist as Insider." *Alabama Law Review* 36 (1985): 835–43.

———. *Populism to Progressivism in Alabama*. Princeton: Princeton University Press, 1969.

Haigh, Roger W. "Defining Due Process of Law: The Case of Mr. Justice Hugo L. Black." *South Dakota Law Review* 17 (1972): 1–40.

Hall, Kermit L. *The Magic Mirror: Law in American History*. New York: Oxford University Press, 1989.

Halpern, Philip. "Robert H. Jackson, 1892–1954." *Stanford Law Review* 8 (1955): 3–8.

Hamilton, Alexander, John Jay, and James Madison. *The Federalist*. Modern Library. New York: Random House, n. d.

Hamilton, Virginia Van der Veer. *Hugo Black: The Alabama Years*. Baton Rouge: Louisiana State University Press, 1972.

———. "Lester Hill, Hugo Black, and the Albatross of Race." *Alabama Law Review* 36 (1985): 845–60.

Haskell, Thomas L. *The Emergence of Professional Social Science: The American Social Science Association and the Nineteenth-Century Crisis of Authority*. Urbana: University of Illinois Press, 1977.

Hays, Samuel P. *The Response to Industrialism, 1885–1914*. Chicago: University of Chicago Press, 1957.

Hirsch, H. N. *The Enigma of Felix Frankfurter*. New York: Basic Books, 1981.

Hockett, Jeffrey D. "Justice Robert H. Jackson, the Supreme Court, and the Nuremberg Trial." In *The Supreme Court Review*, edited by Gerhard Casper, Dennis J. Hutchinson, and David A. Strauss, 257–99. Chicago: University of Chicago Press, 1990.

Hofstadter, Richard. *The Age of Reform: From Bryan to F. D. R.* New York: Vintage Books, 1955.

———. *The American Political Tradition and the Men Who Made It*. New York: Vintage Books, 1973.

———. *The Idea of a Party System*. Berkeley: University of California Press, 1969.

———. *Social Darwinism in American Thought*. Philadelphia: University of Pennsylvania Press, 1945.

Holmes, Oliver Wendell. "The Path of the Law." *Harvard Law Review* 10 (1897): 457–78.

Horowitz, Donald L. "The Courts as Guardians of the Public Interest." *Public Administration Review* 37 (1977): 148–54.

Horton, John Theodore. *James Kent: A Study in Conservatism, 1763–1847.* New York: Da Capo Press, 1969.

Horwitz, Morton J. *The Transformation of American Law, 1780–1860.* Cambridge: Harvard University Press, 1977.

———. *The Transformation of American Law, 1870–1960.* New York: Oxford University Press, 1992.

Howard, A. E. Dick. "Mr. Justice Black: The Negro Protest Movement and the Rule of Law." *Virginia Law Review* 53 (1967): 1030–86.

Howard, J. Woodford, Jr. "On the Fluidity of Judicial Choice." *American Political Science Review* 62 (1968): 43–56.

Hurst, James Willard. *The Legitimacy of the Business Corporation in the Law of the United States, 1780–1970.* Charlottesville: University Press of Virginia, 1970.

Hutchinson, Dennis J. "The Black-Jackson Feud." In *The Supreme Court Review*, edited by Philip B. Kurland, Gerhard Casper, and Dennis J. Hutchinson, 203–43. Chicago: University of Chicago Press, 1988.

Irons, Peter H. *The New Deal Lawyers.* Princeton: Princeton University Press, 1982.

Jackson, Robert H. "Address of the Honorable Robert H. Jackson, Attorney General of the United States." *American Bar Association Journal* 26 (1940): 204–14.

———. "Advocacy before the Supreme Court: Suggestions for Effective Case Presentations." *American Bar Association Journal* 37 (1951): 801–64.

———. "The Advocate: Guardian of Our Traditional Liberties." *American Bar Association Journal* 36 (1950): 607–99.

———. "Back to the Constitution." *American Bar Association Journal* 25 (1939): 745–49.

———. "Bar Associations Viewed by New Vice President." *New York State Bar Association Bulletin* (February 1931): 105–12.

———. "The Bar and the New Deal." *American Bar Association Journal* 21 (1935): 93–96.

———. "Decisional Law and Stare Decisis." *American Bar Association Journal* 30 (1944): 334–35.

———. "The Genesis of an American Legal Profession: A Review of 150 Years of Change." *American Bar Association Journal* 38 (1952): 547–618.

———. "It's Up to Us." *Commentator* (December 1937): 43–48.

———. "Justice Jackson's Final Report to the President Concerning the Nurnberg War Crimes Trial." *Temple Law Quarterly* 20 (1946): 338–44.

———. "The Law Is a Rule for Men to Live By." *Vital Speeches of the Day* 9 (1943): 664–67.

———. "The Lawyer: Leader or Mouthpiece?" *Journal of the American Judicature Society* 28 (1934): 70–75.

———. "The Meaning of Statutes: What Congress Says or What the Court Says." *American Bar Association Journal* 34 (1948): 535–38.

———. *The Nurnberg Case*. New York: Knopf, 1947.

———. "The Product of the Present-Day Law School." *California Law Review* 27 (1939): 635–43.

———. "Progress in Federal Judicial Administration." *Journal of the American Judicature Society* 23 (1939): 60–62.

———. *The Struggle for Judicial Supremacy: A Study of a Crisis in American Power Politics*. New York: Knopf, 1941.

———. *The Supreme Court in the American System of Government*. New York: Harper & Row, 1955.

———. "The Task of Maintaining Our Liberties: The Role of the Judiciary." *American Bar Association Journal* 39 (1953): 961–65.

———. "Wartime Security and Liberty under Law." *Buffalo Law Review* 1 (1951): 103–17.

Jacobsohn, Gary J. *Pragmatism, Statesmanship and the Supreme Court*. Ithaca: Cornell University Press, 1977.

Jaffe, Louis L. "The Judicial Universe of Mr. Justice Frankfurter." *Harvard Law Review* 62 (1949): 357–412.

———. "Mr. Justice Jackson." *Harvard Law Review* 68 (1955): 940–98.

Johnson, Frank M., Jr. "Judicial Activism Is a Duty—Not an Intrusion." In *Views from the Bench: The Judiciary and Constitutional Politics*, edited by Mark W. Cannon and David M. O'Brien, 279–84. Chatham, N.J.: Chatham House Publishers, 1985.

Keller, Morton. *Affairs of State: Public Life in Late Nineteenth Century America*. Cambridge: Harvard University Press, Belknap Press, 1977.

Key, ' O., Jr. *Southern Politics in State and Nation*. New ed. Knoxville: University of Tennessee Press, 1977.

Kloppenberg, James T. *Uncertain Victory: Social Democracy and Progressivism in European and American Thought, 1870–1920*. New York: Oxford University Press, 1986.

Koch, Adrienne. *Jefferson and Madison: The Great Collaboration*. New York: Oxford University Press, 1977.

Kurland, Philip B., ed. *Felix Frankfurter on the Supreme Court: Extrajudicial Essays on the Court and the Constitution*. Cambridge: Harvard University Press, Belknap Press, 1970.

Landynski, Jacob. "In Search of Justice Black's Fourth Amendment." *Fordham Law Review* 45 (1976): 453–96.

Langdell, Christopher Columbus. "Harvard Celebration Speeches." *Law Quarterly Review* 9 (1887): 123–25.

Larson, Magali Sarfatti. *The Rise of Professionalism: A Sociological Analysis*. Berkeley: University of California Press, 1977.

Lash, Joseph P., ed. *From the Diaries of Felix Frankfurter*. New York: W. W. Norton, 1975.

Laski, Harold J. *Authority in the Modern State*. 1919. Reprint, New York: Archon Books, 1968.

———. *A Grammar of Politics*. New Haven: Yale University Press, 1925.

Leuchtenberg, William E. "A Klansman Joins the Court: The Appointment of Hugo L. Black." *University of Chicago Law Review* 41 (1973): 1–31.

Levinson, Sanford V. "The Democratic Faith of Felix Frankfurter." *Stanford Law Review* 25 (1973): 436–48.

Levy, Leonard W. *Emergence of a Free Press*. First published as *Legacy of Suppression: Freedom of Speech and Press in Early American History*, 1960. Rev. and enl. ed. New York: Oxford University Press, 1985.

Lowi, Theodore J. *The End of Liberalism: Ideology, Policy, and the Crisis of Public Authority*. New York: W. W. Norton, 1969.

Lustig, R. Jeffrey. *Corporate Liberalism: The Origins of Modern American Political Theory, 1890–1920*. Berkeley: University of California Press, 1982.

MacLeish, Archibald, and E. F. Prichard Jr., eds. *Law and Politics: Occasional Papers of Felix Frankfurter, 1913–1938*. New York: Harcourt, Brace, 1939.

Magee, James. *Mr. Justice Black: Absolutist on the Court*. Charlottesville: University Press of Virginia, 1980.

Mason, Alpheus. *Harlan Fiske Stone: Pillar of the Law*. New York: Viking Press, 1956.

McCloskey, Robert G. *The American Supreme Court*. Chicago: University of Chicago Press, 1960.

McConnell, Grant. *Private Power and American Democracy*. New York: Knopf, 1967.

Meiklejohn, Alexander. *Free Speech and Its Relation to Self-Government*. New York: Harper & Bros., 1948.

Mendelson, Wallace. "Hugo Black and Judicial Discretion." *Political Science Quarterly* 85 (1970): 17–39.

———. *Justices Black and Frankfurter: Conflict in the Court*. Chicago: University of Chicago Press, 1961.

———. "Justices Black and Frankfurter: Supreme Court Majority and Minority Trends." *Journal of Politics* 12 (1950): 66–92.

———. "Mr. Justice Black and the Rule of Law." *Midwest Journal of Political Science* 4 (1960): 250–66.

———. "Mr. Justice Frankfurter on Administrative Law." *Journal of Politics* 19 (1957): 441–60.

———. "Mr. Justice Frankfurter: Law and Choice." *Vanderbilt Law Review* 10 (1957): 333–50.

Morrison, Stanley. "Does the Fourteenth Amendment Incorporate the Bill of Rights? The Judicial Interpretation." *Stanford Law Review* 2 (1949): 140–73.

Mowry, George. *Theodore Roosevelt and the Progressive Movement*. Madison: University of Wisconsin Press, 1946.

Murphy, Paul L. "The Early Social and Political Philosophy of Hugo Black: Liquor as a Test Case." *Alabama Law Review* 36 (1985): 861–79.

Murphy, Walter F. "Mr. Justice Jackson, Free Speech, and the Judicial Function." *Vanderbilt Law Review* 12 (1959): 1019–46.

Murray, Robert K. *Red Scare: A Study in National Hysteria, 1919–1920.* Minneapolis: University of Minnesota Press, 1955.

Nielson, James A. "Robert H. Jackson: The Middle Ground." *Louisiana Law Review* 6 (1945): 381–405.

O'Brien, David M. *The Public's Right to Know: The Supreme Court and the First Amendment.* New York: Praeger, 1981.

———. *Storm Center: The Supreme Court in American Politics.* New York: W. W. Norton, 1986.

Parrish, Michael E. *Felix Frankfurter and His Times: The Reform Years.* New York: Free Press, 1982.

Paul, Arnold M. *Conservative Crisis and the Rule of Law: Attitudes of Bar and Bench, 1887–1895.* Gloucester, Mass.: Peter Smith, 1976.

Phillips, Harlan B., ed. *Felix Frankfurter Reminisces.* New York: Reynal, 1960.

Pollack, Norman, ed. *The Populist Mind.* New York: Bobbs-Merrill, 1967.

Posner, Richard A. *Cardozo: A Study in Reputation.* Chicago: University of Chicago Press, 1990.

Pound, Roscoe. *An Introduction to the Philosophy of Law.* 1922. Reprint, New Haven: Yale University Press, 1954.

———. "Liberty of Contract." *Yale Law Journal* 18 (1909): 454–87.

———. "Mechanical Jurisprudence." *Columbia Law Review* 8 (1908): 604–23.

———. "The Need of a Sociological Jurisprudence." *The Green Bag* 19 (1907): 607–15.

Preston, William. *Aliens and Dissenters: Federal Suppression of Radicals, 1903–1933.* Cambridge: Harvard University Press, 1963.

Pritchett, C. Herman. *Civil Liberties and the Vinson Court.* Chicago: University of Chicago Press, 1954.

———. *Constitutional Civil Liberties.* Englewood Cliffs, N.J.: Prentice-Hall, 1984.

———. *The Roosevelt Court.* New York: Macmillan, 1948.

Purcell, Edward A., Jr. *The Crisis of Democratic Theory: Scientific Naturalism and the Problem of Value.* Lexington: University Press of Kentucky, 1973.

Quandt, Jean B. *From the Small Town to the Great Community: The Social Thought of Progressive Intellectuals.* New Brunswick, N.J.: Rutgers University Press, 1970.

Ransom, William L. "Associate Justice Robert H. Jackson." *American Bar Association Journal* 27 (1941): 478–82.

Rauch, Basil. *The History of the New Deal.* New York: Creative Age Press, 1944.

Rodell, Fred. *Nine Men: A Political History of the Supreme Court from 1790–1955.* New York: Random House, 1955.

Rogers, William Warren. *The One-Gallused Rebellion: Agrarianism in Alabama, 1865–1896*. Baton Rouge: Louisiana State University Press, 1970.

Rumble, Wilfrid E., Jr. *American Legal Realism: Skepticism, Reform, and the Judicial Process*. Ithaca: Cornell University Press, 1968.

Russett, Cynthia Eagle. *The Concept of Equilibrium in American Social Thought*. New Haven: Yale University Press, 1966.

Sabine, George H. *A History of Political Theory*. 4th ed. Hinsdale, Ill.: Dreyden Press, 1973.

Saloutos, Theodore. "The Professors and the Populists." *Agricultural History* 40 (1966): 230–40.

Schlesinger, Arthur M., Jr. "The Supreme Court: 1947." *Fortune* (January 1947): 73–212.

Schubert, Glendon. *The Constitutional Polity*. Boston: Boston University Press, 1970.

———. "Jackson's Judicial Philosophy: An Exploration in Value Analysis." *American Political Science Review* 59 (1965): 940–63.

Schwartz, Bernard. "The Administrative World of Mr. Justice Frankfurter." *Yale Law Journal* 59 (1950): 1228–65.

Shannon, David A. "Hugo LaFayette Black as United States Senator." In *Justice Hugo Black and Modern America*, edited by Tony Freyer, 121–37. Tuscaloosa: University of Alabama Press, 1990.

Shklar, Judith N. *Legalism: Law, Morals, and Political Trials*. Cambridge: Harvard University Press, 1986.

Silverstein, Mark. *Constitutional Faiths: Felix Frankfurter, Hugo Black, and the Process of Judicial Decision Making*. Ithaca: Cornell University Press, 1984.

Simon, James F. *The Antagonists: Hugo Black, Felix Frankfurter and Civil Liberties in Modern America*. New York: Simon & Schuster, 1989.

Skowronek, Stephen. *Building a New American State: The Expansion of Administrative Capacities, 1877–1920*. New York: Cambridge University Press, 1982.

Small, Albion W. *General Sociology: An Exposition of the Main Developments in Sociological Theory From Spencer to Ratzenhofer*. Chicago: University of Chicago Press, 1905.

Small, Albion W., and George E. Vincent. *An Introduction to the Study of Society*. New York: American Book Company, 1894.

Snowiss, Sylvia. "The Legacy of Justice Black." In *The Supreme Court Review*, edited by Philip B. Kurland, 187–252. Chicago: University of Chicago Press, 1990.

Steamer, Robert J. "Mr. Justice Jackson and the First Amendment." *University of Pittsburgh Law Review* 15 (1954): 193–221.

Stevens, Robert. *Law School: Legal Education in America from the 1850s to the 1890s*. Chapel Hill: University of North Carolina Press, 1983.

———. "Two Cheers for 1870: The American Law School." *Perspectives in American History* 5 (1971): 405–548.

Stimson, Shannon C. *The American Revolution in the Law: Anglo-American Jurisprudence before John Marshall*. Princeton: Princeton University Press, 1990.

Story, Joseph. *Commentaries on the Constitution of the United States*. 1833. Reprint, Durham: Carolina Academic Press, 1987.

Sugarman, David. "Legal Theory, the Common Law Mind and the Making of the Textbook Tradition." In *Legal Theory and Common Law*, edited by William Twining, 26–61. London: Basil Blackwell, 1986.

Thayer, James Bradley. "The Origin and Scope of the American Doctrine of Constitutional Law." *Harvard Law Review* 7 (1893): 129–56.

Thomas, Helen Shirley. *Felix Frankfurter: Scholar on the Bench*. Baltimore: Johns Hopkins University Press, 1960.

Thornton, J. Mills, III. "Hugo Black and the Golden Age." *Alabama Law Review* 36 (1985): 899–913.

Tocqueville, Alexis de. *Democracy in America*. Edited by J. P. Mayer. Translated by George Lawrence. Garden City, N.Y.: Anchor Books, 1969.

Truman, David B. *The Governmental Process: Political Interests and Public Opinion*. New York: Knopf, 1951.

Twining, William. *Karl Llewellyn and the Realist Movement*. South Hackensack, N.J.: Rothman, 1973.

Twiss, Benjamin R. *Lawyers and the Constitution: How Laissez Faire Came to the Supreme Court*. Westport, Conn.: Greenwood Press, 1973.

Urofsky, Melvin I. *Felix Frankfurter: Judicial Restraint and Individual Liberties*. Boston: Twayne Publishers, 1991.

Wasby, Stephen L. *The Supreme Court in the Federal Judicial System*. 3d ed. Chicago: Nelson-Hall Publishers, 1988.

Weidner, Paul A. "Justice Jackson and the Judicial Function." *Michigan Law Review* 53 (1955): 567–94.

Weinstein, James. *The Corporate Ideal in the Liberal State, 1900–1918*. Boston: Beacon Press, 1968.

Westin, Alan Furman. "The Supreme Court, the Populist Movement and the Campaign of 1896." *Journal of Politics* 15 (1953): 3–41.

White, G. Edward. *The American Judicial Tradition: Profiles of Leading American Judges*. New York: Oxford University Press, 1976.

———. "Felix Frankfurter, the Old Boy Network, and the New Deal: The Placement of Elite Lawyers in Public Service in the 1930s." *Arkansas Law Review* 39 (1986): 631–67.

———. *Patterns of American Legal Thought*. Charlottesville, Virginia: Michie, 1978.

Wiebe, Robert H. *The Search for Order, 1877–1920*. New York: Hill & Wang, 1967.

Wood, Gordon S. *The Creation of the American Republic, 1776–1787*. Chapel Hill: University of North Carolina Press, 1969.

Woodard, Calvin. "The Limits of Legal Realism: An Historical Perspective." *Virginia Law Review* 54 (1968): 689–739.

Woodward, C. Vann. *The Strange Career of Jim Crow*. 3d ed. New York: Oxford University Press, 1974.

Wyatt-Brown, Bertram. "Ethical Background of Hugo Black's Career: Thoughts Prompted by the Articles of Sheldon Hackney and Paul L. Murphy." *Alabama Law Review* 36 (1985): 915–26.

Yarbrough, Tinsley E. *Mr. Justice Black and His Critics*. Durham: Duke University Press, 1988.

Index

About the Author

Jeffrey D. Hockett is assistant professor of political science at the University of Tulsa. He received his Ph.D. from the University of Virginia. His 1989 article, "Justice Robert H. Jackson and Segregation," received a Hughes-Gossett Memorial Award from the Supreme Court Historical Society.